A READER'S GUIDE TO
Wallace Stevens

A READER'S GUIDE TO

Wallace Stevens

Eleanor Cook

PRINCETON UNIVERSITY PRESS

PRINCETON AND OXFORD

Copyright © 2007 by Princeton University Press

Published by Princeton University Press, 41 William Street, Princeton,
New Jersey 08540

In the United Kingdom: Princeton University Press, 3 Market Place, Woodstock,
Oxfordshire OX20 1SY

All Rights Reserved

Library of Congress Cataloging-in-Publication Data
Cook, Eleanor.
A reader's guide to Wallace Stevens / Eleanor Cook.
p. cm.
Includes bibliographical references and index.
ISBN-13: 978-0-691-04983-0 (cloth : alk. paper)
ISBN-10: 0-691-04983-1 (cloth : alk. paper)
1. Stevens, Wallace, 1879–1955—Criticism and interpretation—Handbooks,
manuals, etc. I. Title.
PS3537.T4753Z62295 2007
811'.52—dc22   2006044637

British Library Cataloging-in-Publication Data is available

This book has been composed in Adobe Garamond and Helvetica Neue

Printed on acid-free paper. ∞

pup.princeton.edu

Printed in the United States of America

1 3 5 7 9 10 8 6 4 2

For John Hollander

and

Natalie Charkow Hollander

and in memory of

Anthony Hecht

CONTENTS

PREFACE

Wallace Stevens is, by common consent, one of the great Moderns, those major writers in the earlier part of the twentieth century who changed once and for all the way their art is practised. Among poets, there are at least four such Modern masters: W. B. Yeats (b. 1865), Robert Frost (b. 1874), Wallace Stevens (b. 1879) and T. S. Eliot (b. 1888). Other names such as Ezra Pound or William Carlos Williams or Marianne Moore might be added. Among this group, Stevens seems the youngest and the strangest, though he was older than Eliot. But he matured slowly as an artist, and he did not engage in literary polemics designed to further his art, as did Eliot and Pound.

Reaching for a volume by Stevens, readers can be baffled and turn away, as with any new art. Or new art of a certain kind, for much of Yeats and Frost, even when new, was more accessible than much of Stevens. Yet Stevens continues to attract readers, including some who were at first puzzled. His ways of combining words, his wit and seriousness, his pithy and telling affirmations, his gift for titles, his conception and development of a "supreme fiction": any or all of these keep drawing readers, including the most diverse readers. Stevens is far from being a poet read chiefly in the academy, demanding as he can be. Perhaps his great attraction is that he knows how to be simple too. Some of the work is straightforward and sensuous, in a Keatsian line of inheritance. (I know people who take it along on holidays—maximum value for minimum space.) Or perhaps the academy underestimates the number of serious readers outside its domain.

This guide is designed for all these types of Stevens's readers—the knowledgeable, the studious, the enthusiastic, the occasional, the curious, the baffled but persistent. Among students at school, it is designed for those at about a first- or second-year college level (or an advanced high school senior) plus those among their teachers who are puzzled by Stevens. Among more knowledgeable readers, those who specialize in Stevens will find both familiar and new material here.

The best reader's guides seem to me to offer both general and specific information, with some judgments and some help in interpretation up to a point. Thus here. Readers will have no difficulty separating matters of fact and matters of judgment or interpretation. This book is centered on the body of work itself, while including whatever biographical and historical information sheds light on the work. It looks primarily at the poems as literature. That is, it offers a guide to help the reader work out what a given poem is saying, and how. (I'm aware of challenges of the intentional fallacy in such a statement, and would simply say that I like to follow a poem's apparent intentionalities.)

This is the reading of a poem that necessarily comes first, before any theoretical approaches such as deconstruction, new historicism, or feminist readings. (Needless to say, these latter approaches may condition or modify an initial reading, but then lots of things modify initial readings, and should.)

The first aim of this guide is to add to the pleasure of reading Stevens through an increased sense of what a given poem is saying. It also tries to demonstrate in passing why Stevens is regarded as a master of his art—how he is innovative, how he finds a voice of his own, how he alters our sense of A or B or C, and more.

Notes to the poems are chronological, concentrating on the six major collections, and following the order of poems in Alfred A. Knopf's *Collected Poems*, plus the late poems. For the latter, notably those published after the *Collected Poems* went to press, I have relied on the Library of America edition, "Late Poems (1950–55)." To these, I have added the poems in *The Necessary Angel*. The glosses are keyed to pages in both the Knopf *Collected Poems* (and *Opus Posthumous* and *The Necessary Angel*) and the Library of America *Collected Poetry and Prose*. The text of the poems in the Library of America edition is much more accurate than the text in the Knopf *Collected Poems*, which has never been corrected. (Where useful, I have noted the correct text, but by no means always.) The layout of the Knopf editions is, however, more spacious, and the publication of the *Collected Poems* and *The Necessary Angel* was overseen by Stevens himself.

A word or two of caution. First, glosses necessarily try to elucidate the more puzzling words and phrases in Stevens's poems. This may give the impression that his work is nothing but. On the contrary, some of his finest work is straightforward and accessible. Second, all entries list the place that a poem first appeared in print. I have relied on the standard bibliographical work for this information; this guide should not be used as a substitute for close textual editing.

ACKNOWLEDGMENTS

My first acknowledgment must be to the scholars and critics and readers who have added immeasurably to our knowledge and appreciation of Wallace Stevens. This guide could not have been written without them, though limitations of space do not permit individual acknowledgment. (Very occasionally, I have acknowledged a source for a point of fact in the briefest possible way. Citations by author alone refer to items in the bibliography.) Next, the libraries with hidden treasure troves, large and small, as below. First and foremost among these comes the Huntington Library, the main repository of Stevens's books and papers, whose staff makes working there such a pleasure. Beyond other libraries acknowledged below, I should also like to thank the Beinecke Library, Yale University, and the Clara Thomas Archives and Special Collections, York University.

I am grateful to the Social Sciences and Humanities Research Council of Canada for a Research Grant that greatly assisted in the preparation of this book. My two graduate assistants, Sophie Levy and Roseanne Carrara, both of them poets as well as scholars, saved me much legwork and more. At Princeton University Press, Mary Murrell and Hanne Winarsky have been exemplary editors: guiding, patient, encouraging, and full of good humor. I am also grateful to Princeton University Press at large, to Ellen Foos, to my copyeditor and fellow birdwatcher Jon Munk, and to the helpful readers for the Press. As always, my family has given immeasurable support.

For permission to quote from unpublished material in the Huntington Library's possession (including all WAS listings), I am indebted to the Huntington Library. For permission to quote from all other unpublished material, I am grateful to Stevens's grandson, Peter R. Hanchak, and to the following institutions. Details are provided with quotations in the text.

Several paragraphs in the appendix are adapted from my "Accurate Songs or Thinking-in-Poetry," in *Teaching Wallace Stevens: Practical Essays*, ed. John N. Serio and B. J. Leggett (copyright University of Tennessee Press, reprinted by permission).

Dartmouth College: Rauner Special Collections, courtesy of Peter R. Hanchak and Dartmouth College Library.

Houghton Library: manuscript material by Wallace Stevens, shelf-marks fMS Am 1333 and bMS Am 1543 (two quotations) by permission of Peter R. Hanchak and the Houghton Library, Harvard University.

New York Public Library: from the Berg Collection of English and American Literature (see "The Emperor of Ice Cream") and from the Montague-Collier

Family Papers, Manuscripts and Archives Division (see head note to "Notes toward a Supreme Fiction"); both by permission of Peter R. Hanchak and The New York Public Library, Astor, Lenox and Tilden Foundations.

State University of New York at Stony Brook: courtesy of Peter R. Hanchak and Special Collections, Frank Melville Jr. Library.

University of Massachusetts Amherst: courtesy of Peter R. Hanchak and the Department of Special Collections, W.E.B. Du Bois Library, University of Massachusetts, Amherst.

Victoria University Library (in the University of Toronto): Annotations to Northrop Frye's copy of Stevens's *Collected Poems* (Northrop Frye Collection) are quoted by permission of the library.

ABBREVIATIONS

I

CP   *The Collected Poems of Wallace Stevens* (New York: Alfred A. Knopf, 1954).

L   *Letters of Wallace Stevens*, ed. Holly Stevens (New York: Alfred A. Knopf, 1972; paperback, Berkeley: University of California Press, 1996).

LFR   "Letters to Ferdinand Reyher," ed. Holly Stevens, *Hudson Review* 44 (1991): 381–409.

LOA   *Wallace Stevens: Collected Poetry and Prose*, ed. Frank Kermode and Joan Richardson (New York: Library of America, 1997). This edition includes all the poetry, all the essays, most other prose, and a few letters.

LWSJRF   *Secretaries of the Moon: The Letters of Wallace Stevens and José Rodríguez Feo*, ed. Beverly Coyle and Alan Filreis (Durham, N.C.: Duke University Press, 1986).

MBG   "The Man with the Blue Guitar."

NA   Wallace Stevens, *The Necessary Angel: Essays on Reality and the Imagination* (New York: Alfred A. Knopf, 1951).

NSF   "Notes toward a Supreme Fiction."

OE   "An Ordinary Evening in New Haven."

OP   Wallace Stevens, *Opus Posthumous*, 2d ed., ed. Milton J. Bates (New York: Alfred A. Knopf, 1989). Supersedes 1957 edition, ed. Samuel Morse.

SP   Holly Stevens, *Souvenirs and Prophecies: The Young Wallace Stevens* (New York: Alfred A. Knopf, 1977). Early letters and journal entries beyond those in *Letters*.

SPBS   *Sur Plusieurs Beaux Sujects: Wallace Stevens' Commonplace Book*, ed. Milton J. Bates (Stanford and San Marino: Stanford University Press, Huntington Library, 1989).

WAS   Wallace Stevens papers, Huntington Library.

WSJ   *Wallace Stevens Journal.*

II

(Journal titles are abbreviated according to the standard listing in the *Publications of the Modern Language Association*.)

AV: Authorized (King James) Version of the English Bible (1611); biblical books take their usual abbreviations (e.g., I Cor: I Corinthians). See also bibliography.

Bartlett: *Familiar Quotations*, ed. John Bartlett, 14th ed. (Boston: Little, Brown, 1968).

Brewer: *Brewer's Dictionary of Phrase and Fable*, rev. Adrian Room (London: Cassell, 2001), and earlier editions. (E. Cobham Brewer died in 1897.) The various editions are worth checking; they indicate what is not completely familiar, what is no longer interesting, et cetera, at a given time.

cf.: compare (Lat. *confer*).

EB: *Encyclopedia Britannica*, 11th ed. (1914), a classic in its own right, and contemporaneous with Stevens.

e.g.: for example (Lat. *exempli gratia*).

Eng., Fr., Ger., Gk., Heb., It., Lat., Sp.: as in standard dictionary usage, English, French, et cetera.

ibid.: in the same place (*ibidem*).

Lewis and Short: *A Latin Dictionary*, comp. Charlton T. Lewis and Charles Short (Oxford: Clarendon, 1879).

NPEPP: *The New Princeton Encyclopedia of Poetry and Poetics*, ed. Alex Preminger and T.V.F. Brogan (Princeton: Princeton University Press, 1993). The poetry-reader's Bible, more advanced than Abrams (see bibliography); entries vary according to author.

OCD: *The Oxford Classical Dictionary*, 3d ed., ed. Simon Hornblower and Antony Spawforth (Oxford: Oxford University Press, 1996).

OED: *The Oxford English Dictionary*, 2d ed. (Oxford: Clarendon, 1989). An up-to-date version is available on-line.

PL: Paradise Lost, in *John Milton: Complete Poems and Major Prose*, ed. Merritt Y. Hughes (Indianapolis: Bobbs-Merrill, 1957).

Webster: *Webster's Third New International Dictionary* (Springfield, Mass.: Merriam-Webster, 1986).

A READER'S GUIDE TO
Wallace Stevens

Biography

Individual poets, whatever their imperfections may be, are driven
all their lives by that inner companion of the conscience which is,
after all, the genius of poetry in their hearts and minds. I speak of
a companion of the conscience because to every faithful poet, the
faithful poem is an act of conscience. (OP 253, LOA 834, 1951)

Wallace Stevens lived from 1879 to 1955. He was born in Reading, Pennsyl-
vania, of chiefly Dutch and German ancestry. He recognized family traits in
himself. "The Dutch are all like that," he once wrote, "as weird as the
weather"—a simile that bears watching (L 146, 1909). He recommended
studying one's family tree as a way of becoming absorbed in American history,
and he spent time and money studying his own in his later years. He took
pride in "being one of these hard-working and faithful people" (L 782,
1953). (The word "faithful" turns up more than once when Stevens talks
about his own art.) He remained deeply interested in the language and habits
and beliefs of his ancestors, including the fact they saw visions. In a book
where the writer's original spelling had been retained, Stevens found the word
for "pork" spelled "borck," recognized it as "pure Pennsylvania German," and
stayed up reading the book "night after night, wild with interest" (L 521,
1946). He thanked a friend for "super-duper" baroque postcards from Mu-
nich and Geneva, which reminded him of his mother's side of the family.
"Pennsylvania Germans have visions during their work with the greatest regu-
larity," he told her (L 842–43, 1954).

Stevens's father was a lawyer and businessman, involved in civic affairs and
turning his hand to verse occasionally. His health became troubled in 1901, he
lost a good deal of money in 1907, and he died in 1911 at sixty-three, feeling
defeated by life, as his son later surmised (L 458, 1943). A few of his letters,
arch and admonitory by turns, are printed in Stevens's *Letters*. ("You are not out
on a pic-nic—but really preparing for the campaign of life" [L 18, 1898]. "I am
convinced from the Poetry (?) that you write your Mother that the afflatus is
not serious—and does not interfere with some real hard work" [L 23, 1899].)

Stevens's mother, Margaretha Catharine Zeller, was cheerful, active, and devout; she read to her children from the Bible each night, and she died in her faith. Stevens remembered the freshness of her person in "everything she wore," and her vigor and sense of being alive (L 172, 1912). She was the kind of mother to whom a fifteen-year-old son could sign a letter, "with love to yourself—yourself's partner and you and your partner's remaining assets I myself am as ever, Yours truly, Wallace Stevens" (L 7, 1895). (The remaining assets were his two sisters, at home.) Or, aged sixteen: "Forever with supernal affection, thy rosy-lipped arch-angelic jeune" (L 10, 1896). A few of her letters survive, in the fine hand of those taught penmanship in school. She teased her daughter about courting. ("No doubt you and Mr. Stone will do some *meandering*" [18 April 1909, Huntington Library].) She encouraged her to travel. ("I wish you might go to Europe; *borrow* the money and pay it back when you start teaching. I say go if you can" [18 May 1909, ibid.].) Stevens would write in the same vein to his future wife. And his mother loved birds, as did Stevens, at least for a while. "I have seen them [robins] and welcome them," she wrote when ill (29 March 1912, ibid.). Four months later she was dead, and Stevens had lost both parents within a year and a day. Stevens's account of his mother's last days is very moving (L 172–74, 1912). She was about sixty-four, and when he himself had passed that age, by that time the last living member of his family, memories of her came back (see "The Auroras of Autumn" III).

There were five children, three sons and two daughters, Wallace Stevens being the second oldest. The youngest, Mary Katharine, died at thirty on 21 May 1919 while nursing in France after World War I, and Stevens took the death hard. He had to turn away, overcome with emotion, at the sight of war-mothers in a Memorial Day parade, each carrying a gold-star flag; it was because of "my present state of mind on account of [K]atharine" (WAS 2014, 31 May 1919).

From 1897 to 1900, Stevens attended Harvard as a special student, then briefly tried journalism in New York, before opting for law school; he went on to work in insurance law. As a fledgling lawyer he lived in a boarding house in New York. The acquisition of a small table in his room was an event. He could write on it, "instead of [on] a suit-case on my knee," he told his fiancée in 1909 (WAS 1839, 28 April). Presumably he was saving money during his long engagement. In 1900, he had bought a small copy of the Psalms, signed it, "W. Stevens N. York December 13—1900," then couldn't resist adding the price, "4 cents!" He knew what it was to be short of money and he was careful with it. In 1916 he joined the Hartford Accident and Indemnity Company, where he became a vice-president in the home office in 1934. He lived in Hartford for the rest of his life. In 1909 he married Elsie Kachel Moll from Reading, after a long-distance courtship of five years; they had one child, a daughter Holly, born in 1924.

Stevens was a vice-president who, aged sixty-three, sometimes washed the dinner dishes and scrubbed the kitchen floor, among other household chores. ("Floor scrubbing" could even engender poetry [L 450, 1943].) He learned about dust in the first year of his marriage when his new wife was away: "a huge matter. It settles . . . continuously, as . . . one learns day by day things unsuspected and amazing!" He signed the letter, "Your—learner—and student of dust" (WAS 1911, 7 June 1910). He had an instinct for domesticity. A reticent man, needing times of quiet and isolation, he also needed to center himself in a home and a family. At twenty-four, a few months before he met Elsie, he found himself wildly lonely, in a "Black Hole," and he knew very well why: "The very animal in me cries out for a lair. I want to see somebody, hear somebody speak to me, look at somebody, speak to somebody in turn. I want companions. I want more than my work, than the nods of acquaintances, than this little room. . . . Yet I dare not say what I do want. It is such a simple thing. I'm like that fool poet in [Shaw's] 'Candida.' Horrors!" (L 69, 1904). This is from the journal Stevens kept when young, a journal mostly given up when he began writing regularly to his future wife. The journal is candid and often uncertain; it records doubts and fears and resolutions and emotions. It records observations, sometimes of New York City, sometimes of the countryside. A few paragraphs read like exercises, set-pieces that Stevens may have thought of expanding or editing had he remained a journalist. He talked to himself, testing thoughts and moods. In 1906, he could not "make head or tail of Life." He was, he complained, as boring on this topic as "a German student or a French poet, or an English socialist!" Why weren't things "definite—both human and divine"? Then, choosing jobs where things are certainly definite, he wrote that he might "enjoy being an executioner, or a Russian policeman" (L 86–87).

The letters to Elsie Kachel Moll form a class in themselves, extending over the five-year period of their courtship and engagement, and later. (Long engagements were not unusual in the nineteenth and early twentieth centuries, and understandable, given middle-class financial and child-bearing habits.) She later destroyed a number of letters, saving only extracts. What we have shows an amorous, sportive, fantastical Stevens, sometime talking as much to himself as to his lady. But he does reach out to her: recalling times together, telling her of his desires, reassuring her about being a wife or about religious matters or about family background. (He came from an established Reading family; she did not, and Stevens's family disapproved of the match. She joined the church, but he had no intention of doing so, though he liked the idea of the church's existence.) He sometimes addressed her as "Bud" and signed himself "Your Buddy," a term of endearment between lovers at the time. She reciprocated. He cavorted before her as Pierrot, as Tom Folio, as Ariel. It was part of his "antic disposition." (See, for example, L 114, 1908.) As with Yeats's jester in "Cap and Bells," these were displays of love. A young woman inclined to worries and melancholy was being diverted and made to laugh. "Wallace is crazy. Don't mind him," she wrote to her parents on her honeymoon, in a postscript to an exuberant card from Stevens (SP 246). There were other selves too: his bewigged self (WAS 1830, 9 July 1909) or the Tireless Historian, the Devil of Sermons within me, the Giant.

The union would prove very troubled in its middle years. For over ten years at the start, there are touching signs of the ways Stevens worked at his marriage. Nonetheless, signs of estrangement began in the early 1920s, subsided with the birth of a child in 1924, then returned by the early thirties. The estrangement became serious and prolonged. Stevens remained reticent about it, though he allowed himself a few bitter poems in the early thirties, poems he never collected. His wife's difficulties can only be surmised. Henry Church, one of the very few close friends to whom Stevens spoke of his marital problems, wrote to him about his wife's virtues (WAS 3413, 27 March 1943) and later teased him about being a domestic tyrant (WAS 3426, 24 August 1943). This time Stevens did answer directly, defending himself (L 453).

In their later years, things eased, and there is a new tone to Stevens's remarks about his wife. A three-week holiday in Hershey proved to be "one of the happiest holidays we have ever had" (L 534, 1946). Confined to home after a fall on the ice, Stevens wrote that his wife "was a true angel" and that staying "at home with her . . . was a happy time" (L 663, 1950). Returning from trips to New York, he found "the house full of the good smell of fresh cookies" (L 743, 1952) or "a newly-baked loaf of bread, round and swelling and sweet to smell" (L 854, 1954). And he was enjoying his grandson, Peter, who would sit in his lap while Stevens invented stories about animals—including "one about an elephant with two trunks, one tenor, one bass" (L 744, 1952).

Stevens's early letters move quickly, but his mature letters should be read slowly; the later the date, the slower the pace. Otherwise it is possible to miss his pithy, sometimes tongue-in-cheek sentences in which a lot is implied. He loved aphorisms and his style shows it. Stevens, like any poet, also knew the arts of precision and of silence. ("It might occur to you that I should like to review this book. I should not.") There are a fair number of letters up to his marriage in 1909, just before his thirtieth birthday. There is also the early journal. In Stevens's middle years, from 1909 to 1934 (age thirty to fifty-five), the letters fall off. But for the last twenty years of his life, we have a large number of letters. It is this latter group that requires a reader to slow down.

Stevens was not a chatty letter-writer. He never suffered from a loose tongue: the opposite, if anything. (He referred to his "own stubbornnesses and taciturn eras" as coming "straight out of Holland" and impossible to change. But, he wrote, he always tried to undo any damage he might have done [L 422, 1942].) On paper, he showed little sustained interest in the gossip, minor self-displays, leisurely detail, and openness that make for a good letter-writer as usually conceived. When Stevens does unburden himself, the glimpses are all the more affecting. Congratulating a friend on the birth of a second child, he added (the only such remark I recall seeing), that there was nothing he would have liked more, "but I was afraid of it" (L 321, 1937). (His wife was thirty-eight when she bore her first child.) In his pleas with his daughter that she stay at Vassar during the war and complete her studies, he spoke as he rarely did about living "the good in your heart" and devoting her life to it, even if she never spoke of it. The agitation of the time—military, political, and social—"acquires all its force, all its sanction, from one thing only and that is the love of the good" (L 426, 1942). His daughter decided to leave Vassar nonetheless. About 1907, his own father had apologized to Stevens's sister, Elizabeth, because he had not managed his finances well enough to send her to college: "thus my dream of Vassar for you went to nought!" (Bates, 10). An ironic memory for Stevens, though he did not mention it.

The early letters and journal show a great fullness of response: from the senses, from the feelings, of thought. Aged nineteen, he recorded a walk through the garden "with Sally in a half enchantment over the flowers" (L 28, 1899). He distinguished scents. (Bergamot has a "spicey smell," and mignonette a "dry, old-fashioned goodness of smell.") He saw shapes. (Snapdragon "reproduces a man in the moon or rather the profile of a Flemish smoker.") His love of flowers stayed with him all his life, and an interest in flowers remained a bond between him and his wife. He loved his food, as we might infer from his poetry, and that too remained a bond with his wife, who was a good cook. "Generally speaking, grocery stores have considerable interest for me," he told a friend (LFR 384, 1920). His friends sent him fruit from Florida or different teas from abroad or told him of various honeys. Or he himself ordered items from Paris (see "Forces, the Will & the Weather") or elsewhere.

Shortly after his parents' death in 1911–12, Stevens began to write remarkable poetry, fresh, striking, with a voice of its own, technically impressive. He had been writing poetry for at least fifteen years, but the early work is conventional and only mildly interesting. Suddenly, in a leap much like Keats's inexplicable leap, he started to publish extraordinary poems: "Sunday Morning," "Peter Quince at the Clavier," "Domination of Black." Stevens's fellow craftsmen recognized a new presence in their midst. "Have you given the poems of Wallace Stevens in the Oct. *Poetry* any attention," Hart Crane asked in 1919. "There is a man whose work makes most of the rest of us quail. His technical subtleties alone provide a great amount of interest. Note the novel rhyme and rhythm effects" (*O My Land, My Friends: The Selected Letters of Hart Crane*, ed. Hammer and Weber [1997], 26). (For the poems, see the head note to "The Paltry Nude Starts on a Spring Voyage.") At the same time, Stevens said little to his business associates about this passion. In

1923, he published his first collection of poems, *Harmonium*, with Alfred A. Knopf. He would remain with Knopf for the rest of his life, in all publishing six collections before his *Collected Poems* in 1954. With Knopf's permission, he also published initial limited runs of poems with small presses whose designers and printers he admired. *Harmonium* made its way only slowly. Stevens was not a literary polemicist like Pound and Eliot, nor was he widely active in the literary world. (Pound was impressed enough with his work to invite him to contribute some writing in 1927, but Stevens declined. By this time he had a new baby and had entered a silent period [letter to William Carlos Williams, 7 Sept. 1927, Beinecke Library]. Pound later had second thoughts [Filreis (1994), 147].) In mid-1924, he received royalties of $6.70. "I shall have to charter a boat and take my friends around the world," he commented (L 243).

Stevens would later find it a struggle to persuade people that there was nothing really peculiar in his combination of activities. Chaucer was a senior civil servant in various capacities, Shakespeare a successful theater manager, Milton from 1649 to 1660 the Secretary for Foreign Languages, Eliot for some years an executive with Lloyds Bank, and Williams a medical doctor. Yet critics tended to stereotype businessmen, Stevens complained, so that someone in business who writes poetry seems "queer." He had supposed this to be an "American attitude," only to discover it in French and Belgian critics too (L 562, 1947). In 1951, he reflected on how hard it seemed "for people to take poetry and poets naturally. One is either tripe or the Aga Khan of letters" (L 716). Late in life, he suggested to an interviewer that "poetry and surety claims aren't as unlikely a combination as they seem. There's nothing perfunctory about them for each case is different" (Lewis Nichols, *New York Times*, 3 Oct. 1954).

Stevens must have found his other life energizing or he could not have started over again at the end of a working day, reading or writing. In fact, he commonly started the day by reading a few pages. He was an early riser and loved the dawn, especially just before sunrise. (There are poems on that magical time of day, such as "Not Ideas about the Thing but the Thing Itself.") He pursued his reading like a born scholar (see below, on the figure of the rabbi). Even when occupied with a new baby, he managed to read a book from time to time, "for, as the Chinese say, two or three days without study and life loses its savor" (L 245, 1925). Sometimes he concentrated on an area that interested him: "My hobby just now is the 17th century" (L 176, 1912).

Art and insurance, his vocation and profession, could clash. In 1935, an acquaintance, a printer, was touring nearby

> on foot and *in shorts* . . . and promised to call on me. The office here is a solemn affair of granite, with a portico resting on five of the grimmest possible columns. The idea of Mr. Ney and his wife toddling up the

front steps and asking for me made me suggest that they might like
to stop at some nearby rest-house and change to something more
bourgeois. This is merely one of the hilarious possibilities of being in
the insurance business. After all, why should one worry? (L 283)

But then, Stevens had just become a vice-president, and this was the 1930s,
long before the 1960s relaxed the attitude toward dress.

Not that Stevens was a worshipper at the business shrine. "The only other
people I see are contractors and lawyers and similar blood-curdling people"
(WAS 2024, 12 June 1920). In 1953, he attended a national insurance con-
vention "of our principal men," and reported sitting "in a smoke-ball (of ci-
gars, pipes, cigarettes) day after day, listening to platitudes propounded as if
they were head-splitting perceptions" (L 804). But he was very good at his
day job, and he clearly wanted to do it well. (See LOA 792–99, 1937 and
1938, for two short articles Stevens wrote about his profession.) Eventually he
earned a reputation as "the most outstanding surety-claims man in the busi-
ness" (Brazeau, 77), "the dean of surety-claims men in the whole country"
(ibid., 67). Once, when the Hartford president asked his vice-presidents to
identify problem areas in their departments, Stevens stood up and replied,
"The surety-claims department has no problem," and then sat down. Nobody
challenged him (ibid., 59). Stevens's salary, incidentally, was nothing like to-
day's salaries for top executives. In 1944, he was paid $20,000, and his salary
never reached $25,000 (Sharpe, 3); using the wages and benefits index,
$20,000 in 1944 is worth about $500,000 today (2006).

Like all of us, Stevens was conditioned by his time and place and occupa-
tion. He drank too much and told off-color jokes on occasion, including a
Harvard occasion (probably in order to relax things). One Harvard professor
reacted with high dudgeon, another with amused understanding. Perhaps
"slightly risqué," was Harry Levin's judgment (Brazeau, 171). He was capable
of isolated anti-Semitic remarks, though some of these sound a matter of class
as much as anything. At the same time, he took his daughter to a synagogue
to hear a rabbi (a "wise man") speak (WSJ 16 [1992]: 212), while the rabbi is
a constant exemplary figure in his poems. Similarly, the isolated remarks
about African-Americans sound largely about class, though certainly not in-
variably.

He grew up before houses and streets were lit by electricity, and he loved
the effects of light and shade and dark all his life. During his last illness, at
home between hospital stays, he lay on his back in the garden, watching the
sky. The enchantments of the night sky went back decades. "A half-misty
Fantin-La Tourish night" (L 92, 1906); "Our moon returns. Dear Elsie, hark! /
Once more we whisper in the dark" (L 107, 1907–8); "So let us call that
golden, misty moon rising over Picardy [in a painting] our own" (L 135, 1909).
But Stevens was a devotee of sun more than moon. "Thursday morning sat in

a shaft of light in Livg's [Livingood's] office—he read Milton's *Paradise Lost* to me.—The sun was better than the poetry—but both were heavenly things" (L 46, 1900). The sun one fall was "almost a September sun (I know them all)" (L 158, 1909). As for color, "God! What a thing blue is!" (L 72, 1904). A hyacinthine macaw interested him chiefly because he could then "see what color hyacinthine really is!" (L 184, 1915).

He loved the touch of air and water on his skin. Florida air was "pulpy," he wrote (L 192, 1916). And he cherished memories of swimming all day long, a memory shared with other North American children, and not just North American (see Wordsworth, "Oh, many a time . . . ," *Prelude* 1850, I.288). He swam morning, noon, and night, "for hours without resting and, in fact, can still." He and his friends lay on the walls of the locks, baked themselves, and then rolled into the water to cool off (L 125, 1909). Years later, he could still recall the warmth and the laziness. In 1906, he returned; he floated underwater, looking at "the blue and brown colors there and I *shouted* when I came up" (L 98, 1907). Even without these letters, we could guess that "A Lot of People Bathing in a Stream" was written by someone who loved to swim, to come up from under the water and look through it, to float in it, head above the water-line or below it.

When he was young, he longed to travel, and he spoke of his dreams to his fiancée. He looked over a map of eastern Canada for half an hour one evening, following the rivers and lakes, and referring to steamship lines. What appealed were Quebec, the St. Lawrence River, and especially the Bay of Fundy ("where the tide falls seventy-five feet and people get off boats by ladders"). He dreamed of spending a few months there, "in real woods, hunting and fishing." But that would be after seeing London with his future wife (SP 237–38, 1909). Most of these dreams came to nothing. First money, then war, then the Depression and another war intervened. There came a time when Stevens preferred not to travel after all, partly because his wife suffered from motion sickness (Holly Stevens, "Bits of Remembered Time," 657). They did manage a long trip south through the Panama Canal in 1923. And Stevens traveled on business early in his career, though time to take in his surroundings was limited. All his life he nourished an imaginative life in favorite spots he had never seen: Paris, Lausanne, Basel, for example. He would always remember an early camping trip to the interior of British Columbia. "In the last few weeks before his death," his daughter wrote, "he spoke of the trip frequently to me" (SP 117). It was in August 1903; Stevens was twenty-three years old. He went across Canada by train, then spent a month at a hunting camp in the Rockies. "Wrapped in my Hudson Bay blanket, I look like a loaf of bread by the fire" (L 65). A Hudson Bay blanket (in production since at least 1798) is made of white wool with one or more bright stripes at the end. Stevens's white blanket is, of course, an *unbaked* loaf, set in a warm spot by the campfire to rise. He came from a time familiar with the baking of bread.

Given his susceptibility to light and color, Stevens was bound to like paintings. He had firm views about them from the start, looking for what he later called "force." The same word was a test for other kinds of art. When he had enough money to buy paintings, he did so, acquiring a number through a Paris dealer, Anatole Vidal, and later through his daughter Paule Vidal, so that he did not see them before they arrived. He had to know something about the artist's work (he read art magazines with care); and the painting had to please his dealer, on whose taste he relied (L 777, 1953). He could do better this way than by purchasing them in New York. People who think of art objects as decorations or commodities will not understand the need that impelled Stevens. He was aware of what surrounded him. He was not interested in displaying works of art; he wanted them in order "to do me good" (L 280, 1935). "I feed on these things," he wrote (L 548, 1947). A gift from China of a carved wooden god-like figure delighted him (see the description, L 230–31 [1922], and pictures in Qian, *The Modernist Response to Chinese Art* [2003], 158). Studying him, said Stevens, was "as good as a jovial psalm"; among his benedictions, he told Stevens "not to mind one's bad poems" (ibid.). In buying contemporary art, Stevens was also encouraging artists whose work he liked—similarly with buying books from good small presses, or having his favorite books specially bound by an outstanding binder.

Like any good writer, Stevens was a prodigious reader. He "read left and right when young," and he remembered what he read. Reading was simply a natural habit, so natural that Stevens recorded a couple of weekends when he did *not* read, or write either (L 561 and 744, 1947 and 1952). As he said in 1954, "It adds tremendously to the leisure and space of life not to pick up a book every time one sits down" (L 845). He was nearly seventy-five and working full time as vice-president of the Hartford.

A list of Stevens's reading in his teens and twenties compiled from his journal and his letters is extraordinary. What did he read? Poetry, of course, and fiction and essays. He read a large number of periodicals, later subscribing to many, including various foreign ones. He read French periodicals and books, and French became in effect his second language. He also read German, though more easily when young (L 758, 1952). He taught himself some Spanish, and he had enough Latin to pursue things written in that language; in 1953 he bought Thomas à Kempis's *Imitatio Christi* in Latin (L 766). He read travel literature, philosophy, and so on. We can discover his favorite writers without much trouble. Goethe was an early and lasting favorite (L 22, 1899; L 457, 1943). Turgenev was "special" to him (L 509, 1945); he would reread Hardy if he had his copies nearby (L 147, 1909); "one of my early idols was Thomas More . . . the sense of his civility" (L 409, 1942). We can also tell something of his favorites through the echoes of them in his poetry.

Paradoxically, Stevens was aware of the danger of too much reading. The desire to read is insatiable, he said to his young Cuban friend, the writer José

Rodríguez Feo. "Nevertheless, you must also think" (L 513, 1945). It is possible for those who do not read much to know more than those who do. Take, for instance, Rodríguez Feo's mother. "She wanted to name a newly born colt Platon," her son wrote, "but I told her that the name was too precious and she said that it was musical and went well with his languid eyes" (L 602, 1948). "How much more this mother knows than her son who reads Milosz and Svevo," Stevens commented to his good friend, Barbara Church (ibid.).

When Stevens began to write, American literature was hardly respectable and the British command of writing in English was overwhelming. How to write poetry in the English language in a country very unlike England in its landscape, fauna, and flora? A writer may add all kinds of novel birds and beasts, but if the mindset and the forms come from overseas, then American or African or Australian or Canadian or Caribbean or Indian poetry in English will still sound British. Stevens's task was to find the idiom that was his own, and of his own time and place. If he could do this, he would thereby create an American poetry. He did not start from any nationalist sentiments (see OP 309–10, LOA 803, 1939; also OP 315–16, LOA 828–29, 1950).

Given Stevens's response to the outdoors, it is not surprising that his poetry often walks us around the skies, through a day, through the seasons, pausing here or there at one object or one place. We could make a fine seasonal anthology from Stevens' poems, including one on "deep January" ("No Possum, No Sop, No Taters") and a favorite of mine on February ("Poesie Abrutie"). The place may be New England or Florida (in the earlier poetry) or Europe or unspecified. Yet if this is "nature poetry" (to go by an old term), it does not sound anything like Wordsworth or Frost. "Nature poetry" is a poor term, in fact, because "nature" is a hydra-headed word. What *is* nature? Nature can be "Pretty Scenery" or Nature can be "the whole Goddam Machinery," as Frost puts it in "Lucretius versus the Lake Poets." (The best rule of thumb for dealing with this hydra-head comes from C. S. Lewis [*Studies in Words* (1960), 43]. In any given context, ask what is the implied contrary of "natural." For example, is it "unnatural" or "artificial" or "supernatural" or "civil"? The same rule of thumb is useful for large words like "freedom," "order," or "elite.") Stevens's poems sometimes offer a strange take on nature. Yet they are not usually fanciful. In fact, he claimed in 1935 that every Florida poem of his had "an actual background," adding that the world as perceived by a man of imagination might well appear to be "an imaginative construction" (L 289).

When talking about his work, Stevens regularly used the terms "reality" and "imagination" and the "interactions" between them. He liked this last term especially, and it turns up in various forms ("interdependence," et cetera). "Reality" and "imagination" are such huge terms that they are not very helpful. Stevens defined them variously, explicitly or implicitly, on a sliding scale of meaning, and he clearly liked this flexibility. He talked more about reality and the imagination in his earlier years, and more about interaction as he developed his art. (Toward the end of his life, he looked back and decided that his "imagination-reality" concern was "marginal to [his] central theme," which he defined as "the possibility of a supreme fiction" [L 820, 1954].) Imagination for Stevens is one of the great human powers. Not by itself, though. He had little time for an imagination that tried to ignore reality. It is "fundamental," he wrote in a 1942 essay, for the poet to be "attached to reality" and for the imagination to "adhere to reality" (NA 31, LOA 662). That is why his late "necessary angel" says, "I am the angel of reality" rather than "I am the angel of imagination" ("Angel Surrounded by Paysans"). To be sure, it is "the world within us" that keeps the outside world from being "desolate." But there is an "interchange between these two worlds . . . migratory passings to and fro, quickenings, Promethean liberations and discoveries" (NA 169, LOA 747, 1951). The process is two-way.

By my count, Stevens had two subjects, plus an abandoned third. From the start he wanted to write poetry of the earth, poetry of its place, especially poetry of the natural world. The way that he conceived it, however, changed over the years. His other, and finally main, subject was what he called a "supreme fiction." His abandoned subject was love poetry. He began to write it early, developed it, published it in *Harmonium*, then said good-bye to it in "Farewell to Florida," though in some ways he never left it. Of course there are other subjects too. But the other subjects tend to gravitate toward Stevens's main interests.

"O quam te memorem virgo?" ("What name should I call you by, O maiden?") asks Aeneas (*Aeneid* I.237). In *Harmonium*, "The sea of spuming thought foists up again / The radiant bubble that she was" ("Le Monocle de Mon Oncle"). It is Venus, in both writers. In Virgil it is the goddess herself, though her son does not recognize her. In Stevens, it is Venus remembered, especially through Botticelli's famous painting of the birth of Venus. Stevens's relation with the goddess, so intense at the beginning and so differently intense at the end, was troubled in his middle years. He was born to be a love poet, and to give us what high Modernism too often lacks: a poetry of eros. Stevens had the makings of a Ben Jonson, a love poet of a most interesting kind: of shades of love after the rose-colored glasses of first youth begin to make out shade. It is eros that draws Stevens. "In Stevens, sexuality is never an act; it is a state, a condition," Richard Howard once remarked (seminar, 1990). Just so.

> If sex were all, then every trembling hand
> Could make us squeak, like dolls. . . .

Stevens is smiling, groaning, acting out his Dutch-uncle role, and his French-uncle role too, in this aftermath to a lovers' quarrel, "Le Monocle de Mon Oncle." He is musing over the forms of love in a crowded, demanding, and moving love-poem. The poem was written early (1918) when Stevens was still discovering how difficult a goddess Venus could be.

Was his wife, after all, his muse, but in an unexpected way? Stevens's first major work is marked by a new honesty about Venus, as also about religious matters. Reality had intervened to challenge the erotic and other platitudes that fill Stevens's early work.

"Peter Quince at the Clavier" appeared in 1915. The title implies that Shakespeare's comic rustic, Peter Quince, may be speaking, but the story is of Susanna and the Elders. The point of view is far from simple. Stevens, in some ways the subtlest of men, liked to play the role of a bumbler, especially in matters of love. (Perhaps he was, sometimes.) Peter Quince is only one of several unexpected personae such as Crispin the Comedian. In *A Midsummer Night's Dream*, Peter Quince solemnly directs a comical play-within-a-play where two separated lovers communicate through a chink in the wall, until they finally meet, only to die. What can this comical play have in common with the story of Susanna and the Elders? One answer is: walls and private places, and their effects on love and lust, and death too. As if this is not enough complication, Stevens begins by sounding as if his own persona is speaking: "Just as my fingers on these keys / Make music. . . ." Whether Stevens ever played a clavier except in a fiction, I do not know. He did play a piano, one that he bought with great pride for his wife in 1913, for she was a good pianist. He records playing jigs on it during her absence in the summer (WAS 1950, 28 Aug. 1913). Stevens's poem refers only obliquely, in musical metaphors, to the famous trial of the Elders and their execution ("Death's ironic scraping," "viol"). At the end, his language becomes Miltonic or biblical. His layering of voices and stories suggests a very complex response by a man to a woman's beauty, ending with a dominant response of praise. Stevens was capable of all this in 1915, just as he began to write major poetry. It was the same year that Eliot published "The Love Song of J. Alfred Prufrock," where the final response is certainly not one of praise. These two complex responses to female figures by two New England men bear comparison. There are more straightforward passages of erotic force, for example, in "Gray Room" (1917), which Stevens did not collect, and in "The Plot against the Giant" (1917), which he did.

Stevens's engagement with poetry of the natural world and love poetry came together when he visited Florida, with which he had a virtual love affair. He was attracted from the beginning. The Stevens who whimsically cast himself as an erotic bumbler had found something different: a climate of erotic force, crude and vital. It affected him like a woman of erotic force, crude and vital. At first, as in "Nomad Exquisite," one force inspires another. But Florida's sensuality could be excessive, "lasciviously tormenting, insatiable." Stevens spoke of eros "fluttering" at the end of "Le Monocle de Mon Oncle" in 1918. But Florida's eros did not flutter, and Stevens was drawn to it. It was time to say farewell to "seem" and turn to actual being: "Let be be finale of seem" ("The Emperor of Ice Cream"). Though this poem specifies no setting, Elizabeth Bishop thought it was set in Cuba. It was time to celebrate actual dreams ("Hymn from a

Watermelon Pavilion"). Banana flowers had their own erotic force, "Darting out of their purple craws / Their musky and tingling tongues" ("Floral Decorations for Bananas"). The fruit of the banana tree used to be called "muse" (OED, last recorded use, 1602). She might come in this guise too.

These are poems written from 1919 to 1922. Over a decade later, Stevens announced a divorce, and the break was painful. Florida had not been easy: "Her home, not mine . . . / I hated the vivid blooms / Curled over the shadowless hut, the rust and bones." Nonetheless "I loved her once . . . Farewell. Go on, high ship" ("Farewell to Florida"). This is no tourist talk. Stevens is saying good-bye to his erotic muse and to love poetry. He was fifty-six years old, and his love poems had turned too merely personal and bitter to be good poetry. Staying with this subject threatened to eat away at his poetic world, his own gifts. ("She can corrode your world, if never you," "Good Man, Bad Woman" [OP 65, LOA 558–59, 1932].) His own place was New England, after all.

Yet we could make a small anthology of Stevens's few erotic lines and poems. Say, an erotic-invitation poem, a twentieth-century variation on Herrick's "Gather ye rosebuds while ye may": "Unsnack your snood, madanna, for the stars / Are shining on all brows of Neversink" ("Late Hymn from the Myrrh-Mountain"). The rest of the poem consists of lines that serve equally well for a human woman or for nature as a female form. So do others such as "The Woman in Sunshine." Sometimes Stevens writes with powerful yearning: "It is she that he wants, to look at directly, / Someone before him to see and to know" ("Bouquet of Belle Scavoir"). "The thought that he had found all this / Among men, in a woman—she caught his breath—" ("Yellow Afternoon"). Or there is his "blue woman" or personified spring weather, who remembers eros well, and does "not desire . . . that the sexual blossoms should repose / Without their fierce addictions" (NSF III.ii). She achieves what is not achieved earlier: she holds the reality of actual sexual force and the imagination and beauty of it together and yet separate, in a living relation. The delicate and the sensual are not at odds, as in some of Stevens's early erotic poems. Strange as it may sound, all these lines were written after Stevens's ritual farewell to Florida-cum-Venus. In one sense, he never abandoned his erotic muse. She still lived in his memory, and she regularly reappeared in displaced forms.

Stevens's best-known poems still tend to come from his first collection, *Harmonium* (1923): "Sunday Morning," "The Emperor of Ice-Cream," "The Snow Man," "Domination of Black," "Peter Quince at the Clavier," "Le Monocle de Mon Oncle," the Florida poems, and more. They are extraordinary, yet Stevens was not satisfied. Something in him found these poems "outmoded and debilitated" by 1922. He wanted "to keep on dabbling and to be as obscure as possible until I have perfected an authentic and fluent speech for myself " (L 231). Younger poets like Hart Crane were already in awe of his technical ability. But Stevens put himself to school, lying low for the better part of a decade, while he and his work underwent a major change. As Yeats and his work gradually did after Maud Gonne's marriage to someone else in 1903. As Eliot and his work did after he converted and was baptized in the Church of England in 1927. Yeats was thirty-eight and Eliot was thirty-nine. With Stevens, the major shift came in his fifties.

Harmonium is full of intelligence, passion, conviction, humor, and sense-effects. These often find expression in oblique ways, in strangely fabled ways, in cunningly modest ways. Stevens is largely a hidden poet, and by choice. Something still remains in this early Stevens of the dark rabbi, as in his 1918 description of a younger man who likes to observe "the nature of mankind, / In lordly study" ("Le Monocle de Mon Oncle"). The early enigmatic Stevens could be misread, for example, as simply a hedonist or a dandy. Yet it is true enough that if he had persisted in the range of subject and voice of the *Harmonium* poems, we would have had an accomplished poet, with a fierce but unfocused intelligence, an intricate and delicate and fastidious sensuousness, a sometimes idiosyncratic temperament, and a formidable technique. This would have been cause for gratitude; few poets attain so much. But Stevens was capable of more.

In Stevens's poems from about 1920 on, there is an increasing sense of something not getting out. It may be heard in some of the *Harmonium* poems—for example, "Banal Sojourn," with its thrice-repeated "malady" at the end. Stevens tried to exorcise this struggling spirit by retracing his poetic career to date, first in "From the Journal of Crispin" (OP 46–59, LOA 985–95, 1921), a genial poem submitted for a prize, then abandoned and consigned to a trash can. (The landlady fished it out; see Martz in Doggett and Buttel, 3–4.) Stevens then revised the poem as "The Comedian as the Letter C," a distinctly ungenial poem (not recommended for beginners). Stevens harrows his younger selves, the one who liked romance and the one who liked realism, the one who wanted an ideal mistress, the one who yearned for the sublime. His playful titles sometimes play over areas where he is vulnerable, as here or as with the erotic ("Le Monocle de Mon Oncle") or as with the sublime ("Tea at the Palaz of Hoon"). In 1921 Stevens wrote one of the best poems ever on what we call "writer's block," "The Man Whose Pharynx Was Bad": "I am too dumbly in my being pent."

After *Harmonium*, Stevens's next collection, *Ideas of Order* (1935, 1936), sounds oddly bare and oddly rough in places. Paradoxically the voice sounds stronger, though this book is half the length of *Harmonium* and has fewer remarkable poems for its size. There is a peculiar honesty to these poems. They sound less self-sufficient than earlier work, for they struggle with the self and with the times, whether private or public. Stevens had by now become a father, he had established himself in his profession, he had bought his first and only house, and he was among those financially secure even in the Depression. Nonetheless we hear something unexpected in his inner life: what he did not have and would not have, yet also what he did have. The trade edition of 1936 opens with "Farewell to Florida" and closes with an evening poem, also a leave-taking, "Delightful Evening." The collection records loss, sometimes personal loss: "Farewell to Florida," "Ghosts as Cocoons," "Sad Strains of a Gay Waltz," "The Sun This March," "Autumn Refrain."

Stevens reflected on such changes in himself and in others. He had second thoughts about his earlier selves. He repeated his earlier words, as if talking to himself. The repetitions may be explicit ("Hoon" in "Sad Strains of a Gay Waltz") or they may be glancing—footnotes to himself from an inveterate note-taker. Poets too change their minds, and poems need to be read in the context of a whole body of work. Stevens complained sometimes about being stereotyped and fixed at one stage of his writing. *Ideas of Order* is just that (unless we prefer Judge Powell's title, *Ordeals of Ida*). At a time of great social and economic disorder, at a time of new personal order, Stevens here steps back to meditate on ideas of order. Thinking about ideas of order is one way of confronting loss, of deciding how to live with changes that are not always welcome. Stevens's sense of loss was partly public (the misery of the Depression, and the dangerous volatility of political systems around the world), and it was partly private (erotic loss).

Demos, Mars, Clio; politics, war, history. Stevens's poetry has wide implications for all of these, and occasionally talks directly about them. Yet we do not return to his poems on these subjects as we return to Yeats's "Easter 1916" or "Meditations in a Time of Civil War" or "Remorse for Intemperate Speech." Or as we return to Wilfred Owen's "Anthem for Doomed Youth", "Strange Meeting," and "Dulce et Decorum." Or to W. H. Auden's "The Shield of Achilles" or T. S. Eliot's meditation in *Little Gidding* or Elizabeth Bishop's "Roosters."

As for his politics, in the 1900 election he "voted the Democrat ticket—Bryan," having turned twenty-one the month before (L 48). His later politics was conservative, though his political sympathies were wide. He admired Harold Laski (L 441, 1943) and Dwight Macdonald (L 486, 1945). He admired, or said he did, the aims of the left ("the most magnificent cause in the world") though not its various practices or its political philosophy (see L 287, 1935; L 620, 1948). (In order to judge Stevens's remarks, it is essential to know something about the political and economic struggles of the thirties in America and Europe.) He believed in "what Mr. Filene calls 'up-to-date capitalism' " (L 292, 1935). He believed in "social reform and not in social revolution" (L 309, 1936). His sympathies lay with the A. F. of L. rather than the C.I.O. He mused over these questions for some time, concluding that communism was "just a new romanticism." He said that he was no "revolutionist" even if he did "believe in doing everything practically possible to improve the condition of the workers," as well as supporting "education as a source of freedom and power," and regretting that "we have not experimented a little more extensively in public ownership of public utilities" (L 351, 1940).

He was divided in his view of Truman's victory in 1948. Personally, it meant more taxes, hence fewer savings and less security for himself and his family. But he admired "the vast altruism of the Truman party." If he regretted having to think twice about buying pictures, "still one could not enjoy books and pictures in a world menaced by poverty and enemies." "Enemies" meant the Russians—if they were enemies, that is. "One never knows. Perhaps they are merely undertakers" (L 623). (Presumably Stevens was enjoying a pun on the standard Marxist phrase "late capitalism.") In 1953, contemplating social upheavals, including the pressure of increasing population, he had the sense that "the time for speaking of birds has passed" (L 780). Yet he would go on to speak of birds. The earliest bird of the day and the year with its "scrawny cry" belongs to 1954 ("Not Ideas about the Thing but the Thing Itself"), and the "gold-feathered bird" at the edge of the mind belongs to 1955 ("Of Mere Being").

Stevens knew well what his subjects were. While he might be "on the right," he did not think "as, say, a prebendary of Chichester thinks" (L 351). Actually, Stevens went on, this talk of the right and the left was "most incidental" for him. His "direct interests" (a propos of the prebendary of Chichester) were quite different. "My direct interest is in telling the Archbishop of Canterbury to go jump off the end of the dock" (ibid.). It was 1940, and Stevens, increasingly absorbed by what he calls the "spiritual" role of the poet, was turning toward the subject of his great 1942 sequence, "Notes toward a Supreme Fiction."

Yet if Stevens's "direct interests are with something quite different," his indirect interests took a wide sweep. He could and did write on questions of politics and of war. A thirties politician turns up in "The Man with the Blue Guitar" x. Stevens's biblical language ("behold / The approach"), together with the word "pagan," help us to place this politician. He is a demagogue, proclaiming himself as the new savior. The people are fooled and yet not fooled. Individuals are skeptical, but in a crowd they accept what the crowd appears to believe. In 1946, Stevens was asked to identify the major problems facing the writer in the United States. The first, he responded, is that "all roles yield to that of the politician," and the politician wants everybody to be just as absorbed in politics "as he himself is absorbed." The poet must "maintain his freedom," as all individuals should (OP 311, LOA 814). Stevens's poet-figure in "The Man with the Blue Guitar" climbs a steeple and defies the slick, parading politician, "hooing."

Stevens knew the allure of the political dreams of the thirties: "Here is the bread of time to come." But: "Here is its actual stone" (MBG xxxiii). "What man is there of you, who if his son ask bread, will give him a stone?" asked Jesus. He also said: "Man shall not live by bread alone," when offered the chance to convert stones to bread. Bread and stone turn up together in different stories, well worth pondering in times like the thirties. "The Man with the Blue

Guitar" followed *Ideas of Order* at once, in 1937. It is a pivotal poem, its thirty-three sections simple in some ways, demanding in others, and packed with thought as Stevens positioned himself for the last quarter of his life. He ended the poem with a parable of bread and stone, and with a resolution that sounds like a covenant made with himself. From this time on, Stevens now wrote steadily until the end of his life.

Throughout Stevens's work, we can find the theme of the individual as against the crowd. Or of the actual individual as against abstract logic. His sense of particulars and of exceptions to general rules is very strong: this peach, that eccentric, this hermit, the feel of rain. It is part of a long American heritage. In the mid-thirties especially, his mind was running on these questions. In 1937, he wrote a poem called "United Dames of America," a blanket name for organizations like the Daughters of the American Revolution. The poem asks all such organizations how they respond to the visions of a hermit or of the rare politician who is strong enough to think independently. Alas, such organizations tend to use words like "paradigm" and to think about groups, not individuals: "Never the naked politician taught / By the wise." Stevens gave "United Dames of America" an epigraph from Jules Renard: "Je tâche, en restant exact, d'être poète" (I try, in staying precise, to be a poet). The word *exact* in French carries wider signification than in English, among others, that of "being true to reality."

Stevens's most effective form of political engagement in his poetry is the fable, and his favorite fable centers on abstract Utopian theory oblivious to everyday particulars and needs. Konstantinov, a member of the Soviet secret police, "would not be aware of the lake. / He would be the lunatic of one idea" ("Esthétique du Mal" xiv [1944]). Lenin by a lake does not see the lake except in terms of future power ("Description without Place" iv [1945]). Stevens, who desired a poetry of the earth, was wary of all Utopias, Marxist, Christian, or other. "The way through the world / Is more difficult to find than the way beyond it," he wrote in 1950 ("Reply to Papini"). Nor was he interested in idealizing the poet as guide through the world. The poet is not "the nucleus of a time." Rather, the poem is—"the poem, the growth of the mind // Of the world" (ibid.).

Stevens also wrote of war. How could he not? He lived through both world wars, as well as the Depression and the wars of the "dirty thirties." Like Eliot he was moved by Eugène Emmanuel Lemercier's popular *Lettres d'un Soldat* (1916), translated as *A Soldier of France to His Mother: Letters from the Trenches on the Western Front* (1917); in 1918 he himelf wrote a sequence, using Lemercier's title, "Lettres d'un soldat." Only a few of its parts pleased him enough to collect, the best being retitled "Death of a Soldier" and shorn of its epigraph. Poems meditating on war continued, through the Spanish Civil War ("The Men That Are Falling") to World War II. Stevens admired individual heroism, but not uncritically, as witness "Examination of the Hero in a

Time of War." He detested the war-time melding of religious and patriotic fervor, and attacked it in "Dutch Graves in Bucks County." He wrote a fifteen-part poem in response to a soldier's call for a poetry of pain, "Esthétique du Mal." Though uneven and sometimes cramped, it includes some of Stevens's best work; its meditative, indirect approach to war is the one most congenial to Stevens.

Stevens's letters testify to his horror of the war from 1939 onward. In 1940, he spoke of "the great evil that is being enacted today" (L 373) and of "the great disaster in which we are all involved" (L 381). This was before the United States went to war, but Americans were acutely aware of what was happening in Europe. In a lecture in May of 1941, Stevens mentioned how "we know of the bombings of London" and how "we should know of the bombings of Toronto or Montreal" (NA 21, LOA 655, published 1942); he knew that Canada had been at war since 1939. Occasionally his touch was off, and even admiring readers are uneasy. See, for example, the note on the epilogue to the 1942 poem "Notes toward a Supreme Fiction," which addresses a soldier and draws a parallel between the poet's war and the soldier's war.

In 1942, Stevens published both the collection *Parts of a World* (1942) and the sequence *Notes toward a Supreme Fiction*, the latter in a limited edition by the Cummington Press. He judged these to be his best work so far (L 475, 1944; and cf. L 501, 1945). *Notes*, he said, meant more to him than *Parts of a World* (L 433, 1943). And not only to him. It is an extraordinary achievement. Stevens chose it to end his next collection, *Transport to Summer*. Still, *Parts of a World* shows Stevens moving from strength to strength, laying the groundwork for yet more powerful work to follow. Some poems like "The Poems of Our Climate" are major achievements. Some poems treat vividly the particulars of everyday life, often visually as if in a painting ("The Poems of Our Climate," "Study of Two Pears"), sometimes also through taste or smell ("A Dish of Peaches in Russia"). A good deal of food appears (seed-cake, almonds, peaches, nougats), as does the trope of words as food. Stevens also begins work with the word "common," moving along the full spectrum of its meaning and associations, work that will culminate in "An Ordinary Evening in New Haven" in 1949. Voices and themes in the poems show a poet more closely engaged with matters that concern him than in *Harmonium* and *Ideas of Order*. *Parts of a World* is also a collection filled with a sense of war, even though most of its poems were written before the United States declared war on the Axis powers in December 1941. Stevens demanded more of himself here. He was disappointed in most of the reviews, especially because nobody "seems to enjoy the poems" (ibid.). As too often, his kind of humor went unappreciated.

Stevens's later meditations on history increasingly turn to the question of supreme fictions, notably of Judaeo-Christian belief. American history also engaged his attention, especially New England history. What drew him was the history of ideas. How did it happen that Calvinism came to dominate a certain time and place, say, early New England? Calvinism may not be very close to the thinking of John Calvin, yet there he stands or there stands some mindset we call "Calvinist." "Things are as they seemed to Calvin or to Anne / Of England, to Pablo Neruda in Ceylon," or to Nietzsche or to Lenin ("Description without Place" III). Queen Anne was also a figure who gave a name to a style, an attitude. (And who once owned Greenwich Village, as Stevens notes in his 1907 description of the place [L 103].) The Queen Anne style is a considerable contrast to Calvinism, yet both found roots in North America once. Not now, of course, "An age believes / Or it denies." "Description without Place" was written in April–June 1945, just as the war in Europe was ending. It was a time when discussion of the history of ideas was especially acute.

In 1947, the collection *Transport to Summer* appeared. Beyond "Notes toward a Supreme Fiction," it includes "Description without Place," as well as two other remarkable sequences, "Esthétique du Mal" and "Credences of Summer." The shorter poems are equally strong. All in all, the book represents five years of extraordinary creative power. It is as if writing "Notes" somehow released his full gift. The reviews were gratifying.

Stevens described himself in 1953 as a "dried-up Presbyterian" (L 792). He decided early that he belonged to no church, on which see "Sunday Morning." And he retained all his life a mischievous, sometimes iconoclastic, polemical streak, especially noticeable when belligerent religious conformity threatened. For himself, the heavens were clearer when swept free of the old Christian inhabitants; he threw away an old Bible with evident relief when housecleaning in 1907 (L 102). During his mother's bedtime reading from the Bible, "often, one or two of us fell asleep" (L 173, 1912). Stevens must have been among the sleepers, since he found himself having to consult the library in order to be sure who Saul was—"confound my ignorance" (L 176, 1912). Yet the same Stevens was quoting the Psalms in his journal (L 86, 1906), dropping into churches from time to time, holding on to his copies of Psalms and Proverbs. The English Bible was part of him, and he felt the force of the ancient words. In his fifties, Stevens turned back to reexamine his heritage in the light of this question, which absorbed him to the end of his life.

What happens when people stop believing in God? As with all such over-large questions, the answer depends on where we start. What does it mean to believe in God in the first place? What God is believed in? The question has force because the old authority of Christianity has now so widely dissolved in the Western world. Biblical stories and verses are fading from common knowledge. The doctrines of Christianity do not command the general assent they once did, nor are they often the focus of intense public interest. (Public religious focus on questions that are peripheral to Christian doctrine or unimportant in the Gospels only reinforces the point.) For many, religious observance has come to be ceremonial, marking the transition times of birth, marriage, and death. (Not that ceremonial practice is without importance, on which see Philip Larkin's poem "Church Going.")

For all that Stevens is a major American poet, his idea of a supreme fiction has not been taken in much beyond classroom discussion. For him, as for others, Christianity was no longer compelling. Like many another, he mused on what might take its place as a force of authority. At first, he seemed to suppose, like Matthew Arnold, that poetry could take the place of religion, a vague humanist view of the kind that Eliot fought (see "Arnold and Pater" in his *Selected Essays*). Some such attitude lies behind Stevens's invention of the phrase "supreme fiction" in 1922 ("Poetry is the supreme fiction, madame," "A High-Toned Old Christian Woman"). But the memorable phrase was not seriously explored until twenty years later in "Notes toward a Supreme Fiction." By that time, Stevens had also mused on humanism, though not to Eliot's conclusions. Stevens wanted a fully human belief that would include religious invention. "Notes" is organized around three notes that head the three sections: "It Must Be Abstract," "It Must Change," "It Must Give Pleasure." At one stage, he planned a fourth note, "It Must Be Human," but in the end did not use it.

The sequence has a rounded spherical shape, with a clear sense of beginning and end. There are glancing references in canto i to biblical beginnings in Genesis, and, in the final canto, to biblical endings in the Book of Revelation. Throughout, Stevens engages with the great demanding debates of theology and metaphysics, in poetry and elsewhere, echoing the language of the English Bible, Dante, Milton, Coleridge, and more. His "magnificent agnostic faith" (in Geoffrey Hill's exact and just phrase [*The Lords of Limit* (1984), 16–17]) works from the premise that the human imagination has invented God. For him, the writers of the biblical books are among the great Western poets. He was convinced that we have not yet taken in the implications of such a view (NA 173–75; LOA 748–49, 1951). This emphatically does not imply a materialist or simple antireligious stance.

If the sine qua non of belief is the existence of a transcendent God beyond ourselves, then Stevens's supreme fiction will appear to be a contradiction in terms. Supreme being, yes. But a fiction is something invented by the human imagination; by definition, it cannot be supreme to a Christian believer. For Stevens, the human imagination has recorded and created and interpreted the history and law and hymns and prophetic sayings and wisdom literature of the Hebrew Scriptures and Old Testament. And the gospels, apostolic acts, epistles, and apocalypse of the New Testament. His second premise is that people always believe in something, whether they are aware of it or not, and that we need to believe in something. If we possess "a will to believe ... it seems to me that we can suspend disbelief with reference to a fiction as easily as we can suspend it with reference to anything else." Some fictions, Stevens added, "are extensions of reality" (L 430, 1942). "The willing suspension of

disbelief ": this is Coleridge's classic phrase for the way we respond to imagi-
native work such as his "Rime of the Ancient Mariner," works presenting
"persons and characters supernatural" (*Biographia Literaria*, chap. 14). *The
Will To Believe* is William James's 1897 title. Stevens is combining the two.

If then, people need to believe in something and can no longer believe in a
transcendent God, what are they to believe? Stevens's answer is: a fiction,
something fictive. If this meant that the idea of God was an illusion, he was
not greatly troubled. For him, there were harmful illusions and benign illu-
sions, and "the idea of God" was an example of "benign illusion" (L 402,
1942). Arnold's simple substitution of poetry for religion has one great weak-
ness: the obvious fact that poetry or imaginative literature simply did not have
the force of religion in Victorian society, nor did it seem likely to attain such
force. "Biblical imagination is one thing and the poetic imagination, in-
evitably, something else" (NA 144, LOA 731, 1948). Imagination, Stevens
said late in life, is the *next greatest* power to faith. This important qualification
needs to be remembered; it turns up in 1949: "next to holiness is the will
thereto, / And next to love is the desire for love" ("An Ordinary Evening in
New Haven" III). And it turns up in 1951: "Men feel that the imagination is
the next greatest power to faith: *the reigning prince*" (NA 171, LOA 748, my
italics). To be sure, Stevens's phrase, "the reigning prince," bears watching. A
reigning prince is something more than a crown prince, though something less
than a reigning king. Stevens is leaving open the question of eventual reign.

This was no casual matter for Stevens. His instincts were not secular, be-
cause the word "secular" defines itself in opposition to the sacred, and Stevens
did not divide the world that way. He yearned fiercely for something sublime,
something noble, to use an old-fashioned word. He was not prepared to in-
vent or to endorse a supreme fiction himself. How this might come about, he
could not foretell, though he could imagine how. In 1942, he imagined, not a
supreme fiction, but the young writer who might do what he himself had not:
find some story, some formulation, that would command allegiance and give
fulfilment ("The Figure of the Youth as Virile Poet"). For himself, in 1942,
there were only notes about a supreme fiction, or rather, not "about" but "to-
ward." He did not have in mind the vagaries of fashion but rather the long-
standing appeal of some systems of thought or belief, some viewpoints. He
had no mystical notion of a zeitgeist, and he had no patience with cant or in-
flated formulations. He pretty clearly has in mind the parallels of Christian-
ity's beginning, as in the Incarnation and Christmas imagery in "Notes to-
ward a Supreme Fiction" I.IX or the use of Constantine at the end of "An
Ordinary Evening in New Haven."

For Stevens, the desire for a supreme fiction (or for holiness or celestial love,
as above) is a need of the human spirit so great that it amounts to a violence.
In a well-known description, he spoke of nobility as "a force . . . a violence
from within that protects us from a violence without. It is the imagination

pressing back against the pressure of reality. It seems, in the last analysis, to have something to do with our self-preservation" (NA 35–36, LOA 665, 1942). Possibly he was too sanguine about the human spirit.

Late in life, Stevens commented on the rabbi that appears regularly throughout his poetry. He had always found "the figure of the rabbi . . . exceedingly attractive." Why? Because this is the figure of someone "devoted in the extreme to scholarship" and also using it "for human purposes" (L 786, 1953). Some figures in Stevens's work, like the rabbi and the scholar, are parts of his own self that act as mentors. He was touched when young by Chénier's poem, "La Flute," describing how a master tutors a young flute player, and he translated it (L 124, 1909). He could also laugh at his own tutoring self, the "Devil of sermons, within me"—this after hectoring his bride-to-be (L 124, 1909). Or at the Doctor of Geneva who finds that the ocean is nothing to sneeze at ("The Doctor of Geneva"). Or at the lecturer on "This Beautiful World of Ours" who "composes himself / And hems the planet rose and haws it ripe" ("The Ultimate Poem Is Abstract"). There is a whole rogues' gallery filled with preaching and professorial faces in Stevens's work.

But there are other, quieter, more secret, more congenial figures. They do not hector or chase down an audience. They are absorbed in some quest, like Stevens himself. Henry James talked about *mon bon*, his wonderful term for his "'guardian spirit' and figure of inspiration. When he used the term in conversation he would raise his hat" (*Complete Notebooks*, ed. Edel and Powers [1987], 87). Proust also spoke of a young man within him, one of his selves, alive only when he wrote ("Contre Saint-Beuve"). Stevens had more than one such figure.

"Like a dark rabbi, I / Observed . . . In lordly study." Thus Stevens in 1918. Words of studying run all through "Le Monocle de Mon Oncle" and the poem closes on the figure of the rabbi, but this rabbi is not a mentor. In the thirties, figures of an interior mentor and an artistic conscience begin to appear in Stevens's work. They too have to do with ideas of order: "Oh! Rabbi, rabbi, fend my soul for me / And true savant of this dark nature be." So ends Stevens' 1930 poem, "The Sun This March," with a petition that is part of his rededication to poetic work. The rabbi clearly helped.

It is the rabbi as a scholar to whom Stevens cleaves. Not just any scholar, but a scholar whose spiritual life is centered on his study and whose practical life follows from what is gleaned there. Or the rabbi in the traditional sense as master or teacher. (Jesus is addressed in the Gospels as Rabbi, and twice as Rabboni, the highest such term.) "Poetry is the scholar's art," Stevens wrote ("Adagia," OP 193, LOA 906), and he knew the scholar's passion. (See above his remarks on reading, and the Chinese saying about study and life's savor [L 245, 1925].) Little wonder that the figure of the rabbi attracted him. The Protestant clergy, Stevens's own forebears, also used to be known for their devotion to the serious study of the Bible. It was to this kind of inner faithfulness that Stevens appealed when asking his daughter to reconsider her decision to leave Vassar during the war years (L 426, 1942). The rabbi continued to appear in Stevens's work. In "The Auroras of Autumn" (1948), he is called upon to end the poem, and in "Things of August" (1949), he opens the poem as part of its wonderful first line: "We'll give the week-end to wisdom, to Weisheit, the rabbi." By this time (Stevens had just turned seventy), he can be playful, playful as in possible titles of the rabbi, playful as in the pleasures of studying with the rabbi.

Stevens also invented a "hidalgo," a "Spanish gentleman" (OED) and "a son of the lower Spanish nobility" (Webster). He was another of Stevens's own selves, again present from the start. At first, Stevens sometimes liked him and sometimes did not, as with the Spanish masks he assumed (Don this or that). Later he found a new role for this Don Quixote part of himself, the guitar-playing, courtly, witty, deeply feeling and finally artistic self: an idealized Picasso, say, or a Santayana. Not the role for a vice-president of a major United States insurance company. But then Stevens hardly thought his person should be defined by a job description. The hidalgo was a possible conscience for an artist, a figure "Who watched him, always, for unfaithful thought. . . . To keep him from forgetting" ("An Ordinary Evening in New Haven" xxv). Stevens once wrote, in a comment on "The Man with the Blue Guitar" (xxix), "I desire my poem to mean as much, and as deeply, as a missal" (L 790, 1953). He did not compare his poetry with a missal or anything like a missal in *Harmonium*, nor are there mentors in *Harmonium*. By 1939, his sense of the future involved "a confidence in the spiritual role of the poet" (L 340).

Stevens's last collection before his *Collected Poems* (1954) appeared in 1949: *The Auroras of Autumn*. He reassured a correspondent that he was not writing a seasonal sequence, that is, an autumn volume following his 1947 *Transport to Summer*. He also said a little defensively (he was nearly seventy-one) that there was nothing "autobiographical about it" (L 636, 1949). He had a sense of not moving in "the circles of spaciousness" quite as grandly as in his younger days, but there is no falling-off in these poems. The remark speaks more to his ambition than his achievement (L 669, 1950). The collection includes three sequences, the title-poem, "The Auroras of Autumn"; the long sequence, "An Ordinary Evening in New Haven"; and the charming late-summer sequence, "Things of August." The closing poem, "Angel Surrounded by Paysans," is one of Stevens's most memorable. *The Auroras of Autumn* won the National Book Award. Stevens would receive it once again in 1954 for his *Collected Poems*, which were also awarded the Pulitzer Prize.

In 1946, Stevens asked to be remembered to his good friend, Barbara Church, who was returning for a stay at her house in France. Stevens thought of her "as of someone returning to a home long desired" (L 532). "Heureux qui comme Ulysse . . .": "Happy the man, who, like Ulysses . . . / Is come . . . / To live among his kinsmen his remaining days!" Stevens translated du Bellay's beautiful sonnet of 1558 when he was twenty-nine years old, living in a room in New York, and still thinking of Reading, Pennsylvania, with some nostalgia (L 150–51, 1909). When he was seventy, he spoke of the "exile at the bottom of the heart," echoing the cry from the great psalm of exile, Psalm 137: "If I forget thee, Jerusalem—and then [a man] works for years at a task of this sort with all the cunning of his love" (L 681, 1950). He was speaking of a gifted printer and designer, and of himself. The language of exile, with occasional homecoming, runs quietly—or mostly quietly—all through Stevens's poetry and prose. (It is not nostalgia for Reading, though Stevens remembered his native city and state vividly and affectionately, and referred to landmarks there in his later poetry.) In part, it is the condition of any artist. Marianne Moore, a good friend, wrote to Stevens, paraphrasing Auden:

> I . . . would say with W. H. Auden, "writers are not passive recipients
> of good fortune, art is a vocation for which a price must be paid. In
> being a writer one leaves the family hearth. . . . Each must go his way
> alone, every step of it, learning for himself by painful trial and shaming
> error, never resting long, soon proceeding to risk total defeat in some
> new task." (Garbled by me, but what I feel—plus the fun and
> exhilaration of one's sundry experiments.) (WAS 62, 2 Mar. 1953)

In part, this was the condition of the American artist. "Our most disastrous lacks . . . ," said Randall Jarrell, "these things were the necessities of Stevens' spirit." Our most disastrous lacks, to follow Jarrell, were "delicacy, awe, order, natural magnificence and piety" (134). Have things changed?

Where might Stevens have found a home? First, in his family, and so it was at last, but not as he once imagined. Then too among friends, and so it was also at last, with the few friends he could talk with, though the talk came at intervals and sometimes on paper. And third, in his own country, after all, his own place: "I like to hold on to anything that seems to have a definite American past. . . . One is so homeless over here in such things and something really American is like meeting a beautiful cousin or, for that matter, even one's mother for the first time" (L 626, 1948).

The lovely late poem "Credences of Summer," includes a strong sense of homecoming and being at home. As with Keats's "To Autumn," time stops in a sense, or, as Stevens says, in one direction. This happens in Stevens's natal state, Pennsylvania. Since things stop, "The directions stops and we accept what is / As good" (IV).

Homecoming is always peculiarly intense in Stevens's poetry, and so is its contrary, exile or desolation. It was so for Eliot, himself a voluntary exile who filled *The Waste Land* with exiles, but at last found a home in his ancestral country. It was so for Elizabeth Bishop. "One dear perpetual place" is how Yeats felt. Stevens seems more rooted in one place than any of these writers except Yeats, yet he was just as susceptible in his own land to thoughts and feelings of strangeness. In his small copy of the Psalms, which he read through in 1900 (to follow the dates inscribed at start and finish), he marked a good deal, but he copied out one text only. On the inside back cover, he wrote: "I am a stranger in the earth: hide not thy commandments from me," from Psalm 119. This formulation finds its way into Stevens's poetry.

Yet the late poetry also includes a sense of being at home on this earth, in Stevens's own part of it, New England. And loving it, as he once loved Florida—or rather, not that way, for the terms have changed. Asked in 1954 for a brief biographical note, Stevens replied that his work "suggests the possibility of a supreme fiction, recognized as a fiction, in which men could propose to themselves a fulfilment" (L 820). "Propose to themselves a fulfilment": Stevens's words are carefully chosen, and his poems and deeds stand by them. In work after 1942, he moved toward his always-desired poetry of the earth in a different way. A supreme fiction widely accepted, a communal supreme fiction, a new kind of religious adherence: this lay in the future, beyond his time. Meanwhile there was life to be lived here and now, and poems to be made. Yet the possibility of a supreme fiction informs his later work, so that the sense of an ordinary, everyday world is also extraordinary. His true subjects come together: a poetry of the natural world, a poetry of eros, a supreme fiction, all in one as poetry of the earth. Not one of these subjects exists the way it did at the start. And each one enriches the others.

Harmonium

Harmonium was published by Alfred A. Knopf in September 1923, with a second, slightly enlarged edition in 1931. The 1923 edition is dedicated "To my wife," and the 1931 edition "To my wife and Holly." Later collections bear no dedications. The 1923 collection gathers together sixty-eight poems published from 1915 to 1922 (C49–C79 in Morse, Bryer, and Riddel). Three poems from 1923 were cut in the second edition, "The Silver Plough-Boy" (OP 17, LOA 42), "Exposition of the Contents of a Cab" (OP 41, LOA 52), and "Architecture" (OP 37–39, LOA 66–67). *The Collected Poems* (1954) reprints the 1931 edition, where the 1923 poems end with "Nomad Exquisite" (CP 95), followed by fourteen additional poems, then by "Tea" and "To the Roaring Wind," which end both editions.

Stevens's subsequent collections generally publish most poems in approximate chronological order, but this one does not. A 1915 poem, "Tea," is the penultimate poem in both editions, while the latest poem chronologically, "Floral Decorations for Bananas," appears about halfway through. The order of the opening poems is skilfully designed. The overall order conceals Stevens's growing sense of frustration and malaise, most evident in the long poem, "The Comedian as the Letter C," which was rewritten and much expanded in the summer of 1922 (L 229), but appears about a third of the way through *Harmonium*. (See also the note to "The Snow Man.")

The harmonium is a musical instrument invented about 1840, "a keyboard instrument, the tones of which are produced by free metal 'reeds', tongues or vibrators', actuated by a current of air from bellows, usually worked by treadles; a kind of reed-organ" (OED; for more information, see EB, "harmonium"). It is a good word for poetry, given the longstanding tropes of pastoral reeds, the reeds of Pan et cetera, for poetry, as well as the organ-tropes of Milton, Dickinson, and others. The word is derived from Greek and Latin *harmonia*, so that it also suggests questions of harmony, including the older idea of the harmony of the universe, as it moves in accordance with the unheard heavenly music of the spheres. Note especially the next sentence in the OED: "Strictly distinguished from the American organ by the fact that the air is driven outwards through the reed-pipes, whereas in the latter it is sucked inwards; but the name is sometimes extended to include the American organ." This means that the word is also a happy trope for American poetry in 1923, because it distinguishes it in kind from British poetry. The troping of musical instruments runs throughout Stevens's work, on which see Hollander in Buttel and Doggett. (On his wife's piano and her accomplished playing, see the biography.) Stevens's first title was "The Grand Poem: Preliminary Minutiae" (L 237–38, 1923), which Knopf wisely discouraged; he wanted to subtitle his *Collected Poems* "The Whole of Harmonium" (L 831), but it did not happen.

* * *

Earthy Anecdote

Modern School 5 (July 1918), also in *Others* 5 (July 1919) with "Life Is Motion," another Oklahoma poem; CP 3, LOA 3.

To open, a poem with a distinctive Stevens flavor, and a distinctive American voice and place. Generally, this is a poem about two different kinds of energy encountering each other, often read as a fable about nature and art. Specifically, it is a fable or, more precisely, an anecdote that lends itself to different plots, as does "Plot against the Giant," three poems later. Stevens said there was no symbolism in the poem, but added that there was "a good deal of theory about it" (L 204, 1918). On possible "theory," see notes on the title and on "Oklahoma" below. Stevens's sinuous free verse works with skilful repetition and enjambment; the bucks' "swift, circular line[s]" also describe themselves as poetic lines.

TITLE: "Earthy": of the earth, rather than gross; see Stevens's important remarks on "the great poem of the earth" (NA 142, LOA 730, 1948). *Harmonium* opens with the word "earthy," and both editions close with "To the Roaring Wind," an invocation to the element of air. Traditional invocations come at the beginning, and call on the Muse for inspiration. Stevens has changed the order. Though the opening six poems in *Harmonium* do not invoke the Muse, they all focus on muse or genius loci figures that are both earthy and American.
"Anecdote": beyond the common meaning, "a secret or private, hitherto-unpublished narrative"; Stevens worked with this minor genre in 1918–20. (See titles CP 51, 55, 57, 76; OP 31, 43; LOA 41, 44, 46, 60, 539, 550. See also "anecdotal" CP 13, LOA 11, and "anecdote," CP 45, LOA 36, 37.) The Concordance shows no other uses of the word beyond these dates.

"bucks": Stevens objected to an illustration of his poem that resembled "orig-
   inal chaos," whereas he had in mind "something quite concrete: actual
   animals" (L 209, 1918).
"clattering": not usually a sound made by bucks, who more often graze or gallop.
"Over Oklahoma": an oddly skewed preposition that distances this poem
   from realistic narrative, moving its "actual animals" toward tale or fable,
   generically anecdote. The word "Oklahoma" functions in this generic
   context, while also recalling history. (On Oklahoma's turbulent history,
   especially in Stevens's lifetime, see, e.g., *Dictionary of American History*,
   ed. Cutler.) As an Indian name, said to mean "red men" or "land of red
   men," Oklahoma also evokes the tragic Indian history of this area. As an
   old name and a new state (1907), Oklahoma embodies the paradox of
   old and new in one (cf. "Oklahoman" in OE xvi). Rhetorically, "Okla-
   homa" echoes the *k———cla* of "bucks clattering" in a sound scheme,
   one of many schemes on place-names in Stevens.
"firecat": though an actual animal (L 209), mysterious and still resisting sim-
   ple identification. (Minor Indian legends tell of a cougar or mountain
   lion who brings either helpful or destructive fire. Recent retellings use the
   word "firecat," but the relevant Smithsonian historical volumes on the
   American Indian do not record the word.) Cf. the force of poetry or of
   the spirit as a lion or cat in MBG xix, "Poetry Is a Destructive Force,"
   OE xi, etc.

Invective against Swans

Contact 2 (Jan. 1921), with "Infanta Marina"; CP 4, LOA 3–4.

Oddly, no swan appears in this invective against swans. Or not so oddly, for
the poem's silent premise is "All your swans are geese." As elsewhere (CP
142–45, 342–43, 397; LOA 115–17, 299–300, 343), swans are associated
with stale or dead conventions. No fertile earth exists in these Old-World-
style parks. In contrast to "Earthy Anecdote," this poem uses couplets in reg-
ular iambic pentameter, some rhyme, imitative older syntax (e.g., "which that
time endures"), i.e., it is an old-style poem.

TITLE: again the title identifies the genre, again a minor genre.
"A bronze rain from the sun": an aged, autumnal version of Zeus visit-
   ing Danaë in an impregnating shower of gold. The old gods now lack
   potency.
"Paphian": the swan, like the dove, is the bird of Venus.
"chilly chariots": Venus has a chariot drawn by swans; "chilly" wittily revises
   such standard tropes as "snowy chariot."

In the Carolinas

Soil 1 (Jan. 1917), as part of "In the South," Pt. II of "Primordia"; CP 4–5, LOA 4.

While the Carolinas may be a fertile part of the earth, the "Timeless Mother" here (Mother Nature?) is not always welcoming. As with the opening poem, this is a small poem that implies a good deal. A quatrain, then a tercet, then a couplet, all unrhymed, are cast as a short dialogue.

"aspic nipples / . . . vent": not the usual food (breast-milk), but playing between a nourishing meat-jelly and a sense of death; cf. the deadly asp or aspic that Cleopatra laid on her breasts (*Antony and Cleopatra* V.ii.233ff.). The snaky verb "vent" is in charge. In contrast to a nourishing *alma mater*, Stevens suggests an *aspera*, or bitter, mother. (Cf. "Esthétique du Mal": "Life is a bitter aspic.") The breasts of this "Timeless Mother" do not always suggest a land of milk and honey.

"*The pine-tree* . . .": the cryptic reply, presumably by the Timeless Mother, answers only the first sense of "How is it," i.e., "By what means." Or does it? Stevens leaves open the possibility that the reply is also a refusal to answer the second sense of the question, "Why?"

The Paltry Nude Starts on a Spring Voyage

Poetry 15 (Oct. 1919), one of fourteen poems under the title "Pecksniffiana"; CP 5–6, LOA 4–5. The thirteen others are: "Fabliau of Florida," "Homunculus et la Belle Etoile," "The Weeping Burgher," "Peter Parasol" (not in *Harmonium*, see OP 40–41, LOA 548), "Exposition of the Contents of a Cab" (only in 1923 *Harmonium*, see OP 41, LOA 52), "Ploughing on Sunday," "Banal Sojourn," "The Indigo Glass in the Grass" (not in *Harmonium*, see OP 42–43, LOA 549), "Anecdote of the Jar," "Of the Surface of Things," "The Curtains in the House of the Metaphysician," "The Place of the Solitaires," and "Colloquy with a Polish Aunt." Pecksniff, from Dickens's *Martin Chuzzlewit*, is a type for a hypocrite and bully. The suffix implies that this group of poems belongs to an age of Pecksniff or concern him, as in "Victoriana." (See OED, Webster, "-ana," also "Pecksniff.") "Pecksniffiana" suggests that we ask what hypocritical stance each poem is set against. The answer is sometimes easy, sometimes not. The meaning of "Pecksniffiana" as "sayings of Pecksniff" (as in "Virgiliana") does not appear to be in play, yet it is not fully absent either; Stevens refuses to exempt himself from any taint of Pecksniffery.

The poem offers a current American Venus, very much of the earth, if not yet of the stature of her European forerunner. The title and the pun on "on" in line 1 set the tone. A virtuoso display of skill marks the diction.

TITLE: lines 1 and 2 modify and clarify the title; "paltry" is a humorous varia-
tion on a modesty topos, so as not to claim too much.

"But not on a shell, she starts": evoking a memory of Botticelli's "Birth of
Venus," and thereby identifying this "she" as a twentieth-century Venus.
Though now the "paltry nude," she will reappear as "the goldener nude"
in American guise, presumably in Stevens's poetry. Another early use of
the Venus figure, here as subject-cum-muse, retrieved from archaic use
and revised. (On titles run into first lines, especially in Marianne Moore,
see Anne Ferry, *The Title to the Poem* [1996], 266.)

"purple": traditionally, the color of royalty.

"scrurry" (CP 6): misprint for "scurry," correct in LOA 5.

"scullion of fate": scouring the waves, so to speak (Dryden, "ships, that scour
the watery plain," *Georgics* II.625; Geoffrey Hill, "and now the sea-
scoured temptress," "Re-birth of Venus").

The Plot against the Giant

Others: An Anthology of the New Verse, ed. Alfred Kreymborg (New York: Alfred A.
Knopf, 1917), with eleven other poems, ten of which were published in *Harmonium*
(see head-notes, below). The omitted poem is "Gray Room" (OP 28–29, LOA
537–38); CP 6–7, LOA 5–6.

The title and three girls suggest a fairy tale. The three girls, like three graces,
set about civilizing the giant, "this yokel," in a delicately erotic poem.
Echoes of Whitman make clear that the civilizing plot of the three charmers
is not as simple as they suppose. "Giant" was one nickname for Stevens, be-
stowed because of his size (Richardson I.335 and see the signature to a letter
to his fiancée, "Your Giant," L 160, 1909). He also enjoyed the mock-role of
a bumbler (e.g., Peter Quince). Contraries of labials and gutturals are at
work in the diction, and both perform poetic roles, despite the Third Girl's
assumptions.

"Arching . . . puffing. / He will bend": echoing Whitman, "They do not
know who puffs and declines with pendent and bending arch" (*Song of
Myself* 11).

"Oh, la . . . le pauvre!": "Oh, oh . . . the poor thing"; "la" is archaic or dialect
Eng. adding emphasis, and evoking Fr. *là* (there); "la" and "le" not only
play against each other in sound, but also in suggestion, because "la" is
the feminine definite article and "le" the masculine.

"whisper / Heavenly labials": echoing Whitman, "whispers of heavenly
death murmur'd I hear, / Labial gossip" ("Whispers of Heavenly Death"
1–2).

Infanta Marina

Contact 2 (Jan. 1921) with "Invective against Swans"; CP 7–8, LOA 6.

A beneficent muse figure for once, providing a poem of flowing language and flowing water, both fluent. The four stanzas coincide with four sentences, and end firmly with a rhymed couplet.

TITLE: an infanta (Sp.) is an infant and historically a princess who is daughter of the king and queen of Spain; here she is of the sea ("marina") and soon proves to be a type of genius loci. Verbally "infanta" is a rich pun on "fan" as (1) like some palm leaves (cf. Stevens's journal, L 84, 1905: "the fan-like starry palms . . . were new"); (2) fan poetry and courtly fan language, evoked by Stevens's early fan poems like "She that winked her sandal-fan" in "Carnet de Voyage" (OP 6, LOA 523) and cf. "Gray Room" (OP 28–29, LOA 537–38); Stevens once said his early writing was like fan-painting (L 171, 1911); (3) *fans* and *infans* in Latin ("speaking" and "un-speaking," whence our word "infant," on which see Eliot's 1920 poem "Gerontion"). The puns all trope on the ways that this seascape speaks to us, through its personified genius loci, yet also does not speak except through our words.

"sleights of sail": a variation on "sleights of hand," and see further in L 785, 1953; cf. "The Sense of the Sleight-of-Hand Man" (1939).

Domination of Black

Others 2 (Mar. 1916); CP 8–9, LOA 7.

One of Stevens's earliest major poems, but placed in *Harmonium* after six later poems that inform it, as does the major poem, "The Snow Man," that follows. On Stevens's sense of the poem, see L 151 (1928) and the appendix under "Logic." A firelit room is filled with moving colors that evoke the colors of fallen leaves, and indirectly evoke the well-known troping of fallen leaves as spirits of the dead, elsewhere directly alluded to ("Arcades of Philadelphia the Past"). The fireplace as a memory-place is central in many poems and stories, especially American ones. Stevens turns away from conventional developments of this topos with "Yes: but" and with his repeated "against," which also questions kinds of againstness. This is the first use of the first person in *Harmonium*, emphasized at each stanza's end, and a contrast with third-person "one" in "The Snow Man." The "I" sentences map the movement of the poem. The short lines work with some repeated

end-words, and memorable use of repetition and of the rhyme "hemlocks"-
"peacocks."

"Turned . . . Turning": the play on "turn," a favorite word for poets, includes:
    (1) a descriptive use of colors turning in the room; (2) memories of leaves
    turning color; (3) the troping of leaves ("trope" means "turn" etymologi-
    cally); (4) turning leaves or pages of a book; (5) turnings of the end of the
    line (note placement in the line); and later (6) the turning of the earth
    and apparent turning of the planets. Note the insistent anaphora in
    stanza 2.
"striding": so placed in the line that it elicits "striding" over the line-end, i.e.,
    enjambment, literally "walking"; cf. Milton on Death, who comes "With
    horrid strides; Hell trembled as he strode" (*PL* II.676), and Wordsworth
    on the fearful peak that "Strode after me" (1850 *Prelude* I.385).
"the cry of the peacocks": their cry is loud, piercing, and primordial, falling in
    pitch at the end. The old bestiaries attribute it to the bird's dismay over
    its ugly feet, Juno's punishment for the peacock's vanity. Why peacocks
    and hemlocks? Not just the rhyme, but because a peacock's tail at rest ac-
    tually looks like a hemlock bough, where the evergreen needles lie flat,
    overlapping each other. When a peacock flies to or from low boughs, the
    long tail appears to sweep, like a broom.
"planets gathered": Stevens recorded in 1907 that the stars appeared "fear-
    ful . . . at night at sea" (SP 185).

The Snow Man

Poetry 19 (Oct. 1921), one of twelve *Harmonium* poems under the title "Sur Ma Guz-
zla Gracile" (a mixed-language title, meaning "On My Small Gusle"). "Guzzla" is a
variation of "gusle," Serbian for a bowed musical instrument, still popular in Bulgaria,
usually of one string; see "gusle," OED, "gusla," Webster, and *New Harvard Dictio-
nary of Music*, ed. Randel (1986); cf. Prosper Merimée, *La Guzla* (1827). As one ex-
ample of Stevens's arrangement, note the order of these twelve poems when finally
collected: "Palace of the Babies," "From the Misery of Don Joost," "The Doctor of
Geneva," "Gubbinal," "The Snow Man," "Tea at the Palaz of Hoon," "The Cuban
Doctor," "Another Weeping Woman," "Of the Manner of Addressing Clouds," "Of
Heaven Considered as a Tomb," "The Load of Sugar Cane," "Hibiscus on the Sleep-
ing Shores." In the 1923 *Harmonium*, they appear as poems 54, 22, 18, 65, 8, 45, 44,
19, 33, 34, 10, and 16, respectively. CP 9–10, LOA 8.

"The Snow Man" is so placed that it makes a companion poem to "Domina-
tion of Black" in a fine contrast of black versus white, night versus day, fire
versus ice, past tense versus present, "I" versus "one," haunting memory versus

purged memory, charm poem versus riddle poem ("Who am I?" "A Snow Man," with a truncated echo-rhyme, "Am I?" "No Man"). (On charm and riddle poems, see Northrop Frye, "Charms and Riddles," *Spiritus Mundi* [1976].) Not that this poem represents a domination of white: it is a poem written against any domination. As an artist's exercise, it tests how far sensation can be dissociated from emotion, e.g., how far (and why) cold is associated with misery. Stevens much later mentioned enjoyment, which is not apparent in the poem unless in the opening pretty-winter images (L 464, 1944). See the developments in "Extracts from Addresses . . ." IV, "The Plain Sense of Things," and "A Quiet Normal Life." Syntactically, "The Snow Man" is remarkable as a one-sentence poem with shifting parallel phrases. The final memorable line is the culmination of much skilful repetition and internal rhyme. The entire poem is logically compact, and complicated by the a-logical play of paradox at the end.

TITLE: sometimes misspelled as "Snowman," not the same thing.

"regard . . . behold": note the difference in the two verbs, and cf. "behold" in "Nomad Exquisite."

"not to think": like being told not to think of an elephant.

"same bare place": Emerson's "bare common," which elicits a different response, is often cited ("Nature," *Essays: Second Series*, chap. 1)

"nothing himself": how far can a writer become a pure recorder of sense effects, without the self intervening? A snow man can do so. (Cf. Emerson, "I am nothing" [ibid.].)

"the nothing that is": note this is not "nothingness," a weighted philosophical and theological concept. One "nothing that is" is the word "nothing" on the page. On paradoxes of "nothing," see Stephen Booth, *Shakespeare's Sonnets* (1977, index) and Rosalie Colie, *Paradoxia Epidemica* (1966), 219–51.

The Ordinary Women

Dial 123 (July 1922), with five other *Harmonium* poems, "Bantams in Pine-Woods," "Frogs Eat Butterflies . . . ," "A High-Toned Old Christian Woman," "O, Florida, Venereal Soil," and "The Emperor of Ice-Cream," all under the title "Revue"; CP 10–12, LOA 8–9.

An ordinary escapist fantasy (female variety), presumably evoked by a guitar, which sounds throughout in rhyme or imitative sounds. An off-beat "cat-tarhs"-"guitars" rhyme in stanza 1 is reversed in the last stanza, as are the rhymed end-words to stanzas 1 and 2 ("walls," "halls") in the last two stanzas, enclosing the poem in a double scheme of chiasmus (xyyx). The Cinderella setting culminates in "Insinuations of desire, / Puissant speech," whereupon the fantasy vanishes, and guitars subside to cattarhs or colds again. (Cattarhal songs are, of course, harsh.) The poem is built on contraries and plays on coldness, glitter, and lack of fire.

"poverty": perhaps literal, certainly imaginative or spiritual.

"alphabets, / At beta b . . . heavenly script": The magnitude of stars is often measured by the Greek alphabet (alpha, α or a; beta; β or b; gamma γ or g, etc.; constellations often retain their early Greek names); the brightest stars in constellations are alpha magnitude and are lacking here, in a judgment on these escapist fantasies (cf. "make believe a starry *connaissance*" in "Le Monocle de Mon Oncle").

"How explicit the coiffures": "explicit" also in the etymological sense of "unfolded," as in "explicate"; on the use of hair styles, including "coiffures," see "Le Monocle de Mon Oncle" iii, below.

The Load of Sugar-Cane

Poetry 19 (Oct. 1921); see note on "The Snow Man," above; CP 12, LOA 10.

A one-sentence poem of flowing water and fluent syntax, using skilled repetition with parallel phrases and clauses. The effect slows down time, and sharpens sensuous effects in this vivid little sketch, set in sugar-cane country. It makes a notable contrast to the preceding poem: warmth versus coldness, flowing versus vacillation, work versus fantasy, ordinary diction versus precious.

"Turning, bedizened": see note on "turning" in "Domination of Black," above.

Le Monocle de Mon Oncle

Others 5 (Dec. 1918); CP 13–18, LOA 10–14.

An intensely felt poem about middle-aged eros, opening with a lovers' quarrel, brooding over time and mortality, expostulating against romantic illusion, climaxing in an exuberant invitation, and ending pensively. The scope and variety of argument, trope, and tone make it a small handbook for writing love poems. "Mon oncle," a persona for Stevens, examines intimations of mortality, often insistently, in combat against his beloved's "make believe." The numbered stanzas are self-contained as in "Sunday Morning," each with a core argument and typical tropes. For all its partly unresolved feelings, occasional mixed effects, and densities, this poem's felicities make it Stevens's one great love poem. His own comment was bland and evasive (L 250–51, 1928).

TITLE: "The Monocle of My Uncle," or "a certain point of view," in Stevens's flat rendition; see also his remarks on "the excitement of suave sounds" and the "insistent provocation in the strange cacophonies of words" (ibid.).

I

"Mother of heaven": fine hyperbolic swearing ("somebody to swear by," as Stevens said [ibid.]), as mon oncle mocks some unspecified accusation concerning "two words."

"clashed edges of two words that kill": note the suggestion of "(s)words" for "words."

"sea of spuming thought . . . radiant bubble": evoking the beloved as Venus, especially as in Botticelli's "The Birth of Venus."

"saltier well . . . bursts its watery syllable": likely mon oncle's tears, and so troping against Wordsworth's "Thoughts that do often lie too deep for tears" ("Ode: On the Intimations of Immortality," last line). Cf. Herrick's hourglass poem, where the sand is troped as "Lovers tears enchristalled" that "Do in a trickling manner tell / (By many a watrie syllable). . . ." (Stevens owned a copy of Herrick's poems, now at the Huntington Library.)

II

"red bird": general, not specific, though suggesting that the rare red birds of Stevens's temperate climate are birds of pleasure (as indeed they are to the eye), akin to allegorical erotic red birds.

"wind and wet and wing": all common types of trope for song or poetry (e.g., blowing, pouring out a melody, soaring on the wings of song); cf. "torrent" in the next line.

"uncrumple": Eng. translation of Lat. *explicare*, whence our "explicate."

"I am a man of fortune greeting heirs": Stevens invites assessment of his tone, since relations between the wealthy and their heirs vary greatly.

"choirs": birdsong fills the air in spring during the mating season; cf. Stevens's different response to the bird choirs in "Not Ideas about the Thing but the Thing Itself" (1954).

"starry": both as in "starry-eyed" and as in "everlasting"; cf. the use of stars in V, XI.

"*connaissance*": (Fr.) "knowledge," including acquaintance; contrast *savoir*, also "knowledge," but including profound knowledge, and a word Stevens liked ("Bouquet of Belle Scavoir," "The Plain Sense of Things").

III

Art versus nature, as in the art of hair arrangements, e.g., in Chinese and Japanese paintings.

"Utamaro's beauties": the distinctive women with elaborate Japanese hair arrangements in the well-known wood-block prints of Utamaro (1753–1806).

"all-speaking": an Eng. variation on latinate "evoking"—say, "pan-voking."

"mountainous coiffures": eighteenth-century European female hair fashion, piled very high on the head.

"curl": a common figure for troping (cf. George Herbert: "curling with metaphor / A plain intention," "Jordan" II); hence the figure of the barber as poet.

"Have all the barbers . . . ?": A rhetorical question: have all the poets lived in vain that no love in nature (rather than art) has survived? Response: In nature, hair (love) is restyled according to the time and one's age, by means of a new art of curling (troping).

"dripping": the remarks are addressed to "a woman whose hair [is] still down" (L 251, 1928). Hence she is an intimate, just risen. (In 1918, adult women still commonly wore their long hair up on the head during the day; short bobbed hair arrived in the twenties.) The word "dripping" also evokes statues of Venus Anadyomene, wringing out her wet hair.

IV

On the apple as a figure for love.

"impeccable fruit": also "unsinful" in the latinate sense of the etymon, and thus unlike the apple usually assigned to Eden.

"Falls": not from grace and in Eden, but from gravity and on earth.

"Eve": the beloved as Eve rather than Venus, sweeter as potential than as actual, a chilly observation.

"a round": a cycle, as in music, and appropriate for the shape and fate of both apples and skulls.

V

On the planet Venus, and on small earthly lights of love.

"west . . . furious star": Venus, the evening star in the west, associated with the furies of young love as in "spring's infuriations" ("Credences of Summer" i).

"firefly's . . . stroke": the late-spring green-white nighttime flash of the firefly, a mating signal.
"crickets": sometimes associated with mortality.

VI

A very circumscribed view of life after forty, from an apparently vulnerable, resigned male.

"Hyacinth": loved and accidentally killed by Apollo, hence eternally young in legend; metamorphosed into the blue flower, hyacinth.

VII

A "parable" (l. 7) on how heavenly love might (but does not) change our views of erotic love.

"mules . . . come slowly down," etc.: perhaps echoing and revising Goethe (whom Stevens knew and loved [see L index]) in his well-known poem, "Kennst du das Land"? The third stanza opens: "Kennst du den Berg und seinen Wolkensteg? / Das Maultier sucht im Nubel seinen Weg" (Do you know the mountain and its cloudy path? The mule picks its way through the mist).
"honey of heaven . . . heightened by eternal bloom": considering the possibility that the mules are bearing a "specifically divine revelation" (L 464, 1944).

VIII

A "trope" (l. 4) of love as a flowering plant, now producing fruit, which Stevens designates as squashes. Read literally, the trope is a little hard on middle-aged bodies.

IX

Stevens's exuberant, lusty, middle-aged return, troping against love-melancholy, which nonetheless comes back at the end of the poem.

"quiz": tease, regard with an air of mockery, and also look through a monocle.

X

Troping against exuberant love-poetry in the manner of the early Yeats (which Yeats also reacted against).

"gigantic . . . tip": presumably a tree of life, like the great banana tree in NSF II.v, but a little risible nonetheless.

XI

A memorable opening observation on the limited power of sex, for all its force.

"weep," etc.: under the spell of eros or in sexual ecstasy.
"starlight . . . frog": cf. the stars and frog-pond (her eyes and his talk: "her lovely eyes . . . like stars above a miasmatic frog-pond") in Henry James's story, "Eugene Pickering."
"Boomed from his very belly odious chords": presumably a bullfrog, whose sound is far from odious, except in a metaphor. Stevens's division between bright starry images and gross earthly images marks an erotic problem, a division between heavenly eros and actual sexuality; the division is explored in several Florida poems.

XII

Pigeons as the doves of Venus in ordinary form. The blue and white pigeons are one and the same, seen in different lights. The earliest use of Stevens's favorite rabbi figure, here for two earlier selves, first dark, then rose.

"dark rabbi . . . mincing": an engaging trope of a detached, overconfident young observer, as viewed by his older self.
"rose rabbi": on one's younger self as a rose rabbi pursuing "a philosophical ideal of life," see L 251 (1928); the title and arguments also suggest seeing through rose-colored glasses.
"shade": a weighted word for Stevens, especially as an end-word (see Concordance).

Nuances of a Theme by Williams

Little Review 5 (Dec. 1918), with "Architecture for the Adoration of Beauty" and "Anecdote of Canna," all under the title, "Poems"; the former appeared only in the 1923 *Harmonium*, under the title, "Architecture" (see OP 37–39, LOA 66–67); CP 18, LOA 14–15.

TITLE: The theme from William Carlos Williams's "El Hombre" is given in italics in lines 1–4. The more usual expansion would be "Variations on a Theme by X." Stevens's term "nuances" is also a pictorial and musical term.
"Lend no part": troping against Williams's verb "give" in l. 2.

"an intelligence": for the use of the word with an article, see OED 4 ("intelligence"), and cf. "The Comedian as the Letter C," l. 1.

Metaphors of a Magnifico

Little Review 5 (June 1918), with "Anecdote of Men by the Thousand" and "Depression before Spring," all under the title, "Poems"; CP 19, LOA 15–16.

Stevens's title suggested an inflated persona, but the poem develops a puzzled one, so that the title acts as ironic defense, perhaps with negative effect. The chief question is: what metaphors? The Magnifico (magnificent? magnifying?) is a persona comparable to the Prince in "Anecdote of the Prince of Peacocks," a possible self that Stevens guards against. The Magnifico produces no good metaphor, for the A-is-B formula of metaphor keeps turning up as A-is-A. Either this is attempted archetypal metaphor (as in Frye, *Anatomy of Criticism* [1957], 123–25; cf. "major man" later) or it is a problem of identity. Or else, it is a would-be writer, stuck on the bridge of metaphor, since "metaphor" literally means "carrying across or beyond." (Note the emphatic position of "Are," as a one-word centered line in stanza 3.) A 1918 poem, the scene evokes (among other contexts) a wartime officer and his men in Europe (the white wall of the village). It shows a mind logically at work, but imaginatively blocked, unable to connect logic and sensuous detail. This is the earliest of Stevens's metaphor poems, and a forerunner of the fine 1945 poem, "Thinking of a Relation between the Images of Metaphors."

"So the meaning escapes": LOA rightly follows *Harmonium* and separates this line from what precedes it.

Ploughing on Sunday

Poetry 15 (Oct. 1919); see note on "The Paltry Nude Starts on a Spring Voyage," below; CP 20, LOA 16.

An exuberant strong-stress poem, whose hyperbole, high spirits, and addressee, Remus, suggest the genre of tall tale (see Joel Chandler Harris, *Uncle Remus, His Songs and Sayings*). Stevens spoke of its "fanfaronnade" (L 338, 1939), i.e., boisterous or arrogant language, bluster. Repetition and irregular rhyme are skillfully used throughout the five stanzas, expanding appropriately in the center stanza.

TITLE: "Ploughing": literal, and also figurative as a longstanding trope for writing from Isidore (Curtius, *European Literature and the Latin Middle*

Ages [1948, 1953], 313–14) to Seamus Heaney ("The Sense of Place," *Preoccupations* [1980], 137); cf. "Primordia," 6, "Unctuous furrows, / The ploughman portrays in you / The spring about him" (OP 26, LOA 535–36). In 1919, Sunday church attendance was very common and rest from labor was expected, often legislated. To plough on Sunday was an antisabbatarian act, treated casually here. Sunday is experienced more as a day of the sun than a day for church.

"Tum-ti-tum . . .": humming to an emphatic beat, which is the beat of the poem, heightened; Stevens liked to make poetry of phonetic equivalents for various sounds; cf. also the guitar sound of "zay-zay" in "The Ordinary Women"; early critics took him to task for this.

Cy Est Pourtraicte, Madame Ste Ursule, et les Unze Mille Vierges

Rogue 1 (15 Mar. 1915), with "Tea," under the title "Two Poems"; CP 21–22, LOA 17.

A variation on a well-known and frequently illustrated saint's tale. (For the complicated origins of the legend, see EB, "St. Ursula.") Ursula lost her life fleeing the persecution of Christians and/or an arranged marriage, along with eleven thousand like-minded young women. Not surprisingly, she is a patron saint of virgins. Stevens's title, dress, colors, radishes, and flowers evoke some illustrated medieval French version of Voragine's *Legenda Aurea* (see "Colloquy with a Polish Aunt"). But his portrait of such a saint is mischievous, though tender, with eros sublimated only in supposed intent and not in effect. The reading is very different from Apollinaire's rude and riotous "Les onze mille vierges" (c. 1906). The free verse works effectively with phrasal line breaks and irregular rhyme.

TITLE: (Old Fr.) "Here is depicted Madam Saint Ursula and the Eleven Thousand Virgins."

"marguerite and coquelicot": Fr. names for daisy and poppy.

Hibiscus on the Sleeping Shores

Poetry 19 (Oct. 1921); see note on "The Snow Man"; CP 22–23, LOA 18.

Like "The Snow Man," written in a form much favored for later poetry, the unrhymed tercet working with an iambic pentameter line. Both these 1921 poems move in and out of a regular line. This one is a stark contrast to "The Snow Man," while nothing like as forceful. Compare the use of color with that in the preceding poem.

TITLE: Hibiscus, a house plant in Stevens's climate, but growing wild on semitropical seashores.

"I say": see note on "Anecdote of Men by the Thousand," below.

"Fernando": fictitious addressee, whose name suggests a Hispanic locale, and continues the cadence of the preceding "I say now."

"monstered moth": the mind (l. 2); cf. the later development of mind and monster in MBG XIX.

"the blather": with the noise of the water as "voluble, foolish, or nonsensical talk" (Webster), cf. the development in "The Idea of Order at Key West."

"stupid afternoon": a seeming letdown after what precedes it, especially the highlighted diction of "besprent." Stevens trusts the title and preceding 14 lines to give the ambience, and also the etymology of "stupid," from Lat. *stupidus*, itself from *stupere* ("to be stunned or benumbed," also "to be amazed at"), whence also Eng. "stupendous"; the "stupid afternoon" is thereby connected with the stupendous "monstered moth."

Fabliau of Florida

Poetry 15 (Oct. 1919); see note on "The Paltry Nude Starts on a Spring Voyage," above; CP 23, LOA 18.

Stevens liked this poem, in which "the feeling of the words and the reaction and images the words create" count more than the sense (L 341, 1939). It offers a black-white-and-dark-blue color range—a Whistler range—as against the colors of the preceding poem, also from a semitropical region. As with the preceding poem, a surprising word ("droning") closes the poem. The five stanzas, couplets and tercets mostly in dimeter and trimeter, have fine, wavelike rhythmic variations.

TITLE: "Fabliau": a metrical tale in early Fr. poetry, often a beast-fable (the "moon-monsters"?); another title with a generic signal; "of " takes two meanings, as elsewhere in Stevens, so that this is a fabliau about Florida and a fabliau that Florida herself offers.

"barque": playing between a poetic term for a rowboat seen as in a romance, and a modern term for a type of three-masted sailing ship.

"phosphor": playing between the effect of bright moonlight on the waves, and of actual phosphorus luminous in a warm sea.

"moon-monsters": Stevens identified the moon-monsters as "drifting vapors." He approved of the adjective *troublants* (disturbing) to describe them in a Fr. translation, but added that in his mind's eye they were "more *gauches* than *troublants*" (to Henry Church, WAS 3471, 21 June 1939).

The Doctor of Geneva

Poetry 19 (Oct. 1921); see note on "The Snow Man"; CP 24, LOA 19.

Not Balboa or stout Cortez meeting the Pacific with wild surmise, as in Keats's sonnet, "On First Looking into Chapman's Homer." Rather, one of Stevens's learned European doctors, here from Geneva (city of Calvin, city that expelled Rousseau, city beside a lake), a reader of the French classics, a good city burgher. On all counts, the doctor possesses an orderly mind, whose view of the ocean is implied in Stevens's pun on "impounding" (l. 2). In this third seashore poem in a row, the sentence structure is governed by the rhythm of the plot, while the regular iambic pentameter bursts its bounds at appropriate spots.

"impounding": beyond the usual and the legal meanings, note the submerged effect of "pound," which is an action of the water, not the sand.

"stove-pipe hat": U.S. term, originally for a tall, silk hat (first use 1851, OED); with the shawl, it may indicate that the doctor prefers old-fashioned dress (see OED 1902 quotation).

"Lacustrine": on lake-thinking versus ocean-thinking, see note on "Esthétique du Mal" xiv, below ("Lakes are more reasonable than oceans") and "Description without Place" iii, iv, below ("Lenin by a lake," "apocalyptic legions").

"Racine or Bossuet": see Stevens's amusing remark on "the orderly relations of society" as a fit theme for a choir or for Racine (L 305, 1936); elsewhere, he admires Racine (e.g., SPBS 57n).

"unburgherly apocalypse": the doctor's body betrays his orderly mind, and responds to the Pacific in a sudden unpredictable apo-calypse, or uncovering. That is, the doctor sneezes. A re-covering by his handkerchief is required. A French sneeze (*éternument*) is apocalyptic in the sense that it approaches eternity (*éternité*). For Stevens's mixed views of a burgher, see "The Weeping Burgher."

Another Weeping Woman

Poetry 19 (Oct. 1921); see note on "The Snow Man," above; CP 25, LOA 19.

In 1921 this poem followed "The Cuban Doctor," another poem of unspecified personal crisis. The argument hinges on "Leaves you," which is unhappily ambiguous. The poem offers no sympathy, presumably because sympathy is useless—or so the argument assumes.

"the imagination, the one reality": Stevens's two key terms in his early work, juxtaposed in an apparent but momentary oxymoron.

"Leaves you": as a single line, loss of the reason for living ("the magnificent cause of being, / The imagination"); extended over the enjambment, "Leaves you / with him," i.e., leaves the weeping woman with a man "for whom no phantasy moves."

"phantasy": in context, probably a weak contrast to "imagination," as in Coleridge's classic definition of fancy versus imagination (*Biographia Literaria*, chap. 13, and cf. "Le Monocle de Mon Oncle"); whatever the case, the woman's phantasy will not be realized.

Homunculus et La Belle Étoile

Poetry 15 (Oct. 1919); see note on "The Paltry Nude Starts on a Spring Voyage," above; CP 25–27, LOA 20–21.

The title (Fr.) means "Homunculus and the Beautiful Star." A homunculus is a miniature man or a dwarf; Paracelsus thought he could be created artificially, and others thought he existed in minute form in human sperm. The star is Venus. Homunculus, who is related etymologically to the uncle of "Le Monocle" and the "nuncle" of "Floral Decorations," sets about restoring the relation of Venus to philosophers in this arch and charming poem. Around the time of *Ideas of Order*, Stevens thought of the poem as "an early poem of order." The first part of the poem describes "state[s] of confusion" (L 306, 1936).

"drunkards, poets, widows, / And ladies soon to be married": one of Stevens's variations on the famous speech by Theseus on "the lunatic, the lover, and the poet" (*A Midsummer Night's Dream* V.i.7–8), with drunkard substituting for lunatic.

"a wanton . . . Fecund": a very different reading of Venus than in "O, Florida, Venereal Soil."

The Comedian as the Letter C

CP 27–46, LOA 22–37.

A difficult poem linguistically, especially toward the end; for an acquired taste, and chiefly of interest for Stevens's wry view in 1922 of his own artistic development. The earlier shorter version, "From the Journal of Crispin," 1921 (OP 46–59, LOA 985–95), is easier to follow and more cheerful. Stevens allegorizes his partial literary biography as the physical and mental journey of

Crispin, the poem's hero of sorts. The narrative voice often mocks Crispin, in the mixed tone of speeches to one's earlier "greenhorn" self (I.27). (Cf. Browning's *Sordello* as a similar exploration of false paths and an undesired fate for the writing self; Browning also masked his cautionary tale in difficult language.) A series of running metaphors with multiple puns charts Crispin's progress—metaphors of music, printing, hair and clothing, soil and cultivation and food, etc. The words describing Crispin also chart his progress: a series of comical tropes in Book I, then "sophomore," "hermit," etc.

On a common cycle for the mind, "from romanticism to realism, to fatalism and then to indifferentism," see L 352 (1940). Stevens notes that the cycle may start again with a new romanticism. But, at the time of this poem, he resisted such a move. He had begun to sense that he "was on the edge" and he "wanted to get to the center" (ibid., and see head-note to *Ideas of Order*). Stevens sends Crispin through the cycle, and leaves him at the end of it. On Crispin's haphazard kind of life, with its "mass of irrelevancies," see L 293 (1935).

Throughout, Stevens uses a syntactical rhythm of very long sentences and very short ones, enacting Crispin's hyperbolic responses and sudden deflations. The entire poem is written in unusually regular blank verse, an indirect comment on its plot, since Stevens shows remarkable variety and command of metrical and free-verse forms all through *Harmonium*.

TITLE: the letter C is a "cypher for Crispin," as Stevens says, but much more. The poem is also "THE COMEDIAN AS THE SOUNDS OF THE LETTER C"; various C sounds accompany Crispin including the varieties of TS, Z, X, and so on. These provide a "whistling and mocking" background—"to say it as a lawyer might say it, 'In, on or about the words' " (L 351–52, 1940). In 1935, Stevens spoke of the shades of the letter C as having "a comic aspect" (L 294, 1935)—by the end, a comic aspect with a black edge.

I *The World without Imagination*

Crispin emigrates from France (i.e., European traditions, especially about art) to North America. The sea (punningly see-C) overwhelms him, destroying the neat certitudes of village life. (For another European confronting an ocean, see "The Doctor of Geneva.") The diction appropriately includes archaic or rare terms and Shakespearean hyperbole (ll 2–3, 22–27). This version is very close to Book I of "From the Journal of Crispin."

"Nota": (Lat.) "memorandum" (cf. Crispin "making notes" and as "annotator," II), as in the imperative *nota* of NB (*nota bene*, or note well); also a note of music (middle C?), and cf. *notae litterarum* or characters in writing such as the letter C.

"man is the intelligence of his soil": a proposition about man's domination over nature, which is taken as a given at the start and governs Books I–III.

"ghost": spirit (archaic), as in the Holy Ghost.

"principium / And lex. Sed quaeritur": (Lat.) "principle and law. But it is asked"; familiar legal language; *quaere* and *lex talionis* are listed in the *Concise Oxford Dictionary* for 1914.

"nincompated": a portmanteau word from "nincompoop" and "-pated" as in "addle-pated"; an appropriate echo of "syncopated," since grammatical syncopation is part of the effect.

"Crispin": patron saint of shoemakers (cf. Fr. *chausseurs*, or "chaucers," hence a possible progenitor of a poetic tradition); also a Commedia dell'arte type (see note on Scaramouche in "The Weeping Burgher," below) and a French comic type as valet (e.g., in Le Sage's *Crispin rival de son maître*); also one who desires to "crisp," i.e., "curl," a figure for troping (e.g. Herbert, see note on "Le Monocle de Mon Oncle" III, above).

"silentious porpoises . . . waves that were mustachios, / Inscrutable hair": a late comic version of Ovid's sea-creatures, in a sea that corresponds in shape.

"clickering . . . short-shanks": "clicker" as noun applies to the work of both a shoemaker and a compositor; "shank" is used of both shoes and the body of a type (as against, say, its foot).

"hallucinating horn," etc.: especially because of echoes, still faintly hallooing, from Spenser, Wordsworth, and Keats on Triton and his horn; playing also against "greenhorns" (l. 27).

"distortion of romance": "romance" and the "romantic" are variously defined in Stevens (see note on "Sailing after Lunch," below); here, romance is synonymous with being an "egotist."

"reality . . . imagination": Stevens's early and long-standing contraries, also variously defined; Crispin's limited imagination cannot handle the power of the sea.

"Crispin beheld and Crispin was made new": an echo from the Apocalypse, "Behold, I make all things new" (Rev. 21:5), in comic vein.

II *Concerning the Thunderstorms of Yucatan*

Crispin encounters the fauna and flora of North America, and its dramatic weather, starting in a semitropical zone. He desires to find a voice corresponding in strength and an eye sufficiently accurate, i.e., a new style, for these new phenomena. (Stevens's response to Florida bears comparing.) Stevens deleted references in "From the Journal of Crispin" to Petrarch, Virgil, and Ariosto, and to Crispin as "an artful, most affectionate emigrant / From Cytherea." The poem thereby lost its dimension as a voyage of erotic discovery.

"night-bird": presumably the nightingale, the exquisite songbird well known from European literature but not found in the Americas.

"vanishing autumn in a park": cf. "Invective against Swans."

"exquisite thought": see note on "Nomad Exquisite, below."

"His mind was free": cf. "Farewell to Florida," where similarly the mind is not free.

III *Approaching Carolina*

"The book of moonlight": Stevens's early work associates a moonlit world with imagination, also with eros. This often modifies, as here, into a dialectic between the moon and the sun, which is associated with reality.

"Morose chiaroscuro," etc.: "From the Journal of Crispin" adds a judgment: "A feverish conception that derived / From early writs and marginal heraldry."

"liaison, the blissful liaison": the connecting word for the interaction between humans and their environment is always important.

"Moonlight was an evasion . . . sun and moon": here and elsewhere, Crispin's reactions tend to follow an either-or pattern. Stevens would later write: "The law of contrast is crude," even if it is "one way of making progress" (L 445, 444, 1943).

"tropic": as elsewhere, also punning on "trope."

IV *The Idea of a Colony*

To judge from Stevens's early poems on specific named American places, Crispin's idea of a colony also appealed to him.

"Nota . . .": the opening proposition of Book I is reversed (environment now dominates man), in an either-or reversal that shortly begins to sound like geographical determinism.

"Exeunt omnes": (Lat.) "All leave", a standard stage direction; here also the culmination of six "ex-" words echoing through three lines.

"the whole shebang": a favorite Stevens mix of high and colloquial diction; the OED cites Whitman as first recording "shebang" in 1862.

"The appointed power unwielded from disdain": a pastiche of Miltonic language from *PL*, where "disdain" describes Satan's pride.

"Eden . . . innocence": the Americas as an earthly paradise, one form of primitivism.

"island hemisphere": the Americas as one huge island; cf. "Sunday Morning" VIII.

"salt": as in "worth his salt," also as a synonym for wit (OED 3.c), also recalling Book I.

"skyey sheets": "the most skyey of skyey sheets" describes powerful imaginative writing in L 231 (1922); for "skyey" as a poetic word in different contexts, see OED.

"No, no, veracious page on page exact": "From the Journal of Crispin" adds six lines to end the poem in a firm closure quite unlike the attempted open closure of the revised version ("As Crispin in his attic shapes the book . . . Thereafter he may stalk in other spheres," OP 59, LOA 995).

V *A Nice Shady Home*

This part ends with a prolonged contrast between the sun, the great energizer, and the quotidian, which depletes energy. A "shady home" is hardly propitious. The domestic setting with muse-cum-wife is a diminution, for all its comforts; what Crispin needs now is to find a self "more truly and more strange" ("Tea at the Palaz of Hoon"). Much later, Stevens's muse-cum-beloved figures (the "fat girl," NSF III.x; "Final Soliloquy of the Interior Paramour") also inhabit domestic settings, but simple ones where artistic energy is not depleted. A tour de force of thirteen rhetorical questions (V.36–54) explores and rejects hyperbolic responses to Crispin's diminution.

"Candide": hero of sorts in Voltaire's philosophical novel, *Candide ou l'optimisme* (1759); he begins as an innocent, endures much, and concludes that "Il faut cultiver notre jardin," in a now-proverbial expression; a suggestive C character for Crispin.
"quotidian": an important word in Stevens; cf. "malady of the quotidian" in "The Man Whose Pharynx Was Bad," 1921.
"Although the rose . . . lay beside him": the entire series of phrases and clauses can be bracketed for easier comprehension.
"a humped return . . . from . . . fiscs": the price of the quotidian results in dubious financial reward, as in a humped miser's form (or humped sacks of gold), and just possibly as in a sexual posture (cf. Shakespeare's "exchequer" in a money-sex wordplay, Sonnet 67).
"Exchequering from piebald fiscs unkeyed": one example of concentrated C sounds and tangled meaning. These C sounds go "hissing and screeching all over the place" (L 352, 1940), and also "squeak" (L 294, 1935); "exchequering," said Stevens, contained about as many C sounds as any word he could think of (ibid.); "piebald" continues the series of motley and clown tropes, while "unkeyed" works in the contexts of a literal and/or personal treasury and of jangled music and harmony.

VI *And Daughters with Curls*

On the move toward fatalism and indifferentism, see head-note, and further in L 354 (1940). Crispin as "progenitor" here becomes a progenitor of children rather than poems. The four allegorical daughters have never been read to general satisfaction, despite their distinct characteristics. Read literally, the plot is about the sapping of artistic energy and achievement by busy family life—not applicable to Stevens, whose only child was not yet born or expected. Nor had he ceased writing, though see the head-note to *Ideas of Order*. Among useful suggestions are: four stages in Stevens's own work, marked by different muse figures and different relations between imagination and reality; four stages in American literature similarly marked.

"Portentous enunciation . . . Forgather and bell boldly": as in Book I, an ironic voice piles up hyperbolic phrases about Crispin. The opening imperative mood parodies epic opening sentences that similarly call on the muse.

"door-yard": despite Whitman's elegy for Lincoln, "When Lilacs Last in the Dooryard Bloom'd," Stevens much later denied any "reference to President Lincoln"; he added that "door-yard" is not in common use, except in the South (letter to Charles Tomlinson, 3 July 1951, University of Massachusetts Amherst; see acknowledgments).

"Score this anecdote," etc.: another long imperative sentence, offering one type of ending. Another, even longer sentence follows at once, offering another type of ending with the question, "what can all this matter?" Insofar as it is a rhetorical question, it is depressing.

"The relation comes, benignly, to its end": "relation" in several senses, including the relation of the reader to this poem, and the relation of reality and imagination as seen in Crispin; "benignly" attempts to mitigate some of the poem's severe judgments.

"So may the relation of each man be clipped": a decidedly ambiguous ending; "clipped" takes both its modern meaning of "cut short" and its archaic meaning of "embrace."

From the Misery of Don Joost

Poetry 19 (Oct. 1921); see note on "The Snow Man," above; CP 46, LOA 37.

Stevens called his invention, Don Joost, "a jovial Don Quixote" (L 464, 1944). He is hardly jovial here, though perhaps he once was in his "body, the old animal." Cf. "misery" in "The Snow Man," also a 1921 poem. Stevens focused on the subject in a 1938 poem beginning "That's what misery is" ("Poetry Is a Destructive Force").

"combat": as against Don Quixote: "It seems clear to me . . . that thou art not well-versed in the matter of adventures: these are giants; and if thou art afraid, move aside and start to pray whilst I enter with them in fierce and unequal combat" (Cervantes, *Don Quixote*, I.viii, trans. Edith Grossman, 2003).

O, Florida, Venereal Soil

Dial 73 (July 1922); see note on "The Ordinary Women," above; CP 47, LOA 38.

A poem written against the overwhelming, messy sexiness and fecundity of Florida, here personified as an all-too-earthly Venus. The heavenly Venus, the planet, and the constellation Virgo suggest more discriminating ways to behave. The classical Venus at her fullest is both chaste and fecund. The five 7-line stanzas, mostly in dimeter and trimeter, lengthen to tetrameter at the end in a slowing effect appropriate to a more subtly seductive Venus.

TITLE: LOA restores the comma after "O," cut in CP, but present in all previous printings. Florida personified recalls original Sp. "Pascua florida" (Webster) and the root meaning from Lat. *floridus,* flowery (Milton: "this florid earth"). "Venereal": of Venus, as in "venereal trains" (Milton, *Samson Agonistes* 533), though now chiefly of sexual disease. "Soil": evoking both virgin soil and mother earth. Venus as goddess functioned as the sexually desirable woman and/or the great mother, the generative principle in all nature, as in Lucretius, *De Rerum Natura* I.1–28.

"Convolvulus": genus of plants with winding stems, e.g., bindweed; common moony-flowered weedy vine; a faint acoustic echo of "vulva."

"Tiestas": (Sp.) barrel-hoops.

"Virgin of boorish births": cf. numerous paintings with titles such as "Virgin of the Rocks."

"Donna": fem. form of Sp. Don; title of honor or courtesy for a woman, here Florida.

"a hand that bears a thick-leaved fruit": Venus sometimes carries symbolically fertile fruit in her hand.

Last Look at the Lilacs

Secession 4 (Jan. 1923); CP 48, LOA 39.

A blunt and atypical poem for Stevens, who is not at ease with this tone. Cf. some of the strained effects in "The Comedian as the Letter C," written in the same time period.

TITLE: Lilacs do not make Stevens happy; cf. the "lilacs give the alleys," etc., in "From the Journal of Crispin" III (OP 54, LOA 991), "the lilacs magnify / The easy passion" (NSF II.vii), and "The sad smell of the lilacs" ("Things of August" iv).

"the fragrance of vegetal": a contemporary commercial hair and skin tonic, still in production, was called "Lilac Vegetal."

"Floréal": April 20 to May 19 in the 1793 French Republican calendar; echoing the word "Florida."

"its fantastic star": the planet Venus, also evoking the preceding poem.

The Worms at Heaven's Gate

Others 3 (July 1916); CP 49, LOA 40.

The poem offers an earthy chariot to heaven for Badroulbadour, and an earthy version of the resurrection of the body. Like several other early poems, it is acutely aware of the death of the body. The challenge lies in the tone: not Hamlet-like mordant wit, but a mix of emotion that includes tenderness and eschews the lugubrious. The eight iambic pentameter lines are followed by a full-line ellipsis, which indicates a long pause, then by a single line repeating line 1.

TITLE: A contrary to Shakespeare's song, "Hark, hark, the lark at heaven's gate sings" (*Cymbeline* II.iii.20); cf. "The larks cannot always sing at heaven's gate" (L 27, 1899). Not "hymns at heaven's gate" sung by the lark (Shakespeare, sonnet 29) but, punningly, worms.

"Badroulbadour": the most beautiful woman in the world in the *Arabian Nights*; see Brewer, "Badoura."

"we her chariot": Williams suggested this revision from "as a chariot"; he also suggested a deletion, marked by the ellipsis (*WSJ* 3 [1979]: 72–73).

"genius": see note on "The Idea of Order at Key West," below.

The Jack-Rabbit

CP 50, LOA 40.

Jack-rabbit, Arkansaw black man, grandmother, and buzzard all figure in this spirited tall-tale poem, with a distinctive Stevens flavor. The jack-rabbit's language puns and plays exuberantly, while the realistic down-to-earth Arkansaw reckons with a menacing deathly buzzard. This is another poem of contrary forces, with one force destructive of song.

TITLE: the jack-rabbit is a singer, like Brer Rabbit in the classic American tall tales (see "Ploughing on Sunday").

"caracoles": half turns to right or left, executed by horse and rider, as in *Don Quixote*, "hacer un revuelto caracol" (to move in caracoles, II.LXI, trans. Grossman); echoing "carol."

"on the feat sandbars": punning on musical feet (to say nothing of the jack-rabbit's) and bars.

"Crochet . . . On your winding-sheet": cf. the embroidered pigeons on the sheet in "The Emperor of Ice-Cream," also the embroidery in "Colloquy with a Polish Aunt" and "Explanation."

"buzzard": "in North America . . . corrupted in popular usage to mean our Vulture" (Peterson, "The Names of Hawks," *Field Guide to the Birds* (Eastern), 2d ed. [1934]).

Valley Candle

Others, special number (Dec. 1917), with "Thirteen Ways of Looking at a Blackbird," "The Wind Shifts," "Meditation," "Gray Room" (OP 28–29, LOA 537–38), under the title "Five Poems"; CP 51, LOA 41.

Candles figure throughout Stevens's work; see, e.g., his play, *Carlos among the Candles* (also 1917, OP 163–67, LOA 615–20) and "Final Soliloquy of the Interior Paramour" (1950).

Anecdote of Men by the Thousand

Little Review 5 (June 1918); see note on "Metaphors of a Magnifico," above; CP 51–52, LOA 41.

For the close cultural and geographical identification of people with places, cf. "The Comedian as the Letter C" IV.31–65.

"he said": as in "I say," "we say," etc.; an unidentified pronoun with the verb "to say" is a common distancing device in Stevens.

"Lhassa": capital of Tibet, largely inaccessible in 1918 and so especially exotic; site of British armed intervention in 1908 and later struggles (see EB, "Tibet": "Explorations," "History").

[The Silver Plough-Boy: 1923 only]

OP 17, LOA 42

The Apostrophe to Vincentine

Modern School 5 (Dec. 1918); CP 52–53, LOA 42–43.

Earth and heaven, at first separate, become interpenetrated one with the other, through and in the nude, heavenly Vincentine, as here figured. Similarly with reality and the imagination. This is a painterly poem in its sense of composition and color. The numbered stanzas of irregular line length have repeated end-rhymes on "Vincentine" (13 in 27 lines).

TITLE: Another *Harmonium* title announcing the genre of its poem; cf. also "apostrophes are forbidden" in "Botanist on Alp (No. 1)." "Vincentine" is etymologically the conquering one (feminine).

"figured": in both the painter's and the poet's sense of "figure."

"between": "between / The sheets" is what the reader might expect; Stevens's enjambment veers away.

"what I knew you felt": cf. the end of "Gray Room."

Floral Decorations for Bananas

Measure 26 (Apr. 1923), with "New England Verses" and "How the Constable Carried the Pot across the Public Square," all under the title, "Three Poems"; the other two appeared only in the 1931 *Harmonium*; CP 53–54, LOA 43–44.

Has there ever been such a description of banana flowers as Stevens's last stanza? The poem functions like a near-riddle poem asking: what are the right floral decorations for bananas? Answer: banana leaves and flowers, alive as animals in all their sexual force. The eglantine in stanza 1 stand no chance in this contrast of tropical versus temperate, primitive versus delicate (eighteenth-century style), Gaugin versus Watteau. This is another Stevens poem on how the tropics affect someone from a northern temperate zone. The diction embodies this contrast, which is heightened by hyperbole, rhyme, alliteration, and assonance; the exclamation marks, unusual in Stevens, mark the persona's speech patterns.

"nuncle": jocular term for "uncle" in local U.S. and U.K. diction, also the way a learned fool may address a superior in Shakespeare (*King Lear*, I.iv.170); "nuncle" sets the knowing tone of the poem, which is overwhelmed by the force of the last stanza.

Anecdote of Canna

Little Review 5 (Dec. 1918); see note on "Nuances of a Theme by Williams," above; CP 55, LOA 44.

Not a remarkable poem by Stevens's standards, but with the advantage of a useful Stevens gloss on its beginnings. As he recalled, Stevens was putting in time in Washington, where the flower-beds around the Capitol were full of canna lilies (L 465, 1944).

"X": identified as the President, who continues to think in his sleep; but sleeping thought is different from waking thought because "*it meets only itself.*" Hence the President's "exhilaration" when he awakes and sees the reality of the canna freshly (ibid.). It is not clear from the poem or Stevens's later comment whether the canna may provide any larger allegory.

Of the Manner of Addressing Clouds

Poetry 19 (Oct. 1921); see note on "The Snow Man"; CP 55–56 (title incorrectly says "On" for "Of"), LOA 44–45.

Cf. *Alice's Adventures in Wonderland,* chap. 2, on how to address a mouse, with her memory of the Latin vocative case. Stevens' poem does not quite live up to the promise of its title.

Of Heaven Considered as a Tomb

Ibid.; CP 56, LOA 45.

The trope of heaven as a vault is well known (e.g., Shelley on night as "the dome of a vast sepulchre / Vaulted," "Ode to the West Wind" ii.11–12). Stevens similarly rewrites the vault as a tomb, still inhabited by ghosts of the dead.

"of men": "of " is ambiguous ("from"? "about"?), as befitting ghosts.
"old comedy": see OCD for classical old comedy; the diction and argument also suggest an old divine comedy like Dante's.
"pillared up each day": cf. the guiding pillar by day in the Exodus journey (Ex. 13:21).

"the host shall no more wander": "host" as both a large group and the "host of heaven" where the ghosts' lanterns are the stars; cf. also the wandering of the Exodus journey.

"icy Elysée": Fr. for Elysium, with sound-play on "icy"—the temperature of space, though not the temperature of the classical Elysian fields, or, for all that, of the official residence of the French President, the Elysée.

Of the Surface of Things

Poetry 15 (Oct. 1919); see note on "The Paltry Nude Starts on a Spring Voyage," above; CP 57, LOA 45–46.

" 'The spring is like a belle undressing' ": Northrop Frye commented, "Not a hell of a good line at that" (annotations to CP; see acknowledgments).

Anecdote of the Prince of Peacocks

CP 57–58, LOA 46; see the earlier MS version (1918–1920?) in the Huntington Library, OP 40, LOA 550 (a fuller MS version in the Beinecke Library is closer to the final printing); CP 57–58, LOA 46.

The early version is arch and charming, but has little of the powerful uncanniness of the final version. This is a haunting dream poem, where Berserk is more dangerous for the Prince than the buzzard is for the jack-rabbit in "The Jack-Rabbit." Note the *c* and *p* sounds in the name of this persona, who resembles part of Stevens's own self (cf. Crispin, Peter Quince, etc.). The contrast of moonlit and sunlit worlds, and their relation to art, is developed later in the powerful poem, "The Motive for Metaphor." The poem uses strong stress (or pure accentual), the poetic meter of the time of a Berserker.

TITLE: see note on "Earthy Anecdote," above.
"moonlight": the place of the imagination for early Stevens; blue ("milky blue") is consistently its color.
"Berserk": This personified "berserk" is descended from a Berserker (a powerful Norse warrior fighting in a mad frenzy), but is more subtly scheming than his impulsive forebear. Alas, his effect is all the more deadly. Also a figure for an internal part of the self.
" 'You that wander ... On the bushy plain' ": cf. "So long you wandered on the dusky plain" (Andrew Lang, trans. du Bellay, "To His Friend in Elysium").

"blocks / And blocking steel": cf. William James's well-known opposition to a "block universe"; cf. also "steel" in "The Motive for Metaphor."

A High-Toned Old Christian Woman

Dial 123 (July 1922); see note on "The Ordinary Women," above; CP 59, LOA 47.

One of a group of antipietistic poems written about this time, e.g., "Of Heaven Considered as a Tomb." Stevens develops a heaven designed to suit the less orthodox. The poem is addressed provocatively to someone who will not appreciate it.

title: "High-Toned": the full phrase was spoken by a Southern friend, Judge Powell (Brazeau, 100); the punning anticipates Stevens's governing trope, the music of a conventional heaven versus the jovial music of an "opposing law."
"the supreme fiction": first use of Stevens's well-known phrase, here simply in a general affirmation opposed to canonical sacred Scriptures; later, much developed in the thirty cantos of "Notes toward a [not "the"] Supreme Fiction" (1942).
"the opposing law": opposing "the moral law"; in context, bawdiness, jazz, good food, and revelry.
"tink," etc.: "tink" is echoic (earliest OED record from Ben Jonson) as is "tink-tank"; "tunk" is Stevens's contribution, as if he were extending the series by echoing the vowels in the conjugation of Germanic strong verbs like "ring, rang, rung" (see also "Page from a Tale").
"wink": cf. "When most I wink" (Shakespeare, sonnet 43), a "studied refusal to recognize evil" (Stephen Booth, *Shakespeare's Sonnets* [1977], on 43.1). Stevens's stars wink and twinkle to various ends.

The Place of the Solitaires

Poetry 15 (Oct. 1919); see note on "The Paltry Nude Starts on a Spring Voyage," above; CP 60, LOA 47–48.

Stevens called this "a poem actually in motion . . . with the activity of thought in solitude" (L 463, 1944). Cf. other "solitude" and "solitaire" poems, e.g., "Solitaire under the Oaks." Bloom cites Emerson's essay, "Society and Solitude" (94). Stevens's shapely free verse is framed by very similar couplets, and consists of one short and one eleven-line sentence; of the thirteen lines, six end in an onomatopoeic "-tion" sound.

The Weeping Burgher

Ibid.; CP 61, LOA 48.

On Stevens's antagonism against conventional "burghers," cf. the "un-burgherly apocalypse" in "The Doctor of Geneva." This burgher bitterly re-grets that he has never expressed the selves within him. Compare "Another Weeping Woman."

"Scaramouche": Fr. form of Scaramuccia (literally "skirmish"), a stock charac-
   ter in Italian *commedia dell'arte*, a bully and intriguer and military adven-
   turer. In 1920, Stevens ordered several older books about eighteenth-
   century Italy, especially its theater; they include descriptions of the stock
   theatrical "masks" or personae (LFR 385).
"black barouche": Scaramouche is commonly dressed in black, as Pierrot is
   commonly dressed in white; Pierrot is an early Stevens persona (L 106,
   1907–8; 134, 1909; 166, 1910). Northrop Frye calls stanza 2 a "black and
   white version of Philistinism" (annotations to CP; see acknowledgments).

The Curtains in the House of the Metaphysician

Ibid.; CP 62, LOA 49.

Compare the treatment of motion here with that in "The Place of the Soli-taires." Query: how does a metaphysician deal with the topos of the drifting curtains, or even possess such curtains in the first place? This is one of Stevens's single-sentence poems, in ten lines of varied stress.

"the drifting of these curtains": a romantic topos in writing, painting, and
   film; cf. also the effect of "the drifting of the curtains" in "A Dish of
   Peaches in Russia."
"long motions": also describing the poem's structure, with its "long open
   sounds," as in l. 6 ("silence, wide sleep and solitude" [L 463, 1944]).

Banal Sojourn

Ibid.; CP 62–63, LOA 49.

A poem of a humid heat-wave, dominated by parasites, whether earwigs or mildew. As with the mildew of "The Man Whose Pharynx Was Bad" (1921), natural pests provide tropes for writerly pests or writer's block. Or tropes for a general block, as in Stevens's startling last line. Stevens called the poem "a poem of exhaustion in August," which may typify "the mildew" of any season or experience grown monotonous, including "the experience of life" (L 464, 1944). In 1917 the title, "Banal Sojourn," figured in the parodic play, "Bowl, Cat, and Broomstick" (OP 173, LOA 629). Working with long lines, some archaic diction, and mostly short sentences, the poem culminates in the repeated "malady" that anticipates "the malady of the quotidian," again in the more powerful "The Man Whose Pharynx Was Bad."

"grackles crack": with this onomatopoeic effect of the grackle's name and sound, cf. "Autumn Refrain."
"Our old bane": traditionally Satan (cf. "the Satan ear" below); adding to the sense of "banal" in the title.
"wigs despoiling the Satan ear": ordinarily, earwigs despoil an ear of corn; the conjunction of "Satan ear" recalls Satan, "like a Toad, close at the ear of Eve" (PL IV.800).

Depression before Spring

Little Review 5 (June 1918); see note on "Metaphors of a Magnifico," above; CP 63, LOA 50.

Contrast with the exuberance of "Ploughing on Sunday," also written in short-line free verse, with echoic words.

"ki-ki-ri-ki": imitative of a cock calling.
"rou-cou": (Fr) "coo," imitative of dove-song or other cooing song, here female.
"no queen comes / In slipper green": unlike Stevens's later "green queen [who] comes" in "Description without Place" i.

The Emperor of Ice-Cream

Dial 123 (July 1922); see note on "The Ordinary Women," above; CP 64, LOA 50.

The entrancing title, succinct vignettes, and memorable refrain make this a favorite poem, much explicated and sometimes overallegorized. It is centered on the corpse of an ordinary woman laid out on an inexpensive table, and her simple funeral arrangements. Compare Williams' "Tract" (1917). Ice-cream, which is cold and tasty, informs death, which is cold and dumb. Stevens liked the poem. He spoke of its "deliberately commonplace costume" that nonetheless has "something of the essential gaudiness of poetry" (L 263, 1933). (On "gaudiness," see "Montrachet-le-Jardin," "plus gaudiest vir.") He also noted that he did not like "niggling" when he wrote, but rather liked "letting myself go," as in this poem (L 264, 1933). In 1931, Stevens spoke of the poem as "a respite from the imagination": "let us take life as we find it." (See the entire letter to R. P. Blackmur in Holly Stevens, "Flux," *Southern Review* 15 [1979]: 773–74.) See also L 341 (1939) on the poem as essentially "about being as distinguished from seeming to be," and not about ice-cream. In 1945, the Amalgamated Ice Cream Association asked Stevens what it meant, presumably with an eye to advertising (L 502). In 1951, Stevens declined a suggestion that the title provide the theme for a Houston ball: "The final reality is not death but life, as it is, without any pretenses. The roller of big cigars is the ordinary laborious man; the wenches dawdling are women in their ordinary occupations; the boys are every-day children. No one is seduced. There are no parades. But over all a will dominates: the will of the extraordinary. The point of the poem is to isolate and make crisp the commonplace. The emperor as a symbol is the simple symbol of a physical good. . . . To make people at a ball conscious of the excitement of reality . . . seems like asking a good deal" (to John Rawlings, 21 Nov. 1951, New York Public Library, Berg Collection; see acknowledgments).

"concupiscent curds": Stevens rightly preferred the Fr. translation "*des laits libinineux*" to "*des crèmes délectables*" (L 340, 1939); the phrase points to life's concupiscence and, by the contrasts in the poem, to "life's destitution"; this, Stevens added, gave them "something more than a cheap lustre"—a craftsman's firm judgment on his work (L 500, 1945).

"fantails": fantail pigeons (L 340, 1939).

"Let be be finale of seem. / The only emperor is the emperor of ice-cream": resonating against Hamlet's remarks, also on a corpse and a meal, "Your worm is your only emperor for diet," and in turn his earlier "Seems, madam! Nay, it is. I know not 'seems'" (*Hamlet* IV.iii.22 and I.ii.76). Stevens called himself "poor Yorick" in 1920 (L 219), and earlier said that the subject of death absorbed him (L 206, 1918).

The Cuban Doctor

Poetry 19 (Oct. 1921); see note on "The Snow Man," above; CP 64–65, LOA 51.

On the inescapability of certain hostile forces. The implied plot involves a learned Cuban doctor and a skilled, primitive Indian (probably North American). It sounds at first like a Wilkie Collins' plot, as in *The Moonstone*. But on reflection, it resembles more the common experience of finding some inimical force (especially internal or psychological) in the very place we went in order to escape it. Compare the two forces in "Anecdote of the Prince of Peacocks."

"worm": in the archaic sense of a serpent.
"summer's . . . horn": commonly the cornucopia or horn of plenty.

Tea at the Palaz of Hoon

Ibid.; CP 65, LOA 51.

A poem on a remembered visionary experience of the sense of calling, as of a prophet, as of a poet, as of any strong vocation. The last line catches the paradox of finding one's own self "more truly" but also "more strange." The exotic or whimsical title sounds like something from the *Arabian Nights*, and keeps the sublime memory and its biblical language from solemnity. Stevens's strange, true sublime self (early style) is caught and defended in "Hoon." On Stevens's thoughts about Hoon in 1935, see "Sad Strains of a Gay Waltz." For a major development of the argument here, see "The Idea of Order at Key West." The four iambic pentameter tercets move generically from a dramatic monologue to a soliloquy.

TITLE: Who is Hoon? Stevens's tongue-in-cheek response in 1955 identified Hoon as Hoon or just possibly "the son of old man Hoon," who sounds like a Dutchman (L 871). He added that the name Hoon was probably a "cipher for 'the loneliest air' [l. 3] of sky and space." Hoon as cipher suggests that the loneliest air is also a place where the nourishment or inspiration of poetry may be ingested. (For poetry as tea, see also the little poem, "Tea.") Stevens had a passion for long walks in rural or wild settings. "Palaz": cf. It. *palazzio* and low Ger. *palas*.
"Not less . . . was I myself": the logic opposes an argument (from the unidentified "you"?) that we are not "really" ourselves in visionary or exalted states (see appendix, under "Logic").
"in purple I descended / The western day": purple is the color of royalty and bishops and exalted personages (cf. also Stevens: "The purple robe must, of course, be laid aside now and then; but never, I hope, entirely lost sight of" [to Elsie, WAS 1866, 6 July 1909]); "descended" in the west like the sun or Apollo; more humanly, like a prophet or poet or visionary descending from a mountain (Hoon is called "that mountain-minded Hoon" in "Sad Strains of a Gay Waltz"). A mountain-top as a place of vision is a familiar topos.
"ointment": as in oil anointing a prophet, priest, or ruler, e.g., the reigning monarch of the United Kingdom; the word "Christ" (from Gk. *Xristos*, translating Heb.) means literally "the Anointed One."

"beard," "hymns": with "ointment," biblical language, emphasized by later repetition.

"came not but from myself ": note the difference between the highly subjective argument here and Wordsworth's "what they half create, / And what perceive" ("Lines [on] . . . Tintern Abbey," 106–7), or, for all that, Stevens's later thinking; not, however, radically subjective, because of "there" in the last line.

"more truly and more strange": "more truly" is familiar language, "more strange" is stranger; note the slightly startling grammatical shift from adverb to adjective.

[Exposition of the Contents of a Cab: 1923 only]

OP 41, LOA 52

Disillusionment of Ten O'Clock

Rogue 2 (15 Sept. 1915); CP 66, LOA 52–53.

An engaging early poem, written against the smothering dullness of staid "white night-gown" living, devoid of anything "strange" ("strange" links it to the preceding poem). With respect to a translation into French, Stevens commented that he was thinking of "something bizarre." He added that, for himself, he liked words that "sound wrong" (L 340, 1939). The poem is an early example of his work with the negative as a form of argument, emphasized here by line breaks, line-end repetitions, and anaphora.

"purple with green rings," etc.: the function of color throughout Stevens is worth attention; note here the resemblance to clown costumes.

"ceintures": (Fr.) "waistbands."

"an old sailor, / Drunk and asleep": cf. Baudelaire's "Ce matelot ivrogne" ("Le Voyage").

"In red weather": "Red sky at night, / Sailor's delight"?

Sunday Morning

Poetry (Nov. 1915), reordered as stanzas I, VIII, IV, V, VII; CP 66–70, LOA 53–56. Among Stevens's first major poems, "Sunday Morning" appeared in a shortened form in *Poetry*, as requested (see L 183, 1915), and was so known until 1923.

The poem plays on two senses of Sunday: (1) the day of Christian worship, and (2) the day of the sun. Stevens's homiletics are naturalistic and antisupernatural (see L 464n, 1944), preferring a Virgil-Keats line of inheritance to a biblical, Miltonic line. Each stanza is numbered, self-contained, and centered on a single proposition (e.g., "Death is the mother of beauty"). The first and last stanzas form a contrasting diptych. Generically a modulated ode (see Fowler), and demonstrating Stevens's early command of a Tennysonian eloquence and of the iambic pentameter line, "Sunday Morning" has remained a favorite. Stevens returned to its subject in the forties, notably in "Notes toward a Supreme Fiction."

"Complacencies": cf. the etymological meaning of "well pleased," as in Milton, "my sole complacence" (*PL* III.276).

"ancient sacrifice," also "the blood and sepulchre" (l. 15): references to the crucifixion of Jesus Christ.

"She": the unidentified, embowered woman, whose Sunday-morning reverie provides the occasion for the poem and debating points for the "I."

"Winding across wide water, without sound": cf. Milton, "I hear the far-off Curfew sound, / Over some wide-water'd shore" ("Il Penseroso" 74–75).

"our blood, commingling, virginal, / With heaven . . . hinds discerned it, in a star": references to the Christian Nativity, with Jesus as both human and divine, the Virgin Mary, the shepherds, and the star of Bethlehem.

"shall the earth / Seem all of paradise that we shall know?": cf. Milton, "for then the Earth / Shall all be Paradise" (*PL* XII.463–64)

"golden underground . . . heaven's hill": topoi of paradise in classical and Christian accounts.

"sure obliteration . . . littering leaves": topoi of death, playing on senses of "leaves," and etymologically on "obliteration" and "littering"; the willow is symbolically the tree of death and also of unrequited love.

"disregarded plate": silver plate, "so-called family plate" (L 183, 1915); in *Poetry* 1915: "She causes boys to bring sweet-smelling pears, / And plums in ponderous piles . . . ," a variation on the topos of offering fruit to the beloved (cf. Virgil, *Eclogues* II.52).

"A voice that cries, 'The tomb in Palestine . . .'": assertion denying the resurrection of Jesus, introduced by a clause in biblical language.

"We live in an old chaos . . . inescapable": naturalistic overviews of this earth.

"Deer walk . . . extended wings": an extended sentence of exquisite rhythm, alluding to Keats's "To Autumn," stanza 3; "quail": cf. Ex. 16:23, Ps. 105:40; "casual flocks of pigeons . . . wings" thoroughly revises the tradition of the single, causal Holy Spirit in the form of a dove, bringing light and life (e.g. Milton, *PL* I.19–23, Hopkins, "God's Grandeur" 13–14, and cf. the Milton-Keats-Hopkins birds of "In the Element of Antagonisms").

The Virgin Carrying a Lantern

CP 71, LOA 56–57.

A slight spy poem, sounding like a somewhat weak offshoot of "Peter Quince at the Clavier." The poem is marked by over-easy parodic rhyme, close to nursery rhyme ("Moses supposes his toeses are roses").

"There are no bears . . .": echoing Theseus's speech, a favorite with Stevens, from Shakespeare's *A Midsummer Night's Dream*: "How easy is a bush suppos'd a bear!" (V.i.22).

Stars at Tallapoosa

Broom 2 (June 1922); CP 71, LOA 57.

Playing on lines, including the imagined lines that link stars into constellations, lines of an eyelid, the line of the night-horizon, lines of waves, lines of wave detritus, lines of shot arrows, lines of poetry, Whitman's lines. The poem is a coda to "Le Monocle de Mon Oncle," and an elegy for Stevens's Whitmanian and erotic muse.

"not the cradle . . . deep-oceaned": cf. Whitman, "Out of the Cradle Endlessly Rocking."
stanza 2: the correct text is that of LOA (for CP's "simplicity." read "simplicity,"; for CP's "on" read "no").
"secretive hunter": evoking (among other things) the constellation of Orion, the hunter (cf. the "arrows" in ll. 15, 17).

Explanation

Others: An Anthology, ed. Alfred Kreymborg, 1917; see note on "The Plot against the Giant," above; CP 72–73, LOA 58.

A charming though sad poem, which implies much in a few lines. The poem is a dramatic monologue in little, where a female speaker tells her mother what she is doing, as she works at a traditionally female occupation. The conversational tone indicates attachment between the German mother and her daughter, but no more by way of explanation for the daughter's clear, unfulfilled needs. Compare "Disillusionment of Ten O'Clock" and elsewhere for the suggestiveness of colors in clothing.

"Ach, Mutter . . . Nein, Nein . . . Liebchen": (Ger.) "Ah, mother . . . No, No . . . darling."

Six Significant Landscapes

Others 2 (Mar. 1916); see note on "Domination of Black," above; for a manuscript version titled "Eight Significant Landscapes," see OP 21, LOA 995; CP 73–75, LOA 58–60.

Six quite different ways in which an outer or inner landscape may be significant. The skilful short-line free verse works with phrasal and clausal breaks.

i. "In China / . . . larkspur": see Stevens's comments on the "irreality" of a place like China in 1909, whose "little realities" seem "wonderful and beyond belief" (L 137, 1909), as well his interest in Chinese responses to landscape paintings (ibid.). See also his remarks in 1915 about studying the flowers in the New York Botanical Garden; he found larkspur very Chinese (L 184).

vi. "square hats": as in academic mortar-boards; the metaphor of putting on a certain hat to do a certain job is literalized (cf. the sombrero in "The Pastor Caballero").

Bantams in Pine-Woods

Dial 123 (July 1922); see note on "The Snow Man," above; CP 75–76, LOA 60.

A spirited hyperbolic challenge from one bantam to the reigning chief cock. Hence, any challenge from "the little fellow" (Chaplin's persona) to the big guy; from the *eiron* to the *alazon* in classical comedy (the *eiron*'s irony vents itself in wild punning here). The poem treats bantam versus cock in every sense of the word: literal bird, cock of the walk or braggadocio, and (faintly, as if echoing Shakepearean bawdry) male sexual organ. A battle between poets is only one example of Stevens's possible battles here. He wanted this poem to open the group of six poems in the *Dial*. The five couplets exuberantly rhyme and pun, as well as echoing Shakespeare's most extravagantly punning play. A good dictionary is essential for pursuing the many multiple readings (of "tang," "bristle," etc.).

TITLE: "Pine-Woods": with Stevens's usual pun on "pine" as "yearn for" (whence possibly "Pine-Woulds"?).

"Chieftain Iffucan of Azcan": inviting multiple readings, e.g., "If-you-can," "As-can."

"caftan . . . hackles": describing a rooster's head and neck.

"Fat! Fat! Fat! Fat!": cf. Rosaline in the battle between the sexes in *Love's Labour's Lost* on the king's and lords' inadequate wit, "gross, gross; fat, fat" (V.ii.269); the men, in ludicrous disguise, are attended by "Blackamoors with music" (cf. the "blackamoor" here, l. 4).

"hoos": in Stevens, usually a derisory sound, as in MBG x.

Anecdote of the Jar

Poetry 15 (Oct. 1919); see note on "The Paltry Nude Starts on a Spring Voyage," above; CP 76, LOA 60–61.

A powerful anecdote poem, where Stevens's odd grammar should be explored, not naturalized. Compare, e.g., the different effect of "I set a jar down on a hill / In Tennessee." Tennessee evoked in Stevens a different response than Florida. He was "of two minds about . . . this midway South" (L 206, 1918). See also L 208 (1918) for O. Henry on whether anything ever happened in Tennessee—not, Stevens commented, "without outside help." The unadorned jar seems unlikely help (though consider the beauty of simple gray Korean or Japanese pottery), yet it becomes a center and an ordering force, as human art takes dominion over nature, at least in the circumstances here. The poem might be called "The Idea of Order in Tennessee." Keats's "Ode on a Grecian Urn" is often compared, though note the different focus. Irregularly rhymed tetrameter quatrains, with short sentences and a high percentage of monosyllables, give a neat, pared, aphoristic effect.

"placed": as if to say "placed on a mantelpiece," "placed in a cabinet"; the entire state of Tennessee thereby becomes a possible setting for a jar.

"placed a jar in Tennessee": Stevens likes to put pressure on prepositions, using their inconspicuous force in unexpected ways; cf. "All over Minnesota, / Cerise sopranos, / Walking in the snow . . ." ("Primordia," OP 25, LOA 534).

"surround": the jar is not "about" anything in nature, but rather causes the wilderness to be "about" it or "surround" it, in another sense of "about."

"round upon the ground": note the shifting perspective from "round . . . upon a hill" (l. 2), and the shift again in the following line to "of a port in air"; note also the contrast of plane and elevation in the perspective, as if

one were looking at an architect's drawings or (more precisely) looking at
the jar with full aesthetic attention.

"port": "bearing," as in Hawthorne, whose ancestor "trod the unworn street
with such a stately port" (*The Scarlet Letter,* chap. 1, "The Custom-
House," para. 8) or in Milton, where "their port was more than human"
(*Comus* 396); also "purport"; see OED, Webster.

"of a port": Robert Hass notes that his grandmother referred to her husband
as being "of a port," to describe, approvingly, his bearing and his substan-
tial presence (2004, quoted by permission).

Palace of the Babies

Poetry 19 (Oct. 1921), under the title "Pecksniffiana"; see note on "The Snow Man,"
above; CP 77, LOA 61.

Compare the argument with that of "Stars at Tallapoosa."

Frogs Eat Butterflies. Snakes Eat Frogs. Hogs Eat Snakes. Men Eat Hogs

Dial 73 (July 1922); see note on "The Ordinary Women," above; CP 78, LOA 62.

The rhyming title is amusing, but the poem is not an Ogden Nash big-
flea–small-flea poem. The subject is metamorphosis, and not of the upward
type that ends with a butterfly-psyche. The poem moves like its nosing swine
and its nosing river and its planters' "indolent, arid days." It owes its powerful
sluggish effect to syntax (one 18-line sentence), diction, sound, repetition,
and regular stanzas (most have a 12-, an 8-, and a 9-syllable line). Compare
the effects of "The Load of Sugar-Cane."

"rattapallax": perhaps an echoic invention from *rataplan* (Fr.), the rat-tat-tat
of a drumbeat.

Jasmine's Beautiful Thoughts underneath the Willow

CP 79, LOA 62–63.

Despite the auspicious name of Jasmine (cf. "jasminerie . . . jasminatrice,"
L 229, 1922), not an especially memorable poem.

Cortège for Rosenbloom

Measure 1 (Mar. 1921); CP 79–80, LOA 63–64.

On how heaven is conventionally painted, and how "it all comes down to the proverbial six feet of earth" for everyone, see L 223 (1921). Stevens called the subject of his poem "this chestnut" (ibid.). He wrote what is in effect a funeral march, written against literalist belief in a heaven, which is here merely the sky. The setting is generally northern and European, as of a painting from Russia or a scene from *Boris Godunof.* The poem is another death poem from this period that stresses the death of the body. Stevens uses strong stress, as to a heavy drumbeat, settling into two-stress lines in the second half. "Dead" and "tread" end thirteen of the forty lines.

"Rosenbloom": apparently a general name, often Jewish.
"color of horn": the color of a dead body; cf. "horny feet" in "The Emperor of
   Ice-Cream."
"infants of nothingness": in 1944, Stevens said that "infants" signifies children,
   and nothingness signifies "without imagination" or "of the strictest prose"
   (L 464, 1944). Stevens likes to use the word "infant" in its etymological
   sense of "unable to speak" (Lat. *infans*), here unable to speak as a grown-up.
"chirr": the gongs make a prolonged trilling sound, as of a grasshopper, rather
   than appropriate sonorities.

Tattoo

Others 2 (Mar. 1916); see note on "Domination of Black," above; CP 81, LOA 64.

"filaments of your eyes / On the surface of the water": older paintings show
   the eye's filament extending to the object of sight; the trope grows from
   old theories of light and vision.

The Bird with the Coppery, Keen Claws

Broom 1 (Dec. 1921); CP 82, LOA 65.

A curiously edgy poem. In isolation it reads like a modern version of a Romantic bird. In conjunction with Stevens's other work at this time, it reads like an attempted allegory that is not fully successful. The dominant "parakeet of parakeets" with blind eyes rules by laws of "pure intellect" and by "will," so that it can sound like a parody of a Calvinist God. (Some have also heard a play on "paraclete of paracletes.") The six tercets rhyme lines 2 and 3, in an unusual effect for Stevens; the pronounced alliteration adds to the edgy sense.

Life Is Motion

Others 5 (July 1919), with "Earthy Anecdote," which is reprinted; CP 83, LOA 65.

Stevens's second Oklahoma poem, complete with down-home names, clothing, dancing, and whooping. The cries extract the vowels from "Oklahoma." The poem is an example of a fine, short, and short-line, strong-stress poem. For a different effect of the two-stress line, cf. the second half of "Cortège for Rosenbloom."

"the marriage / Of flesh and air": ending the poem with unobtrusive but very
    fine tropes: generally, on the pleasure of motion, as in dancing; also on
    the actual physical interaction of flesh and air in the act of breathing
    (where life is indeed motion) or of uttering sound.

[Architecture: 1923 only]

OP 37–39, LOA 66–67

The Wind Shifts

Others, special number (Dec. 1917); see note on "Valley Candle," above; CP 83–84, LOA 68.

A series of similes in a quietly remarkable, compact, strong-stress poem, turning on a simple formulation like the nursery rhyme's "This is way we . . ." Five different similes invite five different pictures or stories, moving slowly downward.

Colloquy with a Polish Aunt

Poetry 15 (Oct. 1919); see note on "The Paltry Nude Starts on a Spring Voyage," above; CP 84, LOA 68.

TITLE: "colloquy": heightened beyond a merely casual conversation; "Polish Aunt": another avuncular figure (see note on epigraph, below).

EPIGRAPH: (Fr.) "She knew all the legends of Paradise and all the tales of Poland," from *Revue des deux mondes*, the long-established French literary journal, to which Stevens subscribed.

"Voragine": Stevens was impatient with the notion that his reference was too esoteric. His "obscurantism" or the other fellow's "stupidity" depended on which way the wind blew. He then turned scornful. The well-known *Golden Legend*, "subject of Caxton's w-k [well-known] work and W. Morris's chef d-o. [chef d'oeuvre]" should be "fairly well-known even to book reviewers" (L 216, 1919).

"pantaloons": loose trousers; Pantaloon is a stock character in Italian comedy (see note on Scaramouche in "The Weeping Burgher," above), a beslippered, foolish, old man; whence the sixth age of man in Jacques' famous speech (*As You Like It* II.vii.158).

"the imagination": the nephew's limited imagination extends to women, and it works by contraries; inconsistently, he does not extend it to saints' legends.

Gubbinal

Poetry 19 (Oct. 1921); see note on "The Snow Man," above; CP 85, LOA 69.

Another poem on a reductive view of the world, which refuses to see "that strange flower" or "that savage of fire," the sun. The poem uses short lines, short words, and short sentences.

TITLE: from "gubbins" (British, obs.), meaning "trash," "scraps," especially fish-scraps; also historically, barbarians in the Dartmoor district; hence a poem from such a viewpoint.

Two Figures in Dense Violet Night

CP 85–86, LOA 69–70.

The painterly title turns into a dramatic monologue with advice on how to be more truly seductive. The best way is to use words, words that express what the other wants to hear. By the end, this has dwindled to a desire for any verbal expression at all, even about the time of day. "O, Florida, Venereal Soil" also treats the subject of seduction, and the conditions are worth comparing in this lesser poem.

Theory

Others: An Anthology, ed. Kreymborg (1917); see note on "The Plot against the Giant," above; CP 86–87, LOA 70.

A theory briefly and succinctly stated, applicable only so far.

"I am what is around me": see also Stevens's 1917 letter on his play, *Carlos among the Candles*, as illustrating a related theory. He observed that the influence of one's environment is a commonplace, but that the idea also "applied to the minutiae of one's surroundings" (L 201n, 1917).

To the One of Fictive Music

New Republic 32 (15 Nov. 1922); CP 87–88, LOA 70–71.

An early example from a series of muse poems throughout Stevens's work (though he abjured the word "muse"; see below), e.g., "Final Soliloquy of the Interior Paramour." Stevens will later rewrite and revise the high Romantic theme of this hymn (whether apostrophe or address), here still conceived a little too easily. The point of the poem, he wrote in 1928, was that "the imaginative world is the only real world"; this, despite our need to return to everyday life regularly (L 252). He would later emphasize the mutual interaction between imagination and reality. The tone is influenced by rhapsodic writers like Shelley. The poem works with flowing syntax and much near-rhyme, frequently with incantatory effect.

TITLE: "of " is twofold, so that the music is both imagined and generated by fictions; note the difference between "fictive" and "fictitious."
"Sister and mother and diviner love": Hera is both sister and spouse of Zeus (Hesiod, *Theogony* 453–58), as Juno is of Jupiter (Virgil, *Aeneid* I.47).
"sisterhood of the living dead": Stevens called this "the music of poetry" that makes its own fictions, and also a muse—a word he regretted the next day (L 297, 1935).
"No muses exist for me." He would say no more, except that the figure named in the title "is one of the sisterhood" and that the others are similar figures (L 298, 1935).
"weaving": as in *texere* (Lat. "to weave"), whence *textus* ("a text"); the pun is common.
"girdle": like the potent aphrodisiac girdle or belt of Aphrodite or Venus (see Homer, *Iliad* XIV.214–21).

"fatal stones": uncertain, but part of the distancing of this all-too-powerful figure.

Hymn from a Watermelon Pavilion

Broom 2 (June 1922); CP 88–89, LOA 71–72.

A poem on "the two dreams, night and day," where the good of the actual daytime dream prevails. Compare moonlit and sunlit worlds elsewhere in *Harmonium*, associated respectively with imagination (sometimes mere fancy) and reality (sometimes the merely reductive). The ending of *MBG* offers a powerful resolution to "a wrangling of two dreams" (XXXIII.5).

TITLE: "Hymn": on Stevens's work with genres, see the appendix under "Who Speaks to Whom? Genre." "Watermelon Pavilion": as against a "dark cabin" where watermelons are purple; in a watermelon pavilion, watermelons are presumably red within (cf. "red feather") and green without (cf. "leaf-green").

"feme": "woman" (cf. Fr. *femme*), obsolete except in legal use; a word attractive for its archaic and thereby ceremonious tone; its adjective, "leaf-green," is a fresh, spring-like color, like the queen's "slipper-green" in "Depression before Spring."

"blackbird . . . creaks": North American blackbird song is likened to a rusty hinge by Peterson: thus with regard to the yellow-headed and the rusty blackbird, and cf. grackle "song" in *Field Guide to the Birds* (Eastern), 2d ed. (1934).

Peter Quince at the Clavier

Others 1 (Aug. 1915), with "The Silver Plough-Boy" (1923 *Harmonium* only), under the title "Two Poems"; CP 89–92, LOA 72–74.

An erotic poem of difficult argument and disjunctions, unlike the other remarkable 1915 poem, "Sunday Morning." Stevens's version of the story of Susanna and the Elders (see the Apocrypha, "The History of Susanna," or the Roman Catholic Old Testament) is complicated by the teller, presumably Peter Quince or a Peter Quince. Named for the rustic in Shakespeare's *A Midsummer Night's Dream*, who presents a play about frustrated lovers, this is a Stevens persona uncertain about sexual desire. (Compare the struggling earlier poem, "Dolls" [OP 4, LOA 517, 1913–14?], which treats sexual guilt with strained humor and escapist fantasy.) The four sections are like program music, each different, with the musical terms indicating the narrative.

TITLE: "Peter Quince": as well as resembling Shakespeare's rustic, this is one of Stevens's self-deprecating personae with *p* and *c* sounds (Crispin, Pecksniff); "Clavier": a generic German name (*Klavier*, from Lat. *clavis*, key) for stringed keyboard instruments in Bach's day (as in his *Well-Tempered Clavier*), later the pianoforte. The combination of Shakepeare's bumbling rustic and the delicate clavier sets the tone—or rather, invites the reader to ascertain it.

I

Tetrameter tercets with occasional rhyme, a clavier interrupted by bass violins playing pizzicati.

"Just as my fingers on these keys": literal and figurative (music as poetry); Stevens played the piano, though not very well, unlike his wife, a skilled pianist (L 181, 1913). See L 81, 1904–5, on their letters during courtship as resembling "some strange instrument" with delicate and endearing music that both played.

"Music is feeling . . .": not in the strict sense, nor in the logical sense if we read ll. 1–8 as a syllogism; but Stevens's "music" and "a music" are just different enough to make this only a near-syllogism.

"like the strain / Waked in the elders by Susanna": a musical strain, the strain of the elders' eyes and their desire, the strain of this astonishing simile. Why should music that evokes desire for a woman then evoke this story of attempted rape, near execution of the victim, and her final vindication by an astute judge? (Beyond the apocryphal book, see numerous paintings.) Stevens's musical punning on the lust of the red-eyed elders (I.12–15) suggests attempted humor, but it falls rather flat, even for Peter Quince, given the opening tone.

II

Short-line irregular stanzas of two sentences each provide the "melody" and "quavering" of general sexual desire. They are suddenly muted, then invaded by the crash and roar of cymbal and horns that indicate the attempted rape, as does the truncated last stanza. Stevens invents Susanna's sexual desire; cf. Ste Ursule's unwitting desire, also from 1915 ("Cy Est Pourtraicte . . .").

"And roaring horns": the last line of a truncated stanza, which invites the reader to supply a final line or lines rhyming on "night" or "turned" ("flight," "fight," "burned," "spurned," etc.).

III

The five tetrameter rhymed couplets, with reversed opening and closing rhymes, give a refrain music of tambourines to indicate scandal. Stevens was disdainful of the pedant who pointed out to him that no Byzantines existed as such in Susanna's time (L 250, 1928).

IV

Three stanzas (as in LOA) of flowing syntax, played on the viol in praise of Susanna. The elders' bass strings are now scraping like death, their death by execution for false accusation.

"The body dies; the body's beauty lives": cf. Milton on the phoenix: "And though her body die, her fame survives, / A secular bird, ages of lives" (*Samson Agonistes* 1706–7).

"clear viol": the musical instrument also recalls Susanna's near violation; cf. Eliot's later "inviolable voice" concerning the song of Philomel and her rape (*The Waste Land* III, 1922).

"a constant sacrament of praise": evocative of a biblical diction of praise, e.g., "bringing sacrifices of praise" (Jer. 17:26) and "offering sacrifice of praise" (Heb. 13:15).

Thirteen Ways of Looking at a Blackbird

Others, special number (Dec. 1917); see note on "Valley Candle," above; CP 92–95, LOA 74–76.

Stevens emphasized that this gathering of poems was intended as a collection of sensations, not of epigrams or ideas (L 251, 1928). Each section invites the reader to realize one strong visual effect, as if perceiving or making a drawing centered on one or more blackbirds. Relations between black and white, motion and stillness, and other opposites or contraries vary throughout. This is an early poem on interaction, for which see the note on "Les Plus Belles Pages," below, and the appendix, "On First Approaching Stevens's Poems." Blackbirds are mentioned in an early letter as one of the "Pleasant Things to drive dull care away" (L 112, 1908); cf. also L 44 (1900). The numbered sections of short-line free verse are frequently compared with Japanese haiku and tanka in their effects. Stevens, however, said he did not have haiku in mind, adding that Japanese prints interested him more (Qian, *The Modernist Response to Chinese Art* [2003], 86–87). The grammar bears watching.

TITLE: Thirteen is an unlucky number in the West, but not in Japan.

III

Note other bird movements in Stevens's poems, like the movements in "Sunday Morning" or in "The Sense of the Sleight-of-Hand Man"; for early, though conventional, interest in the subject, see L 30, 32 (1899).

IV

"Are one": one way in which "A man and a woman / Are one" is in the biblical sense of man and wife as one flesh (Gen. 2:24, etc.); Stevens's addition of the blackbird turns this section into a question of what it means to say, "Are one."

V

"whistling": the sharp, clear call of a blackbird differs from the "rusty hinge" sound of some blackbird song (see note on "Hymn from a Watermelon Pavilion," above, and NSF II.vi). Bird calls and bird songs are, of course, quite different.

"or just after": catching, with exquisite precision, two closely linked but different sensations and emotions.

VI

Compare Coleridge, "Frost at Midnight."

VII

Haddam: Haddam, Connecticut. Stevens informed his Italian translator in 1953 that the "thin men of Haddam" are entirely fanciful. He added that he just liked the name, which, to his ear, had "a completely Yankee sound" (L 786). As elsewhere, Stevens highlights an American place-name by making it sound unusual; the "thin men of Haddam" sounds like the start of a fable, partly because Haddam sounds like a place in the Middle East, though the name is said to derive from Hadham, United Kingdom; the thin men desire otherworldly birds, ignoring what is before them, women included.

X

"The bawds of euphony": Stevens's harsh trope reflects his mistrust of euphony—for good reason, given his own gift for eloquence; cf. "old romance . . . a euphony in a museum / Of euphonies" ("Examination of the Hero in a Time of War" iii), and "euphonius bane" ("The News and the Weather" ii).

"cry out sharply": "express themselves . . . naturally, with pleasure, etc." (L 340, 1939).

XI

"glass coach": a mysterious vehicle, part fairy-tale coach (indirectly recalling Cinderella's) and perhaps part glass-windowed railroad coach; it travels "over Connecticut" (not "through" or "across," more usual prepositions); Stevens's technique here bears comparison with "Earthy Anecdote" ("Over Oklahoma," etc.).

"a fear pierced him": the first use of this verb, a strong word in Stevens.

XII

The couplet is intended to embody the compulsion that often lies behind our acts (L 340, 1939).

XIII

Stevens was uncertain whether one translation conveyed despair or not (ibid.).

Nomad Exquisite

CP 95, LOA 77.

A forceful Florida poem, with no reservations. The poem is built on one extended simile, resembling the form of an epic simile. It borrows the language of creation in Genesis ("brings forth") and other biblical diction ("hymn," "behold," "blessed," "meet for the eye of "). The slightly strange lexical combinations (e.g., "immense dew") and the utterly unexpected alligator help to set the tone. This is a one-sentence exuberant flaming-forth, the nomad's own type of hymn.

TITLE: A Stevens persona who both roams ("nomad") and quests ("exquisite") in search of pasture, while aware of appearing slightly precious. "Exquisite": both the usual and the etymological meanings are in play (Lat. *exquisitum*, from *exquiro*, "to seek out, to search or test," as in Mozart, *Vesperae Solemnes* [K 339], "*Magna opera Domini, exquisita*" ["Great are the works of the Lord, sought out"]; also "far-fetched," "artificial."

"angering for life": playing against the expected "hungering."

"green . . . gold": also the symbolic colors of spring.

"come flinging": as if near the nuptial bower in Milton's Eden, where "wings / Flung Rose, flung Odors," and where "Flung" rhymes with "Sung" (*PL* VIII.517–19); if an echo, suggesting "singing" as a resonance to add to the three "-ing" words in this stanza.

last line: a first draft, 15 Jan. 1919, read "Fruits, forms, flowers, flakes and fountains" (*The Palm at the End of the Mind*, ed. Holly Stevens, 401); in both versions, Florida elicits fertile f- and fl- words.

"flakes of flames": commonly observed in fireplaces; thus "Flames with many a flake" (Spenser, "Epithalamium"), "flakes of fire" (Tennyson, "Tithonus"); note how the revision concentrates and strengthens the effect; it also explicitly introduces flames, perhaps because of their association with the artist's forge, from Vulcan to Yeats's Byzantium poems.

[Tea, 1923]

[To the Roaring Wind, 1923]

The Man Whose Pharynx Was Bad

New Republic 28 (14 Sept. 1921); CP 96, LOA 81.

The first of fourteen poems added at this point to the second edition of *Harmonium* (1931); some of the fourteen are surprisingly weak, but not this one. It is an extraordinary valedictory poem on writer's block, published on the eve of Stevens's six-year poetic silence. The diction very quietly echoes Lear's speech on the heath, Hotspur facing danger ("Out of this nettle, danger, we pluck this flower, safety"), Spenser on broken poetic pipes (January Eclogue, *Shepherds Calendar*), and Tennyson on a trapped poet ("The Golden Years"). The sore-throated man can hear all too well, but can hardly speak himself. The quatrains have uncanny echoing effects.

TITLE: playing over tropes for poetic voice (larynx, syrinx, windpipe, sore throat, tongue-tied, dried-up [see Lat. *fistula*]); cf. "Playing a crackled reed, wind-stopped, in bleats" ("Owl's Clover," "Sombre Figuration" II.9, 1936, OP 97, line omitted in LOA 167).

"dumbly in my being pent": a rebounding echo from Milton through Coleridge and Keats on effects of being "pent" in a city (Cook [1988] 93–94); Stevens here revises the city topos to include confining villages.

"malady of the quotidian. . . .": as elsewhere, the preposition is ambiguous; the ellipsis marks the omission of four additional lines from the 1921 version, which had five stanzas instead of four (see LOA 996).

"mould": like mildew, a fungus growth, but unlike mildew, not solely destructive; also a play on mould as a shaping form.

The Death of a Soldier

Poetry 12 (May 1918), as part XI (untitled, but with an epigraph) of "Lettres d'un Soldat" (OP 35–36, LOA 544); CP 97, LOA 81.

A strong poem on its own. The 1931 title draws on the original epigraph from Lemercier's *Lettres d'un Soldat* (see LOA 1006): "La mort d'un soldat est près des choses naturelles" ("The death of a soldier is close to things that are natural"), whose larger context Stevens changes.

"three-days' personage": in North America, often the approximate time between death and funeral rites; cf. also Socrates on funeral orations for the death of a soldier (*Menexemus* 235 b–c) and the three-day interval between Christ's death and resurrection.

"pomp": cf. also French *pompes*, as in *entrepreneur de pompes funèbres* (funeral director).

"The clouds go": the phenomenon of the upper wind moving clouds, while a lower wind dies down, is a common sight, and here a fable. Following the death of his good friend, Henry Church, Stevens made a similar observation to his widow in a letter of condolence ("*the* world as distinguished from our world goes on," L 592, 1948).

Negation

Ibid., part IX (OP 34, LOA 543), with the same title, preceded by an epigraph from Lemercier; CP 97–98, LOA 82.

This weaker poem from the series would profit from its original epigraph, as would "The Surprises of the Superhuman," which follows. It is written against Lemercier's "justice impersonelle" and "destinée utile et harmonieuse" in the epigraph, which reads, translated: "The only sanction for me is my conscience. We must trust [*confier,* not LOA "submit"] in an impersonal justice, independent of any human aspect, and in a destiny [*destinée,* not LOA "fate"] that is useful and harmonious, in spite of all the horror of the form it takes."

"too": as in blind Chance? The assertions and tone recall the Victorian favorite, Fitzgerald's *Rubáiyát of Omar Khayyám,* owned by Stevens (SP 34).

"meticulous potter's thumb": of the creator (l. 1), as in Isa. 64:8 and numerous poems.

The Surprises of the Superhuman

Ibid., part VI (OP 32–33, LOA 541), with the same title, preceded by an epigraph from Lemercier; CP 98, LOA 82.

See note on "Negation," above. Again written against a Lemercier epigraph, notably his "confiance en la justice eternelle" and "l'humaine idée." Translated, the epigraph reads: "I have firm hope, but especially I have confidence in eternal justice, whatever surprises it brings to the human idea we have of it." The poem's iambic pentameter couplets have an epigrammatic tone.

"palais de justice": cf. Lemercier's remarks on "justice," above.
"Übermenschlichkeit": superhumanness.

Sea Surface Full of Clouds

Dial 77 (July 1924); CP 98–102, LOA 82–85.

One of Stevens's variation poems (cf. "Variations on a Summer's Day," etc.), consisting of five portrayals of the sea surface off Tehuantepec, Mexico. With the painterly effects, the poem evokes Monet's paintings of the façade of Rouen Cathedral in different lights. The sea surface evokes color descriptions and associations that are both accurate and suggestively fanciful. The response of the poem's persona is sometimes hard to ascertain. In the fall of 1923 Stevens and his wife took a sea voyage through the Panama Canal, passing by the Gulf of Tehuantepec (L 241–42). The five sections all begin with "In that November off Tehuantepec," and have a second stanza whose structure repeats and whose end-words read "chocolate," "green," "machine."

I

"In that November off Tehuantepec": Stevens had to inform one correspondent that "off Tehuantepec" is not fanciful; "one crosses the . . . Gulf of Tehuantepec" en route to California (L 288, 1935; see also L 241–42, where it is noted that the actual crossing was in late October).

"*C'était mon enfant, mon bijou, mon âme*": "It was my child, my jewel, my soul."
"flotillas": things that are floating (L 389, 1941).

II

"*C'était mon frère du ciel, ma vie, mon or*": "It was my heavenly brother, my life, my gold."

III

"*Oh! C'était mon extase et mon amour*": "Oh! It was my ecstasy and my love."

IV

"*C'était ma foi, la nonchalance divine*": "It was my faith, divine nonchalance."
"Salt masks of beards and mouths of bellowing": cf. "The Comedian and the Letter C" I on Triton and similar sea-creatures.

V

"Chinese chocolate": in 1941, Stevens said the phrase was meant to evoke something incongruous, "a big Chinese with a very small cup of chocolate" (L 389). If this is accurate, the poem is sometimes flawed by the nearly impenetrable overingenuity of parts of "The Comedian as the Letter C."
"*C'était mon esprit bâtard, l'ignominie*": "It was my bastard spirit, shame."
"conch . . . trumped": again, cf. "The Comedian as the Letter C" I on Triton.

The Revolutionists Stop for Orangeade

CP 102–3, LOA 86.

Stevens does not sound at ease with this subject or this mode.

"Capitán profundo, capitán geloso": (Sp., except for It. "geloso" rather than Sp. "celoso") "Profound captain, jealous captain."

New England Verses

Measure 26 (April 1923); see note on "Floral Decorations for Bananas," above; CP 104–6, LOA 87–89.

A series in one of Stevens's favored forms, the epigram. The eight pairs of rhyming couplets each have contrary titles, so that the reader is invited to consider the kind and degree of these and other contraries.

III, IV

"*Soupe Aux Perles*," "*Soupe Sans Perles*": "Pearl Soup" (or "Soup with Pearls"), "Soup without Pearls"; oyster soup is *soupe aux huîtres*; but *soupe aux perles* is a puzzle for the chef, unless it is lucky oyster soup or (unlikely in context) pearl barley soup; given the surrounding luxury, it also sounds like dress for a formal dinner.

"Health-o": a toast or exclamation, in a current idiom; cf. "Will-o" (for "Well-o," LFR 382, 1917) and "Well-o" (L 232, 1922); "Right-o" is still a current expression.

"fromage": cheese; "ginger and fromage" revises "cheese and guava peels" (*Measure* 1923); either way, suggesting gourmet fare.

IV

"I crossed in '38 in *The Western Head*": who is this "I"? If a contemporary, he or she is at least eighty-five; 1838 is the date of the first transatlantic crossing by steamship; two ships from rival companies crossed, the *Great Western* being one; shipping records show no *Western Head*.

"which way you crossed": the "tea-belle" reckons that those crossing the Atlantic, east to west, include new settlers, not wearing their pearls for dinner at the captain's table.

V

"weltanschauung": (Ger., well known and here naturalized by using lower-case *w*) "worldview, outlook."

VII

"*Artist in Tropic*": with the usual pun on "tropic" as a place of trope.

"Phœbus Apothicaire": "Phoebus Apo—" should end as Phoebus Apollo, the same sun god that figures in NSF I.I; instead, Apollo becomes an apothecary (in 1923, Fr. "Apothécaire"), in something close to a portmanteau word playing on Apollo-Apollinaire (the Fr. poet).

"beatitude . . . multitude": the sun as appropriate apothecary for the tropics (or the land of trope), offers his own kind of beatitude, also for a multitude like the well-known ones in the Gospels; the beatitude itself represents a new turn for Stevens, best seen in *Ideas of Order*.

XV

"Scène Flétrie": "Withered Scene"; cf. "autumn . . . shrivelled forms" ("The Reader").

XVI

"Scène Fleurie": "Flowered Scene."
"Pinakothek": a picture-gallery (from Gk. "pinacotheca"); in this spelling, evoking the well-known galleries in Munich, the Old and New Pinakothek.

Lunar Paraphrase

Poetry 12 (May 1918), as part VII of "Lettres d'un Soldat," with the same title, but preceded by an epigraph from Lemercier (OP 33, LOA 543); CP 107, LOA 89–90.

Stevens's poem combats Lemercier's epigraph, which reads, translated: "Such was the beauty of yesterday. Shall I speak to you of the preceding evenings, while along the road, the moon outlined for me the embroidery of the trees, the pathos of the wayside crosses [*calvaires,* not LOA "hills"], the pity of these houses whose ruins one knows, yet which the night causes to rise again [*surgir*] like an evocaton of peace."

"the body of Jesus hangs . . . Humanly near": as elsewhere, Stevens portrays a human Jesus, not the Christ that Lemercier's "calvaires . . . surgir" intimate; his antiorthodox homiletics read feebly compared with Lemercier's metaphors and descriptions from the front in World War I; nor do they gain strength from shearing off the epigraph; see "The Good Man Has No Shape" for a much better poem on a purely human Jesus.

Anatomy of Monotony

CP 107–8, LOA 90.

A treatment of themes familiar from "Sunday Morning" and elsewhere in *Harmonium*.

TITLE: echoing Burton's *Anatomy of Melancholy*, where "anatomy" is used in the Renaissance sense of "a systematic treatise"; the echo reinforces the sense of monotony through its sound-scheme.

The Public Square

Measure 26 (April 1923), as "How the Constable Carried the Pot across the Public Square"; CP 108–9, LOA 91.

A moonlit scene like some of T. S. Eliot's, e.g., "Rhapsody on a Windy Night." Compare "Lunar Paraphrase," which also turns against Stevens's once-magic moon.

"The bijou of Atlas, the moon": presumably for the Atlas who carries the world on his shoulders.
"porcelain": in 1923, "bedroom."

Sonatina to Hans Christian

CP 109–10, LOA 91–92.

TITLE: "Sonatina": diminutive of "sonata" (It.), a shorter, easier, and often lighter form of the sonata. Stevens owned recordings of two sonatinas by Busoni (1866–1964; *WSJ* 3 [1979]: 85), who was among those who revived the term; he read and annotated Busoni's *Letters to His Wife* (copy at the Huntington Library; *WSJ* 2 [1978]: 56).
"Hans Christian": Hans Christian Andersen (1805–75), whose well-known fairy tale "The Ugly Duckling," informs this poem.

In the Clear Season of Grapes

CP 110–11, LOA 92.

TITLE: cf. the powerful treatment of such a season in "A Postcard from the Volcano" "in autumn, when the grapes . . ." (l. 4).

Two at Norfolk

CP 111–12, LOA 92–93.

"gurrituck": untraced.
"Johann Sebastian": Johann Sebastian Bach.

Indian River

Soil 1 (Jan. 1917), as part 9 of "Primordia," part of "In the South," untitled; CP 112, LOA 93.

A short, hypnotic charm poem, with much internal rhyme and a long line, to mime the hypnotic charm of Florida's inland waterway running parallel to the Atlantic coast. The last line breaks the rhythm and moves beyond the earlier diction with two unusual phrases, the second being the poem's only metaphor.

"no spring in Florida": on Stevens's preference for the variety of his familiar four seasons and long autumn, which "the lotus-eaters of the South must pine for," see L 211 (1919); he later acknowledged he was mistaken about Florida having no spring (L 676, 1950).

"boskage perdu": "lost boskage."

"nunnery beaches": not an expected "-ery" adjective like "flowery," but ambiguous, suggesting whiteness and purity, yet echoing other negatives like "none."

Tea

Rogue 1 (15 Mar. 1915); see note on "Cy est Pourtraicte, Madame Ste Ursule . . . ," above; CP 112–13, LOA 77.

One of two seemingly (but far from) slight poems that close both editions of *Harmonium*. The poem offers a very effective implicit leave-taking. Though tea is mentioned only in the title, the poem pointedly refers to leaves and to a tea-growing country, Java. For the poem's import, cf. all the troping of leaves through the collection, recalling centuries of such troping ("Domination of Black," etc.). Paul Muldoon's poem "Tea" makes explicit Stevens's delicately implicit trope of drinking tea as a metaphor for reading (ingesting a drink from leaves). Stevens was a tea-fancier, though the more important fact about tea is that it is the most common beverage drunk in the world, except for water. An eight-line, one-sentence, free-verse virtuoso performance, "Tea" acts as a sending-off for *Harmonium* like older poems beginning "Go, little book . . ."

"elephant's ear": tropical bedding plant such as Colocasia esculenta or caladium, whose huge leaves give rise to the popular name, because of their shape. The name accords with Java, place of tea-plants and elephants both, and an early center for the tea-trade.

"Java": beyond the above, note that Java once had a sophisticated court culture; its subtleties and appreciation of artists made it the kind of culture that Stevens especially liked.

To the Roaring Wind

Soil 1 (Jan. 1917), as the last poem of "Primordia," with the same title; CP 113, LOA 77.

Is this an address to the wind or an invocation to a muse or both? Wind is traditionally a source of inspiration (from Lat. *spiritus*, wind). (Compare Frost, "To the Thawing Wind," presumably thawing frost.) Invocations to the muse conventionally come at the start of a book rather than the close, but Stevens chose to end by handing his book over to his poetic voice. Four short lines (the last monosyllabic), with much near-rhyme and alliteration, give a charm effect. But the argument, presented succinctly in the vocative case and the interrogative and imperative moods, requires alertness, unlike many charm effects. Stevens ends his volume with an imperative injunction.

"Vocalissimus": the superlative form, in the masculine singular vocative case, of the Lat. adjective *vocalis*, "that utters a voice, sounding, vocal, singing," also in a rare poetic use, "causing or inspiring speech or song" (Lewis and Short).

Ideas of Order

Published in a limited edition in July 1935 by Alcestis Press, then in a trade edition in October 1936 by Alfred A. Knopf, with three new poems ("Farewell to Florida," "Ghosts as Cocoons," "A Postcard from the Volcano"). Stevens returned to continuous poetic activity only in 1933, as is clear from this book's publishing history. The 1936 collection gathers thirty-six poems, twenty-eight of which were first published between 1933 and 1936; one was first published in 1932, one in 1930, and one ("Academic Discourse at Havana") in 1923.

Stevens wrote a comment for the dust jacket of the Knopf edition, observing that the current "economic changes, involving political and social changes" are changes that "raise questions of political and social order." Inevitably, a poet will be involved in such questions, but *Ideas of Order*, Stevens explained, also concerns order in a wider sense. His first example is "the general sense of order," especially when established ideas are challenged. His second is "the idea of order created by individual concepts," as in "The Idea of Order at Key West," and the third is "the idea of order arising from the practice of any art."

Stevens called *Ideas of Order* "a book of pure poetry" (ibid.), as he defended the role of the imagination in difficult times like the thirties. (For the full statement, see OP 222–23, LOA 997.) By "pure poetry," he meant something wider than the strict definition of Henri Brémond in his influential 1926 book, *La poésie pure.* (See his discussion of Brémond in "The Irrational Element in Poetry" vi, OP 227–28, LOA 785–86, 1936.) Art or scholarship as a reminder of normal civilized life is a motif during turbulent times, including this period (see, e.g., Graham Greene, *The Confidential Agent*).

For the words "order" and "disorder" in *Ideas of Order*, see "Sad Strains of a Gay Waltz" and "The Idea of Order at Key West." (The Concordance provides a listing for all the poetry.) There are scattered remarks on "order" and "disorder" in Stevens's letters. They include the quotation, " ' man's passionate disorder,' " and Stevens's subsequent interest in disorder, though personally he disliked it (L 300, 1935). On "competent" poems as introducing order, and on an individual sense of order, see L 293 (1935). On the "order of the spirit," that is, "one's own fortitude of spirit" or the true " 'feste Burg,' " see

L 403 (1942); lacking such fortitude, "one lives in chaos," Stevens added. Compare also "A Collect of Philosophy" on "the habit of probing for an integration" as "part of the general will to order" (OP 276, LOA 862, 1951).

In any remarks about the word "order," context is crucial. "Order" is a curious word in that it can evoke contrary emotions, depending on the associations. The order in a police state, the order in a well-run household, biological orders, and so on. How do we react? A good many people had ideas of order in the thirties, as Stevens knew. He had some of his own. And lest readers take a thesis-ridden approach to *Ideas of Order*, Stevens mentioned that the arrangement of the poems was simply "based on contrasts." Some poems had nothing to do with "a phase of order"; "after all, the thing is not a thesis" (L 279, 1935).

* * *

Farewell to Florida

Contemporary Poetry and Prose 3 (July 1936), added to the 1936 ed.; CP 117–18, LOA 97–98.

An impassioned farewell to Florida, in which the speaker protests too much. A clause with the word "except" in stanza III shows the struggle. Poetically, this is a farewell to Florida as Stevens's erotic muse. He testified in 1943 that he used to find Florida "violently affective" (L 450). Generically "Farewell to Florida" is a valediction (see Fowler, index), where any convention of praise is much modulated by Stevens's ambiguity. The poem is marked by telling repetitions and a strongly pulsing ship-on-sea rhythm.

I

"Key West": as the island at the outermost tip of Florida, one edge of the country; cf. the American seashore poem in Whitman, Eliot, Ammons, etc.

II

"Her mind had bound me round": at the end, the poem moves toward another binding of the mind; with the conjunction of "bind" and a ship's "deck" in stanza IV, cf. Ulysses (a Stevens persona), bound to the mast in order to hear the Sirens' song and not die.

III

"trees like bones": the correct text, as in LOA.

Ghosts as Cocoons

Added to the 1936 ed.; CP 119, LOA 98–99.

Written at a time when, as Stevens put it, there was a "profound desire to be released from all our misfortunes" (L 347, 1940). Both the short sentences and the variety of grammatical moods work well for this subject.

TITLE: where are the cocoons? Both ghosts and cocoons are commonly white, but a ghost is an apparition of past life, while a cocoon encloses future life; see the ghost in l. 16, and the final couplet, appropriate for bride or cocoon.

"The grass is in seed": a trope for "Those to be born," i.e., "the people of the future," who, Stevens commented, "need to know something of the happiness of life" (ibid.)—not something generally apparent in 1936.

"the bride": i.e., the poem's "sun and music" (l. 6), which Stevens associated with love and happiness (ibid.).

"It is easy to say to those bidden—": echoing the biblical language of the parable of the marriage feast, "Tell them which are bidden . . . come unto the marriage" (Matt. 22:4); the parable suggests what is broken off here, and perhaps a darker lesson as well.

"butcher, seducer": Stevens gave as an example of the "butcher, seducer," etc., "the inept politician"; he associated the figures with "evil and unhappiness" (ibid.), sketching his fable in broad lines.

"pearled and pasted, bloomy-leaved": a bridal figure, also a cocoon at the stage when the chrysalis is close to emerging as a butterfly; both are figures of hope.

Sailing after Lunch

Alcestis 1 (spring 1935), with "Meditation Celestial & Terrestrial," "Waving Adieu, Adieu, Adieu," "The American Sublime," and "Mozart, 1935," all under the title "Five Poems"; the first poem of *Ideas of Order* in the Alcestis edition of 1935; CP 120–21, LOA 99–100.

Sailing and, more generally, boating often provide tropes for poetry, as in Rimbaud, "Le Bâteau ivre," or Jay Macpherson, *The Boatman*. For sailing as voyage for an aging writer, contrast Emerson's "Terminus." For the wind as inspiration, see "To the Roaring Wind," which closes *Harmonium*. Note how the sailboat trope avoids the either / or of nature or art. Sailing is an art that learns to read nature and to work with it, as in T. S. Eliot's sailboat in *The Waste Land* V. The poem uses irregular end-rhyme and pronounced stress, imitating sailboat rhythms, notably in the last stanza where the wind catches the sail. Nonetheless, the poem does not appear to be fully realized.

"*pejorative*": Stevens noted that people tend to speak of the romantic in "a *pejorative* sense." But, he added in 1935, "poetry is essentially romantic," though the romantic of poetry must be continually renewed (L 277, and see L 279). See also remarks on the romantic in "A Poet That Matters" (on Marianne Moore, OP 217–22, LOA 774–80, 1935) and in SPBS 31 (1934); "Sailing after Lunch" and "A Poet That Matters" are said to express the same thing (L 282, 1935). Stevens later abandoned the term, "romantic," arguing forcefully for the imagination as "one of the great human powers," and setting the romantic against it. "It is to the imagination what sentimentality is to feeling. It is a failure of the imagination precisely as sentimentality is a failure of feeling" (NA 138–39, LOA 727–28, 1948).

"My old boat goes round on a crutch ... under way": because there is no wind or a different tack is needed?

"hear the poet's prayer": cf. Pope on Orpheus, "He sung, and hell consented / To hear the Poet's prayer" ("Ode on St. Cecilia's Day" 83–84).

"The romantic": see note on "*pejorative*," above.

"my spirit": again, recalling etymologically the wind that a sailboat needs, and the inspiration that a poet needs (Lat. *spiritus*, "breath").

"pupil": close to a pun on the pupil of the eye, given the wheel; the "people-pupil" punning is a little distracting.

"transcendence": with the renewed romantic, "the most casual things take on transcendence" (L 277, 1935); the adjective "slight" modifies an Emersonian use of the word.

Sad Strains of a Gay Waltz

New Republic 83 (22 May 1935); CP 121–22, LOA 100–101.

A strong elegiac lyric, echoing and referring to Stevens's earlier writing, and indicating new directions for his work more persuasively than "Farewell to Florida." The poem ends on "shadows," a weighted word for Stevens.

TITLE: compare the use of "strain" in "Peter Quince at the Clavier."

"desire ... empty of shadows": cf. "What I feel ... desiring you, / Thinking of your blue-shadowed silk, / Is music" (ibid.).

"mountain-minded Hoon": see "Tea at the Palaz of Hoon"; Hoon, a visionary self for Stevens, is now identified as a solitary, hardly surprising for someone of his gifts.

"sudden mobs . . . sudden clouds": cf. "Farewell to Florida," stanza IV.
"Requiring order beyond their speech": cf. " 'But play, you must, / A tune beyond us, yet ourselves' " (MBG I).

Dance of the Macabre Mice

New Republic 83 (5 June 1935); CP 123, LOA 101.

One of Stevens's statue poems, heavily ironic in the "hungry dance" of these 1930s mice over the Founder of the State.

Meditation Celestial & Terrestrial

Alcestis 1 (spring 1935); see note on "Sailing after Lunch," above; CP 123–24, LOA 101–2.

A poem on returning spring, like "The Sun This March," where exaltation and joy indicate a personal as well as a seasonal return.

TITLE: note the effect of the unusual ampersand rather than "and."
"in the jungle": in the tropics of Central and South America, where many
   warblers spend the winter.
"hilarious trees": given the next line, a strong etymological sense of "cheer, hilarity" (Lat. *hilaritas*), and thereby a memory of a standard epithet for
   Aphrodite, "laughing" or "laughter-loving Aphrodite" (e.g., Homer, *Iliad* XIV. 211).
"the drunken mother": punning on "drunken" as intoxication with life and
   providing food (cf. "In the Carolinas" for a very different view of the
   earth-mother).

Lions in Sweden

Alcestis 1 (Oct. 1934), after "The Idea of Order at Key West," followed by "Evening without Angels," "Nudity at the Capital," "Nudity in the Colonies," "A Fish-Scale Sunrise," "Delightful Evening," "What They Call Red Cherry Pie," all under "Eight Poems"; the first seven were dispersed throughout *Ideas of Order*, and the last (OP 68, LOA 561) omitted.

A discourse on majestic images that affect us, cast as an address to one Swenson (see below). Stevens takes a lion as the prototypical such image. He is recalling Dufy's illustrations for the original edition of Apollinaire's *Le Bestiare*, 1919.

"Swenson . . . bank": the name is probably adopted from one known in 1934 because of a banking scandal. Eric P. Swenson, CEO of the National City Bank of New York, was the son of a prominent Swedish financier (Filreis [1994], 70); the scandal may have been the starting-point for this poem.

"sovereigns of the soul / And savings bank": a conjunction like R. H. Tawney's in *Religion and the Rise of Capitalism*, punning on "sovereign" as a ruler and a coin.

"Fides": (Lat.) "Faith," one of the three Christian virtues, along with hope and charity. Fides, sculpted for a savings bank, has a different kind of faith in mind, as with any financial institution using words derived from *fides* (e.g., "fidelity").

"Justitia": (Lat.) justice, one of the four classical virtues, along with (usually) prudence, temperance, and fortitude ("Fortitudo," l. 7).

"Patientia, forever soothing wounds": the Lat. root (*patio, patere, passus,* to suffer) gives us the words "patience" and also "passion" in the sense of suffering (known chiefly through the Passion of Christ); both meanings are in play here.

"Still hankers after sovereign images": cf. "Some Friends from Pascagoula."

"Monsieur Dufy's Hamburg": referring to Apollinaire: "O lion, malheureuse image, / Des rois chers lamentablement, / Tu ne nais maintenant qu'en cage / A Hamburg, chez les Allemands" (O lion, unhappy image, / Lamentably, of dear kings, / Now you are born only in a cage / In Hamburg, among the Germans" (*Le Bestiare*).

How To Live. What To Do

Direction 1 (spring 1935); CP 125–26, LOA 102–3.

A poem on the true heroic, centered on the image of a rock. In 1935, Stevens called it his favorite poem from *Ideas of Order*, "because it so definitely represents my way of thinking" (L 293); cf. note on "Anglais Mort à Florence." It is not a general favorite, however, partly because of its doctrinaire tone and somewhat weak troping. Stevens called "A Fading of the Sun" "in a way, a companion piece" to this poem (L 295, 1935).

"No chorister, nor priest": as elsewhere in the poem, Stevens makes clear this is a rock without any religious connotation, whether from the Hebrew Scriptures, the Christian Bible, or elsewhere.

Some Friends from Pascagoula

CP 126–27, LOA 103–4.

A genuine "sovereign" image (unlike those in "Lions in Sweden") for two African-Americans from Mississippi. The subject is like Tennyson's in his well-known "The Eagle," filtered through the experience of two human fellow-creatures of the habitat, with stage directions. The poem is "neither merely descriptive nor symbolical," Stevens wrote. If someone lives "without existing conventions (beliefs, etc.)," such a person "depends for ideas of a new and noble order on 'noble imagery.'" This poem tries to provide such imagery "in a commonplace occurrence" (L 349, 1940). In 1942, Stevens reflected on the word "noble" in "The Noble Rider and the Sound of Words" (NA 1–36, LOA 643–65).

TITLE: Pascagoula, Mississippi, at the mouth of the Pascagoula River, on the Gulf of Mexico, a likely setting for a bald eagle (see their range in Peterson, *A Field Guide to the Birds*, and elsewhere); one of the few references to American place-names in *Ideas of Order*, in contrast to *Harmonium*.

"kinky clan": the tone precludes irony in what is probably an attempt at local color, but is distracting at best.

Waving Adieu, Adieu, Adieu

Alcestis 1 (spring 1935); see note on "Sailing after Lunch," above; CP 127–28, LOA 104.

A more memorable poem of Stevens's way of thinking than "How To Live. What To Do." One evening, Stevens decided "to describe a deathbed farewell under the new regime." He was very pleased with the result, he said, then added cautiously, "for the moment" (L 273, 1935). Note the skilful use of participles and gerunds.

TITLE: "Adieu": a final good-bye, as against an everyday good-bye, which is "au revoir."

"the ever-jubilant weather": not in the least symbolic, as Stevens affirmed. Human beings "are physical beings in a physical world." We enjoy the weather as "one of the unphilosophical realities," and the "state of the weather soon becomes a state of mind" (L 348–49, 1940).

The Idea of Order at Key West

Alcestis 1 (Oct. 1934); see note on "Lions in Sweden," above; CP 128–30, LOA 105–6.

The title poem for this collection and its most powerful, marking Stevens's return to poetry with a new, strong voice. The poem lays old ghosts and spirits, including old views of a genius loci (see note on "beyond the genius of the sea," below), moving beyond the relation of art and nature in *Harmonium*'s opening poems. It also repossesses Florida as a place of voice, after Stevens's troubled relation with her, recalled in the opening poem of *Ideas of Order*. Stevens wrote that in this poem, "life has ceased to be a matter of chance," in contrast to "The Comedian as the Letter C" (L 293, 1935). The first three stanzas each open with a declaration that is a thesis, emphasized by making sentence coincide with line. Their argument is tight, their rhythm is ocean-like. The poem then settles into two longer verse paragraphs, expanding on the opening theses, before addressing the auditor in two stanzas marked by increasing intensity.

"She": an unknown singer, happily appearing as if she is a pure force of nature (cf. Wordsworth's singing Highland Lass in "The Solitary Reaper") but rejected as such at the start.

"beyond the genius of the sea": genius loci or spirit of the place. On the history of the word "genius," from an "attending spirit" whether for good or ill, through a "spirit of a specific place," to the modern attenuated meaning, see C. S. Lewis, *Medieval and Renaissance Literature* (1966), 169–74. Line 1 moves at once against one romantic view of nature and art, as in Byron's stanzas from *Childe Harold's Pilgrimage*, beginning "Roll on, thou deep and dark blue ocean—roll!" (IV, stanzas 179–83).

"Like a body wholly body, fluttering / Its empty sleeves": not a spirit without a body, but an inverse ghost, recalling death's traditional wide-sleeved garb.

"ever-hooded": descriptively, the shape of a large wave cresting and about to break, as in Hokusai's famous print; iconographically, again recalling death's traditional garb (cf. "Time is the hooded enemy" in "The Pure Good of Theory" 1); conceptually, reminding us we cannot absolutely know outside reality, here "the veritable ocean."

"The sea was not a mask. No more was she": moving against any symbolic or sacramental reading of sea or woman as charged with hidden significance; moving even against sea or woman as persona (Lat., actor's mask).

"medleyed sound": moving against any hearing of human song and sea-sounds as one medley, partaking naturally in this form.

"grinding water": on the shore, as in "I heard the shingle grinding in the surge" (Tennyson, *The Holy Grail* 808); also recalling (through similar sounds) Arnold's well-known sea in "Dover Beach" with its "grating roar," while moving against his melancholy late-Romantic stance; cf. other tropes for the sound of the sea earlier in, e.g., "Hibiscus by the Sleeping Shore," "Fabliau of Florida," and also below in "Doctor of Geneva."

"gasping wind": cf. all the tropes for wind in *Harmonium*, and note how Stevens avoids any ready tropes here, especially any involving inspiration.

"She was the maker": moving against the idea of the poet as inspired bard and prophet, and to an old description of the poet as maker, whether as Gk. *poietes* (maker, poet) or from OE *sc(e)apan* (to shape); cf. "artificer" later, and the repeated uses of "maker" and "made." In 1947, Stevens wrote that a friend's poems disclosed "your character as a Schöpfer, as they say down home" (letter to Byron Vazakas, 7 Mar. 1947, Beinecke Library).

"Whose spirit is this? we said": as the singer sings and walks alone, without benefit of an inspiring wind or other such breath, her listeners might well ask.

"her voice that made / The sky acutest at its vanishing": "acute" is a strong word for Stevens; in his edition of Horace's *Odes*, T. E. Page says that *acuta* (Ode III.iv) is the Lat. equivalent for the standard Gk. epithet for the muses, *ligeia*. Stevens refers to Horace (L 104, 1907; 377, 1940) and quotes him (SP 143). Cf. "the power of the acutest poet" (NA 32, LOA 663, 1942), "the acute intelligence of the imagination" (NA 61, LOA 681, 1943), the degree of perception where the real and the imagined are one "possibly accessible to the . . . acutest poet" ("Adagia," OP 192, LOA 906). Here, note also that an acute angle in geometry vanishes altogether at its acutest.

"Ramon Fernandez": although Ramon Fernandez was a well-known critic, published in France and in T. S. Eliot's *New Criterion*, Stevens claimed that he did not intend to refer to him. He did know of him and had read some of his work, but (he said) simply "chose two everyday Spanish names" (L 798, 1947, and see 798n., 823).

"the lights in the fishing boats . . . Mastered the night," etc.: in 1911 Stevens observed a similar effect by the docks in New York, with the stars and "the lanterns on the masts [that] flickered" (L 171). Note the use of ordinary working boats in this visionary scene—another type of sailing craft to add to those that open *Ideas of Order*.

"Fixing emblazoned zones and fiery poles": on the fishing boats; also as seen against the sky and the sea, and so fixing the earth's zones and poles.

"Oh! Blessed rage for order": one of Stevens's best-known phrases, at first sounding like an oxymoron, but hardly so, as the next line makes clear ("rage to order words of the sea"). Stevens's passion for his art remained fierce, and he did not take tepid artists (or tepid anyone) seriously. In his work with the word "rage," a word for the sea biblically and elsewhere, Stevens turns his back on Crispin's timidity in the face of nature at its most forceful. See note to *Ideas of Order* for other possible contexts for the phrase.

"ghostlier demarcations": the context suggests for "ghostlier" the root meaning of "spiritual" (i.e., "of the spirit"), a strong word in Stevens; cf. also the poem's earlier ghostly figures. The lines of latitude and longitude that mark the earth's "zones" and "poles" are also "ghostly," for they are seen neither on land nor on sea. Yet they are crucially connected with reality, for they help us to master it, as those on the fishing boats well know. So also with a good poet's words.

"keener sounds": also associated with keening, as it might be, by a ghost.

The American Sublime

Alcestis 1 (spring 1935); see note on "Sailing after Lunch," above; CP 130–31, LOA 106–7.

By way of contrast with the preceding poem, a slight, sardonic poem on the lack of an American sublime. A sublime landscape is all very well, but the true sublime rests in the spirit.

"General Jackson": General Andrew Jackson (1767–1845), later president, whose statue in Washington is on Lafayette Square, facing the White House; Stevens's opinion of the statue was low ("there is not the slightest trace of imagination," NA 11, LOA 648, 1942), but here it represents at least some attempt at an American sublime.

"wine . . . bread": the food of the Eucharist or communion, and also traditionally simple, basic sustenance.

Mozart, 1935

Ibid.; CP 131–32, LOA 107–8.

The poem, said Stevens, concerns "the status of the poet in a disturbed society, or, for that matter, in any society" (L 292, 1935)—a subject close to his heart. Paradoxically, the need for art during times of crisis becomes more pressing. Mozart was not a personal favorite (L 604, 1948), but he is needed here for, e.g., the paradox of young and old (see below). "Mozart, 1935" provides an oblique partial answer to the preceding poem.

"hoo-hoo-hoo," etc.: four echoic sounds, evoking thirties music.

"Be thou the voice": anaphoric repetition recalling Shelley's "Be thou me, impetuous one," from "Ode to the West Wind," also echoed in NSF II.vi, but here a wintry wind rather than Shelley's autumnal one.

"Not you. Be thou . . . Be seated, thou": the artist qua artist takes on the mantle of a "thou," an older and more formal "you," asserting the possibility of an American sublime.

"We may return to Mozart. / He was young, and we, we are old": the everyoung and ageless music of Mozart, in contrast to the ongoing, grinding burdens of the Great Depression.

Snow and Stars

New Act 2 (June 1933); CP 133, LOA 108.

Attempted humorous invective against often-admired winter effects, somewhat wearing in its ill humor. The tetrameter tercets come with with banging rhymes and rhythms.

"grackles sing": the discordant sounds of grackle song are not happy in Stevens (cf. "Banal Sojourn," "Autumn Refrain").

"avant": (Fr.) "before."

"spiss . . . spissantly": obs. "spiss" (thick, dense); cf. rare "spissitude" (density) and "inspissation" (used by T. S. Eliot, "Dante," 1929, *Selected Essays* 240).

The Sun This March

New Republic 62 (16 Apr. 1930); CP 133–34, LOA 108–9.

A remarkable poem on returning poetic voice, troping on light and sound. The closing petition, in imperative mood and a full rhyme, is especially memorable.

"conceive": also with an intimation of physical conceiving.

"turn . . . turning . . . returns": see note on the word "turn" in "Domination of Black, above."

"Cold is our element": echoing Shelley's Prometheus, "Pain is my element," but not the full context: "as hate is thine; / Ye rend me now: I care not" (*Prometheus Unbound* I. 477–78).

"Rabbi, rabbi": see biography on the rabbi figure in Stevens's work.

"fend": "defend," an archaic or poetic use (Emerson, "Boston Hymn," 1863).

"savant": as rabbi, and because "poetry is the scholar's art" ("Adagia," OP 193, LOA 906).

Botanist on Alp (No. 1)

Direction 1 (Oct. 1934) with "Hieroglyphica" (not in *Ideas of Order*), under "Two Poems"; CP 134–35, LOA 109–10.

The botanist makes a happy persona for a poet, as the botanist also "live[s] by leaves" (see note on "leaves" in "Domination of Black," above). Stevens added the following poem in 1935, so as to make one of his paired exercises. Here: place a poet-botanist on the top of a high mountain in 1934, and examine the results of that examination. This poem explores yet further the possibility of an American sublime.

"Claude": the painter Claude Lorraine (1600–1682), as Stevens confirmed (L 293, 1935); Claude's classical ideas of landscape beauty were dominant until the time of, e.g., Constable and Turner in England.

"apostrophes are forbidden on the funicular": Stevens could use apostrophe himself ("An Apostrophe to Vincentine"). To forbid an apostrophe like "O Muse" while surveying a standard sublime panorama is another matter. The tone is mixed, but the argument clear, in this funny memorable line.

"Marx has ruined Nature, / For the moment": through Soviet control of art that likes capital-*n* Nature, and more widely through political judgments inappropriately applied to such art. See L 292 on how Marxism might "destroy the existing sentiment of the marvelous." If this should happen, Stevens believed that Marxism would create another such sentiment; he was right (1935).

"in Claude . . . pillars . . . arches . . . composition": his invention, the Claude glass, provided a framing device like the viewfinder in a modern camera; his paintings emphasized the panoramic effect (cf. line 1) by including framing structures like pillars and arches.

"*riva*": (It.) bank, shore.

Botanist on Alp (No. 2)

CP 135–36, LOA 110.

By way of contrast, a somewhat doctrinaire poem on the familiar theme of leaving behind religious views of heaven and earth, and finding "earthier" satisfaction. Glittering crosses lose their symbolic meaning and become "merely . . . a mirror of mere delight," in a pronounced series of puns corresponding to "tum, tum-ti-tum" and introducing the first "de-light" pun in *Ideas of Order*. Note the different forms of the two paired poems.

Evening without Angels

Alcestis 1 (Oct. 1934); see note on "Lions in Sweden," above; CP 136–38, LOA 111–12.

Revisiting the argument of "Sunday Morning," sometimes insistently. As in the preceding poem, light is purely earthly light, from the sun, with no religious connotation whatever, in a world entirely bare of angels. Old ghosts and spirits are also laid, as elsewhere in *Ideas of Order*.

Mario Rossi: contemporary Italian philosopher; the epigraph is from Rossi's "Essay on the Character of Swift" (1932) in his *Life and Letters* (SPBS 34–35), though Stevens did not at first remember where he found it (L 347, 1940).
"where the voice . . . moon": cf. the last two lines with the opening poem of *Transport to Summer*, "God Is Good. It is a Beautiful Night."

The Brave Man

Harkness Hoot 4 (Nov. 1933), with "A Fading of the Sun," under "Two Poems"; CP 138, LOA 112.

A striking personification of the sun and by implication of night-time fears. The fourth stanza on "fears of my bed" describes the common enough night experience, where things look much worse than on waking. The poem's five sentences coincide with its five tercets.

A Fading of the Sun

Ibid.; CP 139, LOA 112–13.

The point of the poem, Stevens wrote, was that "we should look to ourselves for help," rather than crying to the gods or to God. He disliked any sense of the "abasement" of human nature, even such crying for help (L 295, 1935). See note on "How To Live. What To Do," above. The poem uses occasional pronounced rhyme and simple diction, as if offering a lesson. It is the first of three somewhat didactic, somewhat weaker poems.

Gray Stones and Gray Pigeons

Westminster Magazine 23 (autumn 1934), with "Gallant Château" and "Polo Ponies Practicing" (the latter uncollected during Stevens's lifetime), under "Three Poems"; CP 140, LOA 113–14.

Stevens reluctantly and a little clumsily abstracted the sense of the poem: "everything depends on its sanction, and when its sanction is lost that is the end of it." But, he added quickly, the poem is what is printed on the page. The absent archbishop personifies or embodies a world (L 347–48, 1940). The poem emphasizes gray through repetition and rhyme.

"robes folded in camphor": to preserve the stored robes from being eaten by moths.

"Among fireflies": a tiny, flickering, natural light, as against divine light or earthly light given by God in "Let there be light" (Gen. 1:3); as against Milton's great invocation to light, *PL* III.1–55; as against the archbishop's view of things.

Winter Bells

CP 141, LOA 114.

As the strength of the church declined, Stevens thought that it might come to mean simply propriety for many people—about on a par with a capon and Florida as part of living. The Jew was conceived as a man of "exacting intelligence" who nonetheless "drifts from fasting to feasting." Stevens added that "it is a habit of mind with me to be thinking of some substitute for religion" (L 348, 1940). In light of the last sentence, "Winter Bells" may be seen as an exploration of the subject of "Notes toward a Supreme Fiction," though a rather ineffectual one.

"To be flogged": figuratively, as in "fasting" in Stevens's commentary above, but also a reminder of times when Jews were flogged for their beliefs.

"*mille fiori*": (It.) a thousand flowers, also a kind of glass.

"regulations of his spirit": "an allusion to Descartes" (L 348, 1940), the first of several references and allusions to Descartes in Stevens's poetry and prose, here to *Regulae ad directionem ingenii*. Descartes is a figure for human reason in NSF I.iv, though he was also a sufficiently orthodox Christian, and so an appropriate figure here. See also "Life on a Battleship" (OP 106–9, LOA 198–201, 1939) and "The Figure of the Youth as Virile Poet" (NA 55–56, LOA 677, 1943). (Note with respect to the latter that Boileau's remark on Descartes is not from Freud's *The Future of an Illusion* as Stevens supposed. It comes from F. W. Bateson, *English Poetry and the English Language*, 56; Stevens made a note of it in his copy, now at the University of Massachusetts, Amherst, Library.)

Academic Discourse at Havana

Broom 5 (Nov. 1923), as "Discourse in a Cantina at Havana"; under this title, *Hound and Horn* 3 (fall 1929); the earliest version, submitted on request but without result, was longer (L 335, 1938); CP 142–45, LOA 115–17.

A poem from the era of "The Comedian as the Letter C," with a similar tone in places (e.g., III, "Jot these milky matters down") and a similar disjunction between exuberant rhetoric and thematic despondence. As such, the poem is rather disruptive in this collection. Litz quotes an unpublished letter to R. P. Blackmur of 18 Oct. 1930, saying that the poem was omitted from the 1931 *Harmonium*, "since it seems to be cramped" (143). Stevens later called the poem "rather pulpy" and lacking "siccity" (Tate's word), which he liked (letter to Allen Tate, 1943, see SPBS 33). Stevens visited Havana twice in 1923 (L 234–36, 1923; 483–84, 1945).

TITLE: another generic title; cf. the kind and degree of irony with that in, e.g., "Extracts from Addresses to the Academy of Fine Ideas."

I

"A difference from nightingales, / Jehovah and the great sea-worm": as in, e.g., T. S. Eliot? A parodic glance at older sublime themes, e.g., of "the great sea-worm" or biblical Leviathan.

II

"Life is an old casino in a park": cf. Laforgue on existence as an abandoned casino: "Hier l'orchestre attaqua / Sa dernière polka. // Oh! L'automne, l'automne! / Les casinos / Qu'on abandonne / Remisent leurs pianos! (Yesterday the orchestra attacked / Its last polka. / Oh! autumn, autumn! The casinos / We abandon / put back their pianos! "Légende").

"swans": as in "Invective against Swans," a bird emblematic of an old and stale perspective.

"Rouge-Fatima": Elder Olson recalled from 1951: "He told me that he had originally intended to put in something like Helen of Troy but decided the poor girl was overworked, especially in poetry, and so he thought of another beautiful woman" (the last wife of Bluebeard). Stevens corrected Olson's mistaken pronunciation to "Fátima." To a query about "Rouge," he is said to have replied, "Oh, that's just to dress her up a bit" (Brazeau, 210).

III

"goober khan": peanut king; "khan" is an honorific title, once imperial, as in Kubla Khan, whose empire was centered on Mongolia. (Stevens noted the many Chinese in Havana in 1923, including a Chinese peanut-vendor [L 235].)

"wench / For whom the towers are built": probably a variation on the archetypal princess in a tower, familiar from fairy-tales (e.g., "Rumpelstiltskin") and lyric poems.

IV

"Waken, and watch the moonlight on their floors," etc.: see the later powerful development in NSF I.iii.

"an incantation that the moon defines . . . an infinite incantation of ourselves": "cantina" modulates into "incantation" by sound, not etymology (OED "cantina," "canteen"); re "incantation," note the old association of moon and enchantment (see Frye, "Charms and Riddles," *Spiritus Mundi* [1976]).

Nudity at the Capital

Alcestis 1 (Oct. 1934); see note on "Lions in Sweden," above; CP 145, LOA 117.

See Stevens's explication in L 347 (1940). At the end he commented, "The extension of this into statements of principle ought not to be difficult" (L 347, 1940). The last sentence also describes the function of a good epigram. The poem shows masterly, compact play with sound effects.

Nudity in the Colonies

Ibid.

See note on the preceding poem.

"nouveautés": (Fr.) novelties, innovations.

Re-Statement of Romance

New Republic 82 (6 Mar. 1935); CP 146, LOA 118.

With the opening argument, cf. the opening of "The Idea of Order at Key West." The strong use of enjambment between stanzas 1 and 2 introduces a "you" quite unexpectedly.

TITLE: as "Re-Statement," note the "pale light" in the last line and the moon of romance earlier in Stevens's poetry.

The Reader

New Republic 81 (30 Jan. 1935); CP 146–47, LOA 118.

Stevens later observed that he often had in mind "an image of reading a page of a large book" when he was writing a poem (L 642, 1949). With the scene here, cf. "Domination of Black." This is the first of a series of impressive reader poems.

"shrivelled forms": cf. autumn's "*scène flétrie*" in "New England Verses" xv.

Mud Master

CP 147–48, LOA 119.

Cf. "Frogs Eat Butterflies. . . ." for a similar scene. Note again Stevens's use of the negative.

"bulging green . . . Sky-sides of gold": cf. "Nomad Exquisite."
"snarls": both growls and tangles as with a line (also a line of poetry?).
"pickanines": Stevens thought this form of the word reflected its Spanish root, *pequeño*, small (Lensing [2001], 219n.).

Anglais Mort à Florence

CP 148–49, LOA 119–20.

A powerful elegiac poem, starting with the memorable one-line opening sentence in regular iambic pentameter. Stevens slowly lengthens the line and introduces repetition, as if within the mind of an aging man. "Most people stand by the aid of philosophy, religion . . . but a strong spirit (Anglais, etc.) stands by its own strength. Even such a spirit is subject to degeneration"

(L 348, 1940). A thrice-repeated line in the last three stanzas acts as a refrain, like a refrain of memory within the Englishman's brain.

TITLE: (Fr.) An Englishman Dead in Florence.
"the naked moon / Was not the moon he used to see," etc.: also true for Stevens; a theme best known from Wordsworth's "Ode: On the Intimations of Immortality," though experienced there by a younger man.

The Pleasures of Merely Circulating

Smoke 3 (spring 1934); CP 149–50, LOA 120.

On a spectacle of order so huge that it looks like disorder or the fortuitous, see L 348 (1940). Stevens affirmed that, for all its "apparent fortuitousness," it holds together (ibid.). The light-hearted rhyming effects have a Gilbert-and-Sullivan air, especially given the song, "For he is an Englishman" from *H. M. S. Pinafore* ("He might have been a Prussian," etc.). The pleasing, light-hearted effects play against ominous reminders of the thirties, including the different fates of Swedish, German, and Spanish babies.

Like Decorations in a Nigger Cemetery

Poetry 45 (Feb. 1935); CP 150–58, LOA 121–28.

A fifty-part series of epigrammatic poems, each standing singly, unlike the paired poems of "New England Verses." Stevens said that most were composed during his walks to and from his office (L 272, 1934). His gift for epigram may be seen especially in III, XVIII, XXV, XXVIII, and L. The series is chiefly unrhymed, though see the effective aaa rhyme in XIV. The poem includes a rare dedication, to Stevens's Southern friend (see note on title); Powell rightly called the series an olio (a medley or a hodgepodge), thus connecting the form with the title (Brazeau, 100–101).

TITLE: Referring to "the litter that one usually finds in a nigger cemetery"; the phrase was used by Judge Arthur Powell during the preceding winter in Key West (L 272, 1934). The "litter" may have significance, though not to outsiders, for which see, e.g., Faulkner, "Pantaloon in Black" from *Go Down, Moses*. "Nigger" was a term more widespread at the time, sometimes colloquial, but chiefly disrespectful or contemptuous when used outside African-American English or an imitation of it. The respectful form at the time was "negro," also in Judge Powell's reminiscences (Brazeau, 100–101). "Negro" is Stevens's more usual, though hardly invariable, term in his letters. The poetry uses both, depending on context. See also "Prelude to Objects" and "The News and the Weather."

III

"eccentric": note also the mathematical meaning, hence the implicit difference from any view of the world that emphasizes a center.

IV

"rules of the rabbis": "another allusion to regulations of the spirit" (L 348; see note on "Winter Bells," above).

VI

In Stevens's explication, he confirms that "two unrelated ideas" about death are brought together here. First, "we do not die simply." We are attended, Stevens said, by a figure from which we might well turn away. Second, people should not die like what Stevens calls "a poor parishioner"; people should meet their death "for what it is" (L 349, 1940).

XI

On "the ubiquitous 'will' of things" (ibid.).

XII

"Ananke": the goddess *Anagke*, or Necessity, in ancient and classical Greek. Stevens made the connection with Horace's "Necessitas" in Odes I.35 (SPBS 35). Freud uses the word in *The Future of an Illusion*, and Stevens annotated his 1928 copy in the margins ("ἀνάγκη = external reality," p. 93), as well as on the dust-jacket (SPBS 35n.). In a 1934 letter to Stevens, Rossi (see note on "Evening without Angels," above) talked of the "imperscrutable Ananke" (a "magnificent" adjective, Stevens thought [ibid.]). The word "Ananke" also turns up several times in "Owl's Clover" (1936, see the Concordance).

"stride": see note on "striding" in "Domination of Black, above."

"horror of the frost . . . hair": Lat. *horreo* (whence "horror"), when used of hair, means "to stand on end"; also an echo of "hoar-frost."

XIII

"Gemütlichkeit": good nature, geniality, as in social gatherings of a back-slapping kind.

XV

"a page of Toulet": Paul-Jean Toulet (1867–1920), author of *Comme un fantaisiste* (1918) and *Contrerimes* (1921); Stevens owned his *Le Mariage de Don Quichotte* (1922) and *Journal et Voyages* (1934), and copied a 1934 extract on him in SPBS (49, 49–51n.).

XVIII

"grapple . . . muscular poses": evocative of the famous statue of Laocoön grappling with the sea-serpent.
"museums": as elsewhere in Stevens and in others, the repository for past works of art, invaluable though also potentially stifling for current art. The "destroyers" who "avoid the museums," including literary museums, would not recognize skilled reworkings of a tradition.

XIX

Stevens is hard on his favorite word, "portals."

XXII

"Clog": dance in clogs in a country dance, sometimes requiring considerable skill (first citation in OED and Webster from 1925 in Fitzgerald, *The Great Gatsby*, chap. 7).

XXIV

"Tweedle-dum . . . Tweedle-dee": for the history of the pair best known from Carroll's *Alice in Wonderland*, see OED, "tweedle."

XXV

"Oriole, also, may be realist": Stevens insisted that nature's pleasing effects constitute reality to the same degree as its harsh effects. For example, a bird singing on a sunny day is "the same thing as a dog barking in the dark" (L 693, 1950; the point is developed throughout "Esthétique du Mal").

XXVI

"*Cochon!*": (Fr.) "Pig!"

XXVII

"Academy": The Royal Academy of London, famed arbiter of paintings for its exhibitions.

"iron dogs": Stevens was greatly taken by "the castiron animals on the lawns" when he came to Hartford (L 349, 1940, wrongly ascribed to xvii).

XXIX

As elsewhere, ghosts can embody the spirit of the past for Stevens. He was firm about rejecting a spirit that one has merely inherited and finding a spirit of one's own—a spirit "based on reality" (ibid.).

XXXII

"finikin": for the tone, cf. "finical phraseology" re Marianne Moore (NA 97, LOA 702, 1948) and "finikin" in OE xxxi.

XXXVI

Too cryptic for most readers. Stevens tried to help, saying that death could be like a child that dies "halfway to bed." He identified "the phrase . . . spoken" as the voice of death, and the "starry voluptuary" as the child in heaven (L 349, 1940).

XXXVIII

Stevens noted that this part and others use figures of autumn but are not concerned literally with autumn (ibid.). They offer advice not to show pictures of a season, even Corot's paintings, when the season is still flourishing. These are much better seen when the season has gone. His one-word summary, "Despair" (ibid.), may be incorrectly numbered.

XL

"in line": both as standing in line and referring to a poetic line.

XLII

On an anthropomorphic god, which Stevens calls "a projection of itself by a race of egoists" (ibid.).

XLV

"*Encore un instant de bonheur*": (Fr.) "Once more, a moment of happiness."

L

The aphoristic opening sentence of this last epigram is memorable in itself, and introduces the word "wisdom" into the series. In retrospect, the series may be read as a wisdom collection, like Stevens's private collection, "Adagia." The words "wisdom" and "wise" are key words in Stevens.

A Postcard from the Volcano

Smoke 5 (summer 1936); CP 158–59, LOA 128–29.

The first of five remarkable closing poems, each valedictory and each with its own sense of closure. This is a powerful poem on the passing of generations, noting what lives on, even when a younger generation is unaware of it and living by means of it. It is no tourist's postcard, but the voice of the Stevensian persona from within the volcano addressed to future generations, as if after his death; cf. Yeats's late poems. The skilful syntax, in intricately rhymed tercets, is appropriate to this narrative of inheritance.

TITLE: turning on the central trope of a volcano as a powerful image of voice, a longstanding trope (on its history and possibilities, see Cook, 1988, 193–94).
"shuttered mansion-house": one of Stevens's dwelling-places for the spirit.
"weaving budded aureoles": literal and/or figurative; like weaving daisy-chains, but here making a halo-like wreath of buds, appropriate for children.

Autumn Refrain

Hound and Horn 5 (winter 1932); CP 160, LOA 129.

A tour de force of sound and sense, moving on from Keats's "To Autumn." This is a refrain poem appropriately working with echo and allusion, and thereby engaging with the forerunners of this topos of birdsong in an earthly paradise, chiefly Keats's "Ode to a Nightingale," also Milton (echoed by

Keats) and Whitman. If a writer's fear of silence is evident, so also is a fear of false voice. Again, this is a poem of leave-taking and loss, yet with a "residuum" left. It takes the form of a sonnet (varying the Miltonic sonnet, with the turn in mid-line 7, not mid-line 8), with irregular mid-line and end rhymes, and two extended lines (6 and 14).

TITLE: "refrain": given the argument about stillness and voice, a likely pun on the noun and the verb ("to cease"); for the specialized meaning of "refrain" as "birdsong" in several languages, see Leo Spitzer's long note in *Classical and Christian Ideas of World Harmony* (1963), 180n.

"skreak": variation of "screak," now chiefly dialectic.

"grackles": even the parodic or ironic voice of "Banal Sojourn" is no longer available; note, however, the vigor of the language, a constant paradox in writing about loss.

"the yellow moon of words about the nightingale": see head-note, above; suggesting Whitman's mocking-bird song in "Out of the Cradle Endlessly Rocking," with its repeated "yellow half-moon"; for a personal memory, see L 149–50 (1909), where, in a letter to his future wife just before their marriage, Stevens creates at length an ideal spot, or *locus amoenus*, with nightingales, moon, and a "sweet outpouring of liquid sound"; the letter includes reference to "what we have never heard" (cf. l. 7).

l. 7: in 1932, followed by the line: "The stillness that comes to me out of this, beneath".

"stillness": note here, and in repetitions of the word, that stillness is not the same thing as silence.

"grates these evasions": note the omission of a preposition: grates *out* or *on* or *up*? Possibly, given Stevens, all three, as a refrain makes sound (grates on an instrument or on the ear) and also breaks etymologically (grates up); with the earlier *scr-gr* sound, "grates" echoes Milton's "Their lean and flashy songs / Grate on their scrannel pipes of wretched straw" ("Lycidas" 123–24, describing false preachers).

"residuum": cf. usage in L 508 (1945).

A Fish-Scale Sunrise

Alcestis 1 (Oct. 1934); see note on "Lions in Sweden," above; CP 160–61, LOA 130.

Stevens informed his friend, James Powers, a fellow lawyer at the Hartford, that he had put him and his wife into a poem. "I know that you do not read poetry, except on doctor's orders," he wrote; still, the poem would "be a souvenir, not so much of the bat we went on in New York as of the distorted state in which that bat left me" (L 301, 1935, cf. ibid., 269–70, and see Brazeau 90–91 for a charming reminiscence by Margaret Powers). The firmly stressed tetrameter second lines help to anchor the long first lines of the unrhymed couplets.

TITLE: presumably a mackerel sky (cirrocumulus clouds), perhaps a similar feeling in the stomach, as also in the last line.

"instruments of straw": pastoral wind instruments; cf. note on "grates these evasions" in "Autumn Refrain," above.

"La Paloma": (Sp.) "the dove," title of "perhaps the most popular Spanish song ever written" (Grove's *Dictionary of Music and Musicians*), composed 1859 by Sebastien Yradier; apparently the song requested at the New York club (Brazeau 90).

Gallant Château

Westminster Magazine 23 (autumn 1934); see note on "Gray Stones and Gray Pigeons," above; CP 161, LOA 130.

Printed with the circumflex accent on "château" on the Contents pages of *Ideas of Order* and CP. (In both books, titles over the poems are printed in capital letters and accents are omitted, as is customary.) The accent is omitted in LOA without explanation. The word is partly assimilated, so that the accent is optional. Stevens uses both "chateau" (CP 263, LOA 236) and "château" (CP 460, LOA 393). A French title would read "Château Galant." Stevens reverses the French word order, just as he reverses the standard quest plot where the knight arrives at the palace and claims the princess.

"curtains": with the lack of wind, breath, *spiritus* or inspiration, cf. "The Man Whose Pharynx Was Bad," etc.; here the quest has been accomplished, even though the ending is unexpected.

Delightful Evening

Alcestis 1 (Oct. 1934); see note on "Lions in Sweden," above; CP 162, LOA 131.

Stevens's farewell poem for *Ideas of Order* is appropriately an evening poem, punning on "light" and "night." It is a little good-bye wave to Stevens's volume and to a head-holding philosopher who is having trouble with metaphor. (For a true "savant," see the rabbi in "The Sun This March.") It is also a light-hearted good-bye to Stevens's own pensive Germanic self, when it gets out of line.

TITLE: the first line wishes Herr Doktor a "felicitous eve," rather than the conventional "good evening"; the title encompasses this wish ("delightful") and the reaction to it, which puns on "de-light-full"; cf. the punning at the end of "Botanist on Alp (No. 2)."

"Herr Doktor": Stevens identified his character as any philosopher, "particularly one of the German type" (L 347, 1940).

"grieve // At the vernacular of light": the causes of Herr Doktor's grief become fully apparent only at the end; "the vernacular": in contrast to Latin or a similar studied language, since the response to light is deeply instinctive rather than taught.

"twilight overfull / Of wormy metaphors": a surprise to end the poem and the volume; figurative language as wormy, i.e., wiggling, hidden in the dark, turning, and eating up good, substantial food as well as good, substantial philosophical language. Herr Doktor presumably seeks enlightenment through reason, and so sees the waning of actual light into twilight as grievous. Note the later development of the twilight-metaphor association in "The Motive for Metaphor."

The Man with the Blue Guitar and Other Poems

In October 1937 Alfred A. Knopf published this volume, comprising "The Man with the Blue Guitar," followed by *Owl's Clover*, "A Thought Revolved," and "The Men That Are Falling." *Owl's Clover*, first published by Alcestis Press in 1936, was much revised and shortened for this collection.

For Stevens's sense of the collection, see his note for the dust-jacket (LOA 998). Note, in remarks about the title poem, the wide definition of the word "poet." While the blue guitar of the series is a symbol of the imagination, he wrote, it often simply refers to the "individuality of the poet, meaning by the poet any man of imagination."

Stevens cut *Owl's Clover* altogether from his *Collected Poems* in 1954. For its effect as part of this collection, balancing "The Man with the Blue Guitar," see LOA 152–70.

Some lines in the book have blank spaces. The dust-jacket claimed this was an "experimental device" indicating a pause or emphasis. This, Stevens commented, "is pure nonsense" (L 325–26, 1937, and see L 783, 1953; see also the head-note to *Parts of a World*). An attempt to solve a small problem in the layout had metamorphosed into a full-blown theory in some publicist's fanciful brain.

* * *

The Man with the Blue Guitar

Twentieth-Century Verse 3 (Apr. 1937), poems v and xxvi, titled as in notes below, under "Two Poems; *Poetry* 30 CHK (May 1937), as poems ii, ix, xv, xvii, xviii, xxiv, xxvii, xxviii, xxix, xxx, xxxi, xxxiii.

For six rejected poems in the series, see OP 101–4 and see LOA 998–1000; one was published in 1942, the others remained unpublished during Stevens's lifetime. In 1937, each poem was printed on a separate page, a useful effect, for it concentrates the necessary attention on one poem at a time. In the *Poetry* version, Stevens's focus on the 27th to 33rd sections is well justified, for all the intermittent strengths throughout. In the arrangement of the series, one poem leads into another, sometimes simply by contrast (L 359, 1940).

In his dust-jacket note (LOA 998), Stevens identified the subject of the series as "the incessant conjunctions between things as they are and things imagined." A letter of 1937 mentions writing thirty-five or forty short poems over the winter, "of which about 25 seem to be coming through." Their subject, "the relation or balance between imagined things and real things," was, said Stevens, "a constant source of trouble to me." He then added, helpfully, that perhaps the subject is better described as "the painter's problem of realization" (L 316, 1937). (For the painter's problem of "realization," see Cézanne's reflections on *réaliser* and realization in his *Letters*, ed. John Rewald, rev. ed. [1976], 299, 300, 309. Stevens owned a copy of Cézanne's *Correspondance* [L 451n.], read widely about him, and viewed all the pictures he could [LFR 391, 1921].) Compare also L 828 (1954) on Stevens walking in a nearby park and trying "to realize: réaliser, the weather." He later explored the subject in "The Relations between Poetry and Painting" (NA 157–76, LOA 740–51, 1951). Stevens summed up the general intention of the series again in 1953 for a translator. He noted that the statements in xxx "are all succinct, necessarily" (L 788, 1953). They are generally succinct throughout.

"The Man with the Blue Guitar" is a pivotal, crucial series, richer than it may appear, in which Stevens worked out a path for his future writing. The poems are permeated with a sense of the 1930s, though indirectly. Repeated key words and phrases include "things as they are," as well as "sun" and "moon." The sun is associated with reality and the moon with imagination, as in pure, white, immaculate, otherworldly imagination, an earlier view that Stevens is now rejecting in an important move. The word "play" is also repeated, as Stevens enlarges the sense of playing a guitar to encompass an actor playing a role, and, at large, poetry as play that is also serious in the paradox known as *serio ludere*. Stevens twice offered extensive paraphrases, deliberately limited, and largely omitting the poem's tensions, tonalities, and emotional range (L 359–64, 1940; L 783–94, 1953). He cautioned that "The poem is the poem, not its paraphrase" (L 362, 1940), and called one paraphrase "a sort of murder" where one says a number of things "that are true only when they are not said this way" (L 360, 1940).

The poem has been associated with Picasso's 1903 "The Old Guitarist," where of course the guitar is brown (but then "blue" in Stevens is usually a color indicating imagination). He himself said he had no particular painting of Picasso's in mind (L 786, 1953). David Hockney has illustrated it. Stevens himself played on the guitar from an early age, though not very well, he said (L 95, 1907; 110–11, 1908); he sometimes identified his writing as guitar-playing (L 767, 1953).

The thirty-three poems of varying length use tetrameter couplets, made very flexible through variety in the feet, skilful use of syntax and enjambment, and intermittent rhyme, both end and internal. Sounds and rhythms throughout indicate the kind of music each poem is playing, and sometimes the volume; painterly effects are also strong.

I

The series begins with the guitarist and an audience that requests a tune, and not just any tune. Stevens then initiates the dialogue that will shape the poem, here offered in direct quotations. The rest of the series uses indirect quotation or paraphrase, except for poems x and xxix. This first poem is in five couplets, like the next three.

"bent over his guitar, / A shearsman of sorts": the guitarist resembles a tailor (shearsman), bending over his instrument as the tailor bends over his cloth (L 783, 1953); the tailor, like Crispin the shoemaker, can serve as a figure for the poet (thus for Dante in *Paradiso* XXXII.139–41) or for any imaginative man (see head-note to this volume, above).

"things as they are": best understood, in the first instance, in the commonsense meaning, while also raising questions about the nature of reality; evoking numerous other uses of this and like phrases, e.g., Arnold's "To see the object as in itself it really is." As E. H. Gombrich demonstrated in *Art and Illusion*, it is impossible to paint "things as they are." Note the modulation into "A tune" (titled "Things As They Are"?), and "A tune . . . *Of* things as they are" (my italics).

"A tune beyond us, yet ourselves": the requirement sounds impossible at first, yet "beyond themselves . . . is exactly the way" people are (L 359, 1940). That is, people's better or aspiring selves are also part of them; "things as they are" should not automatically be read in a reductive way. Stevens added that the feelings expressed here "demonstrate the subtlety of people" (ibid).

II

The guitarist sets limits to what he can do, to the world he can create and the hero he can celebrate. The main trope is a curious one, in that it kills and then displays its trophy bird (L 359, 1940).

"I cannot bring a world quite round": "cannot bring . . . quite round" or realize as a complete imaginative world, an achievement of very few writers; also "round" as adjective modifying "world," thus the shape of a perfect sphere; yet a world not quite round is the way things are, since our sphere is slightly flattened at the poles.

"patch": "patch together" is a Germanic synonym for latinate "compose" in the epilogue to "Notes."

"I sing a hero's head . . . but not a man": revising the well-known Virgilian epic formula at the start of the *Aeneid*, "Arms and the man I sing," and thereby moving away from heroic epic to what turns out to be "serenade." Is a serenade what the audience wants rather than an epic or is the player himself wary of epic?

"hero's head . . . almost to man": not quite reaching "man number one" (III), but only to a "hero's head." Stevens added that it is impossible for an artist "to do more than approach 'almost to man'" (L 789, 1953).

III

A pause to contemplate what it might be like to pin down "man number one," just as one nails up a dead bird as a trophy. The emphasis is on a savage fierceness in both acts; not a serenade, but banging and jangling.

"man number one": Stevens later said that he had in mind "Man without variation. Man in C Major. The complete realization of the idea of man. Man at his happier normal" (Poggioli, 174).

"nail . . . across the door / Its wings spread wide": not as in Pennsylvania, some hawk displayed "to frighten off other hawks," but rather a New England bird, "nailed up merely as an extraordinary object" (L 359, 1940).

"To strike his living hi and ho": that is, the liveliness of lively human experience, expressed in a natural way (L 783, 1953).

"To tick it, tock it, turn it true": "an exact record of the liveliness" (ibid.); as usual, also a pun on "turn" as "trope."

IV

By way of contrast, a poem on a multitude of people rather than man number one. This time the guitar is picked or it produces a buzzing effect, in a different take on "things as they are." Stevens claimed in 1953 that reality here "changes into the imagination . . . by reason of one's feelings about it" (L 793).

"A million people on one string?": Stevens thought of this as a rhetorical question: "It is not possible to confine all the world (everybody) to reality. They will pick beyond that one string . . ." (Poggioli, 175). As in I, people want "A tune beyond us," and will make one for themselves if need be.

"feelings crazily, craftily call, / Like a buzzing of flies in autumn air": onomatopoeic, suggesting guitar effects, and cf. also III.7–10; here if anywhere, reality changes in the imagination, producing such onomatopoeia, though the trope of flies does not help.

V

A move against "the greatness of poetry," notably in the form of the old great epic poems that assume a world governed ultimately by gods or God. Though the guitar merely chatters now, its aim is to take the place of older hymns. (See L 360, 1940.) The title in April 1937 was "The Place of Poetry."

"the torches wisping in the underground": a turn against great poems treating an afterlife in the underground, e.g., those of Virgil, Milton, and especially Dante, where the shades of the dead take the form of flames; "wisping" is a fine sight-and-sound combination, making a verb of "wisp" in a way that diminishes the noun's force, while also suggesting "whispering."

"structure of vaults upon a point of light": moving against, e.g., Dante's heaven, centered on a point of light that is God; *punto* ("point") is a key word in Dante; the lines also describe the construction of a Christian cathedral.

"There are no shadows": set against shades of the dead, whether classical or Dante's or Eliot's; also against the doctrine that this world is a shadow compared with heaven's true light.

"The earth for us is flat and bare": cf. "Bare earth is best" in "Evening wthout Angels"; but "flat"? As in "flat air" in "The Common Life"? "Flat" may indicate the start of Stevens's second thoughts about an earth stripped bare of any sign of the older gods and God.

VI

This poem opens by returning to a phrase from I, "A tune beyond us," which it explores further in the light of the previous poem. Play on the words "place" and "space" link it with v, and make it another poem on "The Place of Poetry." It takes seven couplets, like the following poem.

"moment": a key word in Stevens, often weighted, as in this revision of the word "final" in the preceding line; "final" is also modified in the next line in "seems final"; Stevens is working against the idea of ultimately final things in an older teleology.

"The thinking of art . . . The thinking of god": "The artist—the imaginative man has quite a different point of view from that of the religious man" (Poggioli, 175).

"smoky dew": Stevens intended "so much dew that it looks like smoke" (L 793, 1953); earthly dew is evanescent.

VII

A new move, introducing sun and moon in their difference, both actual and symbolic. The guitarist argues with himself about the difference, and the conclusion is not happy. The poem ends with the strings "cold on the blue guitar." Though Stevens does not use the word "imagination," the crucial question is whether the imagination is (or should be or can be) detached from "things as they are."

"The moon shares nothing": turning against the moonlit imagination of Stevens's early work, and its world of pure whiteness, "immaculate" and "detached" and unreal.
"It is a sea": recalling also the pull of the moon on the sea, and the sea's salt sterility; both give "a sense of isolation" (L 362, 1940).
"The immaculate, the merciful good": extended to suggest religious symbolism as well, here also "Detached from us, from things as they are" like the moon; with "immaculate," cf. "unspotted" in XIII and XV.

VIII

This poem moves from the sun-moon argument to stormy weather. Now the guitar is heard from again, though merely in a "lazy, leaden twang." Like the next poem, this one disputes any necessary connection between imagination and its environs. Stevens called VIII and IX "companion pieces," linked by being opposites. In the first, where the setting encourages the imagination, it produces nothing of significance. Still, its chords catch "the *milieu*, though they are incapable of doing anything with it" (L 362, 1940).

"my lazy, leaden twang / Is like the reason in a storm": again, a very limited role, merely suggesting "the tumultuous brightness," etc.; "even so it is like reason addressing itself to chaos," for it gathers things into a focus (L 791, 1953, and see the rest of the letter). Stevens is judging art that is less than it might be, yet nonetheless adequate and useful to a degree.
"And yet it brings the storm to bear": in the morning after a night-time storm (L 783, 1953).

IX

By contrast, the imagination is here faced with "a kind of universal dullness" that is not promising, but "seizes upon it and makes use of it, dominates it, takes its place, becomes the world in which we live" (L 362–63, 1940). (For the phrase "universal dullness," see the last line of Pope's *The Dunciad*.) Here poetry masters its environment, natural and other, yet is conditioned by it.

Stevens is continuing the move against an imagination detached from "things as they are." "The actor" makes his first entry in the series and in Stevens's poetry. His behavior is worth watching here and elsewhere.

"The maker of a thing yet to be made": for "maker" as the old term for a poet, see note on "maker" in "The Idea of Order at Key West," above.

"the dress of his meaning": dress is a common trope for meaning or for style, as, e.g., in Stevens's various hats (see note on "Six Significant Landscapes" VI, above).

"The weather of his stage": "The imagination is not a free agent," but depends on reality, as, for example, "the weather" here (L 789, 1953).

X

Another new move, returning to an audience, but this time an audience watching a parade for some contemporary hero, perhaps a thirties politician. The context presents a new challenge for the guitarist, as for imagination and art. The guitar rolls a drum to announce the guitarist's challenge in response. The poem is extended into eight couplets, a longer parade.

"clap the hollows full of tin": banging tin cans to fill the spaces ("hollows") of the parade, in a near pun on "hollow" (L 793, 1953).

"behold / The approach of him whom none believes," etc.: not an agreed-on hero of Stevens's later supreme fiction, but the kind of hero who appears in parades. No one, wrote Stevens, believes such a hero is "a truly great man," but "everybody pretends to believe" this. He gave as examples "a politician, a soldier, Harry Truman as god" (L 789, 1953).

"A pagan in a varnished car": revising heroic triumphal cars (chariots).

"'Here I am, my adversary'": Stevens identified the adversary as the "*second-rate creature*" who is described just above (ibid.).

"'hoo-ing the slick trombones'": a derisive, challenging sound (ibid.); for "'hoo-ing'" as pejorative, see ibid., where it is likened to "booing or hooting." Stevens adds that "the pejorative sense of slick is obvious"—a slick thirties jazz sound and the slick sliding of a trombone's tubes.

XI

The guitar plays chords, which give rise to a reflection on "chord" and "discord." The poem contrasts the chord that merges all things, and so "falsifies," with the discord that separates all things, and so "magnifies" difference. (See L 363, 1940.) Stevens's aim is a balance, and ultimately "the supreme balance between these two," which, he said, concerns us all. He observed that the idea could be extended into social or philosophical spheres, though he did not have this in mind (ibid.).

"the belly's dark / Of time, time grows upon the rock": the era to come, which is "the point of the poem" (ibid.). Time is identified as life, and the rock as the world (ibid.); cf. the function of the rock much later in "The Rock."

XII

This time, the guitar as tom-tom, drum-like (or else a drum?), though eventually "I strum the thing." Again, an audience is present, here a multitude implicitly challenging the guitarist to find his true voice. Stevens noted the series of antitheses in the poem. He cautioned that there was no reference to contemporary poetry; the poem has to do with society (L 360, 1940).

"Tom-tom, c'est moi": (Fr.) "Tom-tom, that's me."
"his breath that lies awake at night. . . . that timid breathing": like the ephebe in 1942? "In silence upon your bed. . . . cowed" (NSF I.v).
"Where / Do I begin and end?": a question that sounds like T. S. Eliot, another "Tom-tom."

XIII

Stevens identified the subject of the poem as pure imagination or "the intensity of the imagination unmodified by contacts with reality." He then added a crucial clause: "*if such a thing is possible* [my italics]" (L 785, 1953). Stevens's earlier love of a moon-centered imagination and pure poetry helps account for his harshness here, in his conviction that contact with reality is necessary. This is the shortest poem so far, at four couplets.

"corrupting pallors," etc.: how words like "immaculate" and "white" can be coercive or even corrupting; cf. the lexis of the moon in vii.
"ay di mi": "purely phonetic," and without any Spanish connotation (L 783, 1953).
"Blue buds or pitchy blooms": "blue" metamorphoses into "blooms" in this act of corrupting, so that the blue of the sky and the pitch-dark of night are all one; the language also suggests a thought of heaven and hell.
"unspotted": Germanic equivalent of "immaculate" (cf vii.10, and also "my unspotted fire of love to you" [*Pericles* I.i.53]).
"imbecile": a harsh revision of the well-known "lunatic" association with the moon, and of the conjunction of "The lunatic, the lover, and the poet"

in *A Midsummer Night's Dream* V.i.7–8 (see note on "Homunculus et la Belle Etoile," above).

"heraldic center of the world": another attack upon the concept of a "center" for everything.

"blue, blue sleek with a hundred chins": blue in this context is evidently fat, presumably from fattening on such words as those above.

"the amorist Adjective aflame": blue, as it acts in this context; *amoureuse flamme* is a common Fr. phrase.

XIV

A poem of contrast, first of a world lit by a "German chandelier" (see note, below), which Stevens identified with the viewpoint of the sciences (L 363, 1940). Second, and more happily, of a world lit by a candle, a domestic setting providing nourishment for body and spirit. Not searchlights, but "chiaroscuro." The series also moves back to a simple playing of the guitar.

"a German chandelier": a trope perhaps clearer at the time; Stevens glossed it as "German laboriousness" (L 363, 1940), "an oversized over-elaborate chandelier" (L 783, 1953), hence the world as seen by such a light.

"A candle is enough": the candle of the imagination, in contrast to the chandelier (ibid.).

XV

After the peaceful and propitious ending to xiv, a sudden turn to crisis, crisis of the self and of society. No guitar sound is heard, apart from "Catching" at a current song, as if singing a catch. The poem is centered on a painting, which becomes actuality even as it remains a painting. It ends on a foreboding question, one of six in six couplets.

"this picture of Picasso's": a prototypical painting.

" 'hoard / Of destructions' ": Picasso was quoted in 1935 as saying that older paintings were a sum of additions, but that in his case a painting was a sum of destructions ("somme de destructions," *Cahiers d'art* X, 1935, and see LOA 1000). Stevens later inferred from this saying by Picasso an analogous saying about poetry: if "a picture is a horde of destructions," then "a poem is a horde of destructions" ("The Relations between Poetry and Painting," NA 161, LOA 741, 1951).

"Good-bye, harvest moon": Stevens later identified this as a popular song "entitled Good-bye, Good-bye Harvest Moon" (L 783, 1953). Surely it is "Shine on, shine on, harvest moon," the very popular 1908 song (lyrics by Jack Norworth, music by Nora Bayes).

"Things as they are have been destroyed": cf. "'destruction'" in l. 2 and the note, above.

"Is my thought a memory, not alive?": not actively thinking, but simply remembering and repeating what has been thought before, either by us or by someone else; cf. remarks on the constructive faculty and memory in NA 164–65, LOA 744 (1951).

"spot on the floor": cf. "unspotted" (XIII.5) and "immaculate" (VIII.10); note internal rhyme with "thought."

"wine or blood": the poem plays between actuality and painting, as if we peered at a canvas and looked at a floor at the same time; also recalling wine as food in the peaceful scene in XIV; also evoking the specific linking of wine and blood in the Christian sacrament, which draws together historic actuality and symbolic commemoration (or else transubstantiation).

XVI

At this midway point, the series continues downward, envisioning a life in war and at war. The guitar vanishes and is replaced by a somewhat similar ancient and medieval stringed instrument (the "psaltery"). The psaltery is best known from biblical translation (Ps. 33:2, etc.), but also from Shakespeare's *Coriolanus* V.iv.49, a suggestive context for this poem. Here it is bluntly played and does not respond (see note, below).

"The earth is not earth but a stone, / Not the mother . . .": moving toward the grim view that earth is an oppressor who grudges the living simply for living, and even grudges them their death. Recalling by contrast the riddle of Themis, correctly answered by Deucalion. Stevens will return to the trope of stone in the last poem, rewriting it.

"to chop the sullen psaltery": to write with difficulty, because, said Stevens, "of excess realism in life" (L 360, 1940); "chop": to aim a hacking or hewing blow at; given the context, "psaltery" suggests the acoustic echo of "assault."

"To improve the sewers in Jerusalem": a powerfully reductive metaphor of possible activity for the "bitter at heart" in the archetypal holy city; thus also the following line re "nimbuses."

"honey on the altars": honey was used in ancient libations to the dead or to Persephone and Hades (OCD, "honey"); here, a libation to the earth Stevens loved, now become a stone, dead, and taking with it any muse or music. On Stevens's personal love of honey, see LFR 384 (1920).

"and die, / You lovers that are bitter at heart": probably lovers of the earth, in the first instance, and thereby also lovers of the guitar; now the lovers are both the sacrificers and part of the sacrifice itself; "bitter" in contrast to the sweetness of "honey."

XVII

The turn toward strength begins here, and culminates in XIX. Stevens returns to simple essentials, the body and its spirit, for which he proposes the word "animal" (see below). Such an animal plays a fierce leonine music on the guitar.

"It is / An animal": "animal" in older, etymological sense of "living being"; "Anima = animal = soul. The body has a shape, the soul has not. The soul is the animal of the body" (Poggioli, 179).

"The angelic ones": unidentified, probably typic, e.g., Abbé Brémond (chap. 12 of his *Prière et Poésie* is titled "Animus et Anima").

"Speak of the soul, the mind": "soul" in Latin is *anima* or *mens* (whence "mind"); Stevens continues play on the etymology of "animal"; the paradox is that we sometimes oppose body and soul, whereas our language identifies them.

"on that its claws propound, its fangs / Articulate its desert days": the soul as animal appears to take the shape of a lion, playing leonine guitar music; the desert is the home of the lion in NSF I.v.

"north wind blows": "wind" with its familiar *spiritus* etymology that connects it to the spirit that is here an animal.

"a worm composing on a straw": Stevens claimed that the north wind "blows with little or no sound," even when most deadly (L 360, 1940)—a rather odd, oblique comment, as if he were having second thoughts about tropes from the natural world for the artist-spirit; "straw": pastoral wind instrument, in contrast to "horn."

XVIII

An assertion of essential need, a dream "(to call it a dream)" in which to believe. The act of believing in it means that the dream is "no longer a dream" but "a thing," one among "things as they are." Stevens plays with different definitions of "dream," then turns away from definitions and toward simile, as the blue guitar, "After long strumming on certain nights," gives what he needs.

"on certain nights": with a pun on "certain," as elsewhere ("Credences of Summer" I).

"The wind-gloss": Stevens's compound is doubly surprising because of enjambment; not the touch of the hand on a guitar, but of the "very senses as they touch" this hard-to-name thing. Art at certain times touches all the senses, or rather they touch the inexplicable wind-shine that is also a wind-poem or a wind-interpretation of things (see OED, "gloss," and see note on "wind" in XVII, above). At one time, Stevens "had an Aeolian harp in the garden, and arranged his bed so that the sound reached him most directly" (Holly Stevens, "Bits of Remembered Time," 654).

"as daylight comes . . . a sea of ex": when morning light comes to the cliffs, the sea changes, ceases to be real, "and is therefore a sea of Ex" (L 360, 1940); Stevens expanded the last clause in 1953: "sea of ex" refers to "the realm of has-been without interest or provocativeness" (L 783, 1953).

XIX

An often-quoted poem that reads almost like a declaration of faith or of principle. It embodies Stevens's working assumption from now on in his poetry.

"That I may": a compacted form of "I wish that I might" (L 360, 1940).

"the monster": i.e., the lion locked in stone, which Stevens identifies with life in general; this is what one wants "to match in intelligence and force, speaking (as a poet) with a voice matching its own" (ibid.). Later he identified the monster with "nature: the chaos and barbarism of reality" (Poggioli, 179).

"not be / Alone": Stevens's explicit conviction by 1937 that imagination always needs reality.

"intelligence": the embodiment of understanding, as in "man is the intelligence of his soil" ("The Comedian as the Letter C," line 1).

"the lion in the lute / Before the lion locked in stone": the guitar has metamorphosed into another *l*-word; "stone" has lost the oppressive force of "stone" in XVI. Cf. the well-known ending of "The Noble Rider and the Sound of Words" on nobility as "a violence from within that protects us from a violence without." Stevens goes on to call it "the imagination pressing back against the pressure of reality" (NA 36, LOA 665, 1942); see also L 790, 1953.

XX

A poem widening the search for a belief, which needs to go beyond ideas to friendship and love. The ending is inconclusive, as the final apostrophe and ellipsis indicate. The "poor pale guitar" makes no sound.

"Good air, good friend": Though "I apostrophize the air and call it friend," still, it is nothing but air, and the poet here needs "a true belief, a true brother." The imagination does not fill this role, but the air as "mere joie de vivre" may possibly do so. This apparently "stands for the search for a belief" (L 793, 1953).

"a brother full / Of love, believe would be a friend": cf. "the clouds, pomp of the air, / By which at least I am befriended" ("Idiom of the Hero").

XXI

Stevens turns away from the need in xx to an old subject, now laid out simply as a renewed aim: "a substitute for all the gods." He is uninterested here in the heavy ironies of earlier anticlerical writing. There is no guitar sound.

"a substitute for all the gods": "It is a habit of mind with me to be thinking of a substitute for religion" (L 348, 1940, "Winter Bells").
"one's shadow magnified": cf. "shadows" in v and below.
"Chocorua": see note to "Chocorua to its Neighbor" (1943), below.
"without magnificence": rejecting the powerful word, a word for Jove in "Sunday Morning" iii, and here implicit in the act of "magnifying."
"The flesh, the bone, the dirt, the stone": a simple rhyme and rhythm, gathering together earth and stone, again no longer oppressive as in xvi.

XXII

One of several poems where the interaction of imagination with reality is figured as a poem setting out on a quest, then returning; cf. xxvi, and "Notes" I.iii, II.ix. Once more, the guitar is silent.

"sun's green": most obviously the green of all vegetation, which needs the sun for photosynthesis; in an unusual phenomenon, the sun may also look green very briefly at sunrise; a painting or poem may also render the sun green if the work of art requires it; similarly with the examples that follow this one.
"universal intercourse": see L 364 on poetry as a passion that "nourishes itself on reality" and on imagination as having "no source except in reality" (1940).

XXIII

Stevens relaxes the intense tone of the preceding few poems in several that now follow. Here he offers wonderfully funny examples of the "universal intercourse" between reality and imagination. One of the challenges is to decide which is which in any given example. Another is whether the voices (including the one "smelling of drink") are singing with a guitar. If they are, we need to devise the appropriate accompaniment for each of them, following the hints here.

"final solutions": written, of course, before the Nazis made this phrase unusable.
"a duet / With the undertaker": Stevens's humor in the contraries that follow is usually ignored.

"Dichtung und Wahrheit": (Ger.) "Poetry and Truth," the title of Goethe's autobiography on his early influences; the phrase asks to be read against what precedes it and what follows it.

"Concerning the nature of things": the translated title of the great work by Lucretius, *De rerum natura*.

XXIV

"missal": Stevens was clear that he wished his poem "to mean as much, and as deeply, as a missal." Such a missal would help with "brooding-sight, for an understanding of the world" (L 783–84, 1953).

"That scholar hungriest": the type of scholar who, "for all his latined learning," would find in brooding-sight "a knowledge that seizes life, with joy in his eye" (L 360, 1940).

"A hawk of life": a phrase that, as it were, seizes in its talons "some aspect of life that it took a hawk's eye to see" (L 783–84, 1953).

"I play": see L 361 on how, "though . . . satisfying the scholar . . . , I pretend not to do so" and simply continue playing. Stevens adds the interesting remark that "there is a kind of secrecy between the poet and his poem which, once violated, affects the integrity of the poet" (L 361, 1940).

XXV

The man of imagination, in Stevens's paraphrase, juggles the earth on the tip of his nose. The world does not realize "that it moves as an imagination directs" (L 361, 1940).

"He held": Who is this he? Any observer, said Stevens. "Copernicus, Columbus, Professor [Alfred] Whitehead, myself, yourself" (L 790, 1953); robes and symbols make him a clown-wizard-magus figure; they and the cats, etc., are props to produce "an effect of comedy. The poet is a comedian" (L 361, 1940).

"upon his nose . . . fling": an old trope; cf. Persius on Horace, "A rare hand he had at flinging out his nose and hanging the people on it" (*Sat.* I.118, Loeb Classical Library).

"this-a-way . . . ai-yi-yi— / And that-a-way": colloquialisms in Pennsylvania; "ai-yi-yi" is just as much Pennsylvania Dutch as it is Spanish (L 784, 1953).

"Sombre as fir-trees, liquid cats": i.e., cats moving as easily as liquid, "solemn black blobs on the mind's eye." "No doubt," Stevens added mischievously, "these sombre cats are merely sombre people going about their jobs" (L 361, 1940).

"A fat thumb beats out ai-yi-yi": stupid people enjoying the spectacle of life, but not understanding it (L 361, 1940). The ellipsis (always to be read as part of the poem in Stevens) marks the contrast between what precedes and the player of "ai-yi-yi."

XXVI

Titled "Inaccessible Utopia" in manuscript. See Vendler's commentary on how the interactions here are realized by means of syntax and rhythm ([1969] 139–40).

"bar": a sand-bar, i.e., the earth "in a sea of space" (L 784, 1953).
"fought / Against the murderous alphabet": the world, continually changing, loses its familiar identity, even its thoughts and dreams. It is "as if these were an alphabet with which it could not spell out its riddle" (L 364, 1940).

XXVII

See Stevens's paraphrase of this poem, whose argument is not self-evident. In effect, the poem questions why we travel over land and sea, when they will come to us if we stay where we are. "Winter really ridicules the wanderer" (L 790, 1953).

"It is the sea that the north wind makes": "The wind makes this particular sea. The noise creates an image of the sea" (Poggioli, 181).

XXVIII

By contrast, another poem that affirms working principles, and also begins to work out what the crucial word "native" means for Stevens.

"I am a native in this world": a key statement; "native" is a strong word throughout his work.
"Gesu": "Jesus" in an obsolete spelling, a spelling that Stevens wanted; the implication is clear (L 784, 1953).
"dead leaves": see note on "Domination of Black," above.
"as I am, I speak and move": among the earliest of such formulations, echoing and revising God's naming of himself to Moses, "I am that I am" (Ex. 3:14); cf. "Re-Statement of Romance," NSF II.viii, III.viii, "The Sail of Ulysses," etc.

XXIX

Another poem of balance, not this time of the world on someone's nose (xxv), but of what a cathedral embodies and what is outside it. The meditation takes the form of quoted remarks from a reader of a Review, sitting in a cathedral. The question of balance is filtered through the reader and the double judgment at the end.

"a lean Review": a prototypical slim Review (lean in content too?), kept unspecified; it appears to provoke the meditation that follows.

"the vaults": cf. the cathedral image of v, "the structure of vaults upon a point of light."

"the festival": followed by a full stop, as in LOA, not a comma, as in CP.

"nuptial song": in the cathedral, the song of nuptials celebrated there; also, e.g., the allegorical marriage of Christ and the church, or music in heaven as in Milton's "nuptial song" in *Lycidas* (176). Outside the cathedral, nuptials are different: see following.

"nuptial song . . . mask": "Religious ceremonies and delights are evasions of reality. External life, the opposite, is all a wedding with reality. The ancient argument goes on forever. It is like a comparison of masks" (Poggioli, 182). Again, note that "evasion," like "illusion," is not necessarily a pejorative word for Stevens; he thought of the idea of God as a "benign illusion" (L 401, 1942).

"The bells are the bellowing of bulls": a turn against the balance envisioned in what precedes; punning on papal bulls; cf. the sound of bells from the village steeple in "Esthétique du Mal" xi.

"Franciscan don": "don" refers to "a clerical figure"; Stevens thought he probably chose the Franciscan because of the order's reputation for "liberality and . . . being part of the world" as against a Jesuit, for example (L 784, 1953); he hastened to add that his first concern was with the general image. Yet another kind of don among Stevens's dons, who are mostly Spanish.

XXX

A summing-up poem, working with what has preceded to "evolve a man." Not now "a hero's head . . . almost to man" (ii) or "man number one" (iii), but simply "man." Stevens has stayed away from such a figure through much of the series, returning only with the idealized imagined reader in xxiv ("that young man / That scholar hungriest"), the observer embodied as a comic wizard and clown in xxv, and the image of the "Franciscan don" in xxix. He is also returning to things as they are for some of an audience—this time to their living conditions in a "suburb" with "One-half of all its installments paid."

"fantoche": puppet, marionette; used "rather arbitrarily," Stevens said, "for a fantastic actor, [a] poet." The cross-piece on a pole is a piece of "realism" (see below) that the fantoche siezes, "rather the way the nightingale, I suppose, pressed its breast against the cruel thorn" (L 362, 1940). On man as "one of the fantoccini of meditation," see L 791 (1953), where Stevens added that there was no conscious reference to Shakespeare. The actor or fantoche in one form is "actually and presently . . . an employee of the Oxidia Electric Light & Power Company" (ibid., see entire entry).

"his eye // A-cock at the cross-piece . . .": "man facing his particular job: in this case, an electric lineman" (Poggioli, 183).

"cross-piece on a pole / Supporting heavy cables": a return with a vengeance to "things as they are" in a familiar urban image of power lines.

"dew-dapper clapper-traps": the lid on a smoke-stack that pours out "bright (dew dapper) flame" (L 362, 1940); the word "clapper" indicates the noise that this rather old-fashioned piece of equipment makes (cf. L 791n., 1953).

"Oxidia is Olympia": Stevens confirmed that these were opposites. "Oxidia (from oxide) is the typical industrial suburb, stained and grim" (L 791, 1953); Olympia is a land like Mount Olympus, home of the classical gods (cf. L 789, and see 788, 1953). "The necessity," he said, "is to evolve a man from modern life—from Oxidia, not Olympia, since Oxidia is our only Olympia" (Poggioli, 182).

XXXI

"The blue guitar" returns, though its nuances are baffling and unattainable here (L 362, 1940).

"pheasant sleeps": a bird from Stevens's neighborhood (L 362, 1940), and see below.

"cock-bird shriek": no gloss needed for anyone who has heard a male pheasant in mating season.

"the lark . . . the museum of the sky": again, the museum as trope for gatherings of older art, e.g., Shelley's "Ode to a Skylark."

XXXII

An often-quoted poem, striking in its use of an opening imperative ("Throw away the lights, the definitions"), its phrase "the rotted names," and its straightforward argument. See L 364 (1940) on the meaning of "being oneself," not in a reductive sense, "but as one of the jocular procreations of the dark, of space" (cf. "A tune beyond us, yet ourselves" in 1). Stevens added that the poem's point was not that this can be done, but that, "if done, it is the key to poetry, to the closed garden, if I may become rhapsodic about it, of the fountain of youth and life and renewal." (The "closed garden" translates *hortus conclusus*, the trope for the beloved in the Song of Sol. 4:12 and the ideal garden of medieval paintings and tapestries.)

"the rotted names": sometimes misquoted as "the rotten names," not quite the same thing.
"the shapes you take": e.g., one of the "jocular procreations."

XXXIII

A remarkable poem in its resolve. The language is like the language of covenant, e.g., Jacob's language in Gen. 28:10–22, where dream, bread, and stone as a bed also figure. It suggests a new and final sense of "The Place of Poetry" (see v). Stevens sounds as if he is taking a vow of vocation, and his subsequent work during his remaining eighteen years would bear this out.

"aviled": "debased, degraded," an obsolete term with religious connotations.
"Monday's dirty light": as the day of the moon, following Sunday, and ending the "moon" theme throughout decisively; commonly the first working day of the week in the West.
"a wrangling of two dreams": cf. the "dream" in xvii.
"Here is the bread of time to come, / Here is its actual stone": the resolution of the language of stone running through the series; the conjunction of bread and stone is familiar from the temptation of Jesus in the Gospels (turn stones into bread); it provides a common allegory (e.g., Brecht, *Der Steinfischer*), especially in times of hunger.
"the stone will be / Our bed and we shall sleep by night": a striking move beyond the desolate earth-as-stone trope in xvi.
"except": also a crucial preposition placed at the end of the line in "Farewell to Florida."
"to play": in the fullest sense (see head-note to the series, above).
"The imagined pine, the imagined jay": "pine" recalls Stevens's familiar pun elsewhere ("pine" as "longing"); the jay is a quietly auspicious bird, free from the weight of Stevens's pigeons or grackles or nightingales; in Stevens's area, it is blue, the color of the imagination; in "The Sense of the Sleight-of-Hand Man," a bluejay provides an occasion for a "grand flight," a "tooting at the wedding of the soul."

[Owl's Clover: see head-note to this volume, above.]

A Thought Revolved

New Directions in Prose and Poetry, ed. James Laughlin IV (Norfolk, Conn.: New Directions, 1936); CP 184–87, LOA 171–73.

The title links four interrelated poems, all antipietistic, reacting against religious and moral notions, especially simplistic ones. The effect is somewhat crude after the subtleties and passion of "The Man with the Blue Guitar."

I

The Mechanical Optimist

Despite the closing injunction to the dying lady to "rejoice," this is a rather jarring poem.

II

Mystic Garden & Middling Beast

Stevens again works with the familiar theme of "Hymns of the struggle of the idea of god / And the idea of man." The result is a shade self-righteous, but with an interesting mixing and realigning of contraries at the end. Stevens again asserts that man made the god or God, placing him on middle earth among the "middling beasts."

"abstraction": cf. NSF I, "It Must Be Abstract" (1942).
"the mystic garden": Milton called Eden one of the "gardens . . . not mystic,"
    i.e., not fictitious (*PL* IX.439–42), as Eden was for Stevens.

III

Romanesque Affabulation

"Son only of man": Jesus is often called both "Son of Man" and "Son of God."
"the Pole / In Paris": a stranger or exile, even in Paris; a Chopin.
"celui qui chante et pleure": (Fr.) "he who sings and weeps"; cf. "L'amant qui chante / Et pleure aussi" ("the lover who sings and weeps as well"), the end of the refrain to Victor Hugo's "L'aube nait," set to music by several composers.
"the race that sings and weeps and knows not why": see preceding note.

IV

The Leader

The final poem makes a sharp tonal change into the harsh bitterness of some thirties work. Stevens can turn his verbal gifts against parts of himself, quite as readily as against the female subject in "Good Man, Bad Woman" or "The Woman Who Blamed Life on a Spaniard" (OP 65–67, LOA 558–60).

"moralist hidalgo": the first appearance of the hidalgo figure is not favorable; Stevens is reacting against his various Dons; the hidalgo will later evolve.
"Whose whore is Morning Star": revising the apocalyptic great whore (Rev. 17:1) and morning star (Rev. 22:16), here combined.
"bone . . . horn . . . morn": note how the near-rhyme suggests ghost rhymes of "born," "hone," and "moan."

The Men That Are Falling

Nation 143 (24 Oct. 1936), and the *Nation* Prize Poem for 1936; CP 187–88, LOA 173–74.

Stevens recorded that he had "the Spanish Republicans in mind" (L 798, 1953) in this strong and moving poem. The Spanish Civil War lasted from 17–18 July 1936 to March 1939. Garcia Lorca, who is quoted in "The Novel," was taken out and summarily shot to death by Franco's forces on 19 August 1936. On August 21, Elizabeth Bishop wrote: "The war in Spain is frightful" (*One Art: Letters*, ed. Giroux [1994], 45). The poem moves on from "The Man with the Blue Guitar," continuing its language of stone and dream and earth versus heaven. The move from the sleeper's desire to other life and another's desire is decisive. The fifteen couplets of compelling rhythm include one 11-line sentence; two early ellipses intimate a great deal.

Parts of a World

Parts of a World was published by Alfred A. Knopf in September 1942, the same month in which the Cummington Press completed *Notes toward a Supreme Fiction* in a limited edition (copyright October). *Parts of a World* collects sixty-three poems written from 1937 to 1942 and arranged largely in chronological order. In his *Collected Poems* (1954), Stevens dropped "Life on a Battleship" (OP 106–7, LOA 198–201) and "The Woman That Had More Babies Than That" (OP 104–6, LOA 201–3) from the original edition (L 830, 1954).

For his rather labored concluding statement to *Parts of a World* on the subject of poetry in a time of war, see LOA 251.

The title, *Parts of a World*, indicates Stevens's perspective. As in "The Man with the Blue Guitar" II, Stevens "cannot bring a world quite round." His various parts do not imply a unified harmonious whole. Stevens questions any general sense that synecdoche as a part stands for a whole. The questioning may come explicitly in argument or implicitly in rhetoric. Poems with the words "part" or "world" contribute to the building of Stevens's own poetic world here. So do poems with the words "piece together," "compose," etc. They also remind us that this collection is a piecing together. But it is not atomistic, not a mere aggregate. If Stevens's world is not an old-style harmonious whole, neither is it fragmented and subject to any passing whim. One poem was specifically written against "the Lightness with which ideas are asserted, held, abandoned, etc." (L 380, 1940).

A number of poems are painterly, and Stevens's remarks about "realizing" poetic effects are a propos here, as well as for "The Man with the Blue Guitar" (see its head-note, above).

Parts of a World, like *The Man with the Blue Guitar*, includes some lines with extended spaces (e.g., "Extracts from Addresses to the Academy of Fine Ideas," "Examination of the Hero in a Time of War"). Despite Stevens's directions for one first printing (L 387, 1941), the Knopf edition continued this practice (see head-note to *The Man with the Blue Guitar*). It was corrected in the 1954 *Collected Poems*.

Parochial Theme

Southern Review 4 (autumn 1938); the first twelve poems of *Parts of a World* were published under the title, "Canonica"; CP 191–92, LOA 177.

An unexpected title to open *Parts of a World*. Not "Universal Theme," but the contrary. This is an oddly fractured poem of disparate "scenes," suffused with violent war-like imagery recalling the thirties and sometimes reminiscent of Jean Renoir's great 1939 film, *La règle du jeu* (*Rules of the Game*). As in Renoir, the sport of hunting is associated with the shooting and hunting by aggressors of the time (hunting, torturing, executing). Against this, Stevens affirms the ongoing, even holy health of the natural world (hunting, health, halloo, chanting), ending with an unusually down-to-earth imperative. The couplets are marked by compelling shifts of rhythm, and strong schematic echoing of *h* sounds. Stevens extends the wind-as-inspiration trope to include voices in the wind (present and past), and introduces the figure of the glass-blower who will reappear in his work. He called the poem "an experiment at stylizing life" (L 434, 1943), a comment that might be used of Renoir as well.

TITLE: "Parochial": playing against the metropolitan, sophisticated connotations of "Parisians."
"pine-lands": as often, "pine" includes to a degree "pine" as "yearning," also echoing in "ponies"; one hunts what one pines for.
"the statues torture": as in NSF II.III and elsewhere, statues provide a trope for authority, here vicious.
"salvation": beyond the usual religious sense, note the political salvations offered in the thirties by fascism and communism.
"horses eaten by the wind": in this poem's context, recalling Picasso's horses in the painting, *Guernica*, a response to the German bombing of the defenseless Spanish town in April 1937.
"guillotine . . . glamorous hanging": outrageously punning on an execution and hanging pictures at an exhibit (a guillotine is both the familiar instrument for beheading someone and an instrument for cutting paper).
"piece the world together": "piece together" is a literal meaning for latinate "compose"; see note on "compose" in "The Poems of Our Climate," below, and note also the use of "world" there, II.

Poetry Is a Destructive Force

Ibid.; CP 192–93, LOA 178.

"Poetry" here takes a wide sense, in effect, anything one "has at heart," including one's convictions. As such, it is quite capable of causing destruction, now or in 1938. The simple diction masks the challenge of a syntax that progresses as cunningly as Dickinson's.

"That's what misery is, / Nothing to have at heart": the grammar offers two possibilities, "This is nothing that you want to have at heart, cheer up" or (reverse word order) "Misery is having a 'nothing' at heart, an absence, a gap." Compare "There was nothing one had" ("Forces, the Will & the Weather"); cf. also "the nothing that is" in "The Snow Man," and also its use of "misery."

"It is a thing to have": playing against line 3, in an unexpected absorbing of difficulty, in order to fight it with equal strength; cf. the two lions in MBG xix.

"Corazon": (Sp.) heart, the "heart" of line 1, now personified.

The Poems of Our Climate

Ibid.; CP 193–94, LOA 179–80.

After the violence of the first two poems, a quiet domestic setting and a still-life painting in one. But as the poem proceeds, an inner battle becomes increasingly evident. The poem is set in one of Stevens's favorite seasons, the first intimations of spring at the end of winter in a northern temperate climate. As often elsewhere, the numbers heading the stanzas mark major shifts, so that the three parts resemble three acts in a play. The poem reads smoothly and clearly, yet each line requires concentration for anything beyond the simplest comprehension.

TITLE: as with the word "weather," "climate" also indicates the climate of an inner world, mental, spiritual, emotional, sensuous.

I

A set piece skilfully presenting a world that is whole and harmonious, except for the qualification after the dash. The beauty of the scene is distanced, as if in detached response. It elicits only two verbs in ten lines, one of dissatisfaction and the other passive.

"Pink and white carnations": a simple description of flowers not "of our climate" in winter, with an intimation of the human body, also often pink and white, and present in the etymology of "carnation" (from Lat. *caro, carnem*); see L 97–98 (1907) for remarks during Stevens's courtship on "pink cheeks," "carnations," "desire," and spring.

"Is simplified": as in the calming effects of harmonious surroundings, and evoking at least two further possibilities: simplifying as in great achievements in science and art, and the simplifying of a heavenly world (see, e.g., Yeats's "Byzantium"), as against "oversimple."

"day . . . a bowl": the trope of the world's sphere as a bowl goes back to the Greeks, as in Anacreon, where it is a bowl of wine to be tilted and drunk; here the bowl of white more resembles an overcast sky.

"white, / Cold, a cold porcelain": an echo of Keats's "cold pastoral" in his "Ode on a Grecian Urn."

II

The setting is now read metaphysically (cf. "the metaphysical," "The *metaphysica*," and the physical in "The Glass of Water," below), a potential there from the start in the diction. The six verbs in a one-sentence, imperative, seven-line poem mark an active response. Stevens plays on words evolved from the Lat. prefix *cum-* beginning here and continuing into III, including a pun on Germanic "come." He works against a "complete simplicity" and the perfection implied by *cum-* in an older world view (see Leo Spitzer, *Classical and Christian Ideas of World Harmony* [1963], 33).

"complete simplicity": confirming that both meanings of "simplified" above are in play, and heightening the felicitous meaning by the prefix from Lat. *cum-*; cf. Eliot, four years later, "A condition of complete simplicity / (Costing not less than everything)" (*Little Gidding* V).

"Stripped one of all one's torments," etc.: much as the simplicity of heaven requires a purging of sin, e.g., in Dante's *Purgatorio*; but closer in argument to Yeats in "Byzantium" (1933; cf. "gong-tormented sea").

"evilly compounded": a sudden expansion of reference; in orthodox Christian doctrine, the self is not ontologically evil, though fallen; for Stevens, who rejects salvation in those terms, it may come to the same thing.

III

"the never-resting mind": working against the repose of Augustine's much-quoted line, "Our heart is restless until it finds its rest in Thee" (*Confessions* I.i).

"Lies": echoing "delight," with a sotto voce pun recalling the reproach that the poet is a liar.

Prelude to Objects

Ibid.; CP 194–95, LOA 179–80.

After the intensities of the preceding poem, a more relaxed tone, and a return to more conspicuous punning ("guerilla I"), as in "Parochial Theme." Stevens builds a cumulative effect, poem by poem. Compare here, e.g., "being nothing otherwise, / Having nothing otherwise," with "Poetry Is a Destructive Force." Note the contrast in syntax in the two parts, and compare with the contrast in syntax between I and II of "The Poems of Our Climate." "Prelude to Objects" is followed by two poems on objects, "Study of Two Pears" and "A Glass of Water."

I

"To go to the Louvre to behold himself": again, as in the museums in "Like Decorations in a Nigger Cemetery" XVIII, a place containing the invaluable and inescapable past, which nonetheless is past and cannot provide a simple formula for identifying one's self; cf. also the function of pictures in "Parochial Theme."

"The S.S. *Normandie*": a famous French transatlantic passenger liner of original design, huge and luxurious, launched in 1932.

"nigger mystics": see note on the title "Like Decorations in a Nigger Cemetery," above; the change of "foolscap" for "wigs" is clear enough, but the import of this phrase is not ("nigger mystics" as against "The rugged black" in II? "nigger mystics" as all too subjective? or?).

II

"foamed from the sea": the etymological meaning of Aphrodite is "born of the foam [of the sea]."

"patting more nonsense foamed . . . , conceive": a sculpting metaphor for the poet, recalling an Aphrodite figure herself and/or statues of her.

"diviner health / Disclosed in common forms": in conjunction with Aphrodite, suggesting that the earthly, everyday Aphrodite is diviner than the heavenly idealized one; cf. "health" in "Parochial Theme"; introducing Stevens's work in *Parts of a World* on the word "common."

"lewdest": taking the earliest meaning of "unlearned," "lay."

"We are conceived in your conceits": the word "conceit" was etymologically conceived from "conceive" (see head-notes in OED); the poet's patting has born fruit; "conceit" takes the meaning of "figure of speech" as in "Le Monocle de Mon Oncle" IX, while not ignoring the common meaning of "vanity."

Study of Two Pears

Ibid.; CP 196–97, LOA 180–81.

A painterly title, possibly including the Latin first line. Compare Renoir's *Three Pears* or Georgia O'Keeffe's untitled 1921 work with two pears. The poem is an exercise in trying to look at two pears in themselves as far as this is possible, trying to "realize" them. The short-line quatrains, each with two sentences, are separately numbered like distinct sections of an older opusculum; thus also the tone of firm resolution on the relation of art, viewer, and reality.

"Opusculum paedagogum": (Lat.) "a little work for teaching purposes."
"viols, / Nudes or bottles": some familiar properties of early twentieth-century painting, all pear-shaped.

The Glass of Water

Ibid.; CP 197–98, LOA 181–82.

Another object, considered in a poetic study that resembles a painter's or sculptor's study: first its physical state, then its metaphysical, including the metaphorical. The word "state" suddenly expands into the political at the end. Compare the contrast of physical and metaphysical elsewhere ("Esthétique du Mal" xv, "Credences of Summer" ii, OE xi). The play of *cum-* derived prefixes and the argument closing "The Poems of Our Climate" reappear in "continue to contend with one's ideas."

"*metaphysica*": Lat. plural; see head-note to "metaphysics," OED.
"the plastic parts of poems": see Coleridge on "the imagination or plastic power," and notes on the term, in his *Biographia Literaria*, ed. Engell and Bate (1983), chap. 10, 168–70.
"Jocundus": "jocund" personified through its etymology (Lat. masculine singular), an unlikely worrier.
"the politicians / Playing cards": possibly recalling then President Franklin Roosevelt and his fondness for poker (Lensing [2001], 267).

Add This to Rhetoric

Ibid.; CP 198–99, LOA 182–83.

Exploring the word "pose," since all speech, painting, music, and poetry unavoidably pose or place things—composing, re-posing, reposing, even imposing, certainly supposing, etc. The poem is full of metaphors, dead and alive, demonstrably unavoidable, except by the natural world—including, as it happens, a woman's figure. Compare the tone indicated by Stevens's collo-quial "Shucks" and "Pfft" with the range of tone in the preceding poems.

"the sun, bull fire": as a ball of fire, as "bully" fire (Tom Sawyer's idiom), also recalling the mythological oxen of the sun (cf. the sunrise poem, "The Latest Freed Man").

"An evading metaphor": playing against "the figure," as metaphor is also a fig-ure; cf. elsewhere Stevens's wish to get beyond metaphor, an impossibility but a useful discipline in pressing the boundaries of his art ("Credences of Summer" ii, OE ix).

Dry Loaf

Ibid.; CP 199–200, LOA 183–84.

A thirties poem acutely conscious of this "tragic time" in war-torn parts of Europe, Africa, and Asia.

Idiom of the Hero

Ibid.; CP 200–201, LOA 184.

"The red and the blue house": given "the hero" and the "workers," suggesting red and blue as colors of the political left and right; in 1938, including the polarized extremes of communism and fascism.

"the clouds, pomp of the air, / By which at least I am befriended": cf. MBG xx.

The Man on the Dump

Ibid.; CP 201–3, LOA 184–86.

A substantial poem, centered on a memorable trope that catches an artist's re-vulsion at images repeated ad nauseam. The poem records an exceptional struggle, with the honesty typical of this volume. This is the first of three po-ems dealing with "the truth," including "truth" as in John's Gospel (see head-note for "The Latest Freed Man," below).

TITLE: Stevens's house was located on a hill running down toward a public dump; during the Depression, a man reputed to be a Russian refugee constructed a shack there "out of old boxes, tin cans, etc.," and lived there for several years (Holly Stevens, "Bits of Remembered Time," 652; L 266, 1933). See also the romantic poet who would find life intolerable in an ivory tower, except for the view of advertising signs and the public dump ("Williams," and note following sentence; OP 214, LOA 770, 1934).

"corbeil": like "bouquet" (l. 3), from Fr.; as "an elegant basket for collecting flowers," also spelled as in Fr. "corbeille"; "corbeil" as architectural term signifies "a carved stone basket of flowers," here in a play between sculpted stone and random vegetative forms.

"Blanche": feminine name for the moon meaning "white," with associations of blanching; cf. "Blanche McCarthy" (OP 17, LOA 529, 1915–16?).

"puffs as Cornelius Nepos reads": Cornelius Nepos, c. 110–24 BCE, Roman historian, friend of Cicero and Catullus, author of the eulogistic, mediocre *De Viris Illustribus* (Lives of Illustrious Men), a schoolbook favorite. Catullus dedicated his first book of poems, "my trifles" (*nugas*, I.1), to him. Stevens's ambiguous grammar offers two similes: (1) "Cornelius" as the object of "reads," i.e., as the text of Cornelius Nepos reads to us now (mediocre, inflated or puffed). (2) "Cornelius Nepos" as the subject of "reads," i.e., as he reads the manuscript of Catullus (fresh as a morning breeze). The twofold simile is like other twofold similes in the poem, on the contraries of ancient and stale versus repeated yet fresh. Stevens was familiar with Catullus (L 104, 1907).

"lard pail": a tin can familiar to cooks who use lard, sometimes a receptacle for freshly rendered cooking fat.

"crow's," "nightingale": from here on, note the allusions to and echoes of Stevens's earlier poems.

"*aptest eve*": as if echoing Milton's "hapless Eve" (*PL* IX.404), and with intricate effect; earlier uses of "apt" are not happy ones (see the Concordance).

"The the.": an ending whose effect is disputed, but certainly includes emphasis on "the" as article ("the truth," not "a truth" or generally "truth"); any reading must take into account the full stop that Stevens places at the end, as against, say, a possible ellipsis.

On the Road Home

Ibid.; CP 203–4, LOA 186.

A poem starting as a gloss on "The Man on the Dump," as the sentence in quotation marks makes clear (" 'There is no such thing as the truth' "). The "I" uttering the sentence and the "you" continuing the discussion are not differentiated, nor are they dramatized as "two figures" very far. Note the pressure on the word "parts," culminating in a crucial sentence for *Parts of a World*, "In the sum of the parts, there are only the parts."

TITLE: at once casual and freighted, especially when placed between the poem set in the dump and the domestic setting that follows.

" 'Words are not forms of a single word' ": opposing, for example, the view in Christian theology that human words are grounded in a single divine Word, identified with Christ (a doctrine elaborated in, e.g., Augustine's *De trinitate* Book XV; thus also in Milton).

The Latest Freed Man

Ibid.; CP 204–5, LOA 187.

Linked with the two preceding poems through perspectives on "the truth," while adding "freed," etc. Stevens is pressing against the underlying biblical text, "And ye shall know the truth, and the truth shall make ye free," from John's Gospel (8:32), whence also the identification of Christ as the Word (see note for "On the Road Home," above); he knew the text well (NA 51, LOA 674, Richardson I.525, and see head-note to "The Old Lutheran Bells at Home," below). The poem returns once more to the subject of "Sunday Morning."

"the doctors in their beds": "doctors" in the older sense of a learned person, a scholar; "Doctors of the Church" include the early Fathers such as Augustine; Thomas Aquinas was known as the "angelic doctor."
"an ox": see the note on "bull fire" in "Add This to Rhetoric," above.
"ox-like struggle": cf. the struggle in "Poetry Is a Destructive Force," above.
"the portrait of Vidal": a painting of Anatole Vidal, the Parisian book dealer and friend who filled Stevens's orders for books and paintings; Stevens commissioned a portrait of Vidal, which is said to have hung in his bedroom (Brazeau, 131n27).
"*Qui fait fi des joliesses banales*": (Fr.) "Who couldn't care less about banal little prettinesses"; untraced, possibly in a letter by Vidal that is now lost.

United Dames of America

New York Times (7 Nov. 1937); CP 206, LOA 188.

EPIGRAPH: (Fr.) "I try, in remaining exact, to be a poet"; see biography on Fr. *exact*, and cf. "accurate songs" (NSF I.ix) and Marianne Moore's remark on "the enchantment of accuracy" (appendix, under "Words").

"leaves": in multiple senses; see note on "leaves" in "Domination of Black," above.

"mass": discussion of the "masses" was widespread in the thirties.

"reef sable": probably a typic place; the reverse word order gives a more formal or heraldic effect; the adjective is unusual for a reef; both words are appropriate for the hermit and modify the tone.

Country Words

New York Times (19 Dec. 1937); CP 207, LOA 188–89.

An attempt at a poem about singing and writing in exile, using the words of the psalm of exile, Psalm 137. The exile for Stevens is spiritual, not literal, and it is bitter. But his wildly punning allusions finally skew his poem, for the original words and their history remain too powerful. He uses a text from Psalm 137 in "Extracts from Addresses to the Academy of Fine Ideas" VII, and later used a phrase from it, "O Jerusalem" (OP 248, LOA 820, 1948).

TITLE: "Country" in the sense of any home, here evidently a home in which one feels an exile.

"canton," "cuckoo cock": evoking Switzerland with its cantons and its cuckoo-clocks; cf. "Swiss perfection" (NSF I.VII); "canton" is also an obsolete form of "canto."

"cunning-coo": echoing "If I forget thee, O Jerusalem, let my right hand forget her cunning" (5).

"Underneath a willow there / I stood and sang and filled the air": alluding to "We hanged our harps upon the willows . . . they that wasted us required of us mirth, saying, Sing us one of the songs of Zion. How shall we sing the Lord's song in a strange land?" (2–4)

"Belshazzar reading right": not the famous words on the wall (Dan. 5), but life-affirming words, with Belshazzar as a true ruler.

The Dwarf

Partisan Review 4 (Dec. 1937); CP 208, LOA 189.

The first of five poems on sharply contrasting parts of the self, seen as small or large, weak or strong. Various pressures (an established pattern of life, a summer plenitude of mind, tedious environments, etc.) exert their conforming force on a mind divided and also aware of immense potential. Here, a seasonal effect (the move indoors in winter) becomes a trope for reduction of the self, confined by circumstance, even (or especially) comfortable circumstance. The couplets make remarkable use of repetition, including occasional rhyme and near rhyme.

"the web": a powerful trope, powerfully developed, with the promise of a "pupa" left unfulfilled (cf. "cocoon" in "Ghosts as Cocoons," "chrysalis" in OE v); the language itself is woven by repetition (right to left in ll. 1–2, as in a weaver's shuttle, cf. "jerked / And tufted"); a text is etymologically something "woven."

A Rabbit as King of the Ghosts

Poetry 51 (Oct. 1937); CP 209–10, LOA 190.

The expansive relaxed rabbit-self, in peaceful August where the suffix "-ful" expands to "full" and "fill." It is disturbed only by the oddly persistent memory of a cat (cf. other vital cats in Stevens, especially those associated with the force of poetry). Stevens liked the poem (L 778, 1953), which argues against any too-dark reading of the happy rabbit-self, saved from complacency by the cat.

Loneliness in Jersey City

Partisan Review 4 (Feb. 1938), with "Anything Is Beautiful If You Say It Is," under the title "Two Poems"; CP 210, LOA 191.

A casual, colloquial poem, from the viewpoint of a tourist in a hotel room, number 293.

"plenty of window for me": perhaps an echo of "I've got plenty of nothing," etc. (*Porgy and Bess*, 1935).
"Encore, encore, encore les dieux . . .": (Fr.) Again, again, again, the gods.

Anything Is Beautiful if You Say It Is

Ibid.; CP 211, LOA 191.

A fairly successful attempt at ennui, nonetheless evoking Eliot's mastery of the subject, especially in the last stanza; cf. "The Ordinary Women."

" 'Pfui!' ": German equivalent of U.S. "Phooey," though implying shame more than nonsense; the concubine may not know German.

"The Johannisberger": a fine white wine from the Rheingau in Germany; along with "metal grapes . . . cheese," playing between actual setting and decorative still life.

"Hans": as to some waiter, echoing Johannisberger acoustically; Hans is a diminutive of Johannes.

A Weak Mind in the Mountains

New York Times (10 July 1938), under the title, "Force of Illusions"; CP 212, LOA 192–93.

A memorable nightmare poem where the mind is gripped in a death-squeeze, as by a butcher, as by a whirlwind. Four distinct scenes, one per stanza, are presented in stanzas 1–3 through terse images, diction, and syntax, then in stanza 4 in an expansive final contrast. The effect is very persuasive.

The Bagatelles the Madrigals

CP 213, LOA 193.

Four questions, juxtaposed two by two, addressed to a serpent (anticipating "The Auroras of Autumn" I) and to "people" in general, plus a final gloss. In all, the four questions make up six quatrains; until the last stanza, all are in the interrogative mood. Given this form, the repeated "In what" may recall Blake's song, "The Tyger," thereby suggesting a defense against serpent-thoughts.

TITLE: juxtaposing two very different forms of music and poetry, (1) light tri-fles, and (2) lyrical poems or musical songs for three to six voices, requiring skilful interweaving. Stevens owned *English Madrigals in the Time of Shakespeare* (1899, bought 1900; *WSJ* 2 [1978]: 50) and recordings of madrigals by Monteverdi (*WSJ* 3 [1979]: 90).

Girl in a Nightgown

CP 214, LOA 194.

TITLE: painterly, with a somewhat puzzling relation to the text.

"booming": cf. uses in "The Latest Freed Man," "On an Old Horn," and NSF II.I.

Connoisseur of Chaos

Twentieth Century Verse 12–13 (Oct. 1938); CP 215–16, LOA 194–95.

A debate about order and disorder by "A" and "B." "Order" was a watchword of the time, sometimes a "new order," often brought about by violence (under communism). Old, right-wing orders could also be violent (under fascism), as A knows (IV.1). For the ending, cf. the ending of "The Bagatelles the Madrigals."

I

"A." "B": If A's proposition is evident, B's is less so, except in an "essential unity" (II) of things (Christian, Hegelian, Marxist, etc.), where there might exist an "order" of disorder, though it strains the word. To be sure, Spinoza did say that "God's idea of order might even resemble our idea of disorder" (quoted K. Burke, *Rhetoric of Religion* [1961], 22–23), but Stevens says "is," not "resembles."

"(Pages of illustrations.)": a crisp and funny injunction; Stevens provides no context, so that "pages" challenges the reader to provide some (and often to wish that Stevens had).

II

"Marchand": Jean Marchand, French painter (1883–1940); Stevens bought his *Les Oliviers*, a landscape painting, from Vidal (see note for "the portrait of Vidal" in "The Latest Freed Man," above).

III

"bishops' books": numerous Christian bishops, e.g., the Bishop of Hippo, St. Augustine.

"squamous": "scaly" (used in Rupert Brooke's 1915 funny piscatory pastoral, "Heaven"); the mind as a large, fishy creature that nonetheless cannot swallow all the squirming food out there; fine enjambment tips a hat to the trope, all in all making one of Stevens's best sentences.

IV

"an order, most Plantagenet, most fixed": the Plantagenet royal house ruled England from 1154 (Henry II) to 1485, when Richard III was defeated by the Tudor challenger, Henry VII, in a much-debated succession.

Stevens's troping is unclear. The Plantagenet order was not fixed forever, but that seems too obvious a contrary, unless to say that three centuries is about as much time as any "fixed" order can expect. Compare "Plantagenet abstractions" in "The Sail of Ulysses" VII.

The Blue Buildings in the Summer Air

Seven 3 (winter 1938); CP 216–17, LOA 196.

"Cotton Mather died when I was a boy": Mather, the great Puritan divine in New England, lived from 1663 to 1728; the remark may be literal or figurative (i.e., the spirit of Mather).

"that mouse in the wall": cf. disruptive mice elsewhere in Stevens, e.g., "The Dance of the Macabre Mice"; cf. also Dickinson, "Narcotics cannot still the tooth / That nibbles at the soul" (no. 501); given the role of Eliot's memorable rats and mice, perhaps this mouse is a relative.

"Over wooden Boston, the sparkling Byzantine": presumably colonial Boston, presumably a steeple.

"theologian's needle": given Mather's doubt about his faith and salvation (I.3), perhaps recalling Mark 10:25 ("It is easier for a camel to go through the eye of a needle than for a rich man to enter the kingdom of God") and its theological interpretation.

"the honey-comb of the seeing man," etc.: here and in V, playing a natural honey-comb of this earth against a honey-comb as Christian symbol; see, e.g., Gjertrud Schnackenberg, *A Gilded Lapse of Time* (1992), 131–32; cf. "Esthétique du Mal" III.

"the leaf the bird brings back to the boat": referring to the olive leaf that Noah's dove finally brings back to the ark (Gen. 8:8–12), a sign of hope and peace.

"Lenin": as elsewhere, the particulars of life conquer some abstractions, including Lenin's abstractions; here perhaps also rather grimly, for Lenin's body was preserved and displayed in the Kremlin. Compare also figurative nibbling as in Dickinson, no. 501, above.

"le plus pur": (Fr.) "the purest one," recalling the meaning of "Puritan."

Dezembrum

CP 218, LOA 197.

A familiar theme in Stevens: the radical cleansing of heaven, not only of religious associations, but here also of the constellations and their classical associations. The result is attained rather too easily.

"the response to desire": desire as eros (given "intenser love"), in a weak parallel with filling "the imagination's need" by repeopling heaven.

Poem Written at Morning

CP 219, LOA 198.

A poem on seeing, as through a painter's eye, or rather experiencing a sight. (Seeing is never a simple recording of data.) Similarly with taste. Compare the example of the pineapple with "Someone Puts a Pineapple Together" (1947). Of the thirteen lines, four are divided, giving the look of stanzas, as if embodying lines 2–3a.

"Poussiniana": things of Nicolas Poussin, influential French classical painter (1594–1665); in 1922, Stevens ordered reproductions of Poussin's works in the Louvre (L 229, and see Richardson II.308); the paintings include depictions of classical buildings with columns in front, like the front of the Hartford Accident and Indemnity building. Stevens does not specify particulars here, so that Poussiniana may include the full ambience of French seventeenth-century classicism, including Racine, as in "The Relations between Poetry and Painting" (NA 172, LOA 749, 1951; for a brief 1948 reference, see NA 152, LOA 737); Stevens wrote in 1912 that he was studying the seventeenth century (L 176), and he owned a copy of Poussin's correspondence (sold by Parke-Bernet at auction in 1959); see also note on the title "Arcades of Philadelphia the Past," below.

"Divide it from itself": by seeing the sunny day as if it is a landscape in a French classical scene or existed within a seventeenth-century view of things.

"By metaphor you paint": note how metaphor paradoxically makes something more itself by identifying it with something not itself.

"cribled pears": sieved pears; "cribled" also has a specialized use with reference to an engraving, so that the term encourages the eye to move between actual and represented fruit.

[Life on a Battleship: see head-note for this volume, above]

[The Woman That Had More Babies than That: see head-note for this volume, above]

Thunder by the Musician

Seven 5 (summer 1939); CP 220, LOA 203–4.

Compare the war-time scene in "Dry Loaf." The poem is written against overly easy accords after viciousness. The composer, if actual, is unidentified. Note how the narrative is affected by the rhythm, e.g., the coincidence of sentence and stanza, the emphasis on the short fourth line.

The Common Life

Poetry 54 (July 1939), with the following five poems, under the title "Illustrations of the Poetic as a Sense"; CP 221, LOA 204.

Part of Stevens's work on the word "common" following "The Comedian as the Letter C" (see L 352 on wanting "to share the common life" [1940]); "common" is used here in a reductive sense.

"Euclid": Greek third-century BCE mathematician, whose *Elements* of geometry still provides the basis for school texts; "a result, / A demonstration," "planes," and "alphabetical / Notations" may all be found there.

The Sense of the Sleight-of-Hand Man

Ibid.; CP 222, LOA 205.

A poem of great charm, readily understood, with no loss of substance. It catches a common experience, the fortuitousness of some truly happy moments.

TITLE: see note on "sleights of sail" in "Infanta Marina," above.
"one's Sunday baths": "Sunday" in the calendar sense plays against "Sunday" as any time one can take a leisurely bath.
"the ignorant man alone": not "stupid"; cf. "ignorant" in NSF I.i, and "The poem reveals itself only to the ignorant man" ("Adagia," OP 187 [not in LOA selections]).
"fluent in even the wintriest bronze": in the usual play on fluent water and a

fluent tongue; with "bronze" as the end of summer, cf. "bronze" in "Invective against Swans," above, and "Yellow Afternoon," below.

The Candle a Saint

Ibid.; CP 223, LOA 205–6.

The second of three poems of sensation where the senses find intense momentary fulfillment, in contrast to the earlier group of poems beginning with "The Dwarf." The seven couplets divide in a three-four pattern, each framed by the refrain, part of a very effective use of repetition.

TITLE: working by juxtaposition, and in oblique relation to the text; both relations are puzzling; one expects a Florence Nightingale figure at first.
"Green is the night": cf. Rimbaud, "J'ai rêvé la nuit verte" ("I dreamt the green night," "Le bateau ivre" 37).
"It is she": cf. the "green queen" in "Description without Place" I.
"Like a noble figure": Stevens's work on the word "noble" appears in "The Noble Rider and the Sound of Words" (NA 1–36, LOA 643–65, 1942).
"above the rabbit and the cat": a reference to "A Rabbit as King of the Ghosts."
"The abstract, the archaic queen": see note on "abstract" in NSF I, "It Must Be Abstract."

A Dish of Peaches in Russia

Ibid.; CP 224, LOA 206.

A poem of intensely apprehended taste and smell, and the memories that these senses release. Proust's scene with the *madeleines* at the start of *A la recherche du temps perdu* (*Remembrance of Things Past*, vol. I, 1913) is the classic treatment of this subject. The allusion to du Bellay makes this a poem of separation in place as well as in time. The question "Who speaks?" prevents any simple identification of the poem's voice, allowing it to represent any exile from any home.

"as the Angevine / Absorbs Anjou": alluding to du Bellay's sonnet of longing for his Anjou home while in Rome, "Heureux qui, comme Ulysse, . . . Angevine" (Happy the man who, like Ulysses . . .); thus also "my village" (l. 13; "mon petit village"); Stevens translated the well-known poem in 1909 (L 150–51), and quoted it in 1951 in connection with one's "native sphere" (OP 277, LOA 863).

"that I, / That animal": playing between "animal" in the usual sense and "animal" as "spirit" (see note on MBG xvii).

"that Russian, that exile": in 1939, Russian exiles from the Soviet Union included Nabokov and many another.

"drifting of the curtains": cf. this romantic topos in "The Curtains in the House of the Metaphysician."

Arcades of Philadelphia the Past

Ibid.; CP 225–26, LOA 207.

One of Stevens's oddest poems, and without obvious attraction. Like the preceding poem, it uses allusion, here a sharply revised allusion to Milton (see note, below) in a very strange setting. Sight metaphorically offers mental insight into ideas, etc.; it was sometimes thought to be the highest of the five senses.

TITLE: "Arcades": probably "the Arcadians" (Lat.), inhabitants of the ideal pastoral land of Arcadia, site of the golden age; one of Poussin's best-known paintings (see "Poem Written at Morning") is "Et in Arcadia ego" ("I too have been in Arcadia"). The arcades of the Philadelphia Museum of Art have also been suggested.

"Only the rich remember the past": patently untrue in a literal sense. Because they belong to a "golden age"? "The past" as a distant past, taught only to the educated rich?

"Queer, in this Vallombrosa of ears": Vallombrosa (literally, "valley of the shadow") in Italy, alluding to Milton's famous simile on Satan's fallen legions, "thick as Autumnal Leaves . . . / In *Vallombrosa*" (*PL* I.302–3). The odd phrase, along with the elided "leaves" and the "queer-ears-hear" sequence, imply that this past also falls on deaf ears.

Of Hartford in a Purple Light

Ibid.; CP 226–27, LOA 208.

An exuberant response to the changing light of dawn over Hartford, first a clear masculine light, then a purple feminine light, much troped.

"Master Soleil": (Fr.) Master Sun.

"tricolor": an "irised" effect as in l. 27, i.e., the iridescent colors of waterdrops; "tricolor" refers generally to three colors, specifically to the French flag (Fr. *tricolore*), an appropriate echo for Master Soleil.

Cuisine Bourgeoise

CP 227–28, LOA 209.

As with "Arcades of Philadelphia the Past," a poem working with a grotesque trope (ll. 1–2), though a good deal more clearly; nonetheless, this style is not Stevens's forte. The "ancient cake of seed" is the seed-cake offered to, or in the name of, the gods or God in a number of traditions; it is thereby the contrary of current cuisine. The two foods lend themselves to various possible allegories of the 1930s, a time when the word "bourgeois(e)" was a freighted word.

TITLE: in 1900, Stevens recorded falling ill after a luncheon from too much "*Cuisine Bourgeoise*" (SP 75).
"mirror . . . eating reflections": cf. MBG xv.

Forces, the Will & the Weather

CP 228–29, LOA 210.

Another poem of great charm and force, catching a familiar mood.

TITLE: "weather" in the usual sense, and in Stevens's extended sense of the atmosphere of one's own world; the punctuation is a quiet challenge.
"nougats": sweetmeats of almonds and sugar, in contrast to the "bitter meat" of the preceding poem; sweet, sustaining bits of food (and experience) though not a full diet. Stevens ordered a box of *fruits confits*, including nougats, from Paris in 1937 (letter, 19 Jan. 1937, University of Massachusetts, Amherst).
"the peer yellow . . . the pair yellow": an intricate play on grammar, language, puns, and echo; noun and adjective can reverse; adjective after noun is Fr. word order, thereby suggesting a peer of France, known as "yellow"; *pair* is Fr. for "peer," and may be general or refer to the twelve legendary peers. This is, then, a persona who resembles one of Stevens's Spanish dons, and is also yellow, the color of the sun, personified as such a peer; punning on Eng. "pair" and also "pear," through the echoes of "Study of Two Pears.
"pair . . . peer": as with "dogwoods" ("dog," "woods"), the poem finds life in the play between words and perceptions, in the absence of ideas.
"not an idea / This side of Moscow": i.e., in the West, now largely at war; ideas in Moscow were officially Soviet, and, after Hitler's invasion in June 1941, desperately bent on the war.
"nothing one had": cf. "Poetry Is a Destructive Force."

On an Old Horn

Nation 149 (30 Sept. 1939); CP 230, LOA 210–11.

A somewhat odd experiment in reversing the bird-human relation. Stevens liked the poem. See his general comments, L. 403–4 (1942), and his explication.

"the tail of a rat": one of the "unexpected transitional features" (ibid.).
"Pipperoo, pippera, pipperum": moving from a bird-call of "pip" to an echoic
    nonsense word to imitation of an invented Latin adjective (properly *pip-*
    perus, -a, -um).

Bouquet of Belle Scavoir

Fantasy, sixth year (summer 1939); CP 231–32, LOA 211–12.

One of several "bouquet" poems in Stevens's work, here a simple and beautiful love poem.

TITLE: "Scavoir": Old Fr. for *savoir* ("knowledge"); the fem. adj. *belle* is incorrect
    grammatically (properly, *beau savoir*), but right poetically. It is as if Belle
    Scavoir were a proper name, or as if this were a peculiarly female knowl-
    edge (or knowledge of a female), powerful enough to undo grammar.

Variations on a Summer Day

Kenyon Review 2 (winter 1940); CP 232–36, LOA 212–15.

Set on the coast of Maine, where the Stevens family took a 1939 summer holiday in the area of the three aboriginal place-names (Holly Stevens, "Holidays in Reality," 108–10; Richardson II.157–58). From time to time, the poem is shadowed by the gathering war-clouds in Europe, but obliquely, through the three place-names that follow shortly after the Maine place-names. (See Holly Stevens, ibid., on her father's conversations with an R.A.F. officer on his honeymoon.) In this poem, the search for "a value that really suffices" has been excluded, but this kind of poem had its own justification for Stevens. He rightly observed that "agreeable things" mean a good deal more than "mere imagism," especially in "a world permanently enigmatical" (L 345–46, 1939). The variation form is more familiar in music; it is apt for high summer when one day resembles another, with variations; cf. "As one improvises, on the piano" (VIII), and see Frye's essay, "Wallace Stevens and the Variation Form."

IV

"Monhegan, Atlantic star": Monhegan Island, Maine, with a lighthouse, and so a lantern with "a bearer"; both before and after this reference, the poem looks out to sea, toward Europe, and at the sea, where the battle of the Atlantic on and under the ocean was raging by the time the poem was printed.

XI

"Pemaquid": colonial settlement, also now with a lighthouse.

XII

"Hugh March, a sergeant, a redcoat killed": killed in an attack in 1695, buried in the Pemaquid graveyard in an unknown location, with many seventeenth-century settlers; "redcoat" in 1939–40 cannot but point toward Great Britain's expected war, which was declared on 3 Sept. 1939.

XVII

"Pine-figures": with a resonance of Stevens's usual pun on "pine" as "longing."

XVIII

"Damariscotta": the tidal estuary of the Damariscotta River; musical word-play makes this word sound fantastical; as elsewhere, such play draws out the mystery of some American place-names.

XIX

"man-boat": a childhood trick familiar to anxious parents; a small boat can seem to move by itself upside down, as a youngster swims underneath, using the air pocket there.

"neater than Naples": Naples is traditionally messy, so "neater" as against Mussolini's 1939 all-too-tidy Naples? (The trains proverbially ran on time.) Or "neater" as a neat concealing contraption? Or "neater" etymologically as "shining," brighter even than the fabled Bay of Naples? Perhaps Stevens is typically putting all such meanings of "neat" in play, as a mimesis of the mind's mixed response to 1939 Naples.

Yellow Afternoon

Seven 7 (spring 1940); CP 236–37, 216.

A poem of the earth, in a three-stanza meditation on what it is that roots and centers the "he" of the poem. It is governed by the unexpected declaration of the astonishing last sentence (incomplete grammar, the conjunction "but," enigmatic movement, enigmatic face, the fine double sense of "she caught his breath"). From origins ("of this"), through possession of a life ("had this"), the poem comes to the present tense and to simple being ("as he is / He is") in a formula Stevens will work with later in "The Sail of Ulysses." A mysterious female figure, intensely apprehended, moves through several poems from this period.

Martial Cadenza

Compass 2 (Feb. 1940); CP 237–38, LOA 217.

"low in the sky / The evening star": alluding to Whitman's great elegy for Lincoln, "When Lilacs Last in the Dooryard Bloom'd," also a war poem, to which this poem is a footnote.

"blank skies over England," etc.: pointedly not lit during blackouts, as all three countries were at war.

"the German camps": military and prisoner-of-war camps (as with England and France), also concentration camps.

Man and Bottle

Hika 6 (May 1940), with "Of Modern Poetry," under "Two Theoretic Poems"; CP 238–39, LOA 218.

The opening and closing sentences are the strongest part of this poem, especially the phrase "find what will suffice," repeated in the next poem. Internal and end rhyme tighten their sense of affirmation. As with other work in this period, memorable lines are not always sustained by their poems.

"suffice": not in a minimal sense; cf. the search for "a value that really suffices" (L 345, 1939); cf. also Whitman, "suffice the poet. . . . suffice" (Preface, 1855 *Leaves of Grass*, para. 4); cf. also the theological sense as in Eliot's "satisfactory" ("Journey of the Magi"), not in specific play here, but part of the word's general strength.

Of Modern Poetry

Ibid.; CP 239–40, LOA 218–19.

Linked with the preceding poem by the opening and closing, but with emphasis on facing a contemporary audience rather than on war. This is a poem of assertions that are like theses, in plain predicative style, with the central trope of a theater with actors, audience, and script.

TITLE: one of six titles in Stevens with the latinate pattern, "Of X" (*De X*, as in Lucretius, *De rerum natura*).

"it repeated what / Was in the script": literally untrue of older writing, at least in one sense of "repeated," so that the formulation requires further thought about kinds and degrees of repetition.

"the theatre was changed": Stevens spoke of a theater as "a reality within a reality" (OP 265, LOA 848, 1951). Note also the remarks on the time before World War I as "a stage-setting that since then has been taken down and trucked away" (OP 229, LOA 788, 1936). Stevens also described Scott's poetry as resembling "the scenery of a play that has come to an end" (OP 254, LOA 835, 1951).

"souvenir": as in "Lions in Sweden," also in the Fr. sense of "a recollection."

"of the time": "[Stevens's] poems are speeches from the drama of the time in which he is living" (quotation from Spender, March 1938, Huntington Library MS, p. 19).

"insatiable": in this aspect, incapable of being satisfied or "finding / What will suffice."

"two . . . becoming one": the full sentence describes and also mimes the process by which we take in words that then become our own, because they are so right for us.

"satisfaction": cf. "insatiable" above and note on "suffice" in "Man and Bottle," above.

"of a man skating": Holly Stevens remembered her father skating on the pond in Elizabeth Park in the winter, "doing lazy figure eights with the greatest of ease" ("Bits of Remembered Time," 655).

"a woman / Combing": Elsie Stevens, when young, had long golden hair.

Arrival at the Waldorf

CP 240–41, LOA 219.

A later, fierce, and frank example of Florida-poem contraries. Rhythmic skill highlights "wild," lexical skill highlights "fake," and both make a memorable last line, anticipating the closing line of "The Motive for Metaphor."

TITLE: "the Waldorf": the Waldorf-Astoria Hotel, New York City, a famed Art
   Deco building and a byword for elegance, was founded in 1893 and
   moved to its present site in 1931; here it is a metonymy for a home
   where the wild country of the soul finds no home.
"that alien, point-blank, green and actual Gautemala": an example of
   Stevens's "great ease in combining abstract words with gaudy visual or
   sound effects" (see Merrill in the appendix, under "Words").

Landscape with Boat

Accent 1 (autumn 1940), with the following poem, both under the title "Two Poems";
CP 241–43, LOA 220–21.

The anti-master-man is related to Mrs. Alfred Uruguay in the much stronger
poem that bears her name. As elsewhere, blue is the color of the imagina-
tion. The title scene, which sounds like a Matisse painting, remains only po-
tential.

"brushed away": cf. Mrs. Alfred Uruguay, and, given title and color here, the
   pun on a paintbrush.
"the truth": cf. the three poems beginning with "The Man on the Dump."

On the Adequacy of Landscape

Ibid.; CP 243–44, LOA 221–22.

Linked by title to the preceding poem. From "frightened" to "insensible,"
then repeated "sensible," the feeling mounts to the memorable last stanza.
The occasion is not specified, but the "red bird" so desired here is also in "Le
Monocle de Mon Oncle" in an erotic connotation. The single long sentence
coinciding with its poem (28 lines) is a virtuoso effect that Stevens likes; the
abcb rhyme is unusual.

"hap-hallow, hallow-ho": echoic, as of owls' various cries, with multiple word-
   play.

Les Plus Belles Pages

Furioso 1 (summer 1941), with the following three poems, all under the title "Four
Poems"; CP 244–45, LOA 222.

A poem central to Stevens's thought, compact, yet conversational and direct. See Stevens's comment on the interrelation between things and its crucial importance. He gives sex as one example of interrelation that is "fecund," and the milkman and moonlight of this poem as another. The best illustration for him is "the interaction of our faculties or of our thoughts and emotions" (OP 281, LOA 867, 1952).

TITLE: (Fr.) "The Most Beautiful Pages," "name of a series of books of extracts from French writers" (LOA 1001).
"Aquinas": Stevens found Thomas Aquinas "a figure of great modern interest." The interaction between "his prodigious logic and his prodigious love of God" gave him special force (OP 281, LOA 867, 1952).

Poem with Rhythms

Ibid.; CP 245–46, LOA 222–23.

Compare the powerful "Yellow Afternoon" and similar poems for the "*image*" and "*love*" that "*compose*" the self. As with the rhythms of living, the poem's rhythms are varied, and with great skill.

Woman Looking at a Vase of Flowers

Ibid.; CP 246–47, LOA 223–24.

A painterly title, in another bouquet poem with a mysterious female figure. An emotional storm of jealousy, then conciliation, is read indirectly through weather and flowers. Compare James Merrill on the writer not needing "to *state* your feelings." If you do feel, and keep your eyes open, "what you feel is expressed, is mimed back at you by the scene" (*Recitative* [1986], 22).

"Hoot, little owl": cf. the little owl in "On the Adequacy of Landscape."

The Well Dressed Man with a Beard

Ibid.; CP 247, LOA 224.

With the often-quoted final line, "It can never be satisfied, the mind, never," cf. "Of Modern Poetry" on satisfaction, and "Man and Bottle" on "suffice," as well as "The Poems of Our Climate" and "Extracts from Addresses to the

Academy of Fine Ideas." The ending prevents any "yes" from moving into a final "yes" that would deaden the mind.

TITLE: Another painterly title, as with Rembrandt's *Bust-Length Portrait of an Old Man with a Beard* or Andrea del Sarto's *Study of a Standing Man with a Beard.*

"no . . . yes": cf. "Esthétique du Mal" x.

"western cataract": the western horizon of the setting sun, playing a waterfall against the earliest meaning of "cataracts" as the flood-gates of heaven (OED 1, cf. "This Solitude of Cataracts").

"douce campagna": (Fr.) "sweet" (It.) "country"; both words are naturalized; "douce" so combined hovers between obsolete "sweet" and "quiet, steady" (thus in J. Tey, *The Franchise Affair* [1948], chap. 1); such a country is like its troping in being both foreign in origin and yet one's own.

Of Bright & Blue Birds & the Gala Sun

Harvard Advocate 127 (Dec. 1940), with the following two poems, all under the title "New Poems, 1940"; CP 248, LOA 224.

On a similar subject, though without the paradox of "most miserable," cf. "The Sense of the Sleight-of-Hand Man." The poem uses Stevens's favored phrase of limitation, "for a moment," and works with the word "element," as he does elsewhere.

"niño": (Sp.) "my boy" or (S. Amer.) "sir," an addressee that may be another part of the persona.

"a bright *scienza* . . . A gaiety": (It.) science or learning; earlier, poetry, as in "the 'gay science' as the Troubadours (I believe) called it" (Tennyson, *Letters* II.87, Apr. 1854). Stevens read H. P. Adams's *The Life and Writings of Giambattista Vico* (1935) and noted on the inside back dust-jacket from p. 72: "scienza nuova a great liberation of creative power" (copy at the University of Massachusetts, Amherst; see acknowledgments).

Mrs. Alfred Uruguay

Ibid.; CP 248–50, LOA 225–26.

A memorable quest poem, contrasting two types of seeker, as in Yeats's "Ego Dominus Tuus." John Ashbery observes that the poem "changes when it is construed as a painting" (Introduction to *Yves Tanguy* [1974], also in his *Reported Sightings: Art Chronicles 1957–1987* [1989]). Mrs. Uruguay like Yeats's Hic quests for herself, while the possessed Coleridge-Yeats youth, a later Don Quixote, comes out of tentative interrogatives into assertive sentences and action. Both embody parts of Stevens's own self. The quester for "reality" by moonlight becomes all negative, not sensing what her lowly donkey instinctively knows, whereas the youth, seeking the sun, can create "the imagined land" in his mind.

TITLE: Uruguay's capital is Montevideo, etymologically a mount of vision, which Mrs. Uruguay climbs while the youth descends, already inspired. A famous poetic Alfred opens his poem, "Let us go then, you and I, / When the evening is spread out against the sky . . ." (Eliot, "The Love Song of J. Alfred Prufrock"). Stevens's first line retorts in Eliot's favorite ragtime: "So what said the others and the sun went down."

"elegance": beyond the usual meaning, note the etymological meaning of "choice"; cf. the use of "elegance" in the last line, and note also NA 78, LOA 691 (1947) on euphuism having its starting-point in the "desire for elegance."

"no and no": cf. no and yes elsewhere in this collection, in Stevens's continuing and rigorous quest to shed what is false, as he tests the necessity for "capable imagination."

"figure of capable imagination": the memorable phrase plays doubly on "figure" and "of."

"Rushing from what was real": Stevens will insist in 1942 that the imagination depends vitally on reality. See his remarks on Don Quixote as against Sancho Panza, and his conclusion that "it is not a choice of one over the other"; rather, "here, too . . . universal interdependence exists" (NA 24, LOA 657). In this poem, the two personified forces are polarized.

"out of the martyrs' bones": What martyrs? Earlier seekers like Mrs. Alfred Uruguay? Those slain in war, as in "Asides on the Oboe"? Martyrs' bones are commonly objects of veneration; as such, they are sometimes also objects of skepticism.

Asides on the Oboe

Ibid.; CP 250–51, LOA 226–27.

On belief, especially Christian belief, as belief in a fiction. See L 370 on belief as always in a fiction, though, Stevens adds, this does seem "a negation or, rather, a paradox" (1940, on this poem); see also the head-note to NSF.

I

"wide river," etc.: uncertain; Jordan? ("Jordan's river is deep and wide"); the European fiction of America as an "empty land"?

"Boucher": François Boucher (1703–70), fashionable Fr. eighteenth-century painter, when gods were decorative and belief was rationalist; he became director of the Gobelins tapestry works, producer of large, exquisitely rendered, legendary scenes.

"dew . . . immaculate," etc.: the "philosophers' man" appropriates religious imagery (cf. NSF IX); not an embodiment like "major man," but an ideal abstraction, replacing the incarnate Christ.

"hautboy": Fr. root of "oboe"; cf. Baudelaire's use in "Correspondances" (*Les Fleurs du mal*).

II

"transparence . . . peace": cf. the dedicatory poem to NSF.

"'August . . . make thee so'": punning on the name of the month (cf. "Augusta Moon" in "A Golden Woman . . ."); see L 377 (1940).

III

"death and war prevented": another poem suffused with a sense of World War II, even before the United States entered it; war shatters the peace of the poems found earlier, nor can war now be seen in the light of orthodox Christian belief in good, evil, and the fall.

"jasmine scent . . . islands": Stevens thanked his friend, Philip May, for his visit "to the jasmine-scented isle [in Florida], and all that, which I enjoyed immensely" (8 Mar. 1935, Houghton Library bMS Am 1543; see acknowledgments); cf. diamond path and jasmine bower in Keats, *Endymion* II.652, 670; on "jasminerie" (jasmine tea) from China and "la belle jasminatrice," see L 229 (1922). Collectively, exotic and pleasurable.

"bloody martyrdoms": impinging on earlier jasmine lands; perhaps associating war with Gethsemane through "gethsamine," an early form of "jasmine."

Extracts from Addresses to the Academy of Fine Ideas

New Poems: An Anthology of British and American Verse, ed. Oscar Williams (New York: Yardstick, 1941); CP 252–59, LOA 227–34.

A poem growing out of a characteristic that Stevens observed in the world around him: "the Lightness with which ideas are asserted, held, abandoned, etc." (L 380, 1940). The context is left uncertain. The poem includes both personal belief and philosophical ideas. A final wartime image suggests that one such idea may be the broken Munich pact. The series is of interest especially in relation to Stevens's other work, and as showing what personal and social matters are on his mind now.

TITLE: partly a retrospective poem, e.g., in allusions to "The Snow Man" (IV), so that the irony of the charming title is not simple; nor does it persist.

I

On the gap between experience and writing, as of a rose. Yet the vivid blood-rose is also a rose of paper, in that it is powerfully evoked by the words that bring it to life on the page. Writing is self-consciousness, but then, so is a good deal of human life.

II

Again, on the gap between experience and writing, with the term "evil" unexpectedly introduced, reminding the reader that most of Europe and the Commonwealth were at war, as were large parts of Asia. Later lines on deaths and wounds confirm this association of the war on fascism with the word "evil," a word not used lightly by Stevens.

"Secretary for Porcelain": the "Fine Ideas" of the title include those that glaze over evil, with the trope literalized as a porcelain glaze. Like other writers (e.g., Elizabeth Bishop), Stevens consistently apprehends the dangers of wartime rhetoric (cf. "Esthétique du Mal" XI).
"my beards": a charming synecdoche for the Academicians.
"ricanery": adapted from Fr. *ricaner* (to laugh sneeringly), with an echo of "chicanery."
"chu-chot-chu": adapted from Fr. *chuchoter* (to whisper).
"It is good death": Stevens corrected this to "It is a good death" in a letter to Oscar Williams, but not in the accompanying proof (L 387, 1941; Beinecke Library), so that the text stayed the same; "a good death" would have made death particular, evoked older phrasing, and kept the lines well away from capital-*d* Death.

III

The "Fine Ideas" of the churches, as possible answer to II, aimed against writers like Eliot.

"lean cats": also, with their backs raised, like the shape of church arches.
"all men are priests": recalling and revising the Reformation tenet, "the priest-
hood of all believers."
"theses," "intercessor": recalling Luther's famous ninety-five theses, and the
Reformation doctrine of Christ as the only intercessor with God.
"*roi de tonnerre*," "Panjandrum": thunder-king (like Zeus), etc., with diction
shifting the tone to imply a historic decline in the churches, which does
not perturb the cats.

IV

A strong section moving back to experience, here of spring in April, both
gathering up "The Snow Man" (ll. 8–12) and moving on. Compare the move
to particulars in "Connoisseur of Chaos."

"Within the difference": a key phrase, as in NSF III.x, and cf. "Mrs. Alfred
Uruguay."

V

The "Fine Ideas" of dominant philosophies in contention. As in some forties
gangster film, the "philosophic assassins" shoot it out, and one idea survives.
The example of Hitler's "Thousand-Year Reich" is a reminder that Stevens's
humor can have a grim edge.

"chaos": not primordial chaos, and cf. "Connoiseur of Chaos."
"composed": both settled and constructed, notably as music.

VI

"Of systematic thinking": announcing the intended subject, in a latinate con-
struction (cf. "of that," ii.3).

"Ercole": (It.) Hercules; context uncertain; "skin," etc., sounds like Ercole
metamorphosed into the Nemean lion that Hercules killed, whose skin
he wore. Possibly a thinker of brute war?
"single place," etc.: as against heaven and earth, afterlife and this life.

VII

Continuing vi and observing the limits of belief, with Stevens's usual insis-
tence on verity.

"past apocalypse": e.g., the last book of the Christian Bible (Revelation or The Apocalypse), hence a Christian time scheme.

"rejects / Ceylon": the sequence suggests this belief is in a possible muse, religious (apocalypse), the other (Ceylon), the sea (Byronic nature), eros (*la belle*), mountains of inspiration (prophetic, Wordsworthian, or Hoon's).

"*la belle / Aux crinolines*": (Fr.) "the beauty / In crinolines."

"casual reunions," etc.: cf. "The Sense of the Sleight-of-Hand Man"; the troping here is of lovers, as Stevens works out a sense of the poetry of this earth, without transcendent justification.

"different element": note the difference from "difference" in iv.

VIII

A return to the wartime present and the arguments in ii, testing them against the resolution of vii.

"camp": as if all living were combat, mental or physical, lesser or greater, as it often is.

"residuum": powerfully developed from the memorable use in "Autumn Refrain."

"If evil never ends": to shear off belief in an afterlife is not enough if earth is governed by evil.

"How can / We chant," etc.: echoing the psalm of exile, "How shall we sing the Lord's song in a strange land?" (Ps. 137:4).

"men in helmets . . . defeat": if literal defeat, such men would include World War II soldiers—by Nov. 1940 (L 380), the defenders of Poland, Denmark, Norway, Belgium, Holland, and France; if spiritual defeat, those who die an evil death rather than a good death.

Montrachet-le-Jardin

Partisan Review 9 (Jan. 1942); CP 260–64, LOA 234–37.

A poem of this earth, working against orthodox religious doctrine, practice, and tropes, and reclaiming them for the earth. A subject related to the preceding poem's subject, but less knotty and guarded, sometimes exuberant. The sentence rhythm of remarkably constructed long periods, playing against shorter ones, corresponds to the pace of the argument, which is not always easy to follow. The open tone is set by the first line, "What more is there to love than I have loved?", a question that invites the reader to think about its likely context.

TITLE: White wines from Le Montrachet have been famous since the six-teenth century, and a simple Montrachet is a great wine. For a hyphen-ated one, it is necessary to know whether it is from a famous vineyard or a big commune. (See Johnson, *World Atlas of Wine*, 4th ed. [2002].) This one sounds like a domestic vineyard promoting itself. In any case, the combination of actual and imagined suits Stevens's line of thought.

"chidder-barn": untraced.

"blue bulls": Asian, and exotic to an American, but not fanciful.

"syllable," "shadow," "flourisher," "players," "lumps" (cf. "bats" in OE III.18): all important words for Stevens, worth pursuing throughout for his work on them.

"our singular skeleton": troping on thought as both bones and a structure that is governed by brain, nerves, etc.; cf. Richard Wilbur, "To His Skeleton."

"our accustomed cell": cf. Auden's 1939 "In Memory of W. B. Yeats" III: "In the prison of his days / Teach the free man how to praise"; recalling also literal wartime cells of 1942.

"moonlight," "words," "undeciphered": cf. NSF I.III.

"fall // As apples fall, without astronomy": neither the fall of mankind in Genesis nor Newton's falling apple, both weighted with significance for the universe, including the heavens.

"plus gaudiest vir": Lat.-Eng. double superlative for the most, most joyous man; "gaudiest" here mingles Eng. "showy" and Lat. "joyous" (cf. the well-known European student song, *Gaudeamus igitur* ["Let us then re-joice"]).

"super-man": the hero, not Nietzsche's Übermensch; see L 409 (1942), L 485 (1945).

"friseured": "coiffeured," unusual in verb form though found in Burns, "Pa-tient Stupidity"; the OED and Webster list only "friseur," a hairdresser (rare).

"Bastard chateaux": castles definitely not in a true line of inheritance.

"smoky demoiselles": demoiselles enhanced and disguised by smoke, as in a magician's puff or the curl of cigarette-smoke from the hand of a thirties vamp.

"the grace // And free requiting": "grace" is defined in Christian theology as God's "free requiting."

"the naked man in a state of fact": given "Terra Paradise" and "grace" just preceding, an echo of the Christian "state of grace," once a familiar phrase.

"never rounding O": the wind (etymologically *spiritus*) is not symbol of the Holy Spirit or of any rounded perfection as in Browning's once well-known "the perfect round" ("Abt Vogler").

"the great cat": cf. the lion in "Poetry Is a Destructive Force"; after strong af-firmation, Stevens will sometimes withdraw warily, as in NSF III.VIII.

The News and the Weather

Accent 1 (summer 1941); CP 264–65, LOA 237–38.

Divided into domestic news, part I, and the weather, part II. Neither the news about a strike at an auto plant, etc., nor the weather at winter's end, induce happiness for the spirit. Life in 1941 might help explain in part why "the spirit [is] left helpless by the intelligence." The last couplet raises the question of whether the breath that "fetches another year of life" is the purple fragrance that smothers misery, as in a situation well known to a "nigger," or another breath, of fresh air. The purple magnolia fragrance is the smell of euphony, a favorite rhetorical device of public speech in times of war and crisis.

TITLE: News and weather broadcasts at this time would be in a newspaper or on radio or on black-and-white film in a movie theater.

"magnolia . . . nigger": the "magnolia tradition" is the tradition of the Old South; see note on title "Like Decorations in a Nigger Cemetery," above.

"euphonious bane": on Stevens's mistrust of euphony, cf. "the bawds of euphony" in "Thirteen Ways . . ." x.

"at the winter's end": magnolia flowers bloom very early, even before the leaves appear.

"a nigger fragment, a *mystique*": cf. note on "nigger mystics" in "Prelude to Objects," and on the title, "Like Decorations in a Nigger Cemetery," above.

Metamorphosis

New Poems 1942, ed. Oscar Williams (Mount Vernon N.Y.: Peter Pauper, [April] 1942), with the following five poems, all under the title "Six Discordant Songs"; CP 265–66, LOA 238–39.

The title is a key word in Stevens's criticism, where it is connected with metaphor. Here, it becomes a play on the autumn months in "a poem of disintegration" that Stevens always liked (L 753, 1952), and with good reason. Using folk-song and charm-verse effects, he metamorphoses autumn month-names into more expressive words than the seventh (September), eighth (October), and ninth (November) months. The stanzas mark progressive stages of disintegration and migration, as does the ellipsis. There is a minor French genre called the *métamorphose*.

"yillow": invented variant on "yellow," as in a folk-song refrain.

"worm": a pathetic creature, sometimes used affectionately (Shakespearean diction), addressee unspecified. There is a hint of metamorphosis to or from a literal worm, through "cock-robin," eater of worms.

"Make o": folk-song effect, the wind again voiced in repeated onomatopoeic O sounds.

"oto — otu — bre": latinate effect like Italian or Spanish, but omitting the *c*, so that October becomes a vocative, as if the wind called out "O tu" before subsiding in br-r-r.

"Fro Niz — nil — imbo.": the month of metamorphosis as disintegration, where streetlamps metamorphose into hanged men, and the name of the month itself into variants on and combinations of frozen, nose (*nez*), nil, limbo, limb.

Contrary Theses (I)

Ibid.; CP 266–67, LOA 239.

Separated from its sequel, this poem has as contraries a soldier and autumn harvest as well as Christian art. The tetrameter couplets, irregularly rhymed, use repetition effectively to mark a growing sense of threat, then disaster. The scene is unspecified, but all too familiar at this date.

Phosphor Reading by His Own Light

Ibid.; CP 267, LOA 240.

A fine development of the dark night of "The Reader" (1935), compact and suggestive. See L 642 for Stevens's image, when he wrote, "of reading . . . the large page of a book" (1949). Note the varied use of person, and the skilled use of near rhyme; the near rhyme of "goes" and "glass," e.g., produces the ghost rhymes, "glows" and "gas," both appropriate for phosphorus.

TITLE: literalizing the trope "according to [one's] lights" (OED 6c); this Phosphor seems to grow from earthly phosphorus, which glows in the dark, and to adapt the role of mythological Phosphor, light-bringer or morning star (Tennyson, *In Memoriam* CXXI; and see OCD).

"green": cf. the color of phosphorus, also the sense of "green" in "The Candle A Saint."

"fusky": obsolete form of rare adjective "fusk" or "dusky," as if recalling "musky" and "sombre" from "The Reader"; the adjective shifts the tone of the poem's diction.

The Search for Sound Free from Motion

Ibid.; CP 268, LOA 240–41.

Compare the tone and properties in other sound and motion poems, e.g., "Infanta Marina," and contrast "motionless sound" in "Sad Strains of a Gay Waltz." A diverting poem, inviting thought on the different relations of sound and motion.

"Parl-parled": obsolete Eng., close to Fr. *parler*, to speak.

Jumbo

Ibid.; CP 269, LOA 241.

Stevens's abhorrence of a mere "imager" or "secondary man" is also clear elsewhere (e.g., MBG), and gives impetus to this attack. The disgust, especially evident in the long penultimate sentence, may stem partly from an old fear that he himself retains bits of this creature. Heavy tetrameter stresses throughout both illustrate and parody this kind of music.

Contrary Theses (II)

Ibid.; CP 270, LOA 241–42.

Compare the contrary theses in I, where autumnal nature also gives rise to one unspoken thesis in a different set of contraries.

"martyrs à la mode": with the sardonic phrase, cf. earlier martyrs (e.g., "Asides on the Oboe") and Stevens's sensitivity to wartime rhetoric ("Extracts" II, "Esthétique du Mal" XI).
"abstract": see note on title to NSF I; here the contours form against the shaping of martyrs, etc.
"Alexandrine": the standard line of French heroic poetry (6 feet, 12 syllables), hence "noble," as in Racine.

The Hand as a Being

CP 271, LOA 242–43.

The first of two poems whose females use charm effects. So do their poems, with incantatory rhythms and repetitions, here including lines irregularly repeated like a refrain. Both are in seven tercets, with occasional rhyme; this poem uses a pentameter base for its white magic.

"canticle": also with a resonance of The Canticles or Song of Songs as part of the erotic enchantment here.
"naked, nameless dame," "tree": as in some Eden.
"wove," "glittering hair": cf. also the Sirens; enchanters like to make weaving motions ("Kubla Khan," and cf. "Oak Leaves Are Hands").

Oak Leaves Are Hands

An American Anthology, ed. Tom Boggs (Prairie City, Ill.: Goethe Press, 1942); CP 272, LOA 243–44.

A black-magic spell poem. If the preceding poem offers the erotic muse, this poem raises the specter of the disabling muse. She develops from some of the Florida poems, and will move into "Madame La Fleurie." The tonality here is different from either, a mordant humor, with wild punning. Treating her this way may exorcise her. The form, otherwise the same as in the preceding poem, illustrates what a difference tetrameter can make.

TITLE: the oaks of Dodona could prophesy in their sounds; this oak appears to belong to sinister enchantment, as in Milton's *Comus* ("this dread wood, / The nodding horror of whose shady brows / Threats," 39–40); cf. "brow" (l. 11).
"Hydaspia": area of the river Hydaspes, earlier Greek name for the Jhalum River, which flows into the Indus in modern Pakistan; see EB, "Jhalum," for its storied history; generally, a distant, legendary Asian region; in Virgil, site of an eastern despotic monarchy (*Georgics* IV.211).
"Flora . . . florid": a metamorphosis of one aspect of Stevens's personified Florida.
"bachelor of feen masquerie": A Bachelor of Fine Arts, magical, that is (perhaps fiendish, in masquerade, masks, masques, make-up, etc.).
"metamorphorid": punningly, a metamorphosis into something horrid.
"Mac Mort": Son or Daughter of Mort or Death, Scottish variety; Flora (a Scottish name) is clearly related to Shakespeare's weird sisters in *Macbeth*.
"ancestral hells": punningly "halls."
"weaving . . . arms": punningly waving, and also weaving past and future, spider-like and witch-like.

Examination of the Hero in a Time of War

Harvard Advocate 128 (Apr. 1942); CP 273–81, LOA 244–50.

An examination that is difficult at times of crisis, yet needed. Stevens begins with the hard job of a fighting soldier, then moves to some older concepts of the heroic, outdated but still not obsolete. After the "common hero" (stanza v), he begins to devise the figure of a hero that will work for 1942. A series of tropes in VI indicates desire for an archetypal hero who is also an everyday person (cf. the major man at the end of "Paisant Chronicle"). The figure of the hero then moves through several stanzas, rejecting various scenes or contexts or concepts ("emblem," "image," "allegory"), before coming to the concluding and defining stanzas XII to XV, where "The hero is a feeling," a "man-man." Stanza XVI suddenly enlarges the entire perspective. For stanzas not included in the final version, see LOA 1001–2.

I

"Force is my lot . . . And cold, my element": cf. Shelley's chained Prometheus, "Pain is my element" (*Prometheus Unbound* I.477); the echo continues with lines on snow, rocks, etc. It suggests the constraints of the soldier, who, as soldier, is an embodiment of force and must act as a cold creature, under the orders of Death. Against this is "the will opposed to cold," also recognized by each man.

"Roma ni Avignon ni Leyden": (Sp.) "Rome nor," etc. Rome belonged to the Axis powers, while both France and the Netherlands fell to Hitler in 1940; all were centers in a peaceful, civilized world in their time, Rome most notably.

"brightness of arms": a common figure, here indicating that the soldiers do not abjure their role, even as they envision a different world.

"wings subtler than any mercy, / These were the psalter of their sibyls": cf. "Be merciful to me, O God . . . Yea, in the shadow of thy wings will I make my refuge" (Ps. 57:1); "sibyls" encompass another religious world, say, that of Aeneas, who consults the Cumean sibyl, dwelling in her "cavern." The syncretism allows for a variety of kinds and degrees of belief on the part of the soldiers.

II

"The Got whome we serve," etc.: alluding to "Our God whom we serve is able to deliver us from the burning fiery furnace" (Dan. 3:17, varied 6:17, 6:20); "Got": Old High German for "God." The text is sometimes quoted in war-time, but its efficacy is hardly guaranteed. Stevens translates the implications of war-time rhetoric into sardonic effect in what follows.

III

"a skin from Nubia": from the ancient and powerful empire of Nubia in northern Africa, and so from a "museum."

IV

"The signal . . .": a parallel of piano practice and a submarine drill is clear, as is the underwater trip of the submarine. The ellipsis, as often in Stevens, indicates a significant break and hence the question of what signal. Whether the submarine is sending a torpedo or being hit, or whether the signal is something other, a collapse follows.

"Chopiniana": music as of Chopin, following "shaken," "sways," "frisson," "collapses," i.e., diction evoking an underwater explosion. The reader is invited to choose the most appropriate Chopin music for what will follow, and/or to consider the relation of the ballet "Chopiniana" (1908) as music and as movement.

V

"the entrails / Of a cat": as in ancient haruspication, foretelling the future by reading entrails.

VI

"Devise. Make him of mud / For every day": cf. Adam, whose name means "earthy, taken out of red earth."

VII

"*Gazette Guerrière*," "*L'Observateur de la Paix*": (Fr.) "*War Gazette*," "*Observer of the Peace*"; apparently fictitious, adapted from common newspaper and journal titles, *Gazette* and *Observer*.

VIII

"brown books": as in older foxed or sepia-colored books.

X

"sua voluntate": (Lat.) "of its own will", in contrast to Dante's well-known line, "E'n la sua volontade è nostra pace" ("In His will is our peace," *Paradiso* III.85).

XIII

"not divided": i.e., not an allegorical figure as in XII.11.

"Say that the hero is his nation, / In him made one": cf. Frye's description of archetypal metaphor, "the individual identified with its class" (*Anatomy of Criticism* [1957], 124).

Transport to Summer

Transport to Summer was published by Alfred A. Knopf in March 1947. It gathers fifty-seven poems, written from 1942 to 1946 and arranged "in the order in which they were written" ("Note," x), with one exception. Stevens ended the volume with his powerful "Notes toward a Supreme Fiction," published by the Cummington Press in a limited edition in 1942, reprinted in 1943. He called it "the most important thing in the book" (L 538, 1946). Cummington Press also published a limited edition of "Esthétique du Mal" in 1945.

Marianne Moore called the title "itself a gift" (WAS 52, 16 Mar. 1947). "Transport" includes the three dictionary significations of (1) "literal conveying," (2) "transference of a word to a different meaning," i.e., "metaphor" (which means literal "transport" by bus, truck, etc., in modern Greek), and (3) "ecstasy." Stevens wrote that he meant "reality" by the word "summer"— leaving it up to his correspondent to define "reality" (L 719, 1951). The collection, then, conveys us to reality by means of a physical book, by means of metaphor, and by means of our own transporting imagination and emotion. As part of this, we may also be transported in time and space, as Stevens was in 1954. His visits to a friend's "old-fashioned house" where nothing had been changed "transports me in time." So too, his friend Barbara Church's travels "transport me in space" (L 827–28).

God Is Good. It Is a Beautiful Night.

Harper's Bazaar 2773 (Dec. 1942); CP 285, LOA 255.

An incantatory address to the moon as muse that comes close to an opening invocation, followed by a response. Stevens is revisiting his early haunting moon as muse, but she is now "brown" as she rises, not all immaculate and pure white. With the head that "is speaking," cf. the head in "The Men That Are Falling." With the head that "reads," cf. some of Stevens's other "reader" poems, and with the head that "becomes the scholar again," cf. some of Stevens's "rabbi" poems. This head sounds close to a writer's head, as it begins to play "the rustiest string" of a zither. A strong use of assonance and other repetitions, as well as the imperative mood, contribute to the incantatory effects of the first three tercets. With "Now, again // In your light, the head is speaking," such effects stop, and zither effects begin (sibilants, etc.), as the moon-muse appears to reply.

TITLE: two juxtaposed sentences with the verb "to be," inviting thought about the unstated relations between them (e.g., is the beautiful night a gift of God?). For Stevens, the first sentence is a metaphor (see NA 72, LOA 687, 1947). Two other titles use juxtaposition, but of nouns: "The Candle a Saint" and "The Bagatelles the Madrigals."

"Look round": for line 1 only, suggesting a submerged pun on "round" as an adjective meaning "full."

"brown moon": the moon may appear orange or brown when seen near the horizon, as it rises; cf. also the "brown" image of the moon in "Study of Images II."

Certain Phenomena of Sound

Poetry 61 (Oct. 1942); CP 286–87, LOA 255–57.

Three types of sound-phenomena, and their various kinds of transport to summer, invite comparison:

    I Remembered sounds of a Sunday summer, and actual sounds, in a cumulative series.

    II Two sounds of a summer lunch, as recounted by the host: the voice of Redwood Roamer re-creating his travels and the sound of a sonata; not a series, but a fruitful melding; not sounds of nature, but of works of art.

    III The sound of the names "Eulalia" and "Semiramide" in the sense of a field of associations; a contrast presented by "I, Semiramide" of two legendary women who evolved from historical figures.

I

"locust's wings": cicada's (American usage); like crickets, from the Orthoptera, who "sing" by rubbing body parts together; see note on "Things of August" I.

"do not beat by pain, but calendar": as against Eliot's biblical grasshoppers in *Ash Wednesday*?

"old John Rocket": possibly a descendant of John Rocket, founder of an old Connecticut family.

II

"Redwood Roamer": nickname of another vice-president of the Hartford, from the redwood area of California (Brazeau, 53–54).

"Naaman": Naaman Corn, a company driver for Stevens and others (Brazeau, 53–56).

III

"Eulalia": from St. Eulalia (Gk *eulalon*, "sweetly spoken," one name of Apollo), virgin martyr (d. c. 304), subject of earliest poem in vernacular French (*langue d'oïl*), and of a poem by Garcia Lorca that Stevens quotes in "The Novel" (see note, below).

"So seeing, I beheld you walking, white": cf. the troping and rhythm of "The Apostrophe to Vincentine."

"Semiramide": concerning Semiramis, legendary queen of Assyria, said to have built Babylon and its hanging gardens; thus with Rossini's opera *Semiramide*.

The Motive for Metaphor

Chimera 1 (winter 1943); CP 288, LOA 257.

A rich and much-discussed poem, still partly mysterious as befits any motive for metaphor. Transport to summer here takes the form of metaphor. The poem is a culmination of the debate between the worlds of moon and sun, sharing some images with the early "Anecdote of the Prince of Peacocks." It is divided sharply between two worlds that invite comparison in multiple ways. Its challenges become especially clear with the line "Desiring the exhilarations of changes" and what follows, including the colon and the grammar (what is the relation of "shrinking from" to what precedes and what follows?), as well as the memorable, paradoxical closing line. Compare the related but different workings of Yeats's "Byzantium."

"You": indeterminate, requiring the reader to work out what kind of "you" would be "happy" in the world described in lines 1–12—"an obscure world / Of things that would never be quite expressed"; this is a world of everlasting potential, including unrealized metaphor; "you" is possibly personified metaphor itself.

"The wind moves like a cripple": the strange simile also evokes a Vulcan figure, who appears earlier in Stevens and hovers behind the final stanza here.

"wind . . . among the leaves . . . words": intimating lack of any breath of inspiration, so that it is no surprise that things "would never be quite expressed."

"shrinking from / The weight of primary noon": cf. the fish "shrinking" from the fisherman-poet's spear in another metaphor poem, "Thinking of a Relation between the Images of Metaphor."

"temper," "hammer," etc.: as of the sun or the sun-god Apollo, known as "He who smites from afar" (Homer, *Iliad* I. 14, etc.; Auden, "Good-bye to the Mozzogiorno"); as of Vulcan's forge, the prototype for the crafts-man's workshop, including the poet's; note the percussive rhythm of these lines.

"X": when "X" follows the "A B C of being," it invites thoughts of elementary algebra, where x is commonly the unknown, expressed as a function of a, b, c. "X" at large invites various identifications, which must suit all the adjectives, e.g., a crossing-place or "X" as with any realized and powerful metaphor that masters the world, and so becomes "fatal" ("like some fate," also "fixed").

Gigantomachia

American Decade, ed. Tom Boggs (Cummington Press, 1943); CP 289, LOA 258.

A far less demanding (or rewarding) poem than "The Motive for Metaphor," providing some change in tension.

TITLE: a contest resembling the war of the giants or Titans against the gods or Olympians, here re World War II.

Dutch Graves in Bucks County

Sewanee Review 51 (winter 1943); CP 290–93, LOA 258–61.

Stevens's father grew up in Bucks County, Pennsylvania, where the family (partly Dutch) originated and belonged to the Dutch Reformed Church (L 405, 1942). His paternal ancestors are buried in Feasterville, Bucks County, Pa.; in 1907, he visited "a cemetery full of soldiers and Dutchmen born long ago" near Morgantown, Pa. (SP, 180). The poem is suffused with a sense of the war, in a meditation on these early American settlers and how their past intersects with the present conflict. The implications become increasingly un-expected and unsettling, starting with the fifth refrain, though Stevens retains a link with his past in the end.

"my semblables": "my fellow-men," familiar from Eliot's *The Waste Land* I.74, alluding to Baudelaire's "—Hypocrite lecteur,—mon semblable,—mon frère!", the final line of "To the Reader," *Fleurs du Mal* ("Hypocrite reader, my fellow-man, my brother!"); also used by Joyce in *Ulysses* (p. 383).

"Know that the past . . .": may be read as indicative or imperative, either one appropriate for Stevens as author, and both together showing the author's power over his subject; other refrains also use this ambiguity.

"hullaballoo of health and have": cf. "halloo," "health" in "Parochial Theme"; the two senses of "of " add to the poem's noise, here from two Germanic words.

"Who are," "What is": cf. Eliot's repeated "What is," "Who are" questions in *The Waste Land* V.

"the glory of heaven in the wilderness": appropriately biblical phrasing.

"to picnic in the ruins that we leave": cf. "A Postcard from the Volcano."

"chimeres": old form of "chimeras"; syntactically placed so that apposition can be with "stars" or "my semblables"; hovering between the meanings of a monster or terrifying illusion and a mere illusion (the stars are illusions in the sense that their light is past, not present).

No Possum, No Sop, No Taters

New Poems, ed. Oscar Williams (New York: Howell, Soskin, 1943); CP 293–94, LOA 261–62.

A January poem, ending with a memorable pair of crows. The couplets, and their many short sentences, offer brisk wintry utterances, as if the cold also caused words to contract.

TITLE: Stevens wrote to his friend, Philip S. May, that he lived "in a land of milk and honey" (Florida). Then, turning from a biblical saying to a more particular metaphor, in a land of "possum, sop and taters" (31 Jan. 1940, Houghton Library bMS Am 1543; see acknowledgments).

"He is not here, the old sun": echo of "He is not here, he is risen" (Mark 16:6).

"a syllable": unspecified, probably a crow's caw (suggested by "gawky"), transcribed as a poet's.

So-And-So Reclining on Her Couch

Ibid.; CP 295–96, LOA 262–63.

Three projections of a woman as she is represented in art, ending unexpectedly with a present model and an artist. The poem neatly encapsulates a small history of painting and sculpture, and perforce of writing.

"this mechanism": cf. "Clasp me, delicatest machine" ("Romance for a Demoiselle Lying in the Grass," OP 44, LOA 551, 1919–20?).

"Suppose . . . Projection A": reflection on a work of art, in terms of a Euclidean problem in geometry.

"Born . . . at twenty-one . . . Eyes dripping blue": evoking the birth of Aphrodite from the sea.

"practick": old spelling of "practice, execution," consistent with "Gothic" and the invisible hand.

"confides": cf. "confiders" in the next poem (stanza XVIII); note the series of "con-" prefixes.

Chocorua to its Neighbor

Ibid.; CP 296–302, LOA 263–68.

A monologue that is more meditative than dramatic, uttered by a well-known New England mountain. Large, sweeping, firm statements (as befit a mountain) slowly come to focus on an archetypal heroic figure. The poem works toward perceiving this "shadow," this "collective being" in various "True transfigurers" (stanza XVIII), as it extends Stevens's work in "Examination of the Hero in a Time of War." Compare also the development of "major man" in NSF I.VIII–X. Mountain monologues are unusual, though cf. A. R. Ammons's wry mountain poem, "Apologetics."

TITLE: "Chocorua": a mountain in New Hampshire; William James, an important figure for Stevens (see L, index), died at his summer home in Chocorua in 1910.

IV

"the figure in / A poem for Liadoff": see note on "Two Tales of Liadoff" and cf. "As if Liadoff no longer remained a ghost" (ibid.).

XV

"beyond / Their form, beyond their life, yet of themselves": cf. MBG I.

XVIII

"transfigurers . . . mountain": evoking the Mount of Transfiguration (Mark 9:2); note the scope of these figures in XVII, extended well beyond the military; "the scholar," for Stevens, includes the poet, who works with figuration.

XIX

"more than human," etc.: on Stevens's mapping of what is truly human, cf. also "The Auroras of Autumn" x, and a proposed section title for NSF, "It Must Be Human."

XXI

"megalfrere": "megalo-" (Gk. "great") is a prefix in many scientific terms; "frère" (Fr.) "brother."

"trash," "boorish," "common": care is needed in reading the tone; cf. "common" in "Ordinary Evening."

"glub": "band, company" (obs.), from Lat. *globus*, hence the pun "glubbal"; also echoic sound.

"tramp": cf. the "vagabond" figure in NSF I.x.

XXIV

"fortelleze": var. of "fortalice" (fortress) that sounds like a neologism made of "foretell," "ease," "forte" (strong), "fort"; see note on "fortress" in "The Old Lutheran Bells at Home," below.

XXVI

"roy . . .": obsolete for "prince, sovereign, royal person"; with ellipsis, giving the effect of a word broken off ("royal"? "royalty"?), as the mountain abruptly stops talking, at least "for the moment."

Poésie Abrutie

Ibid., under the title "Return"; CP 302, LOA 268.

The feel of winter in February, to match the feel of January winter in "No Possum, No Sop, No Taters." The fine pair of winter poems encapsulates winter's progress—and our progress through winter—in couplets with many short sentences, here irregularly rhymed.

TITLE: stupid or stupefied poetry.

"Cinerarias": available from greenhouses in winter; "speaking sheen": both the intense color of some cinerarias, and the sound of "cineraria," especially in a poem of mostly octosyllabic lines.

The Lack of Repose

American Prefaces 3 (summer 1943); CP 303, LOA 269.

Not quite the poem we expect for this title, so that "repose" invites rereading. Compare "pose" and "re-pose" in "Add This to Rhetoric," and note the play of "repose" against "disclose."

"secretions": cf. Stevens's work with "secrete" in "Repetitions of a Young Captain" vi and elsewhere (see Concordance).

"one of the gang, / Andrew Jackson Something": named for the seventh U. S. President (1829–37), a Southerner, and a populist hero, whence the term "Jacksonian democracy" or government for the good of the small man.

"Of a parent in the French sense": requiring us to reread "parent" as *parent*, a different sound and signification (Fr. "parent" or "relative").

Somnambulisma

New Republic 109 (28 Aug. 1943); CP 304, LOA 269–70.

A tour de force of the incantatory sound effects of charm poetry, as heard in the waves of the sea, with expert use of repetition.

"somnambulisma": things having to do with somnambulism, a Lat. coinage (1797) in a plural nominative neuter form.

"vulgar": "ordinary, usual"; also "vernacular," unlike the latinate title ("vulgar ocean," not Lat. *oceanus*).

"noiselessly": as on a remembered shore; as if memorable words about waves washing on a shore repeat themselves over and over, when actual (or recalled) waves are seen.

"A geography of the dead": the metaphorical bird becomes a type for all human imagination, for "feeling everything."

"scholar": "Poetry is the scholar's art" ("Adagia," OP 193, LOA 906).

Crude Foyer

CP 305, LOA 270.

With this poem on the relation of thought and happiness, cf. the development in "Of Mere Being," including the use of space. As in other poems of *Transport to Summer*, Stevens shows the process of feeling one's way toward accurate thought, correcting language as one goes along. The poem consists of one 20-line sentence, impressive technically, even for Stevens.

Repetitions of a Young Captain

Quarterly Review of Literature 1 (spring 1944); CP 306–10, LOA 271–74.

A meditation on the reality of war and its relation to each person's own reality. The argument moves on from two different realities, to the "giants" against the "personals," to one theater against another, and then to a third and "civil" alternative. "Repetition" is a rich subject and rhetoric in Stevens (see note on "He that of repetition is most master," NSF III.ix). Note the poem's own repetitions, e.g., the rhythm and slight variation of "It was something overseas / That I remembered" (i–ii), itself echoing Stickney's varied refrain on "It's autumn in the country I remember" ("Mnemosyne").

TITLE: "of " is both subjective and objective, as often in Stevens; i.e., the repetitions are both by a young captain and a young captain repeated; the "young captain" likely owes something to Captain Fernand Auberjonois (see L, index, and Filreis [1991], 29–36).

I

"theater": as elsewhere, a given world as theater (familiar from Shakespeare's "All the world's a stage" [*As You Like It* II.vii.139], etc.); here modulating into the theater of war with the word "overseas," site of the theater of war in World War II from 1939 onward, and earlier 1930s wars.

II

"gapering": portmanteau word from "gape" and "capering," setting up further echoes.

"a blue scene washing white in the rain": "blue," color of the imagination, washes out if reality changes (as in i) and the imagination does not.

III

"Millions of major men": see note on "Paisant Chronicle," below.

"in years of war,": comma, as in LOA and *Transport to Summer*, not a stop as in CP.

"milky millions": the curious image draws on the Milky Way, as well as other tropes of maternal nourishment; cf. "The milkman came in the moonlight" ("Les Plus Belles Pages"), "Warmed by a desperate milk" (NSF III.vii), and the early "In the Carolinas."

IV

"adobe": bricks dried in the sun naturally make an appropriate dwelling-place for angels, whom Stevens associates with the sun.

"Constantly, / At the railway station, a soldier steps away": the two realities also repeatedly confront the soldier, especially on departing for (or from) the front; cf. "Examination of the Hero in Time of War" I.

V

"On a few words of what is real in the world, / I nourish myself ": cf. the note on "milky millions," above, and (for the entire section) cf. "a few words," "giant" and "reality" in OE I.

"the bride come jingling": cf. the bride in "Ghosts as Cocoons."

"ensigns of the self ": note both the civil and military meanings of "ensign."

"half-arc hanging in mid-air . . . half-arc in mid-earth": in the first instance, the mapped horizons of our world as we look up or down and around; also resembling a theater, an eye, etc.

VI

"green": as elsewhere, the color of this earth, neither the moony inversions of blue nor the gold-red-black of military giants.

"Secrete us in reality": against her "secrete" (hide from, the private imagination avoiding reality) and his "secrete" (express, the imagination moving to pure realism), the poem chooses a third way. It changes person to the plural and uses a double sense of "secrete." The petition is that the imagination of many be hidden, yet moving, within reality.

"Discover / A civil nakedness in which to be": "civil" is both "non-military" and "courteous"; cf. the use of "discover" in NSF III.vii and "civil . . . I am" in NSF III.x.

The Creations of Sound

Maryland Quarterly 2 (spring 1944); CP 310–11, LOA 274–75.

"X" is often identified with T. S. Eliot or with an Eliot tradition of poetry, dominant at the time. The poem's nub is in stanzas 7–8.

"make the visible a little hard / To see": cf. "the difficulty of the visible / To the nations of the clear invisible," e.g., believers in Christian transcendence (OE xiii).
"peculiar horns . . . sound": cf. "The actual landscape with its actual horns" (ibid.) and "On an Old Horn."

Holiday in Reality

Chimera 2 (summer 1944); CP 312–13, LOA 275–76.

Two types of holiday in reality, defined partly by opposition. In part ii the opposition is patently to T. S. Eliot's perspective on spring. ("I regard him as a negative rather than a positive force" [L 378, 1940]; "Eliot and I are dead opposites" [L 677, 1950].)

I

"Palabra": (Sp.) "word, speech, palaver."
"Durand-Ruel": art gallery in Paris and New York; "one never felt that his place was vital" (L 668, 1950).

II

"flowering Judas": as against Eliot, who associates it with "depraved May" in "Gerontion."
"Spring is umbilical . . . or nothing, a waste": written against Eliot's "April is the cruellest month . . . mixing memory and desire" (*The Waste Land* I).
"the down-falling gold": petals, hair, etc., and cf. Zeus visiting Danaë as a shower of gold.
"root of the tongue": written against Eliot's "What are the roots that clutch . . . ?" (*The Waste Land* I); the root of the word "tongue" is said to be cognate Lat. *lingua*, whence our word "language."

Esthétique du Mal

Kenyon Review 6 (autumn 1944); CP 313–26, LOA 277–87.

Begun as a response to a young soldier's letter (quoted by Ransom, *Kenyon Review*, spring 1944) decrying poetry that is "cut off from pain" (like Eliot's and Stevens's) and preferring poets that "transcend the aesthetic of poetry" (like Berryman and Schwartz). Stevens noted the letter "about the relation between poetry and what he called pain," and thought about writing "an esthetique du mal" (L 468, 1944). The unstated argument is that aesthetics is always in play when one writes poetry. The title echoes against Baudelaire's *Fleurs du mal* (*Flowers of Evil*), with *mal* in the wide French sense of "evil" and "pain" (both necessary or natural, and inflicted pain), as well as "wrong, harm, hurt, ache, malady, difficulty, trouble." The title also intimates that there is a question of translation when looking at this subject, including translation from experience into poetry. Beyond the general meaning, Stevens meant "Esthétique" in its root sense, "aesthetics as the equivalent of aperçus" (L 469, 1944), i.e., the etymological meaning from Gk. "insight" (OED 1a; see head-note, especially on Kant).

Stevens's combination sounds provocative, especially in war-time. Ransom had written, "when is there a time for art?" in the "fight against evil." But Stevens took both ethics and aesthetics seriously, and he refused in the end to separate them. (Cf. NA 175, LOA 751 [1951], on "the discipline of the arts" as "a moral discipline"; SPBS 77, "L'esthétique est une justice supérieure" [Flaubert]; etc.) The result is what Robert Lowell called an "important . . . poem," reminding him of parts of *Cymbeline* and *The Winter's Tale*, "slow and rapid, joining the gorgeous with the very simple, wise, elaborate, open, tolerant without apathy, understanding with the understanding of having lived long" (review, *Nation* 164, 5 Apr. 1947). He also rightly observed that the sequence is uneven, both in its sections and in its lines.

I

Stevens starts with the sublime and an eruption of Vesuvius, filtered through someone's (whose?) letters home. This is an oblique response to the young soldier. Yet the response to war often takes the form of the sublime, a reaction to the strange combining of terror and awe. War is also sometimes an example of the sublime, e.g., for Kant.

"He was at Naples writing letters home": an unspecified "he"; a foreigner, someone studying the sublime, long associated with nearby Vesuvius (Longinus, Burke, Kant, etc.). Naples was in the theater of war in 1944, so that a first reading would identify the "he" as a soldier. The "he" is also a possible parody of the aesthetic poets, as seen by the young soldier in the *Kenyon Review* or a possible historical figure. Stevens's use of person throughout the sequence blocks easy ad hominem assumptions about pain and war.

"Vesuvius": erupted 18 Mar. 1944, shortly after the Allies gained control of the area. The sights and sounds of an eruption are often compared to the guns of war. Contrasting the fruitful Naples area and its fearful volcano is also common (e.g., Martial, epigram 80; Goethe, *Letters from Italy*). Volcanoes are also ancient dwelling-places for the gods, mouths of hell, and tropes for poetic voice (cf. "A Postcard from the Volcano").

"Cast corners in the glass": volcanic lightning ("fulgurations"), here reflected in the corner of a mirror; the sublime strikes like lightning in Longinus, *On the Sublime* I.1.

"remember the phrases: pain," etc.: if the phrases are an allusion, it remains untraced.

"The volcano trembled": a common phenomenon before an eruption.

"Pain is human": i.e., it is not an inhuman visitation or a punishment for sin; nor is it felt by the earth, as in a theological view of fallen nature (cf. Robert Lowell's "A Quaker Graveyard in Nantucket").

"the most correct catastrophe": as in a theory of the sublime, Longinus, Burke, etc.

II

Linked with I by the proposition, "It is pain that is indifferent to the sky," which develops the central proposition of I, "Pain is human." It is a common reproach to say that nature is indifferent to human suffering. Stevens reverses the logic. This is not, however, a detached meditation like I, but rather a deeply felt response ("the intelligence of his despair," "A kind of elegy").

"At a town . . . he": again, "he" is unspecified, as is the town, except for its acacias, which grow chiefly in tropical or subtropical climates, and in the area of the Mediterranean.

"The shadow": unidentified, but note the reappearance of the word in "The shadows of his fellows ring him round" (VII); shadows of the dead and the suffering intermittently inform the entire sequence.

III

The play on "firm," "hell," and "terra infidel," as well as the stanza form, indicate that Stevens has moved to Dante's *Divine Comedy* as a reference point for his meditation on war and *mal*. The move to Dante widens the poem's viewpoint to include questions of divine purpose. As elsewhere, Stevens disputes Dante's doctrine, while paying tribute to the power of his great imagination (cf. NA 23, LOA 656–57, 1942). For an early attempt at the subject, see the unfinished "For an Old Woman in a Wig," written in terza rima (OP 18–20, LOA 530–32, 1915–16).

"His firm stanzas hang like hives in hell," etc.": Dante's in his *Commedia*, esp. the *Inferno* ("hell," l. 1) and *Paradiso* ("heaven," l. 2); Stevens's tercets faintly evoke his terza rima in sound or sense.
"terra infidel": not terra firma (cf. "firm," l. 1), but, in Dante's view, infidel.
"over-human god / Who by sympathy has made himself a man": as in the Christian doctrine of the Incarnation.
"honey of common summer": as against the "hives in hell" (l. 1).
"find our way": playing against Dante's opening lines, "in the middle of life's way . . . lost" (*Inferno*, I.1–3).

IV

As if to combat the view that he has an insufficient sense of evil, compared with Dante's, Stevens moves to a definition of radical evil. The central proposition is "The genius of misfortune / Is not a sentimentalist," etc., as he works against a sentimental view of evil or a cheap use of the word. Note Stevens's technique of beginning obliquely, then moving toward one focusing statement.

"Livre de Toutes Sortes de Fleurs D'Après Nature": (Fr.) "Book of All Kinds of Flowers as Found in Nature"; as against Baudelaire's *Fleurs du mal*; the literal meaning of "anthology" is "a collection of flowers."
"sentimentalist": on sentimentality as a failure of feeling, see NA 138–39, LOA 728 (1948).
"B.": Stevens liked the music of Beethoven, Brahms, and Berlioz; he also annotated his copy of *Letters to His Wife* by Furruccio Busoni (1938), a pianist and minor composer famous in his day (1866–1924) (*WSJ* 2 [1978]: 78), quoting him in NA 15, LOA 651 (1942).
"that Spaniard of the rose": uncertain; perhaps Pedro Dot (1885–1976; famous Spanish rose breeder), perhaps Garcia Lorca, perhaps some "X de la rosa."
"that evil in the self": evil, properly so called, is not philandering in Stevens's unusual analogy, i.e., not venial; cf. remarks on "an imagination of evil" (NA 154, LOA 738, 1948); evil is human, just as pain is human.

V

A hymn to human love, as a form of comfort. Stevens returns to a sense of the sublime, this time as seen in human love. The edges, bars, and limits of v indicate that he is working with the probable etymological meaning of "sublime," from *sub-* ("up to") and *limen* ("lintel" or "threshold"). As with evil, so with love: both are understood as fully human, without intervention of divine force.

"Softly": also in a musical sense (*piano*); cf. "in-bar," "ex-bar."

"true sympathizers": as against the "sympathy" of an "over-human god" and the "self-pity" in III.

"ai-ai": Gk. interjection of lament; in context, also submerged pun on "I."

"obscurer selvages": brilliant etymological multilingual word-play on "selva oscura . . . selva selvaggia" (Dante, *Inferno* I.2, 5; dark wood . . . savage wood), through Eliot's *The Dry Salvages* (1941), to suggest that the Dante-Eliot line of belief is not "in the middle of life's way" (*Inferno* I.1) for Stevens, but on the edge of things.

"Be near me": beyond the general meaning, also echoing and revising Tennyson, "Be near me when my light is low" (*In Memoriam* L) and Bach's song, "Bist Du bei mir."

"dear relation": cf. "Relations dear . . . / Of father, son, and brother" (*PL* IV.756–57) from Milton's hymn to wedded love.

"in-bar," "ex-bar": like a temple threshold, but barring the superhuman divine rather than the profane.

"Exquisite": see note on "Nomad Exquisite."

VI

Stevens shifts his terms to "perfection" and "imperfection" in this charming, puzzling fable of sun, moon, and big bird.

"Rejected years": cf. "cast away" (l. 25), and "The Well Dressed Man with a Beard."

"corrected," "lapses": astronomical terms, as if Stevens is reconfiguring a Dantean "celestial" (l. 17) sun-light-life matrix of imagery.

"yellow grassman": the sun; cf. "the haymaker" (SP 119) and Dickinson, "Who is the East? / The Yellow Man" (no. 1032).

VII

A canto that opens with a startling trope, as in some metaphysical poets (e.g., Crashaw) or in Eliot's *East Coker* IV. Yet see note on line 1, "How red," etc., below. The mountain is presumably Vesuvius, where the vast, terrifying redness of an eruption (its flames, the reddish glare of its lightning, its red lava, etc.) becomes a figure for all the wounds suffered by soldiers in war. Compare F. J. Temple, *Vesuvius* (1977), on waiting for "a new bloody flower" after the 1944 eruption.

"How red the rose that is the soldier's wound": see head-note, above; on the conjunction of roses and blood in war, see Fussell, *The Great War*, 243–46; Stevens opens his war-hymn in Whitman's manner.

"A woman," etc.: closing on the memories of surviving women, as in Wilfred Owen's "Anthem for Doomed Youth."

VIII

On the death of Satan rather than the more familiar theme of the death of God.

"a tragedy / For the imagination": Stevens dissociates evil from the figure of Satan, and considers the world emptied by Satan's death, as in IX.

"capital / Negation": denial as capital punishment, like decapitation (from Lat. *caput*, "head").

"his revenge . . . filial revenges": Satan's motive is revenge in *PL*; in his terms, "filial revenges" by the warrior Christ, son of God, are to be expected.

"eccentric": an off-center death, in Stevens's usual literalizing pun on this word; the old end of Satan, as in Dante, at least kept him at the center of things.

"underground": for the shades, as in the *Odyssey, Aeneid, Commedia, PL*, and *The Waste Land*.

"How cold the vacancy," etc.: cf. Stevens on the origin and the end of the gods, which he called no "light matter," observing how we too were part of "this experience of annihilation" (OP 259–60, LOA 841–42, 1951).

IX

A somewhat weaker canto on lost imagination, in a world that has become indifferent to it; cf. the use of "indifferent" in II. "Mal" is here poverty or deprivation.

"the folly of the moon": recalling a favorite quotation, "The lunatic [from *luna*, moon], the lover, and the poet / Are of imagination all compact" (*A Midsummer Night's Dream* V.i.7–8).

"indifferent crickets": devoid of human association, especially with the transitory; cf. "Le Monocle de Mon Oncle" v.

"later genesis": the lexis evokes classical and biblical creation narratives; "halcyon" substitutes for the Spirit of God on the waters (Gen. 1:2; cf. Milton's "Dove-like satst brooding," *PL* I.21–22; OED and Webster, "halcyon").

"haggardie": a noun coined from "haggard," originally of a bird (a raptor, fig. "gaunt, deprived, suffering"), as against "halcyon" (bird, fig. "calm, peaceful").

X

A powerful canto centering on psychological/legendary diction for a mother figure, and widening its lexical scope at the end. Stevens sets the figure against the force of "impersonal pain." The sound of "ma-" echoes through the first few lines, ending in "-mal" ("animal").

"the nostalgias": a memorable invented plural for all forms of nostalgia; etymologically connected with the meaning of "mal" (Gk. *nostos*, home; *algos*, pain).

"Woman with a vague moustache": Jung's anima figure has recessive male characteristics.

"the mauve / *Maman*": a female type, as, e.g., in Proust's Mme Swann, *A l'ombre des jeunes filles en fleurs* I.i; mauve, not the purple of the true romantic (OP 214, LOA 770, 1934).

"a mother . . . other mothers": entirely earthly, not Eve, not the Virgin Mary, not Goethe's redemptive mothers at the end of *Faust*.

"she-wolves": like the foster mother of Romulus and Remus, fabled founders of Rome.

"Reality explained": cf. "The imagination with its typical nostalgia for reality" (L 364, 1940).

"understand": understanding as the "last nostalgia" comments on Jung, Freud, etc., and, more widely, on all passion for knowledge.

"innocence . . . if life itself was innocent": innocent of any nocent or injuring intent, in human suffering or dying.

XI

A return to direct reference to the war ("paratroopers," etc.) in three vignettes, followed by a bitter-minded reaction against such "a well-made scene." Among other things, Stevens is testing war-time writing and reporting. A much-quoted couplet divides vignettes and response. This is the first of four cantos exploring possible ways to live with *mal*.

"bitter aspic": see note on "aspic" in "In the Carolinas," above, and cf. the "bitter"/"honey" contrast in MBG xvi.

"The paratroopers fall": the first of the antisentimental war-time vignettes, fighting "well-made" conventional and sanitized scenes.

"mow the lawn": an old pun on *coup de grâce* and "couper le grass" (mow the lawn), mentioned in e.g., Redfern, *Puns* (1984), 164; evoking the topos of all flesh as grass (Isa. 40:6; cf. the grim reaper); recalling the "grassman" (vi).

"waves / Of people": punning on "waves" of the hand, as in Williams's "The Yachts" and Stevie Smith's "Not Waving but Drowning."

"bell-billows . . . Bell-bellow": cf. "Deep calleth unto deep . . . all thy waves and thy billows have gone over me" (Ps. 42:7) and "The bells are the bellowing of bulls" (MBG xxix), preceded by "The shapes are wrong and the sounds are false" (as in these scenes).

"Violets": flowers growing from a grave make up a familiar topos.

"malheur / The gaiety of language is our seigneur": "Poetry is the gaiety (joy) of language" ("Adagia," OP 199, LOA 912); cf. poetry as the "gay science" in Tennyson (see note on "a bright *scienza* . . ." "Of Bright & Blue Birds & the Gala Sun," above).

XII

As if developing x, the "he" of this canto explores three possible mental worlds and their consequences, as another way of living with *mal*. The last is a world without knowledge, where the personal is ignored and the will alone governs, in a stoical acceptance of "whatever is as true, / Including pain." It is unacceptable, given the need for human love.

XIII

A canto starting with a father figure, and generational struggle, but moving on to look at wider human "destiny." The word "evil" reappears in a different context. The "force that destroys us" (what Stevens calls "the assassin") awaits us all at the end. For the canto as possible conversation with Freud, see note on "the politest helplessness," below.

"a punishment . . . as the son's life for the father's": as in a Freudian scheme.

"The assassin . . . disclosed": suggesting a plot with a scene of (self-) recognition or the final knowledge of what we will die from.

"the politest helplessness": as in a civilized response to necessity. Freud uses the noun "helplessness" (*Hilflosigkeit*) twelve times in chapters III and IV of *The Future of an Illusion* in a related argument; Stevens quoted the book in 1942 (NA 14–15, LOA 651).

XIV

The one directly political canto, written when the Soviet Union was still an ally in World War II. Here, *mal*, even as suffering or evil, is unimportant, for the end justifies the means.

"Victor Serge": on the prolific Russian revolutionary writer (1890–1947), whose name was known at the time, see Susan Sontag, *TLS* (9 Apr. 2004). The quotation comes verbatim from his "The Revolution at

Dead-End (1926–1928)," *Politics* 1 (June 1944, copied in SPBS 79), re his meeting in 1920 with Konstantinov, an examining magistrate for the Cheka.

"the lunatic of one idea": cf. Yeats, "hearts with one purpose alone" ("Easter 1916").

"Lakes are more reasonable than oceans": thus in Auden's "Lakes" ("Bucolics" 4): "Sly Foreign Ministers should always meet beside one"; cf. also "The Doctor of Geneva."

"Konstantinov . . . lake": cf. xv and also Lenin beside a lake in "Description without Place" iv.

XV

Centering on the contrast of physical and metaphysical, in a move to the aesthetic as apprehension of the sensuous world (OED "aesthetic" 1a; see also Kant).

"who could have thought," etc.: Stevens told his editor that he punctuated this sentence so as "to indicate abandonment of the question." He was unwilling to end his series in the interrogative mood (L 469, 1944).

The Bed of Old John Zeller

Accent 5 (autumn 1944), with following poem; CP 326–27, LOA 287.

"John Zeller": Stevens's maternal great grandfather (L 469, 1944).

"in the old peak of night": cf. NSF III.vi, and the similar contrast of "luminous" in III.vii.

"sleep and ting-tang tossing": as against the usual bedtime tossing back and forth; a double sound (like a clock going tick-tock, etc.), a field of association for "tang," and a compound that itself tosses back and forth, in a protracted sentence.

Less and Less Human, O Savage Spirit

Ibid.; CP 327–28, LOA 288.

In Stevens's recording of this poem, he reads it slowly and ceremoniously, stressing the double "must" in line 1.

"savage": cf. "Ordinary Evening" iv and "Puella Parvula."

"Plato's ghost / Or Aristotle's skeleton": appropriate vestiges; cf. Yeats on
     Plato's "ghostly paradigm" and "solider Aristotle" ("Among School Chil-
     dren" vi); "Aristotle is a skeleton" ("Adagia," OP 194, LOA 908).
"It is the human that is the alien": cf. "World without Peculiarity."

Wild Ducks, People and Distances

Arizona Quarterly 1 (spring 1945); CP 328–29, LOA 288–89.

"the smoke of the villages": a topos of home, as in du Bellay, "de mon petit
     village / Fumer la cheminée" ("in my little village, the chimney smoking,"
     "Heureux qui comme Ulysse," trans. by Stevens, L 151, LOA 516, 1909).

The Pure Good of Theory

Voices 121 (spring 1945), with the following two poems and "Flyer's Fall," as well as
some reprinted poems, in an issue in honor of Stevens; CP 329–33, LOA 289–92.

The title functions best when considered after reading the four linked cantos:
(1) on time as we experience it moment by moment, then in relation to felic-
ity; (2) on the philosophical quest of a platonic person, sharpened by the
forces of Naziism; (3) on a retelling of the Eden story, as a modern metaphor;
(4) on particulars, which matter to us, and the passionate need of words that
act as a spiritual force in unexpected ways. All four parts use the form of NSF
cantos and are similarly rich and demanding in argument and trope.

TITLE: As often in Stevens, "of " takes a double meaning (see appendix); the
     "platonic person," in i and ii invites us to think of Plato's theories, espe-
     cially because Stevens starts "The Noble Rider and the Sound of Words"
     with a quotation from the *Phaedrus*; Stevens moves against Plato's world
     of pure and timeless Forms, and of pure good, throughout.

I *All the Preludes to Felicity*

TITLE: the full sense becomes clear only at the end, where the musical mean-
     ing of "preludes" is also evident; the memorable opening stanza, of and
     in time, has strong rhythmic effects.
"Even breathing is the beating of time": as in music, as in the preceding
     sounds of horse and walker, as in time as a batterer, with an acute sense of
     passing time as experienced, from time to time, by someone now sixty-
     five years old.

"platonic person": defined by the phrase "free from time," itself defined in II.

"Time is the hooded enemy": as in the conventional hooded skeleton; see note on "ever-hooded" in "The Idea of Order at Key West," above.

"enchantered": invented past participle, as if what an enchanter does is to enchanter; the neologism keeps us aware of agency in any such magic, and colors the word "enchanted" in the next line.

II *Description of a Platonic Person*

TITLE: expanding on the phrase from I, to devise an archetypal platonic person ("who was what people had been and still were"), who is also actual and conditioned by time (see note on "Man that is not born of woman" in III, below).

"avoirdupois": cf. the "fat girl" in NSF III.x.

"z rivers": onomatopoeic line, snaky and rivery in line and sound, with z as "zee" or "zzz."

"a sense and beyond intelligence": playing on different senses of "sense," including Plato's meaning; cf. also "The poem must resist the intelligence / Almost successfully" ("Man Carrying Thing").

"a Jew from Europe": in 1945, very likely an exile or refugee; in context, learned, philosophical.

III *Fire-Monsters in the Milky Brain*

TITLE: unidentified; "fire-monsters" as "the solar chariot," etc.? "the Milky Brain" as a version of "the Milky Way," where the sun exists? "the Milky Brain" as providing essential nourishment, as in the iconography of the Milky Way as a nursing woman whose breasts give milk? In any case, striking metaphor in this canto about metaphor.

"Man that is not born of woman": e.g., platonic, as against "Man that is born of woman is of few days, and full of trouble" (Job 14:1), a text that the Jew from Europe would know.

"Whose mind malformed this morning metaphor": echoing against the sounds and sense of Hopkins, "I caught this morning morning's minion" ("The Wind-Hover: To Christ Our Lord"); Stevens's Adam is himself the maker of any paradise.

"He woke in a metaphor": cf. Keats on Adam's dream, "The imagination may be compared to Adam's dream—he awoke and found it truth" (letter to Benjamin Bailey, 22 Nov. 1817).

"metamorphosis": on the connection with metaphor, see NA 72, LOA 86–87 (1947).

"solar chariot is junk": cf. "The sky is no longer a junk-shop" ("Dezembrum").

"what it believes in is not true": introducing the large question of the kind of truth in metaphor; see Stevens on believing in something one knows is not true, which, he said, "we are doing . . . all the time" (L 430, 1942).

IV *Dry Birds Are Fluttering in Blue Leaves*

TITLE: an illustration of metamorphosis, with two expected adjectives interchanged, in a fluttering toward metaphor.

"It is never the thing but the version of the thing": cf. "Ordinary Evening" I; there is no need to make heavy water of what is obvious to an artist or a scientist.

"time, / Time . . . a moment in which we read," etc.: returning to the subject of I, then developing it in a climactic 15-line sentence with the beast of poetry (like "the lion in the lute" in MBG XIX or the "great cat" in "Montrachet-le-Jardin"), as well as metamorphosis, transport, and a final epiphany in reading.

"a destroying spiritual": presumably "destroying" continually in order to keep the spiritual true; thus the change described in III.

"middle witch": a play on "middle watch."

A Word with José Rodríguez-Feo

Ibid.; CP 333–34, LOA 292–93.

TITLE: José Rodríguez-Feo was a young Cuban poet, and editor of *Origenes*, whom Stevens befriended. For their correspondence, see L and LWSJRF.

"moon . . . presides over imbeciles": Lat. moon is *luna*, whence our "lunatic."

"grotesque": Stevens made the point that there is no "particular relationship" between the grotesque and the subconscious, even though the grotesque has "taken possession of the sub-conscious" here (L 489, 1945).

Paisant Chronicle

Ibid.; CP 334–35, LOA 293–94.

A poem defining "major man," a term that first appears in NSF I.VIII (1942); the definition comes in stanza 3. Stevens distinguishes this use from the use in "Repetitions of a Young Captain," where "major men" simply means "the pick of the young men." In humanism, Stevens added, "major men" are different. Because humanism in the abstract is not enough, the characters of humanism need to be pieced out fictively (L 489, 1945). The end indicates that major man, a fictive being, may find embodiment anywhere at any time.

TITLE: "paisant chronicle": obsolete Eng. "paisant" (peasant) gathers in older and ongoing chronicles, in a prototypical chronicle. Note the paradox that major men are different from a paisant chronicle, yet within a poem of that name, as if to remind us that "the fictive man" is created from actual people.

"major men": note the prohibition of any "easy projection"; as in the title paradox, Stevens works unobtrusively against any false hero-worship.

"Tartuffe": Molière's archetypal religious hypocrite in his play of that name.

"as still a man / As Virgil": punning on "still" so that Virgil remains human, enduring and quiet, an example of major man. On Virgil in Stevens's work, see note on the epilogue to NSF, below.

Sketch of the Ultimate Politician

CP 335–36, LOA 294–95.

Possibly this poem answers the question of what "the imagination that is satisfied by politics" might be like (NA 144–45, LOA 732, 1948).

Flyer's Fall

Voices 121 (spring 1945); see note on "The Pure Good of Theory," above; CP 336, LOA 295.

In spring 1945, the death of a member of a war-time air force.

Jouga

Briarcliff Quarterly 2 (July 1945), with the following poem, both under the title "Two Poems"; CP 337, LOA 295.

One of a group of casual poems, following the rich and sometimes challenging effects of "Esthétique du Mal," "The Pure Good of Theory," and "Paisant Chronicle."

"Jouga": modern Provençal, "play" (Mistral, *Lou Tresor . . . Dictionnaire*), e.g., a guitar, a role.
"Ha-eé-me": untraced, despite inconclusive attempts.

Debris of Life and Mind

Ibid.; CP 338, LOA 295–96.

"bright red woman . . . violent golds": symbolic colors of desire and magnificence, and actual colors in, e.g., an embellished manuscript or Book of Hours.
"brush her hair": cf. a woman's hair in "Depression before Spring" and especially "The Beginning"; Stevens's wife had long, golden hair when young.

Description without Place

Sewanee Review 53 (autumn 1945); CP 339, LOA 296.

A poem developing Stevens's thinking about description in relation to how we exist (cf. "The Latest Freed Man"). His mind is running on the ways we live within a fictive construct. The poem was written as a Phi Beta Kappa poem to be delivered at Harvard in June 1945 (L 506). Stevens mused over the idea, which he found interesting, that we live within "the description of a place" rather than "in the place itself." He thought this was true "in every vital sense" (L 494, 4 Apr. 1945). The seven linked parts of irregular length are focused as follows: (1) A hypothesis that "to seem—it is to be." (2) Actual seemings, which give identity to an age. (3) Potential future seemings. (4) How things seemed to Nietzsche and Lenin. (5) The experience of a place as description without place. (6) Description as revelation. (7) The importance of the theory of description. The poem was written as World War II was ending in Europe, and it bears indirectly but strongly on the times. Stevens proceeds slowly and logically, doubling back on his argument, before going on. He is aided by syntax, with a rhythm of short, logical sentences contrasted with long ones, and by the couplet form, with occasional end-rhyme, sometimes emphatic internal rhyme.

I

"green queen": cf. "Depression before Spring," where the figure is of spring, desire, and new life.
"Her time": as of a monarch, e.g., the time of Elizabeth I of England.

"seeming made the summer change": part of the interwoven near and full rhyme that, with assonance, gives an incantatory effect, which is one way of changing seeming into being.

"golden": green and gold are the older symbolic colors for spring, here being transported into summer by the force of the queen.

II

"the greater seeming of the major mind": cf. "major man" in NSF and "Paisant Chronicle"; also Gombrich's schemata (in *Art and Illusion*) inside which most artists work, while major artists change the schemata themselves.

"merely": in context, both "nothing more than" and "purely" (obs.), as in "Of Mere Being."

"apparition": in a wide sense, not just a phantom; cf. "Angel Surrounded by Paysans."

"delicate clinkings": cf. "Clasp me, / Delicatest machine" ("Romance for a Demoiselle Lying in the Grass," OP 44, LOA 551, 1919–20).

III

"the death of a soldier": cf. Stevens's World War I poem of that name, and note the war-time date of spring 1945.

"commonplace": see note on vi.7–9.

"another breath": cf. the use of "breathes" in the elegiac canto vii of "Esthétique du Mal."

"curling-out of spring": as in spring vegetation (seedlings, ferns), as in metaphor ("curling with metaphors," Herbert, "Jordan" [2]).

"element": "Description is an element, like air or water" ("Adagia," OP 196, LOA 909).

"Things are as they seemed to Calvin," etc.: because the views below still live on.

"Calvin,"etc.: five names that denote radically new outlooks in (1) the Protestant Reformation (John Calvin, 1509–64); (2) a time of enlightenment and architectural design (Queen Anne, 1665–1714); (3) writing (Pablo Neruda, 1904–73, see next note, below); (4) philosophy (Frederick Nietzsche, 1844–1900); (5) the Soviet state (Vladimir Lenin, 1870–1924). Queen Anne, not herself an innovator, gives her name to the age. The five figures invite comparison, one to another. So do the viewpoints they represent.

"Pablo Neruda in Ceylon": Neruda was consul in Ceylon 1928–30. On 19 May 1943, Stevens wrote to Jorge Carrera Andrade about his book (see L 449, 18 May 1943) and his recent article in *Poetry*: "This is my first contact with South American poetry, and it is really a very great event for

me" (Stony Brook Library; see acknowledgments). Neruda is prominent
in the article as a major influence on South American writing. His inclu-
sion midway in Stevens's sequence breaks the chronology, introduces the
Americas into Europe, and leaves Neruda's type of "seeming" open-ended
as he was still alive; Neruda's "seeming" includes experimental poetry,
protest poems, diplomacy, and exile.

"*Museo Olimpico*": Olympic Museum, trope for a place of preservation in our
minds for our mental Olympians; for all their inescapable eminence, the
Olympians and their effects need testing.

IV

"Basel": Nietzsche lived in Basel, as Stevens was aware (L 532, 1946).

"sun of Nietzsche gildering": "catching in a snare" (obs.), evoking "gild."

"perpetual revolution": Nietzschean cycles of time; on Nietzsche, see espe-
cially L 409, 1942; L 431–32, 1942 (on Nietzsche as a way "of getting
out of focus" just as efficacious as "a little bit too much to drink"); also
WAS 3506, 3512, 3537, to Henry Church, 1943–44; NA 150, LOA
735, 1948.

"Lenin . . . beside a lake": Lenin spent time in Geneva in 1903–5 and 1908,
along with other revolutionaries. In her *Reminiscences of Lenin*, Krup-
skaya mentions his talk of the proletariat's victory "during our evening
walks along the shores of Lake Geneva."

"All chariots were drowned": chariots of the past (as in "Invective against
Swans"), of the privileged, and of the oppressor (as in Pharoah's drowned
chariots in Ex. 14:28).

"took bread": casting his bread upon the waters (Ecc. 11:1), Lenin may hope
to find it later, but is now rejected by the prescient swans he wants to feed.

V

The title of the full sequence emerges only now from the logic of the preced-
ing cantos. Stevens illustrates it in present experience, then as the future, for
which "description without place" is very apt. The phrase helps to place
Nietzsche's and Lenin's forward visions in IV.

VI

"Description is revelation": revelation about—perhaps by and/or to—the de-
scriber.

"explicit": etymologically "unfolded," like etymological "unveiled" in "revela-
tion" and "apocalypse."

"text . . . that we might read . . . reconciliation": see head-note on "The

Reader," above, and see entire passage in L 642–43 (1949), including re-
marks on "reconciliation with every-day reality" and "pages of descrip-
tion."

"the plentifullest John": like St. John the Divine, author of the Book of Revela-
tion or the Apocalypse (cf. iv.30), which is also "a concept only possible //
In description" and also a "canon central in itself"; it ends the biblical
canon.

VII

"a cast / Of the imagination": as of a sculptor's model, or as of a fishing-line?
imagining the Statue of Liberty or the largest trout ever? Stevens's lexical
richness outdoes itself here, in possible tropes for the ways we talk about
the past: (1) a throw, e.g., of dice, of a net or a line, a calculation; (2) a set
of actors in a play; (3) the form into which any work is thrown or
shaped, a model, a sculpture; (4) as in a "cast of mind"; (5) a tinge of
color, e.g., of a reddish cast; (6) as in casting a spell; (7) as in casting light
or shadow.

"the invention of a nation in a phrase": as in "life, liberty, and the pursuit of
happiness" or "liberty, equality, fraternity" or "peace, order, and good
government."

"hidalgo": from the Spanish landed gentry (lesser than the caballero of "The
Pastor Caballero"), a favorite Stevens figure for one of his poetic selves.

Two Tales of Liadoff

Pacific 1 (Nov. 1945); CP 346–47, LOA 302–3.

I

"Liadoff": Anatoly Liadoff (or Lyadov, etc.), Russian composer and collec-
tor of folksongs, known for his tone-poems (1855–1914); Stevens
owned recordings of his "Enchanted Lake" and "Russian Folk Songs"
(*WSJ* 3 [1979]: 89); cf. "A poem for Liadoff" ("Chocorua to its Neigh-
bor" iv).

"ex": cf. prefix "epi-" in neologism "epi-tones," and also "ex" ("out") elsewhere
("Nomad Exquisite," "a sea of ex" in MBG xviii, "ex-bar" in "Esthétique
du Mal").

II

"caboose": extending the assonance of "oh beau"; seeing the process as a long
train? Stevens is fond of words with Dutch or Low German origins.

Analysis of a Theme

View 5 (Oct. 1945); CP 348–49, LOA 304–5.

The first of several strong and memorable shorter poems, of great variety. This one is a variation on Stevens "theme and variation" form, and another example in *Transport to Summer* of Stevens's work with theme, theory, etc. It is one of his most charming (and telling) playful poems, ending in a masterly funny stanza, typical of Stevens's tone. The three-line stanza with a short final line allows for fine logical and rhythmic jumps between stanzas.

"Blandina": the name of Stevens's paternal great-great-great grandmother (L 405, 1942).
"Indyterranean": rather than Mediterranean.
"Gardens / Of Acclimatization": Jardin d'Acclimatation, Paris, a botanical and zoological park, inaugurated 1860, with leisure activities (e.g., a children's amusement park) from 1900 on.
"ithy": Gk. prefix, "erect"; pronunciation not signaled, so that the word hovers between Stevens's "mythy" ("Sunday Morning" III) and Carroll's "slithy" ("lithe" + "slimy," "Jabberwocky"); "we enjoy" the sounds too.
"oonts": rare word for camels, perhaps playing on Oort's comet cloud (OED, "Oort," 1941).
"long-haired": epithet for comets (*cometes*, Gk. "long-haired," as in a comet's "tail").

Late Hymn from the Myrrh-Mountain

Harvard Wake 5 (spring 1946); CP 349–50, LOA 305.

A witty, tender, erotic poem, addressed to a woman or a place, from a man (bulky) and/or a place of love. It is written as in the late summer of life, when timothy turns brown and goes to seed.

TITLE: "Myrrh-Mountain": "Until the day break and the shadows flee away, I will get me to the mountain of myrrh" (Song of Sol. 4:6); the aroma of myrrh permeates the Song of Solomon.
"snood": loose, ribbon-edged net for women's long hair, worn at the nape of the neck; sometimes with sexual connotations; see l. 16 on the act of releasing hair.
"madanna": madonna, madam, etc., in a bandanna?; "unsnack" thereby echoes as "unsmock," etc.
"brows": of a face or a steep hill.

"Neversink": a place of constancy (not one where hearts sink), troping on the Neversink Mountain on the edge of Reading, Pa., Stevens's home city, and the fact that the sun does not sink on the brow of a mountain until long after darkness has spread below.

"deergrass . . . timothy": Stevens mentioned in 1899 that they look alike (SP 53).

Man Carrying Thing

Yale Poetry Review 1 (spring 1946); CP 350–51, LOA 306.

A deservedly well-known poem, chiefly from lines 1–2. The title literalizes another of Stevens's ongoing subjects in *Transport to Summer*, metaphor. With metaphor as a twilight figure ending in brightness, cf. the different effects of light in "The Motive for Metaphor."

TITLE: figuratively a metaphor, which is literally a carrying-beyond; cf. I. A. Richards's terms, "vehicle" ("man") and "tenor" ("thing").

"The poem," etc.: a favorite quotation, also in "Adagia" ("Poetry must resist . . . ," OP 197, LOA 910); NB: "resist," not "destroy"; "almost successfully," not entirely.

"brune": obsolete Eng. for "brown," also current Fr. (feminine, as if modifying *la figure*); *brune* as Fr. noun means "dusk," i.e., a "winter evening."

"Figure": man; in a secondary sense, a rhetorical figure such as metaphor.

"identity": identification; metaphor is sometimes defined as identity (A is B).

"motionless": as metaphor, achieved, but with the motive (that which "moves") gone.

Pieces

Ibid.; CP 351–52, LOA 306–7.

As with the preceding poem, a moment of intense personal focus with a similarly urgent tone, here marked by two strong, one-line affirmations (ll. 2, 10) and the cry to the wind. Matters of sound and voice possess the "he," while Stevens develops the usual troping of wind as inspiration into something even more vital and continually necessary.

"Tinsel in February, tinsel in August": different effects: glitter as in silver- or gold-threaded, rather than worn-out Christmas tinsel; e.g., snow-bedecked trees (Feb.) and sparkling midsummer colors (Aug., and cf. "The Woman in Sunshine," etc., for summer gold).

"Come home, wind": with this address, cf. the apostrophe in "To the Roaring
   Wind" and note the differences (tropes, grammar, tone, etc.) about one's
   own voice, here a writing voice.
"a dog that runs away": expanding the sense in which "Come home" is cried.
"a horse," etc.: as if the wind could not be domesticated like a dog, or even
   like a horse; the series of tropes move from concrete to abstract to con-
   crete, domestic to outer atmosphere to family; also from simile to meta-
   phor; the wind as one's writing voice is deeply internal and known, yet
   also a large, impersonal phenomenon.
"milleman": as with "millefiori" glass (stanzas 2 and 3), pieces fused in one to
   give multiple effects.

A Completely New Set of Objects

Ibid.; CP 352–53, LOA 307.

One of Stevens's poems of the forties and fifties that focus on his natal state of
Pennsylvania. Strands of memory, both personal and historical, are inter-
woven in 14 lines. As with "Man Carrying Thing," they are in couplets and
use enjambment between stanzas to control the rhythm of the argument.

TITLE: inviting thought on how and why figures of the past can be called
   "completely new."
"Schuylkill": river flowing southeast in eastern Pennsylvania into the
   Delaware; Stevens recorded rowing upriver (SP 57–58, 1899), before
   coal dust changed its color (L 611, 1948).
"Shadows": shades as ghosts; cf. friends from youth in SP 57–58, and family.
"canoes": like "flotillas," recalling an annual festival on the water during
   Stevens's boyhood, when boats in the dark were lit by Chinese lanterns
   until increasing daylight slowly revealed who was present (Shenton, cited
   in Bates, 289–90); more widely, recalling aboriginal inhabitants.
"Tinicum," "Cohansey": in Dec. 1945 and Mar. 1946, Stevens was looking
   for information about his father's side of the family in cemeteries of
   Tinicum, Pa., and Cohansey, N.J. (Bates, 290).
"The fathers of my makers": the name "Schuylkill" is Dutch; more widely,
   Stevens recalled that one of William Penn's houses stood on one of its
   banks (L 611, 1948).

Adult Epigram

Ibid.; CP 353, LOA 308.

Most of Stevens's work in the genre of epigram comes earlier, e.g., "New England Verses."

"Again, the diva-dame": the diva and/or sibyl; cf. "mad divining dame" (Dryden, *Aeneid* VI.54).

Two Versions of the Same Poem: *That Which Cannot Be Fixed*

CP 353–55, LOA 308–9.

Compare other poems about a realm of potential being, e.g., of metaphor in "The Motive for Metaphor." Here the realm is natural, first the sea, second the elements ending in the sea. Compare also seeing the natural world possessed by ghosts of its former inhabitants, as in "A Completely New Set of Objects." "Two versions" of a poem usually means an early version and a later revised version. Here the comparison includes persona, dramatized speech, addressee, etc. Again, couplets allow for striking enjambment between stanzas (e.g., "a body . . . in wavering water lies, swollen // With thought").

TITLE: "fixed": with a play of the more usual meaning ("made right") against "fixed" as caught in clear perception, or in a work of art or a metaphor, or in belief, etc.; an important word in Stevens.

I

"stentor": cf. "the stentor Martin" in "The Old Lutheran Bells at Home."
"water-carcass never named": except of course in the play of "carcass" and "Lascar."

II

"old John Zeller": see note on "The Bed of Old John Zeller," above.
"Rest, old mould . . .": punning on mould as a form or shape and as matter breaking down; echoing Hamlet's farewell to his father's ghost, "Rest, rest, perturbed spirit" and his "Well said, old mole!" (I.v.182, 162).

Men Made out of Words

Accent 6 (spring 1946); CP 355–56, LOA 309–10.

A terse response to any notion of human reality as a reality without words. Even when not voiced, our lives follow a worded pattern.

Thinking of a Relation between the Images of Metaphors

Voices 127 (autumn 1946), with the following three poems, all under the title "Four Poems"; CP 356–57, LOA 310.

A poem that opens with present birdsong and a collective historical memory, not human but of fishes, instinctive. Personal memory also underlies the poem, though it is not explicit. The poem moves, itself like both fish and fisherman. It moves from the act of fishing implicitly toward the act of making poetry. As elsewhere, the poet repeatedly searches for the perfect metaphor, fishing, looking, listening, spearing, fixing. In the play between fish and fisherman, flux and fixity, cf. "The Motive for Metaphor" (note "shrinking," "strike perfectly," "grow still").

"Perkiomen": a creek downstream from Stevens's grandfather's farm "famous for its bass"; Stevens recalled that his father "used to fish in Perkiomen for bass" all his life (SP 5, 1942).

"one ear . . . all one ear": an act of intense concentration, expressed by a move toward collective metaphor, as in the one soldier who may stand figuratively for all soldiers in a memorial statue.

"bass . . . in one / Direction": accurate, as fishermen know (fish face upstream, so as to catch food more easily); visually, like fish in a work of art, say, a Japanese bowl.

"rou-cou": see note on "Depression before Spring," above, and cf. "Song of Fixed Accord."

"grow still": punning to indicate the nature of metaphor, which sits still on the page and also still grows in our heads.

Chaos in Motion and Not in Motion

Ibid.; CP 357–58, LOA 311.

Troping on a thunderstorm as theater (as they often are) and as affective (as they often are).

"Ludwig Richter": German painter and illustrator (1803–84); for the possible influence of Ruskin on Stevens's view of Richter, see Beyers *WSJ* 18.2 (1994).

The House Was Quiet and the World Was Calm

Ibid.; CP 358–59, LOA 311–12.

See Stevens's other readers, especially the image of a reader in the head-note to "Phosphor Reading by His Own Light," above. This is an exceptionally quiet poem, even for Stevens, with frequent and unobtrusively varied use of the verb "to be."

Continual Conversation with a Silent Man

Ibid.; CP 359–60, LOA 312–13.

The poem implicitly raises the question of who this silent man is and why he is silent. A ghost from the past, as in some preceding poems, and as the flash-back with the cartwheel suggests? The shift in color indicates a shift in the light in which we view things, literally and figuratively.

A Woman Sings a Song for a Soldier Come Home

Quarterly Review of Literature 3 (fall 1946), with the following eleven poems, all under the title "More Poems for Liadoff"; CP 360–61, LOA 313.

The calm tone belies the grim subject of the surviving soldier who has suffered permanent damage that is not physical. But then he lives a deceptively calm life. The situation is outlined in stanzas 1–3, followed by a 12-line sentence focused on the soldier himself. The tercets are compact, as if uttering only what is needed, no more.

The Pediment of Appearance

Ibid.; CP 361–62, LOA 314.

Another walking poem for questers in an allegorical woods. "Pediment" takes a full range of meaning: the architectural ornament (sometimes with sculpture) as of a temple of Appearance, the geological extended rock as of

Mount Appearance, and more generally the base or path as in following appearance in this life. The solidity of "pediment" contrasts with "appearance."

"savage transparence": "transparence" as elsewhere offers complete clarity of vision, while "savage" has the force of primitive vitality (cf. OE iv).
"The world is myself": as against Stevens's insistence that imagination depends crucially on reality; the young men seek a projection of themselves, another sense of "pediment."
"heavy scowl": a sculpted pediment in the end, an inimical form and hostile projection.

Burghers of Petty Death

Ibid.; CP 362, LOA 314–15.

Two contrasting kinds of death, or rather our sense of death. The puzzle lies in the adjective "petty" so applied. Though one—possibly two—words of the title sound pejorative, neither the burghers nor their "slight part of death" is so treated. Stevens offers no judgment, only a contrast and a memorable trope of leaves.

Human Arrangement

Ibid.; CP 363, LOA 315.

The title raises the question of what other types of arrangement exist. Natural? Animal? The two opening compounds remind us that our sense of place is in large part constructed by our perceptions, and that time is a human construct. The eight tetrameter couplets (with variation) consist of only two sentences; they open with pronounced rhyme effect, as if acting out how we may be "bound."

"from nothing": a creation, possibly echoing the Christian doctrine of creation *ex nihilo*.
"curule": like the wonderful chair itself, the word suddenly breaks our lexical expectations; a line of pronounced internal rhyme to match the opening internal rhyme of the incessant rain.

The Good Man Has No Shape

Ibid.; CP 364, LOA 316.

A poem on incarnations through the centuries of the good man, with allusions to the life of Jesus. It is an affirmation of the good man, e.g., the human Jesus, but opposed to the doctrine of the perfect God-man, Jesus as Christ. Hence the double sense of the title, a parallel to the double sense of the sign over the cross (see note on the title, below).

TITLE: Stevens implicitly raises a question that the poem will address. How or why does the good man have no shape, or how would one complete a succeeding clause, "because . . ."? (a) There is no such thing as the good man; it is an ideal. (b) There are good men, not just one good man. (c) The good man takes this or that shape, but no required shape, as, e.g., in the Incarnation of Christ. Or?

"Lazarus betrayed him": It is Judas who betrays Jesus in the Gospels. They also record the miracle of Jesus raising Lazarus from the dead, in a foreshadowing of his own resurrection. Stevens, deeply sympathetic to the human Jesus, abjures the miraculous, seen here as a betrayal of the human.

"To mock him": cf. the mocking sign over the cross, "King of the Jews" (Mark 15:26).

The Red Fern

Ibid.; CP 365, LOA 316–17.

A poem on the resemblances and likenesses, in shapes and colors, that we perceive in natural phenomena; cf. Thoreau on the leaf in the final chapter of *Walden*. Like other poems by Stevens, this one both catches the familiar and makes it a little unfamiliar. (A day beginning is likened to a fern opening out, from its initial curled frond to full-leaved stem, as in clouds at daybreak.) The warning at the end is a little puzzling.

"Infant": as in "Infanta Marina," playing on the Lat. meaning of *infans*, "unspeaking."

From the Packet of Anacharsis

Ibid.; CP 365–66, LOA 317.

Compare changing color effects with those in the preceding poem. The rhyme is emphatic in the first two tercets, and end-internal rhyme in the next two; contrast the style of the final sentence.

TITLE: "Anacharsis": a Scythian prince, type of the wise barbarian, largely legendary, one of the proverbial Seven Sages (see OCD); "packet": cf. "a problem sealed up in a packet" (though not of Anacharsis) at "The Dinner of the Seven Wise Men" (Plutarch, *Moralia*, trans. Babbitt vol. II [Loeb Classical Library, 1928], 146).
"Puvis": Puvis de Chavannes (1824–98); his idealized, soft-colored, classical murals may be seen in the Boston Public Library.
"Bloom": possibly a generic name, probably Hyman Bloom, U.S. painter (1913–), one of the three "Boston Expressionists"; included in the 1942 Metropolitan Museum of Art (New York) exhibition titled "Americans."
"punctual center": exact center, playing on the Lat. root, *punctum*, a point.
"vast accumulation": what we accumulate is what went before, here Anacharsis and Puvis and what Bloom knew from them.
"lines": in context, a painter's lines, with resonance of a poet's lines.

The Dove in the Belly

Ibid.; CP 366–67, LOA 318.

On an internal psychic and physical force, especially a "tempestuous" one that is told to be calm, cf. the "wild bitch" in "Puella Parvula." The dove has a continuous life in Stevens, notably in later poems, where its erotic associations are to the fore. Note the functions of grammar here, given sentences in four different moods; note also how the questions work, e.g., what range of answers is possible (cf. Hollander, "Questions of Poetry," *Melodious Guile* [1988], 18–40).

"appearance": contrast "appearance" in "The Pediment of Appearance."
"Selah": frequent Hebrew word in the Psalms (71 times), probably a musical or liturgical sign; once thought to indicate a pause but now translated as "up," a sign to participants to rise.
"salut": obsolete "salute, greeting" (cf. Fr. *salut*), echoing the sound of "Selah."

Mountains Covered with Cats

Ibid.; CP 367–68, LOA 318–19.

An intriguing but somewhat mystifying poem, especially the relation of the three stanzas to each other.

TITLE: suggesting multiple associations on first glance: the Catskills; mountain-cats in the Rockies, a hunter's dream; above all, the classic children's book, *Millions of Cats* (1928), by Wanda Gág, who had just died in June 1946. One illustration in *Millions of Cats* shows a hill "covered with cats." The book was published when Holly Stevens was about four years old. For the relation of the title to the second and third stanzas, see note on Freud.

"flights / Of red facsimiles": see note on the "red bird," "Le Monocle de Mon Oncle" II, above, and head-note to "On the Adequacy of Landscape," above.

"catalogue": also, in context, possibly a "cat-a-logue."

"invalid": in a recording (ed. Oscar Williams, *Twentieth-Century Poetry in English*, 1959), Stevens pronounces the word as "inválid"; note the possibility of "ínvalid" on the page, and how both meanings work.

"outcast": in Gág's story, the outcast cat is the one finally chosen for a pet.

"Freud": given the language of "impotent" and "potency," and how humans and the imagination keep "seeking to propagate," Freud's cat saying about female sexual parts serves as subtext here. "J'appelle un chat un chat," he wrote in his German text ("I call a cat a cat"; the Eng. idiom is "call a spade a spade"). The subtext lights up the title and earlier parts of the poem.

"seen clear": clear through, being ghosts; for a skilful poem on another well-known shade in the afterlife, see the dramatic monologue, "Lytton Strachey, Also, Enters into Heaven" (the title echoes Vachel Lindsay's once popular "General William Booth Enters into Heaven" [OP 71–72, LOA 564–65, 1935]).

"how truly they had not," etc.: cf. the paradox and apparent oxymoron in the closing lines of "The Snow Man" and "Tea at the Palaz of Hoon."

The Prejudice against the Past

Ibid.; CP 368–69, LOA 319.

"Marianna's Swedish cart": referring to Marianne Moore's "A Carriage from Sweden"; she thanked him for giving her cart "the savor of poetry," then added that his use of words, "strange but also natural," reminded her of why she wanted to become a poet (16 Mar. 1947, WAS 52).

"souvenirs of time, lost time: cf. Proust, *A la recherche du temps perdu*, literally, *In Search of Lost Time*.

"cart . . . part of the heart": as it is through the ghost rhyme of stanza 1, spelled out in stanza 2.

Extraordinary References

Ibid.; CP 369, LOA 320.

The title describes exactly what the proper names in the poem are doing (the names of a child, a people, a place, and a minor classical god). They are acting as references. The domestic setting and mother's voice make them sound ordinary, and so they are, yet also extraordinary. "An Ordinary Evening in New Haven" will later explore fully how the ordinary can also be the truly extraordinary. Here the conjunction is simpler: an Indian fighter, a descendant with a Dutch name in Pennsylvania (where this name is common), a father killed in an unspecified war—all in a 1946 poem, just after World War II. The proper names are of three kinds, Dutch, Amerindian, and classical—three civilizations, interwoven like the "child's three ribbons."

"*Jacomyntje*": from Stevens's genealogy (L 4); cf. the name "Catelyntje," which Stevens called a good Dutch name (L 405, 1942).

"*an Indian fighter*": in the story of conqueror and conquered, an uncomfortable example on first reading. How far and why does the mother take comfort in coming from a line of warriors? What parallel is there between fighting Nazis and fighting Indians as you invade their country? But then, the phrase is ambiguous: was the great-grandfather himself an Indian, defending his territory?

"Tulpehocken": a Dutch-sounding name, translating an aboriginal name (meaning "turtle-land"); as an area, the home of Stevens's ancestor, Franz Zeller (L 470, 1944, also L 541); as river, north of Reading, a site of Stevens's courtship (SP 239, 1909). He wrote about his visit to the old Zeller house and the Tulpehocken Reformed Church in 1948 (NA 99–101, LOA 703–4).

"Compose": in the double sense of "put together" and "make calm."

"Vertumnus creates an equilibrium": supposedly an Etruscan god, Vertumnus ("the turner," "the changer") is associated with the changing seasons (see OCD) and fecundity, sometimes violently so. Etruscan civilization was conquered by the Romans, as Amerindian civilization was conquered by the Dutch and others. Now, peacefully, a remnant, a garden statue, a memory, remains. "Equilibrium" is a term associated with the changing seasons (cf. the equinox), here extended to areas of personal and historical life.

"ribbons," "plaited hair": opening and closing the poem, the trope of braiding beribboned hair suggests the interwoven strands of history and individual lives, past and present, continuity and change; also the interweaving of poetic lines.

Attempt to Discover Life

Ibid.; first pub. *Origenes* (Cuba) 3 (winter 1946), with Spanish translation; CP 370, LOA 320–21.

"San Miguel de los Baños": a spa in Cuba with mineral waters.

"black Hermosas": Stevens identified this as a kind of rose. On their setting in San Miguel, see L 540 (1946).

"dos centavos": two cents; the poem prompts the question "whether the experience of life" is finally worth more than two cents (ibid.).

A Lot of People Bathing in a Stream

CP 371–72, LOA 321–22.

Written by someone who loved to swim, as Stevens did. See L 98 on his boyhood delight in it, including his pleasure in swimming underwater and looking at the colors there (1907; cf. L 125, 1909). The poem explores boundaries, moving through the boundary of water and air, moving through memories of swimming, moving through the boundary of past and present. The pleasure throughout is anchored by the domestic closing stanza at day's end.

"The yellow that was yesterday": a memory, like the stars shining "during the day" (present but unseen), stars whose light originates many yesterdays ago.

"angular anonymids": another example of Stevens's "great ease in combining abstract words with gaudy visual or sound effects" (James Merrill, *Recitative* [1986], 75); "anonymid" is Stevens's invention, making swimmers into water-creatures through the common zoological suffix, "-id."

"patroon": var. patron, owner of landed estate with manorial privileges under the Dutch governments of New York and New Jersey (abolished c. 1850).

Credences of Summer

CP 372–79, LOA 322–26.

Following "the imaginative period" of "Notes toward a Supreme Fiction,"
Stevens next turned to the subject of this poem (L 636, 1949). He recalled
later that in 1946 he felt strongly the need "of a final accord with reality."
"Summer" in the title represents reality (L 719, 1951). The series is remark-
able for its sensuous richness and passionate sense of vocation. The nine sec-
tions all appear in three 5-line iambic pentameter stanzas; different effects
within the same form invite comparison. The poem includes some of
Stevens's strongest rhythmic effects. He later said that his favorite sections
were IV and VII (L 782, 1953), two quite different parts.

TITLE: note the difference between "credence" (as in "give credence to") and
    "belief"; see also appendix.

I

Summer translated into words, including older words, with a Keatsean sense
of time suspended. The opening sentence, coinciding with its stanza, is mem-
orable: pulsating rhythm, latinate syntax, repeated enjambment. By contrast,
stanza 2 has four sentences, three being one-line.

"all fools slaughtered": uncertain (well past Apr. 1, April Fools' Day?).
"Now the mind lays by its trouble": echoing Catullus (whom Stevens read [L
    104, 1907]), "cum mens onus reponit" ("when the mind lays by its bur-
    den," no. 31, Loeb Classical Library), from his rapturous homecoming
    poem; also quoted by Tennyson in the *Memoir* by Hallam Tennyson (I,
    342) that Stevens owned and marked (copy at the Huntington Library).
"last day of a certain year": punning on "certain," as someone of Stevens's age
    well might.
"heart's core": echoing Yeats, "the deep heart's core" from "The Lake Isle of
    Innisfree" (quoted in "A Page from a Tale"), a poem yearning for home;
    Yeats and Catullus give Stevens two slightly different coordinates for
    such a yearning.
"fathers standing round," etc.: cf. Dickinson, "The Shapes we buried dwell
    about / Familiar in the room" (no. 607).
"mothers touching," etc.: cf. mother figures and the sense of touch elsewhere,
    e.g., "The Auroras of Autumn" III.
"lovers . . . soft dry grass": including a memory from Stevens's courtship ("the
    Mirror of Past Events . . . where we had lunch on the dry grass" [SP 239,
    1909]).

II

A section of imperatives (eight out of nine sentences) that give urgency to Stevens's desire to "see the very thing," "the centre that I seek." The diction throughout variously recalls Dante, Eliot, Yeats, and Keats and perhaps others, as Stevens implicitly argues against the first two, modifies Yeats, and extends Keats.

"pine": the usual pun on "pine" (e.g., end of "The Man with the Blue Guitar") is made overt here.

"evasion by a single metaphor": "evasion" need not be pejorative for Stevens, yet a master of words may still feel the challenge of impossible desire—to be free from even one's own gift, to say nothing of metaphors built into the language.

III

"tower": the first single tower in Stevens's collected poems, a remarkable archetypal one. Its starting-point was probably the Tower on Mount Penn near Reading, which had a commanding view; Stevens loved to hike there (SP 49).

"mountain": another archetypal figure, here expanding Stevens's earlier mountains (e.g., "Tea at the Palaz of Hoon," "Chocorua to Its Neighbor"); as with the tower, recalling other prominent uses, e.g., in Dante and Yeats.

"final mountain": not, then, Moses' Mount Sinai or the Mount of Transfiguration or Dante's Mountain of Purgatory.

"end": meaning depends on context (cf. 1); thus, a final end or purpose, though not in older (e.g., Christian) teleology; also death; also complete fulfillment; re series title, in Amos 8:1–2, summer fruit (Heb. *kayitz*) causes him to prophesy the end (Heb. *kayts*) of the kingdom.

"appeased": note etymological connection with peace, also the use of "appeasement" in OE iv, and cf. the "unappeased" spirit in Eliot's *Little Gidding* ii.b.

IV

A memorable section of complete summer fullness in a Pennsylvania farming area, where time, or, as Stevens says, direction seems to stop.

"Oley": See L 719 for Stevens's locating of the region, which, he noted, was partly settled by Huguenots in the seventeenth century. He added that "an accord with realities is the nature of things there" (1951); mentioned SP 168.

"choirs": evoking Keats's "To Autumn," a Stevens favorite, with a comparable sense of time suspended in sensuous fulfillment.

"nothing else compounded": Stevens forbears from raising Keats's question of passing time.

V

"soldier, weather-foxed": "foxed" as in brown spotting on old books, also evoking military foxholes.

"without souvenir": stressing the sense of memory; also of a poetry of the earth that is "Stripped of remembrance," e.g., of heaven and hell.

VI

"visible rock": as against any invisible figurative rock, e.g., God as a rock (frequent in the Psalms, e.g., Ps. 28:1), Peter (Petros) as the rock (*petra*) on whom the church is built (Matt. 16: 18), the parable of the house built on a rock (Matt. 7:24); cf. "mercy," "sure," which echo biblical language interspersed by other diction ("brilliant").

"sure repose": echoing "On the Rock of Ages founded, / who can shake thy sure repose?" from John Newton's well-known hymn, set to Haydn, "Glorious things of thee are spoken."

"mountain . . . sapphires": cf. the "paved work of sapphire stone" under the feet of God in Ex. 24:10; in Ez. 1:26, a throne-like sapphire stone is above the firmament.

"twelve princes": an auspicious number, as in Jesus' disciples, Arthur's Knights of the Round Table, Charlemagne's Paladins, etc.

VII

"in face / Of the object": continuing MBG xviii ("A dream . . . in which / I can believe, in face of the object").

"avert themselves or else avert the object": cf. Stevens's discussion of whether a poem concerning a natural object comes from the poet or from the object (L 302, 1935).

"grips in savage scrutiny": cf. note on a "hawk of life," MBG xxiv.

"make captive," "subjugate," "proclaim": cf. Browning's three types of poet in *Sordello* III.862–68: one who says he sees, one who says what he sees, one who makes others see.

VIII

"trumpet of morning": though the cock is "trumpet to the morn" (*Hamlet* I.i.150) and appears in ix, this trumpet sounds less like a bird and more like some happy contrary to the last trumpet at the end of the world (I Cor. 15:52, Revelation passim), familiar from Handel's *Messiah*. Possibly it is both. Angels are "trumpet-tongu'd," as in *Macbeth* I.vii.19 (cf. Matt. 24:31) and many an illustration.

"like ten thousand tumblers": a common biblical figure for a very large number; see next note.

"tumblers tumbling down": Sancho Panza's comment in *Don Quixote* II.xxii is germane. "Who was the first tumbler?" "Lucifer." ("How art thou fallen from heaven, O Lucifer, son of the morning" [Isa. 14:12]); Lucifer, the "Morning Star . . . Drew after him the third part of Heav'n's Host" for a war in heaven (*PL*.V.710; cf. Rev. 12:4–11).

"division": cf. Stevens's work with the word "divide" in OE v.

IX

After the scope of the "unreal" in viii, a return to the immediate and domestic, though with unexpected associations.

"willow": commonly a tree of sorrow and death (see "Sunday Morning").

"salacious weeds": not an ordinary garden, but as in the "rank sweat of an enseamed bed," whose "weeds" must not be made "ranker" (Hamlet III.iv.92, 151–52); possibly a corrupted Eden.

"emotions . . . abandoned spot": cf. other empty or dilapidated places in Stevens, and also the setting of Eliot's *Burnt Norton*.

"Soft, civil bird": possible address, until the enjambment; cf. the use of "civil" in NSF III.x.

"*douceurs, / Tristesses*": a common pairing in French erotic and also devotional verse.

"suave bush // And polished beast": cf. "The Mystic Garden and the Middling Beast."

X

Summer, through its personae, is celebrated in heraldic style.

"inhuman": not pejorative; cf. "without human meaning" in "Of Mere Being."

"pales": heraldic term for vertical strip(s) or band(s) in the middle of the shield; Stevens had in mind Keats's use of the heraldic term "gules" in "The Eve of St. Agnes" (L 781, 1953).

"fat": as in plenitude; cf. "fat girl" (NSF III.x) and allegorical figures of Plenty or Copia.

"Free . . . of malice": a common religious and civil prayer and desire (e.g., Lincoln's Second Inaugural Speech).

A Pastoral Nun

CP 378–79, LOA 327.

Continuing work with the pastoral mode and with pastoral language, here in both the literary and ecclesiastical sense.

"apotheosis": Stevens's view of apotheosis is mixed (cf. NSF I.ix.2), but he knows well how to imagine the nun's sense of it.

The Pastor Caballero

Furioso 2 (fall 1946); CP 379–80, LOA 327–28.

TITLE: playing against the preceding title in all its words.
"the hat": likely a sombrero. Compare the sombreros and the square hats in "Six Significant Landscapes" vi, and see note; the headgear throughout Stevens's poetry is worth considering.

Notes toward a Supreme Fiction

Pub. Cummington, Mass.: Cummington Press, 1942; CP 380–408, LOA 329–52.

Stevens considered this powerful, rich, and often beautiful sequence to be "the most important thing" in *Transport to Summer* (L 538, 1946). Earlier he called it "the best thing I have ever done" (to Gilbert Montague, 12 Mar. 1943, New York Public Library; see acknowledgments)—a judgment made before most poems in *Transport to Summer* were written, and suggesting that this poem released a surge of creative energy. For the supreme fiction, see biography. (Beyond citations there, note also L 370, 378, 430–49 passim, 1940–43.) There are three notes, each heading a section of ten cantos: I. "It Must Be Abstract." II. "It Must Change." III. "It Must Give Pleasure." In the Cummington Press edition, each canto appears on a separate page, which gives it a proper weight, and that is how they should be read. Some entrancing cantos, like II.viii on Ozymandias and Nanzia Nunzio, are favorites; some remain partly puzzling; a very few are dry; and the epilogue garners mixed responses. But all in all, Stevens's judgment on the poem's significance is justified, and it continues to generate meaning, like all great poems. Lines of argument, tone, characters and types, intelligence of feeling, unexpected moves, echoes and allusions, sounds, comparisons among cantos: all, and more, are worth pondering.

TITLE: each word matters: "Notes," not "Doctrine" or "Summa"; "toward," not "of" or "on"; "a," not "the"; "Supreme Fiction," not "Supreme Being."

"And for what, except for you, do I feel love?": the addressee of this prefatory verse is unclear, and may be the supreme fiction itself. (Stevens says "for what," not "for whom.")

I *It Must Be Abstract*

TITLE: Note the grammatical construction of the three notes. On "must," cf. III.vii, and see Vendler ([1969], 17–18), and more widely, Hollander on poetic imperatives (*Melodious Guile* [1988], 64–84). The word "abstract" also needs thought. See, e.g., L 434 (comparing the "fictive abstract" in the poet's mind to "the idea of God" in the theologian's mind), 601–2, 607–8, 608, 767, 791 (1943–53). Compare also Keats, as in "abstract" from actual life: "This morning Poetry has conquered—I have relapsed into those abstractions which are my only life" (letter of Sept. 1818, *Letters*, ed. Rollins, I 370).

I.1

Stevens first gave this canto the title "Refacimento" (a remodeling of a literary work, here of supreme fictions), adding that the first stage in moving toward a supreme fiction would be "to get rid of all existing fictions" (L 431, 8 Dec. 1942). This strategy governs cantos I through v, which are also linked by the ephebe and by the mentor's didactic tone (it invites some thought).

"Begin": cf. other beginnings such as "In the beginning" or "Let there be light" (Gen. 1:1, 3), etc., including those that start with mentor and pupil (e.g., Dante and Virgil in the *Inferno*); the imperative gives an emphatic start. Linked by sound with the end word, "be," and thereby suggesting comparisons between acts of beginning and a state of being.

"ephebe": in ancient Athens, a beginning soldier and citizen, training for full participation in society; hence any beginner in training, here also a writer.

"perceiving . . . inconceivable": on the differences between perceptual and conceptual memory, see Oliver Sacks, *An Anthropologist on Mars* (1995), 174.

"You must become an ignorant man again": cf. "Adagia": "The poem reveals itself only to the ignorant man" (OP 187), "Ignorance is one of the sources of poetry" (OP 198, LOA 911), "One's ignorance is one's chief asset" (OP 202, LOA 914). Compare also "The Sense of the Sleight-of-Hand Man," and note the echo of Jesus to Nicodemus, "Ye must be born again" (John 3:7).

"Washed": see NA 62, LOA 682 (1943) on washing the imagination clean.

"The death of one god is the death of all. . . . Phoebus is dead": Phoebus
   Apollo, god of the sun among the Olympian gods; the final sentence of
   the syllogism is omitted, i.e., that all gods are dead, not simply the
   Olympians. The sun is used as symbol of Christ in Christian iconogra-
   phy, with a Son-Sun pun in English-language writing.
"autumn umber": the painter's umber, the color of harvest, and punning on
   Lat. *umbra* (shadow, shade) as shadow of the sun and shade or ghost of
   the dead; part of a pronounced humming ("um") sound in ll. 14–15.
"The sun / Must bear no name, gold flourisher": cf. "flourisher . . . ef-
   florisant" ("Montrachet-le-Jardin" 10–11). The mentor appears to dis-
   obey his own injunction (no name) in calling the sun by such an epithet.
   Is poetic naming allowed, but not religious naming? Is he encouraging
   disobedience? Is he showing that it is impossible to avoid naming? If we
   say "must bear no [necessary] name," the logic shifts.

I.II

"celestial ennui": cf. "Même le sublime ennuie" ("Even the sublime is bor-
   ing," Anatole France); not Baudelaire's deadly *ennui*.
"the first idea": moving on from the "idea / Of this invention" (I.I.1) to the
   "quick" of this invention and the idea of firstness (e.g., what or whom
   gave and gives life to this invented world, the role of the sun as in I.I,
   etc.); see note on "thinker of . . . ," I.VII; "the first idea" also appears in III
   to VIII (except for VI), moves to "the idea of man" in X, then vanishes
   from the sequence.
"apartments": dwelling places that are "apart" and "a part" (cf. Proust, "the
   apartment of sleep," V.430). See Stevens's amusing postcard about his
   apartment, which was across from a chapel. He and his wife are "not a
   part of the chapel," but rather "apart from it." Thus the word "apart-
   ment." He added that he hoped this was clear (SP 246, 1909). "Sacred"
   means "set apart," and "abstract" means "to draw . . . apart" (OED 2).
"prodigious scholar": the ephebe, here addressed in genial mock-ferocity.

I.III

The canto is built on radical reversal, which is also its subject. Poetry can ex-
ercise not only the pure, immaculate power of lines 1–12, but also the dark,
riddling power of lines 13–20.

"immaculate . . . candor": play on whiteness and purity through ll. 1–12, in
   an idealized world of poetry and a Coleridgean view of poetry.
"Arabian": the moon (L 433, 1943), perhaps by association with a crescent
   moon.

"his damned hoobla-hoobla-hoobla-how": a riddling chant, with a submerged pun on Coleridge's "Kubla Khan" (cf. "mythy goober khan," "Academic Discourse at Havana"; Coleridge appears in NA 3, LOA 643 [1942] and NA 41, LOA 667 [1943]).

"the unscrawled fores": Stevens identified this as the moonlight's "undecipherable vagueness" (L 433, 1943).

"wood-dove . . . ocean": the cooing of the wood-dove (once erotic) and howling of the ocean echo "hoo," elsewhere a derisory challenging sound (cf. "The Man with the Blue Guitar" x).

"relation": sometimes misread as "relations"; the singular includes the meaning of a "tale."

I.iv

In contrast to the Coleridgean terms of iii, Stevens now turns to Descartes, a prime foe for Coleridge. (On a poetic element in Descartes, see NA 55–56, LOA 677–78, 1943.)

"Descartes": on Descartes as a symbol of the reason, and on the reason as imposed by us on a place, see L 433 (1943). See also notes on "Winter Bells," above, and "Solitaire under the Oaks," below.

"Eve made air the mirror of herself": varying the topos of Eve gazing in the mirroring water at herself (*PL* IV.449–69), adapted from the story of Narcissus (Ovid, *Metamorphoses* III.407ff.).

"as in a glass": recalling St. Paul's well-known verse, "For now we see through a glass, darkly," more precisely, by means of a mirror (I Cor. 13:12), echoed elsewhere by Stevens.

"muddy centre . . . myth . . . articulate": Stevens allows priority to the earth before humans appeared, even positing a myth that appears to be articulate in nonhuman languages (as in I.v.1?). Neither Coleridge's imagination nor Descartes' reason takes precedence.

"sweeping meanings": also "sweeping" clouds away, "sweeping" the strings of the instruments.

I.v

"Reddens . . . red-colored noise . . . red": The lion is an old emblem of anger, and red its color. The violence without elicits a violence from within to match it (see NA 36, LOA 665, 1942), here an animal violence. The ephebe's violence is as yet "dumb violence" (l. 16).

"elephant": also a king of the beasts, like the lion and the huge cinnamon bear (ll. 8–9); all three offer tropes of voice.

"tanks": Stevens noted that in Ceylon a tank is a reservoir, and that some may have been ancient baths (L 434, 1943). He corresponded with Leonard C. van Geyzel, who lived in Ceylon, now Sri Lanka.

"sigil and ward": the ephebe is like "a being of the roofs," someone who keeps their secrets (ibid.); Stevens refers to looking across roofs from his rented room in 1904 (L 67–68).

I.vi

The outer world of early spring becomes a painting, and a painting seems to take on the actuality of an outer world ("colder for white"). Stevens exquisitely revises traditional religious language for spring's resuscitation. Note the shift in tone.

"Not to be realized": on how it is possible to recognize and understand something, without realizing it, see NA 6–7, LOA 645 (1942). Compare also a painter's realization as in Cézanne, *réalisation*. (See head-note to MBG, above) Stevens crosses the language of actual scene and painter's scene throughout this canto.

"Weather by Franz Hals": Hals did not paint landscapes; probably "weather" in Stevens's usual metaphorical sense of one's private "weather" in one's personal world; the world of Hals's portraits is often a cheerful Dutch world.

"yellow thins the Northern blue": in actuality and in painting, where blue should be added in contrast to yellow to depict daylight (see Richter in Gombrich, *Art and Illusion* [1969] 322).

"without a roof": i.e., out from the old structures of belief. Stevens's language in ll. 5–8 works to release earth and weather from old allegories and symbolism: "without / First fruits": first fruits are often a sacrificial offering, and cf. "the first fruits of them that slept" (I Cor. 15:20, used in Handel's *Messiah*); "the virginal of birds": punning on musical, procreative, and Virgin birth.

"the dark-blown ceinture loosened, not relinquished": the earth and sky as Venus, recalling tropes of earth as bound in winter, and statues of Venus loosening her garments or belt. Descriptively, early spring, e.g., clouds, streams.

"My house": one of a series of dwelling-places in the poem, troped as places of one's spirit.

I.vii

There are times of fulfillment without consciousness of the supreme fiction. Three sentences starting with "Perhaps" give three examples: a walk during which something is composed and coalesces; times when perfect balances simply happen, as when a man and a woman fall in love; extraordinary moments of mental awakening.

"a thinker of the first idea": seeing a painting after "the varnish and dirt of generations" has been cleaned off is seeing it "in its first idea." The same process applies to the world (L 426–27, 1942) and to one's family tree (L 499, 1945).

"composing": recalling Stevens's habit of composing when walking, and introducing acting rather than reacting into the series.

"cock crows . . . all is well": recalling the old night-watchman's cry, giving the time and saying "All's well."

"on the left": in older symbolism, the unlucky or sinful side (from Lat. *sinister*), but not here.

"Swiss perfection": with "balances" and "machine," and the echo of "cock," suggesting Swiss clocks and precision.

"Schwärmerei": (Ger.) "enthusiasm," sometimes fanatic enthusiasm (see Coleridge, *Biographia Literaria*, ed. Engell and Bate [1983], 30, note 4). With "Swiss perfection," introducing a touch of irony (smiling, surely) to temper line 16.

"academies": as structures of thought and belief.

I.VIII

Part I closes with three cantos focusing on the subject of "major man." Here, the long rhythmic sentence, lines 12–21, has marked assonance, internal rhyme, and anaphora, so that its appositive phrases and clauses repeat with cumulative effect, like the sea and the words it describes.

"castle-fortress-home": as, e.g., an older fortified castle; metaphorically a strong, substantial, defensible and true dwelling-place for one's spirit. The last of the structures in Part I.

"Viollet-le-Duc": 1814–1879, renowned restorer of ancient buildings and the village of Carcassone, exponent of Gothic revival, author of a multivolume work on architecture.

"the MacCullough": while MacCullough is "any name" and "any man" (L 434, 1943), Stevens confirmed that the name is derived from a Supreme Court Justice (L 448, 1943); "the" identifies someone as current head of a Scottish clan, here the clan MacCullough; note also Emerson, "The great man makes the great thing. Wherever Macdonald sits, there is the head of the table" ("The American Scholar" III, para. 14, LOA ed., 65–66)—or "lies" rather than sits, for the MacCullough.

"major man": Stevens said that his interest in major man and the hero had "nothing to do with the Biermensch," i.e., Nietzsche's work (L 409, 1942).

"Logos and logic," etc.: a remarkable stanza, demonstrating Stevens's wide command of language, including theological language. The logos ("reason," "word") is now most familiar from the Word (Logos) of John's Gospel, i.e., the Word of God incarnate in Christ. Pre-Christian use goes back to the pre-Socratic philosophers, and develops different emphases (see, e.g., EB, "logos"), including the logos as logic. Eliot used a quotation from Heraclitus on the logos as one epigraph for *Four Quartets* (1943).

"crystal hypothesis": unlike the usual troping of a hypothesis as cloudy and awaiting clarity or clear revelation.

"And every latent double in the word": generally the full richness of language, also recalling standard terms in the Christian typological reading of the Bible, where the Hebrew Scriptures become the Old Testament whose words are latent with what will be the patent revelation of the New Testament.

"Beau linguist": "beau" (Fr. "fine," "beautiful,") in a Stevensian combination and tone; see OED for suggestive earlier uses of "linguist."

I.ix

Stevens distances the origin of the major man from apotheosis (including romantic apotheosis), turning instead to revised annunciation and nativity language. The canto is framed by negatives, as Stevens moves toward major man in the abstract.

"invincible foils": "foil" in various senses, also recalling "shook foil," Hopkins's trope for the grandeur of God in his poem of that name.

"Swaddled": the loudest of several echoes from the Gospels, adapted to major man; from the Nativity, "swaddling clothes" (Luke 2:7, 12), and perhaps "Lighted at midnight" (cf. the Christmas carol, "It came upon a midnight clear"); "the good of April" evokes both the spring season and the Easter season; "cock-birds" possibly also recalls Peter's thrice-crowing cock.

"My dame, sing," etc.: the archaic diction also evokes older carols.

"accurate songs": Marianne Moore knew the force of Stevens's surprising adjective, referring to "the enchantment of accuracy" in his work (see appendix); see also the opening sentence of "Three Academic Pieces" (NA 71, LOA 686, 1947).

"Give him / No names": as against Christian doctrine, and cf. canto i.

"purest in the heart": cf. Stevens's moving injunction to his daughter about living "the good in your heart" (L 426, 1942).

I.x

This canto moves major man away from being an "exception" and back toward being "part . . . of the commonal." Stevens's supreme fiction must be able to speak to a community.

"The major abstraction," etc.: echoing the Islamic formulation, "There is one God, Allah, and Mohammed is his prophet," as Stevens widens his allusive framework.

"The major abstraction is the commonal," etc.: Stevens plays among senses of "abstract" in the nine preceding cantos.

"What rabbi," "What chieftain": two possible incarnations of a major man; cf. the rabbi elsewhere in Stevens, and also the chief of the clan, the MacCullough (VIII); the two figures are communal leaders, who interpret (one through study) and whose thinking leads to action (one indirectly).

"slouching pantaloons": re this Charlie Chaplin figure, cf. Stevens on the young poet as a god and the old poet as a tramp ("Adagia," OP 198, LOA 911); cf. also "The eye of a vagabond in metaphor" (II.x.13).

"ephebe": the last appearance of the ephebe, who presumably continues on his path toward full military training and also full citizenship, as in the speaker of III.x.

"confect": playing against "infected" (IX.17); verb obsolete, etymologically "to put together," including writing, as in *Index Aristophanes*, O. J. Todd, *confectus* (1932).

"final elegance": cf. Stevens's work with the word "elegance" in "Mrs. Alfred Uruguay."

"not to console / Nor sanctify": biblical diction, also echoed in Milton, Wordsworth, etc., again barred through negatives.

"propound": not only "to put forward for consideration," but also "to represent by figure or description" (obs.), "to imagine to oneself" (obs.), to put before the proper authority for legal validation (legal); "propounding" is also an old name for the rhetorical figure of prolepsis.

II *It Must Change*

Not about the gods or God or the first idea or major man like Part I, but concentrating more on the forms and tropes of dominant supreme fictions. These are tested, as are questions of change (repetition, randomness, constancy). Part I begins with ideas and ends on "propound," with doctrinal matters emphasized. Part II begins with sensation and desire, and ends with "propose" and "write" in a Theatre of Trope. Revisions are funnier in Part II than Part I.

TITLE: "Change": see *The Encyclopedia of Philosophy* ("change") for an analytical summary of the chief philosophical arguments.

II.I

"the old seraph": the first of a series of angels in the poem, evoking the seraph of the Christian Nativity, familiar from Christmas carols, illustrated over the centuries in "chronologies" (3), and now the same "old seraph." Here he seems to stray out of an illuminated manuscript and into the natural world.

"parcel-gilded": partly gilded rather than the customary pure gold.

"Inhaled the appointed odor": as in biblical "sweet odors," as in "the odor of sanctity" (Brewer, and note angels; also OED and Webster), as in odor from a ritual sacrifice in classical literature.

"doves / Rose like phantoms": playing on the Holy Ghost, traditionally represented as a dove.

"Italian girls wore jonquils": Italian girls as models for countless paintings of the Madonna, here seen in spring. Stevens again revises the iconography of the Annunciation and Nativity.

"bees came booming": as in I.I, a play on "to be"; cf. Dickinson, "The Bee be booming" (no. 1381).

"satyr in Saturn": the seraph, from the highest order of angels, the seraphim, who burn with ardent love for God, is here made subject to change. In a reign like Saturn's golden age, his heavenly love may change to earthly eros.

II.II

"President": unspecified, though capable of a divine fiat like "Let there be light"; cf. Hardy's President of the Immortals (*Tess of the D'Urbervilles*), and the president belonging in a heavenly Elysée ("Of Heaven Considered as a Tomb").

"the bee": extending the spring bees of II.I and the "be" wordplay of I.I; the bee in several contexts, including actual bee, punning bee ("be"), also bee as image of human life, as example of a doctrinal argument on immortality, as traditional example of the fruitful worker, as a trope for voice (with many older echoes), as comment on its own poem.

"drone": punning on the sound and the unproductive bee.

"a deep echo," etc.: including Gray's beetle who "wheels his droning flight" ("Elegy in a Country Churchyard") or Collins's beetle who "winds his small / But sullen horn" ("Ode to Evening"); these are among "the green phrases of its juvenal."

"adjust / The curtains to a metaphysical t": not drifting, as in "The Curtains in the House of the Metaphysician"; the banners outside cannot be so controlled.

"Spring vanishes the scraps," etc.: a rare transitive form of the verb, with a play on "vanquishes," for a trope of winter's last pockets of snow (like white scraps of cloth) finally going.

"Spring . . . memory's dream? . . . sleep?": as against Eliot's assumptions in *The Waste Land* (e.g., I.1–4) about spring, memory, sleep, returning and death, and any reading of nature's cycles as repetitious, wearisome, or ironic. See Stevens's comment in L 434 (1943).

II.iii

Centered on one of Stevens's memorable statues, emblem of our "more vestigial states of mind," and defined by a wicked pun.

"General . . . Place Du Puy": *puy* (Fr., dial. Auvergne, "hill, eminence"), now obsolete except in place names like Place Du Puy; a grammatical troping through a pun on Fr. *depuis* ("for, since"), which talks about things past but takes a present verb ("Depuis cinq ans, je suis . . ." [For five years, I am, i.e., have been . . .]); the trope embodies the theme of this canto.

II.iv

A Whitman-like canto, especially in its ending, on the fruitfulness of opposites that are interdependent, including human beings, natural phenomena, and the working of the imagination. Lexis, grammar, and tone are in Stevens's calm, affirmative, celebratory style, though without the force of some of his celebratory poems.

"copulars": adj. used as noun, perhaps for the *r* sound or to extend associations, e.g., "copulate."

II.v

A memorable poem of vocation, with actual and ideal lands seen as fruit and colors. Stevens liked this poem. He said it would not have been included if he had been trying to imitate Zeno or Plotinus (see L 435, 1943). It is a fine development of his Florida poems.

"sky-wide water," etc.: cf. "wide water" and other modulations of "Sunday Morning."

"the planter": Stevens called the planter "the laborious human who lives in il-
lusions." When the great illusions have gone, such a person "still clings to
one that pierces him" (ibid.); Stevens is observing that this happens, not
analyzing it; "pierces" is a strong word for him (cf. I.iii.21). The planter
thinks like both a planter and a painter, and, of course, a poet (all three
deal in color, including the colors of rhetoric).

"island beyond him": a legendary place of immense fruitfulness, an ideal and
challenge, with Stevens's weighted preposition "beyond."

"like / A mountain, a pineapple," etc.: as on the mysterious island in "Some-
one Puts a Pineapple Together" (1947).

"là-bas": (Fr.) "over there," "down there," often referring to an ideal place; cf.
"*la-bas*" as the South (L 386, 1941), "là-bas" as Stevens's garden (L 558,
1947), "là bas" as New York (L 692, 1950).

"great banana tree": a tree of life, differing from, e.g., Yggdrasil.

II.vi

Offering "the onomatopoeia of a summer afternoon" (L 435) in another of
Stevens's memorable bird poems; related to "It Must Change" insofar as
monotony—even of birdsong and its associations (especially as a trope
for poetic voice)—leads to a desire for change (see comment, L 437–38,
1943).

"Bethou me": Eng. equivalent of Fr. "*Tutoyez-moi*" or "Address me by *tu*,"
i.e., second-person singular rather than general plural *vous*; in formal Fr.
usage (not Fr.-Can.), *tu* is used among intimates, to servants, to God.
Also a punning allusion to Shelley's "Be Thou me" ("Ode to the West
Wind"). This bird not only knows Shelley, but also answers back by
speaking for Nature in a challenge to the writer; a "glade" (l. 6) is a tradi-
tional setting for song.

"said sparrow": Stevens took the idea from the call of a catbird (nasal, pene-
trating [L 435, 438, 1943]), not of a sparrow. Holly Stevens said that her
father taught her to whistle bird-calls when she was a youngster ("Bits of
Remembered Time," 652).

"crackled blade": cf. "Playing a crackled reed, wind-stopped, in bleats"
("Sombre Figuration," OP 97, omitted LOA 167, 1936; recalling Mil-
ton's *Lycidas* 124); the reed is a conventional pastoral wind instrument,
here modified into a blade of grass; the blade usually produces only a
piercing whistle—hardly encouraging for a pastoral poet; "he invites at-
tention from the summer grass," says Stevens (not saying what atten-
tion); it is also mocking the other birds (L 438, 1943).

"blow": Stevens's wily syntax and punning allows the blade to blow a sound
or to blow passively in the wind; his mixed feelings are very evident.

"coppice": a term used by the Stevens for a group of evergreens in their garden (ibid.); recalling also the coppice-gate where Hardy's memorable bird is heard, singing to different effect ("The Darkling Thrush").

"the bloody wren": Stevens knew that wrens are belligerent (L 435, 1943).

"Ké-ké": this sounds like a jay's cry, perhaps as it steals something, like a "felon."

"jug-throated robin pouring out": a wicked combination of puns: the robin is a substitute for the European nightingale (see "Autumn Refrain"), which conventionally sings "jug, jug." The song "pours out" in the standard trope. This bird surpasses Eliot's hermit thrush in *The Waste Land* V, who only sings "Drip drop," etc., while this member of the thrush family pours like a jug.

"minstrelsy . . . granite monotony": on the birds' minstrelsy that becomes monotony, see L 438 (1943).

"Glass-blower's destiny, bloodless episcopus": prototypes of a glass-blower's bottle and a bishop (ibid.); bishops elsewhere largely appear in unflattering light (e.g., "Connoisseur of Chaos"); possibly a sotto voce riposte against Eliot (Cook [1988], 241n.).

"It is / A sound like any other": Stevens, susceptible to birdsong, fought its seductiveness and its associations with both eros and heavenly hope; he called "Bethou" "the spirit's own seduction" (L 438, 1943).

II.vii

"we say": a formulation that encourages second thoughts about what we say; also in I.iii and II.i.

"any seducing hymn": as in the preceding canto (see final note).

"the scholar": cf. "Poetry is the scholar's art" ("Adagia," OP 193, LOA 906).

II.viii

A favorite canto where Stevens sends an angelic female emissary to seek Shelley's Ozymandias. The tone includes a touch of underappreciated humor in the solemnity of this ceremonious pair. Stevens described it as "an illustration of illusion as value" (L 431, 1942).

"Nanzia Nunzio": surname from Lat. *nuntius*, "messenger" (also the meaning of *angelus*, "angel"), whence a papal nuncio (ambassador), It. *nunzio*.

"Ozymandias": from Shelley's sonnet, "Ozymandias," with its huge, smashed, sneering statue bearing the inscription, " 'My name is Ozymandias, king of kings: / Look on my works, ye Mighty, and despair!' " Nanzia Nunzio desires him as an "inflexible / Order," her version of a supreme fiction.

"As I am, I am," etc.: the first "I am" in "Notes"; cf. the biblical echo in III.vIII, also "I am" in III.x; enjambment completes the sentence, for Nanzia Nunzio desires completion; her "I am" cannot stand on its own. Note that both Coleridge and Descartes (I.III and I.IV) memorably used "I am," Coleridge in echoing the biblical "I am" of God in the climactic ending of *Biographia Literaria*, and Descartes in the formulation "Cogito, ergo sum" ("I think, therefore I am").

"I am / The spouse," etc.: as in the Song of Solomon (the only use of "spouse" in the AV) and its allegorical fulfillment in Revelation with the marriage of the Spirit and the Bride. Nanzia Nunzio also resembles the Queen of Sheba, who seeks out Solomon (putative author of the Song of Solomon), for his wisdom. The high ceremonious tone here merges erotic and spiritual yearning.

"gold," "emerald or amethyst": all part of the bride who is the new Jerusalem (Rev. 21:9–21).

"opened her stone-studded belt," "nakedness," etc.: cf. the "ceinture loosened" of Aphrodite spring weather (I.vI), and classical veiled and unveiling women (Calypso, Isis).

"A fictive covering / Weaves always," etc.: working against tropes of naked truth, etc., for the bride of supreme fiction; cf. weaving elsewhere; a text is etymologically "woven"; the comment also glosses Ozymandias's own fiction in Shelley.

II.IX

In I.III, "the poem sends us"; but where does the poem itself live? This canto locates the poem as always between, not in or at. The poem is a field of force, not an inert mass. Stevens's language works whether the poem is being written or read. This intriguing canto is much under-read.

"gibberish" (ll. 1–2): a full range of meaning; the tone includes some irony.

"vulgate": the common tongue, "vulgar" in the etymological sense; also recalling Jerome's Vulgate, his great translation of the Christian Bible into Latin, the common language of the literate in his day.

"He tries," etc.: with this description of poetic language, cf. Eliot's in *Little Gidding* V ("And every phrase / And sentence that is right," etc.).

"the general": cf. l. 8, also "the commonal" (II.x) and "abstract" in the title to Part I.

"et jocundissima": (Lat.) "and most delightful," exuberantly completing Stevens's fine compounding by adding a superlative Latin adjective to the well-known phrase "lingua franca" (It.); *lingua* (tongue) comes from

Latin, so that Stevens "compound[s] the imagination's Latin" with literal Latin.

II.x

In Stevens's Theatre of Trope, seen from a park bench (he loved nearby Elizabeth Park in Hartford), some earlier cantos reappear briefly ("seraph" [I], "these beginnings" [II, singular], "wind" [VI]). From early staleness (cantos I–III), this canto has moved to a repeated "will to change," resulting in triple freshness (ll. 15–17). Compare with I.x, especially the endings.

"A bench . . ." etc.: "A bench as catalepsy is a place of trance" (L 435, 1943); not the first use of "catalepsy" in poetry: see Tennyson, *The Princess* I.20.

"Theatre / Of Trope": where tropes take on a life of their own and act out their dramas; cf. the world in which metaphors live in "The Motive for Metaphor"; note the effect of enjambment.

"artificial . . . like a page of music," etc.: raising questions of artifice: e.g., of a score, i.e., sign (the artifice of notation); of music itself (the artifice of composition and performance). Each simile engages with "artificial" and enhances the sense of trope.

"west wind": recalling the echo of Shelley in canto VI.

"the eye of a vagabond in metaphor / That catches our own": linking the pantalooned figure of I.x with the trope of metaphor, itself sometimes a vagabond (not a homebody, not proper, unpredictable, surprising). Stevens's metaphor itself captures the way we are sometimes captured by a metaphor, as if it looked out at us in a moment of mutual interest.

"casual": glossing Stevens's favorite phrase "for a moment" (and perhaps "casual flocks of pigeons" in "Sunday Morning"?); cf. "casual" later (e.g., "more than casual" in "Paisant Chronicle").

"rubbings of a glass in which we peer": revising Paul's well-known text, "For now we see through a glass, darkly, but then face to face" (I. Cor. 13:12); here the glass may be cleared by us, now.

III *It Must Give Pleasure*

TITLE: "Pleasure" may sound an odd requirement for a supreme fiction, though it is a biblical word, as are several forms of "please." "Joy" is the more familiar biblical word for us; the meaning of "pleasure" has been lowered. Stevens works with "joy" in III.i.4, moving through different kinds of pleasure to "enjoy" in III.ix and a quiet "Pleased" in III.x. On the associations of "pleasure," cf. "Complacencies," the opening word of "Sunday Morning." Too-easy pleasures turn banal like some "celestial ennui" (I.II), while debased pleasures turn ludicrous. Stevens fully meets the challenge of his subject in this richest of the three sections.

III.I

A startling canto in its strong evocation of joyful song and worship, which is suddenly dismissed as facile. Stevens himself might be facile if he ended there, but he goes on to consider the rare moments when we do have a sense of transcendence. What do we do with them? The one-line closing sentence is memorable.

"jubilas": (Lat.) "make a joyful noise," singular / not the usual plural *jubilate* (Ps. 99 [AV 100]:1, "Jubilate Deo," "Make a joyful noise unto the Lord"); as if continuing "the imagination's Latin" (II.IX); re "exult" (l. 3), note the common "jubilate-exsultate" pairing (Ps. 80:2).

"crested and wear the mane of a multitude": the multitude as a lion, also St. Jerome's animal in numerous paintings; Lat. *juba* means both "crest" and "mane."

"Jerome": St. Jerome "begat the tubas" by the act of translating the Bible into the Latin Vulgate (L 435, 1943); "jubilas" (l.1) was also begat by Jerome; the old association of Jubal and Tubal (Gen. 10:21–22) was also exploited by Joyce ("jubalent tubalence," "tubular jurbulence" (*Finnegans Wake* 338, 84).

"to catch from that / Irrational moment," etc.: cf. use of "catches" in II.x, and "irrational" in III.x; Stevens extends "to find" (ll. 11–12, cf. III.VII), moving from a divine to a human cause.

"heaven-haven": Hopkins's title "Heaven-Haven" appears in a remark in a critical review that Stevens recorded in SPBS 51 (1937).

"shaken": note also, in context, the rebounding echo of "Yet once more I shake not the earth only, but also heaven" (Hag. 2:6) through Heb. 12: 26–27 and Handel's *Messiah*.

III.II

A part that was difficult for Stevens to do, but lasted particularly well for him (L 463, 1944). He identified the blue woman, perhaps a little evasively, as "the weather of a Sunday morning early last April" (L 444, 1943). Stevens's lovely seasonal language is of both natural and erotic seasons; cf. the early spring of I.VI, and especially "To the One of Fictive Music." The blue woman sounds of an age with her creator.

"feathery argentines": specified later as flowers of the grape vine, bringing fruit with "ruddy pulses" in this troping of natural and sexual spring fervor, later cooled.

"foam," "foamy waves": the clouds in context evoke the birth of Venus, an evocation dismissed in ll. 12–13.

"enough . . . / remembered": see L 444 (1943) on memory, and how its intensity may be expressed "in terms of coldness and clearness"; cf. "cold" and "heat" throughout the series, also "cool."

"window": mentioned twice; cf. Whitman's woman at her window, full of secret erotic desire (*Song of Myself* 11 ["Twenty-eight young men"]). The functions of windows throughout Stevens's work are worth considering ("Domination of Black," OE, etc.), and worth comparing with functions of windows in painting, e.g., Dutch painting.

"named": always an important act for a poet; see note on III.x, below.

"corals of the dogwood": the flowers are pink and white; the stems of some dogwoods are a deep coral red.

III.iii

Like II.iii, centered on "vestigial states of mind," here of a primitive deity. Stevens's syncretism sits oddly with Judaism and Christianity in this attack on his old *bête noir*, a petrified religion. Note the opening sentence: fourteen lines and no verb.

"A lasting visage in a lasting bush": on the elementary idea of God as a face, see L 438 (1943).

"face of stone . . .": cf. Shelley's Ozymandias (note on II.viii, above); also Jesus' pun on Peter as a rock in Matt. 16:18 (see note to "Credences of Summer" vi, above), and the word "petrification"; any "graven image" of God is forbidden in Ex. 20:3.

"red": here the color of a dying, moribund past.

"dead shepherd": "an improvisation" (L 438, 1943); pastoral, a combination of Christ the good shepherd (harrowing of hell) and Orpheus (journey to hell); Christ was sometimes seen as "the divine Orpheus" (Curtius, *European Literature and the Latin Middle Ages* [1948, 1953], 244).

"carouse": cf. "A High-Toned Old Christian Woman," and the wine drunk later in Part III.

III.iv

Starting with the end of III.i, this canto reasons "with later reason" about heaven and earth, transforming the old metaphor of the marriage of heaven and earth. The time and date indicate a significant union. Catawba is the first named earthly setting, though the adjectives "Swiss" and "Cuban" have appeared.

"dependent on ourselves": not on a divine being; on Lat. *pendere* and Eng. "hang," see Barfield, *Poetic Diction* (1973) 176–81.

"mystic marriage": not the traditional Christian "mystic marriage," as in Andrea del Sarto's "The Mystic Marriage of Saint Catherine" (Gemäldegalerie, Dresden) where a human female is mystically married to Christ.

"Catawba": aboriginal name, said to mean "divided"; a region and river in North Carolina; as so often, Stevens exploits the possibilities of a placename.

"Bawda": metamorphosing "Catawba" into "Bawda"; cf. "our bawdiness" ("A High-Toned Old Christian Woman").

"the marriage wine": given a mystic marriage in a pointed time and place, evoking the marriage wine at Cana, converted from water in Christ's first miracle; familiar also as a favorite subject for paintings and evoked in marriage ceremonies.

"The shoo-shoo-shoo of secret cymbals round": a line packed with puns, import, and good sounds; "shoo-shoo-shoo": imitative of cymbals brushed, as in jazz, also "shoo" or "go away" to any "cymbal-symbols"; "round": "around," the shape of cymbals, also an important shape for most symbolism. More widely, see Hollander, *Vision and Resonance* (1975), 132–33.

"Each must the other take": echoing the vows of marriage, "I take thee," etc.

"ever-hill": compacting the history of troping the everlasting hills (Gen. 49:26) or hills ever called on (Ps. 121: 1–2, cf. L 173, 1912).

"love's characters come face to face": Stevens at last allows a union, completing his echoing of Paul from his famous chapter on love (I Cor. 13:12, and see II.x); "characters": also letters of the alphabet, coming "face to face" in a type face.

III.v

Stevens moves this canto closer to the actual world and his own poetic self, in preparation for the ending. Having rejected a biblical-Miltonic heritage when younger, albeit a much simplified one, Stevens returns to it. He now allows its full strength, testing it for what may be retained and how.

"Canon Aspirin": Stevens called the Canon a "figure" and "not a symbol," adding that his name is meant "to suggest the kind of person he is" (L 427, 1942). He elaborated in 1943 on Canon Aspirin as "the sophisticated man," by which he meant someone who has "explored all the projections of the mind," especially his own. Nonetheless, he does not acquire "a sufficing fiction," and returns to his sister and her children (L 445). The real puzzle is how this man became a canon at all (ibid.). Compare the "candid-canon" association with the canonical in "From the Journal of Crispin" (OP 57, LOA 993), and also "candid" in I.III. Stevens found aspiration attractive when young (SP 220, 221, 1909, quoting Browning's "Rabbi ben Ezra" on "What I aspired to be," also paraphrased in OP 289, LOA 878, 1955); he re-examined it in 1943 (NA 49–50, LOA 673–74), as also here in 1942, where it is troped as a medication.

"sensible ecstasy": the sister in contrast does not explore things (see L 445, 1943).

"two daughters," etc.: the ages of the sister's daughters suggest seasons and weeks, i.e., the natural world.

"pauvred": "made poor," a neologism from Fr. *pauvre* (adj., poor) and cf. Fr. *s'appauvrir* (to become impoverished).

"rejecting dreams": cf. "The Comedian as the Letter C" IV.92–97, on Crispin rejecting dreams when in his realist phase; the sister makes a realistic complement to her brother.

III.VI

The second Canon Aspirin canto, partly a Miltonic pastiche, allows full strength to the Canon's mind and imagination—a mind that conceives a universal harmony.

"nothingness": rejecting dreams finally gives the Canon "a sense of nothingess, of nakedness, of the finality and limitation of fact" (L 445, 1943).

"learning . . . illuminations": the Canon finds it impossible to live as his sister does, by rejecting dreams; he returns to "night's pale illuminations" (ibid.), i.e., mental illuminations, as of moon and stars (associated with imagination), also recalling illuminated manuscripts.

"eye . . . ear": the Canon creates a world within his head, then enters it, "So that he was," etc.; the sphere of the eyeball contains and becomes the sphere of the earth with the vault of heaven; repeated enjambment reverses our sense of up/down, above/beneath.

"ascending . . . Descending . . . bed": the movement is Miltonic; in the end, the Canon comes back to the bed where the children sleep "with every sense of human dependence" (ibid.).

"Forth then . . . he flew": Miltonic in syntax and lexis; "pathetic," as in "pathos"; see ibid. on the Canon's supreme effort to elude human pathos.

"The nothingness," etc.: repeating l. 3, so that the Canon arrives at another nothingness. In the end, "human pathos [and] human dependence" are not eluded, being "part of thought and of imagination" (ibid., and cf. "Esthétique du Mal" XII). It was not, after all, "a choice // Between, but of."

III.vii

The third Canon Aspirin canto begins to distance the poem from even the learned, aspiring, and respected Canon. It ends powerfully, with Stevens's sine qua non, "the fiction of an absolute," and his capital-A angel, now addressed directly.

"imposes orders": cf. Stevens's earlier examination of different orders, in *Ideas of Order*, etc.

"capitols," etc.: in the Canon's mental world, the buildings of a civil society begin to take shape.

"erudite // Of elephants": presumably because of their proverbial memory.

"To discover . . . to find, / Not to impose": cf. Stevens's criticism of surrealism because it invented "without discovering" ("Adagia," OP 203, LOA 919).

"It is possible . . . must / Be possible": demanding lines, despite their apparent simplicity; they raise questions of, e.g., tone and what logic is in play.

"disgorged": the throat also provides the writer's voice (cf. "The Man Whose Pharynx Was Bad").

"Angel, / Be silent": reversing the usual hierarchy, where the angel speaks a divine message; emphasized by enjambment.

"luminous cloud": repeating the adjective raises the volume of the phrase, as also in the echo from Coleridge ("Dejection: An Ode," 54, 62, 71).

III.viii

Gathering up earlier cantos (esp. I.iii), this one reconfigures the language of direction, of angels, of belief and satisfaction. It focuses on an angel whose downward leap takes us with him in utter satisfaction, until the unexpected ending draws us up short. All the sentences are interrogative, though one modulates through its clauses into an indicative with no question mark. Stevens now moves from "we" to "I," and retains the "I" of a poetic persona until the end.

"What am I to believe?": note the form of the question (not, e.g., "What do I believe?").

"Serenely gazing": given the strong evocation of Milton's *PL*, suggesting a projection of Milton himself into his own creation; Milton's type of blindness was *gutta serena* (cf. "drop serene" in *PL* III.25); also echoed by Wordsworth ("mind serene . . . blind" in "Elegiac Stanzas [on] Peele Castle"); all three play on the usual meaning of "serene" ("cheerful," *PL* III. 46).

"violent": "violet" in the Cummington Press ed. (1942, 1943).

"Leaps downward": Satan falls from heaven when expelled, like Vulcan (or Mulciber), but a revised Satan is not helpful here. A Milton who projects himself into his own creation is more likely, especially given archaic "spredden." Coleridge wrote that the "sublimest parts" of *Paradise Lost* are the "revelations of Milton's own mind, producing itself and evolving its own greatness" (*Lectures 1808–1819: On Literature, Collected Works* II, ed. Foakes [1987], 428).

"spredden": "obsolete word for 'outspread' " (Stevens's note to his secretary in the margin of the manuscript, Houghton Library fMS Am 1333; see acknowledgments).

"Am I that imagine this angel less satisfied?": readers, like the creator, can project themselves into an imaginative world, in a "willing suspension of disbelief for the moment" (Coleridge, *Biographia Literaria*, chap. 14); the angel does not land, but remains suspended; see note on "satisfied" in "The Well Dressed Man with a Beard," above.

"expressible bliss": not "imperishable bliss" ("Sunday Morning"), not "accessible bliss" (II.vii), but in context echoing Wordsworth's "highest bliss," thus evoking the final book of "The Prelude" (1850, XIV.113, and see 63–129). Stevens hears Milton as modified by Wordsworth, then modifies both. The move in diction ("majestic," "abyss," "angels," etc.) is a descent in time, as the angel descends through some of the great writing on "supreme fiction."

"an hour . . . , a day, / . . . a month, a year": moving apocalyptic time to a sequence of earthly time in an echo from the Book of Revelation concerning angels ("an hour, and a day, and a month, and a year," Rev. 9:15).

"I have not . . . I am": after II.vii, now claiming and revising God's "I am that I am" (Ex. 3:14).

"Cinderella fulfilling herself ": a sharp descent; cf. Stevens's early quotation from Browning on aspiration (see note on Canon Aspirin, III.v), where he immediately adds "pumpkin-coach" in a similar descent. The connection with "majesty" is Cinderella's fairy-tale wedding to the prince. As if wary of "the spirit's own seduction" (see note to "It is / A sound like any other" at II.vi), even in great writing on his subject—or all the more, because of it—Stevens's persona breaks the angelic experience immediately after his self-affirmation. The move is from myth to legend, majesty and bliss to death, though of course fairy-tales may be read in more than one way.

III.ix

Again gathering up earlier cantos, and extending them, this canto turns to the earth in ordinary circumstances. Birdsong does not challenge or mock as in II.vi, but provides a different model; the speaker surpasses angels in being also human; wine (cf. III.iv, v) can exemplify a "final good"; "enjoy" (repeated) glosses "joy" in III.1 and modulates into the title word "pleasure," now finally emerging. The opening stanzas move from vIII's interrogative mood to the imperative. The concluding sentence is one of Stevens's richest.

"too weedy wren": a feeble wren? In any case, a bit hard to pronounce, issuing in "reedy wren" (cf. II.vI).

"wren," "robin": whistling, no longer in an "idiot minstrelsy" (II.vI), though modified by "forced" (a somewhat puzzling word: perhaps forced by mating instinct?).

"angels": human shapes with bird-wings, hence the connection with both birds and humans.

"Mere repetitions": Stevens's work with "repetition" appears to begin with its reductive sense, and readers will protest over robin song. (Or is "whistle" the cry, not the song? Are the "preludes" to mating or to song or to both?). He at once moves to "vast repetitions final," etc.

"wine . . . a table in a wood": domestic, yet also a human ritual (cf. "A Primitive Like an Orb" III); reverberating against, e.g., Ps. 78:19 (a text aptly recalled by Robinson Crusoe, chap. 4), also Ps. 78:25 ("angels' food").

"leaf . . . spins": ambiguous as to whether the spinning leaf is still attached or not; until l.18, ambiguous whether we also enjoy like the leaf, ourselves spinning; cf. earlier troping of the topos of falling leaves in, e.g., the "turning" of "Domination of Black."

"he that of repetition is most master": "repetition" in the widest sense (of days and seasons and years, of the routine of work, of human generation, of memory, of works of art that both repeat and revise [see Elizabeth Bishop, "North Haven"], etc.). Context is all in any given discussion of repetition. Note also Kierkegaard's concept of repetition as religious (*Repetition*, cited in Frye, *Anatomy of Criticism* [1957], 345). Marianne Moore praised Stevens for his command of "reiteration," "that pitfall of half-poets" (*Complete Prose* [1987], 97).

III.x

A remarkable ending, with the pleasure of a supreme fiction now fully of this earth, in the richest sense. Stevens sets the canto in an earthly city that also embodies a possible New Jerusalem (cf. II.vIII), revising Revelation, the last book of the Bible, just as I.1 revises Genesis.

"Fat girl": the earth in its plenitude (L 426, 1942, and see note on "fat" in "Credences of Summer" x, above), troped as a beloved constant companion, less a muse than a poetic spouse.

"find you in difference," etc.: a quiet "find" that still startles after "find" in III.vII; "difference" invites the question: from what? One answer leads toward the power of trope to capture reality.

"aberration": cf. Stevens's work with "eccentric"; a trope is "familiar yet an aberration."

"Civil, madam, I am": courtesy balances sensation, while the sense of a citizen (Lat. *civis*) is also at work, given this word order. *Civis Romanus sum* ("I am a Roman citizen") is a familiar phrase (Bartlett). The ephebe has attained citizenship, while the rhyme evokes the palindrome "Madam I'm Adam," an appropriate echo for a poet that names (like Adam) and belongs in a New Jerusalem (like the second Adam). This is the final "I am" of the poem.

"underneath / A tree": see L 444 (1943) for Stevens's sense of this phrase; he calls it the opposite of "a moving contour"; cf. the contraries in "The Motive for Metaphor."

"figure": both the earth personified as a woman, variously occupied, knowing different emotions, and a rhetorical figure or trope, also variously occupied, etc.

"irrational": modified into "more than rational," i.e., beyond the scope of the rational.

"the Sorbonne": traditional name of the University of Paris, properly the name of the original College founded c. 1257; Stevens's idealized Paris is a possible earthly New Jerusalem.

"gildered": echoing against "parcel-gilded" (II.i), with a doubled sense of "gild" that stresses human agency (as in, say, "buildered" houses), thereby tempering a memory of New Jerusalem's streets of gold (Rev. 21:21).

"call you by name": the act of naming is always crucial for a poet; note injunctions against naming or the lack of names in Part I (i, vi, ix) and the move to naming in Part III (ii, v, x); note also how "I am" and "it is" (I.i) now issue in "you are," as in a personal or poetic act.

"fluent mundo": flowing, as with water and as with speech; (Sp. from Lat. *mundus*) "world."

"You will have stopped revolving except in crystal": "crystal" has both fluid and solid connotations; crystalline waters move and mirror, and are often a trope for voice; solid crystals may resemble globes, tiny or huge, as in the crystalline sphere that encloses our world in the old cosmology; in nature, crystals grow, thereby figuring a poem's growth in the reader's mind; see also Curtius, *European Literature and the Latin Middle Ages* (1948, 1953), 390. Like the "fluent mundo," the poem is both still and moving, as Stevens enfolds it and hands it to the reader.

Epilogue

Balancing "peace" at the end of the prefatory poem, the epilogue is addressed to a soldier, reminding us that this is a war-time poem. The Cummington edition also reminded readers by printing the epilogue on the rear outside dust-jacket. The epilogue is controversial because of Stevens's parallel of

World War II with "a war between the mind / And sky," i.e., one that he fights. The objection is understandable, but illogical, especially as wars are rooted in beliefs expressed in words. Metaphors of battle are commonly used of mental fights (Eph. 6:10–18; Blake, preface to *Milton*). Perhaps the objection is not so much to Stevens's kind of war, as the fact that his life was not endangered by it (as, say, St. Paul's was). The most telling objection remains James Merrill's (see note to "How gladly . . .", below).

"Patches . . . together": tactile form of "compose" (Fr. *composer, com-*, "together," and *poser*, "to place"); cf. "patch" in MBG II and "piece . . . together" in "Parochial Theme."

"Virgilian cadences," etc.: Virgil is a constant figure in Stevens; see SP 157 (1906), "For an Old Woman in a Wig" (OP 18, LOA 530, 1915–16?), "From the Journal of Crispin" (OP 49, LOA 987), "A Thought Revolved" II, "Paisant Chronicle"; NA 23, LOA 656 (1942), NA 159, and LOA 740 (1951); he is quoted at NA 116–17, LOA 713–14 (1948), OP 255, and LOA 837 (1951).

"How gladly with proper words the soldier dies": perhaps. Merrill adds, "Or kills" (*Late Settings* [1985] 26).

The Auroras of Autumn

The Auroras of Autumn, published in September 1950, was Stevens's last collection before his 1954 *Collected Poems*. It gathers thirty-two poems written from 1947 to 1950. Stevens shifted the chronological order a little, so that his arrangement is worth pondering. Both individual poems and parts of poetic sequences start on separate pages, a layout that influences our reading.

The collection has a certain unity, as we might expect from a title that belongs to both the opening poem and the entire collection. A number of poems speak to each other through shared subjects or rhetoric or diction. Some of the poems have a valedictory tone, especially those working with scenes and names from Stevens's youth. The framing poems at the beginning and end reread the heavens in very different ways. The closing poem, "Angel Surrounded by Paysans," provides a memorable leave-taking like some swift and passing, yet powerful, benediction.

The Auroras of Autumn

Kenyon Review 10 (winter 1948); CP 411–21, LOA 355–63.

Stevens had in mind the nights of early autumn, when the aurora borealis is visible most often in temperate latitudes (L 698, 1950). He later noted the occasional strength of the northern lights in Hartford, adding that they "symbolize a tragic and desolate background" in this poem (L 852, 1954). The tragic and desolate life of the immediate postwar years for many people around the world cannot help but inform such a background. A sense of apocalypse (or "post apocalypse") informs the sequence, on which see Woodland, *Wallace Stevens and the Apocalyptic Mode* (2005). Stevens's work with the apocalyptic culminated in OE.

Scientific research into the auroras was very active during Stevens's lifetime. (See Harald Falck-Ytter, *Aurora* [1999, 1983].) Until the last canto, the aurora permeates the poem (though more obliquely in II–V), notably through the language used by scientists and others to describe it ("arcs, bands, curtains, veils, drapery, rays, and clouds" [*Aurora* 15]). The northern lights are unpredictable in time and duration and movement. Movements of argument, rhetoric, and images in the poem both describe and resemble the aurora's incessantly flickering light, irregular leaping and collapsing, and differing velocity. Stevens retained his favorite stanzaic and metrical form for long sequences, unrhymed iambic pentameter tercets. One of the best glosses is Dickinson's poem, "Of Bronze — and Blaze — / The North — Tonight — " (no. 290); see also note on VII on Ezekiel's vision, below.

I

"This": unspecified, like the bodiless serpent, and so extending the immediate context, where "this" is the night sky with the northern lights in "ribbon-like serpentine forms showing numerous sinuosities" (EB 11). "A fierce serpent writhed itself up over the sky . . . split into three . . . reached and passed the zenith" (Nansen, cited in Falck-Ytter, 10). The constellation Serpens (the Serpent) appears in the northern sky late in the year.

"Eyes open": cf. Dante's trope of the stars as eyes watching the earth.

"image at the end of the cave": finely ambiguous, and so the darkest end of a cave or else the door out; recalling Plato's cave as well as the human skull; cf. "The palm at the end of the mind" ("Of Mere Being").

"a pole": as of the earth's two magnetic poles, on which the northern and southern auroras are centered; cf. also the sky's apparent pole with polestar, and the zenith or pole of an auroral display.

"master of the maze" a serpent of mythic potency, as in many legends— Norse, Amerindian, etc.

"meditations in the ferns": the ordinary snake as earthly form of the mythic serpent, desiring the sun, as we do.

"in his head": in the appearance of his head; also as if from within his head, which perceives scenes of primitive North American life, thereby evoking centuries of history.

II

Cantos II, III, and IV open with "Farewell to an idea," followed by an ellipsis that requires a long pause. Canto III centers on a mother figure, canto IV on a father figure, and both figures extend into canto V. With the farewell, especially in III and IV, cf. Stevens's early declaration of independence: "I never felt free, or strong, until I had cried 'Farewell to my elders!' and their beastly ideas" (10 June 1910, WAS 1912).

"idea": as in "the idea of man" (NSF I.x), etc., the meaning is wider than an intellectual concept. The relation of the idea to what follows is oblique, unlike the later ideas of mother and father. But the sense of a "farewell" leave-taking is not.

"cabin": one of Stevens's literal and/or metaphorical dwelling-places, context unspecified; the following poem quotes Yeats on his desired "cabin," itself indebted to Thoreau's cabin in *Walden*.

"white": as in cabin and flowers seen late into the evening, as in advanced old age, as in the pallor of death and the abandonment of the body as dwelling-place. See L 172 (1912), on Stevens's mother's last illness, including her "much whiter" appearance. The northern lights are commonly white in temperate zones. More generally, see Melville's tour de force, "The Whiteness of the Whale" (*Moby-Dick*, chap. 42).

"blankly": at a loss, also evoking other powerful uses of "blank," e.g., in Milton ("a universal blank," with respect to his blindness, from the invocation to light, *PL* III.48) and Coleridge ("with how blank an eye," "Dejection: An Ode"). Note, among other uses, "blank" in "The Plain Sense of Things," and in contrast, "Mr. Blank" (OE XXXI).

"extremist in an exercise": as if imitating the flickering of the northern lights and their movement up through the extreme outermost of the earth's atmosphere, the ionosphere.

"blue-red . . . green": possible colors of the aurora.

III

The canto is suffused with memories of the last days of Stevens's mother (see L 172–74, 25 June–1 July 1912).

"dreams.": LOA correctly provides a full stop here.

"transparence . . . peace": cf. the dedicatory poem to NSF, line 8.

"She makes that gentler that can gentle be": including even death; in 1912, Stevens misquoted Whitman on " 'gentle, delicate Death,' " repeating the word "gently" (L 174, 1 July 1912); for "delicate death," see "When Lilacs Last in the Dooryard Bloom'd."

"she too is dissolved," etc.: in the dissolving of memory, in the dissolution of the body, both like the dissolving of the aurora's lines and shapes and colors.

"The necklace is a carving not a kiss": punning gently and sadly on an embrace as a neck-lace, whose living memory has now gone.

"The windows will be lighted, not the rooms": because the light comes from the outside only, say, from the aurora, whose rapid movements and color suggest the dissolution of house and books (l. 14).

IV

"of bleak regard": cf. "Adam of beau regard" ("The Pure Good of Theory" III).

"strong in the bushes of his eyes": curiously combining a sense of bushy eyebrows and a memory of the burning bush whence God speaks his "I am that I am" in Ex. 3:1–14.

"bad angels": traditionally, the fallen angels, as in *PL* I.

"supernatural preludes . . . angelic eye": cf. NSF III.vii.

V

"The mother invites," "The father fetches": where and whom? The context presents a challenge for the reader, though the general plot is clear enough. Stevens offers no reason for the deterioration. The canto opens with an attempt to answer the question at the end of iv, as an apparent Prospero-like father calls forth festive hospitality. The father figure then worsens, as if falling through history into present decline. Compare the angel's fall through time in NSF III. viii.

"musicians who mute much, muse much, on the tales": playing on "muse-music," the double sense of "muse," and several senses of "mute," including the physical device that alters volume and tone color in a musical instrument.

"tinny time": extending "tones" into an expected "tinny tunes," thereby playing "time" against "tune."

"pageants . . . curtains": as elsewhere in the canto, informed by the aurora, e.g., its "curtain" effect.

"herds": the "brute-like guests" below, recalling Caliban or Circe's victims.

"Chatillon": Stevens called his possible ancestor, Gaspard de Châtillon, grandson of Coligny, "one of the great Protestant figures of his time" (letter to Paule Vidal, 21 May 1945, WAS 2887). This may be the current form of the Reformation leader, naturalized, as indicated by the omission of the accent.

"hospitaliers": Fr., cf. English "hospitallers," also "hospitable." As with "Châtillon," a sense of admirable origins and present decline.

VI

Cantos vi and vii return to the auroras themselves, with two strong and different ways of reading the heavens.

"It": the aurora borealis, in the first instance; "sometimes [a display bears] very close resemblance to illuminated detached clouds" (EB, "Aurora Polaris").

"Wild wedges": birds, as in Milton's birds who "in figure wedge their way . . . Flying" (*PL* VII.425–8) or in Joseph Brodsky, "Variation in 'V.'"

"as of a volcano's smoke": cf. the description of the aurora in Seneca (quoted

Aurora 46–47), and in a thirteenth-century Norwegian saga (ibid. 51–52, note "smoke").

"palm-eyed": a puzzling epithet.

"A capitol": the sequence suggests that the birds are connected with emerging and collapsing capitols (hence empires), perhaps by augury.

"nameless . . . destroyed": cf. NSF I.i where the sun is "washed" and "must bear no name."

"frame": both one's body and the earth, as in Hamlet's "this goodly frame, the earth" (*Hamlet* II.ii.298).

"he feels afraid": cf. "I felt afraid" ("Domination of Black") and "a fear one feels / In the great vistas of night air" ("Note on Moonlight").

VII

"the just and the unjust": an allusion to Matt. 5:45, thereby to God the Father in heaven, and questions of justice versus mercy ("As grim as it is benevolent," l. 2).

"in the north and enfold itself . . . crystalled": a likely echo of Ezekiel's famous vision (Ezek. 1:4, 1:26), sometimes thought to have been inspired by a rare massive auroral display.

"Goat-leaper": Aristotle called some forms of the aurora "dancing goats" or "jumping goats" in his *Meteorologia*; cf. also the constellation Capricorn, literally "goat-horn."

"heavens adorn / And proclaim it": an allusion to Ps. 19:1, revised; Stevens quoted Ps. 19:2 in 1906 (L 86).

"crown": a full auroral display has a dark crown at the zenith.

"leaps": increasingly, the canto of the goat, moving against the biblical use of sheep and goats (the latter often condemned), and against any figure like the Lamb upon the throne (cf. "enthroned").

"dare not leap by chance": a move past any simple dichotomy of biblical and antibiblical.

"caprice": cf. "goat-leaper" and Capricorn, above; the aurora is regularly described as capricious.

"tragedy": etymon *tragos*, "goat-song," though this is disputed.

"flippant communication under the moon": cf. NSF I.iii.

VIII

Cantos VIII and IX, linked by a run-on sentence, move to reflections on Stevens's theme of the essential innocence of the earth. (Cf. "Esthétique du Mal" x.) The affirmation works against any concept of an earth that fell with mankind from some blissful prelapsarian state.

"never a place": as in Eden or a Golden Age.

"A saying out of a cloud": as in biblical phrasing, e.g., "he [God] called unto Moses out of the midst of the cloud" (Ex. 24:16) and "a voice came out of the cloud" (Mark 9:7, in the Transfiguration scene).

"symbol of malice": cf. "leaven of malice" in I Cor. 5:8 and the Prayer Book of the Church of England; see also note on "malice" in "Credences of Summer" x, above.

"accordion": suggesting harmony through its etymology (cf. "accord," "chord," etc.).

IX

"the enigma of the guilty dream": "of" in two senses, so that the dream may contain the enigma, or the dream itself may be the enigma. Stevens keeps the context of "guilty" general, having affirmed the inherent innocence of the earth in human fate.

"Danes in Denmark": northerners familiar with the northern lights; note also the convivial party of Danes in Coleridge's recollection (cited NA 40–41, LOA 667, 1943).

"knew each other well, hale-hearted landsmen": this group, this "we," must be surmised through context. Stevens wrote in 1949 about always being "desperately in need of the fellowship of one's own kind." He then added that the need was not for intellectual companionship, but what he called "the fellowship of one's own province . . . of the landsman and compatriot" (L 644, 1949). He was expressing his regret at not knowing the poet Theodore Spencer better.

"hanging in the trees next spring?": with "disaster," suggesting a double meaning to hanging, and breaking sharply with what precedes; in context, "disaster" takes its common etymological meaning of influence from the stars (Lat., *astrum*, star), recalling obsolete "disaster" as a "baleful aspect of a planet or star" (Webster).

"glittering belts": suggesting the constellation of Orion, seen in Stevens's latitude in the winter.

X

A change in focus and in tone separates this canto from the preceding nine. Stevens confirmed John Crowe Ransom's observation of the lacuna between IX and X (letter to H. Weinstock, WAS 3357, 21 Sept. 1954). There are, in effect, two endings to "The Auroras of Autumn," the endings of canto IX and of canto X. Canto X offers a much louder, sometimes funny, ending, with a fortissimo flourish in the last stanza. The tone includes a sense of long-meditated wisdom (through the rabbi figure), devoid of any solemnity. It also includes great pleasure in the moment of these words and an implicit defiance of winter and death.

"hall harridan,"etc.: raising the *h* sound, as if reverting to Anglo-Saxon in this stanza, where most nouns and adjectives have a Germanic origin appropriate to the northern focus of the poem; the prepositions in this stanza bear watching.

"in winter's nick": "nick" takes its full spectrum of meaning; note also the idiom, "in the nick of time."

Page from a Tale

Wake 6 (spring 1948); CP 421–23, LOA 363–65.

A narrative account, as from the tale of a ship caught in ice. Like "Auroras," this poem is focused on the north, but here the far north, hence a difficult climate for human habitation, and often fantastic to non-natives. The poem is linked to both the end of "The Auroras of Autumn" and the next poem by the act of reading; with "Auroras," cf. also the cabin. The poem is a contrast in many ways with the opening sequence, allowing for some relaxation of tone despite the story.

"Balayne": obsolete form of "baleen" ("whale," cf. Fr. *baleine*); as ship, possibly the *Baelana* in 1947 when the frozen North Sea trapped ships (Shoenberg, *WSJ* 6 [1982]: 43–45).

"*blau*": blue, azure; "*lind*": soft, gentle, mild; "*lau*": mild (of weather). Fragments of a poem by Heine: "Die Welt is so schön und der Himmel *so blau*, / Und die Lüste die wehen *so lind und so lau* . . ." ("Lyrisches Intermezzo" XXXI, "The world is so beautiful and the heaven *so blue*, / And the breeze that blows *so soft and so mild*"). The poem refers to a dead love at the end. Note the memory of "W. G. P." sitting "with his lamp translating Heine aloud endlessly" (L 65, 1903), during Stevens's wilderness trip in Canada, the farthest north that he ever traveled.

"*Of clay*," etc.: all the Eng. italicized words are from Yeats's famous early poem, "The Lake Isle of Innisfree"; there, in London, he longs for a cabin in his home county in Ireland (pub. 1890, collected 1893, quoted L 120, 1909).

"It might become a wheel": Hans's waking dream of the returning sun in the far north, shared by the men (ghosts?) on the trapped ship. As in parts of "Auroras," the effect of an implacably hostile universe.

"Arcturus": orange-colored, first-magnitude star in the constellation Boötes, appearing above the horizon in the far north as the winter solstice

(Dec. 21) approaches, and remaining visible until August. If the "hard brightness" of line 1 is literal, the sun has reappeared; hence it is January or February, depending on the latitude.

"miff-maff-muff of water": "miff-muff" (OED, dial. or colloq.) means "peevish ill humor"; does the sound of stirring water in Stevens's imitative invention suggest it is miffed? Compare lines 29–30 on water striving to speak and breaking dialect. Here the water appropriately follows the conjugation of Germanic strong verbs (e.g., "ring, rang, rung"); cf. the play on "tink, tank, tunk" in "A High-Toned Old Christian Woman" and on latinate "Pipperoo," etc. in "On an Old Horn."

Large Red Man Reading

Halcyon 1 (spring 1948), with "This Solitude of Cataracts," both under the title, "Two Poems"; CP 423–24, LOA 365.

Three short opening sentences expand into one 10-line sentence, as the ghosts become blooded (and so more like the red man); the grammatical mood shifts from conditional to indicative. Compare the shades revivified by animal blood in *Odyssey* XI. The central trope also embodies the way that "literal characters" (l.12) or letters on the page become animated and take on feeling. The tercets have unusually long lines with much-varied rhythm. This is a powerful poem, mentioned as one that Stevens liked (L 778, 1953).

TITLE: re "Red Man," note also that one Hebrew root for "Adam" means "to be red." "tabulae": (Lat.) ancient writing tablets, perhaps familiar through "tabula rasa."

"purple tabulae": the "blue tabulae" (l. 2) have taken on enough red to alter their color.

"*Poesis*": (Gk) "a making, creation, poetry."

This Solitude of Cataracts

Ibid.; CP 424–25, LOA 366.

The first of several poems where Stevens's imagination is running on past and present images of death and of being, including water: e.g., biblical cataracts, the river of Heraclitus, the ocean of Hesiod, and actual rivers and mountains. Compare also Valéry's "Le Cimetière marin."

"Solitude": cf. Stevens's other solitude poems, though this one differs from most by imagining a desire for a center.

"Cataracts": apparently in the poem's river, though never mentioned. Figuratively connected with later recollection by its echo of Wordsworth's memory of the "cataract" that "haunted" his youth ("Lines Composed . . . above Tintern Abbey" 76); as trope, suggesting a turbulence of feeling; the archaic meaning of "the floodgates of heaven" (*PL* XI.824) connects it with the poem's ending.

"He never felt twice the same about . . . river": playing on the textbook example of the pre-Socratic philosopher, Heraclitus, "You never step twice into the same river," i.e., the world is governed by perpetual flux.

"thought-like Monadnocks": see L 823 (1954) on the effects of a mountain reflected in a lake, in particular, this mountain.

"an apostrophe that was not spoken": an apostrophe as the sign showing the omission of a letter (cat's) is not spoken, though understood; so here, with "apostrophe" as a sudden exclamatory address to a person or thing.

"buttonwoods": the American plane-tree; cf. Milton's platan in Eden (*PL* IV. 478).

"released from destruction": not completely subject to mortality.

"archaic lapis": a blue heaven, as in an old cosmography and theology; "lapis," used of light and sky, re-enters Stevens's work with NSF III.viii; cf. "Someone Puts a Pineapple Together" III, and OE xxvi.

"the oscillations of planetary pass-pass": the way in which the planets seem to go round and round by night and by day (L 823, 1954); playing on Fr. *passe-passe* ("sleight-of-hand"), and also the passing of time.

"azury": on the word "lapis," above, note that "azure" is adapted from Arabian "lapis lazuli," its earliest meaning.

In the Element of Antagonisms

Accent 8 (autumn 1947); CP 425–26, LOA 366–67.

Compare the wind and the north in "Auroras."

TITLE: cf. the idiom of being "in one's element," and "The Owl in the Sarcophagus" I.14.

"genius": see note to "The Idea of Order at Key West," above.

"birds twitter pandemoniums": with a disjunction or "antagonism" between the words "twitter" (echoing "twitter" in Keats's "To Autumn") and "pandemonium" (Milton's invention); also a play against an expected object for the verb "twitter" such as "songs."

"chevalier of chevaliers": a revisionary echo of Hopkins's "O my chevalier," used of Christ in "The Windhover."

"buskin": figuratively associated with tragedy ("buskin," Webster 2b and OED 2b).

In a Bad Time

Hudson Review 1 (spring 1948); CP 426–27, LOA 367–68.

Linked with several preceding poems by the north, here "the order of the northern sky." Note the syntactic work with interrogatives, ending with three imperatives. The pronounced rhyme in lines 12–14 breaks at line 16 to address a debased muse.

"his heart's strong core": echoing and adapting Yeats's "the deep heart's core" (see note to "Page from a Tale," above).
"Melpomene": Greek Muse of tragedy, here "sordid" as a muse of misery.
"heliotrope's inconstant hue": the flower is blue; etymologically (Gk.) "following the sun."

The Beginning

Nation 165 (18 Oct. 1947); CP 427–28, LOA 368.

One of several memorable end-of-summer poems.

"summer": like "perceived"(l.8), a key word in *Transport to Summer*.
"weave / Inwoven": the dress of summer inwoven as the grammar, alliteration, and reference to bells inweave the text and texture of these lines.
"a weaver to twelve bells": cf. the riddling "Oak Leaves Are Hands"; also playing on the etymon of "text" (weave); so phrased as to recall old riddles on the number twelve (months, etc.).
"tutoyers": (Fr.) *tutoyer*, to use the second-person singular *tu*; see note on "Bethou" in NSF II.vi, above. This use of person indicates that tragedy begins to speak intimately—or else that the speakers address tragedy intimately ("of" takes its double meaning)—in either case, beginning to know it like one of the family. Compare the preceding poem.

The Countryman

CP 428–29, LOA 368–69.

Compare "country" and "countrymen" elsewhere in *Auroras of Autumn*. The poem is not addressed to a Muse, but to a river in Stevens's natal state, Pennsylvania. The strong rhythms of a mostly four-beat line suggest the movement of the river and the corresponding movement of feeling elicited by this river of Stevens's youth. The poem repeats "Swatara" or else "swarthy" ten times in all, setting up a refrain in the first line that echoes through the poem. (Contrast the different rhetorical effect of the play on "Damariscotta" in "Variations on a Summer Day.")

"Swatara": Stevens noted that the name is native, and that the Swatara, a stream, flows into the Susquehanna above Harrisburg (L 611, 1948). As elsewhere, he draws out the storied aspect of an American place-name; this one sounds Sanskrit, for something like "swarthy."

The Ultimate Poem Is Abstract

Poetry 71 (Oct. 1947), with "Bouquet of Roses in Sunlight," both under the title "Two Poems"; CP 429–30, LOA 369–70.

"abstract": see note on NSF I, title, above.
"hems the planet rose and haws it ripe": playing on "hems and haws," and the ripe haws of roses; cf. speaker and rose in "Extracts from the Academy of Fine Ideas."
"writhings in wrong obliques": a Carroll-like resonance of "right and wrong" and of his " 'Reeling and Writhing' " (reading and writing, *Alice's Adventures in Wonderland*, chap. 9).
"because at the middle": "because [we were] at the middle."

Bouquet of Roses in Sunlight

Ibid.; CP 430–31, LOA 370–71.

Another bouquet poem, here as if answering the previous poem by repeating "sense" and "enormous." "Sense" expands to become a nonverbal "sense of things," before and beyond metaphor. The unrhymed iambic pentameter triplets vary the accent so much that the regular last line sounds strongly affirmative.

"like a flow of meanings": "sense exceeds all metaphor" but the poem turns to metaphor (in the form of its species, simile) to describe sense.
"as we are": cf. Stevens's variations on "as I am, I am" in his later work (NSF III.viii, "The Sail of Ulysses," etc.).

The Owl in the Sarcophagus

Horizon 93–94 (Oct. 1947); CP 431–36, LOA 371–75.

An elegiac meditation building on Whitman's "When Lilacs Last in the Dooryard Bloom'd." The poem is dedicated to the memory of Stevens's close friend, Henry Church, who died in April of 1947; it was composed "in the frame of mind that followed" his death (L 566, 1947). That the dead are now at rest, sleeping, and at peace: these are common tropes, to which we usually want to add the right kind of good-by. Stevens personifies the sleep and peace of death, then adds a third figure, a mother figure, who "says / Good-by." Her words near the end of canto I are direct and affecting, as is the last stanza of the entire poem on the mind as "a child that sings itself to sleep." While some portions of the sequence are veiled, much is not; some is very moving and germane, as in the examples just given. (See Peter Sacks on Stevens's "deep understanding of the most ancient and hieratic elements of the genre" [*The English Elegy* (1985), 326].) The poem often works with long appositive sentences, including three 12-line sentences.

I

"Two forms . . . And a third form": two personified figures accompany Whitman, as he flees to the singing hermit thrush (pt. 14).

"sleep the brother is the father, too": cf. "This brother even in the father's eye" in a consolatory section of "Esthétique du Mal" (v). Sleep is traditionally the brother of death, as in *Iliad* XIV.231 on Hypnos and Thanatos.

II

"A man walked living among the forms of thought": cf. "Ideas were the bread of life to him," and Stevens's full memorial tribute to Henry Church (L 570–71, 1947).

"twanged": cf. the planter in NSF II.v, "Sighing that he should leave the banjo's twang."

"abysmal melody": "fathomless"; cf. "abysmal instruments" in NSF I.iv.

III

"foldings": Stevens works throughout III with "fold," a rich word in association with sleep (the folding of the eyelids in sleep, the curling of the body, the sense of shelter as in a sheepfold, etc.); cf. Sappho on evening bringing us "home to the fold" (quoted L 248, 1926).

"weaving": extending "folds" to fabric, also recalling texts (see IV, below).

IV

"peace, the godolphin and fellow": how do we personify the peace of death,
"cousin by a hundred names" (1)? It is something very familiar and one
of us, a fellow, but also strange, as in Stevens's strange noun, "godol-
phin"—perhaps generalized from a name well known to racing and
horse-breeding circles, the famed eighteenth-century Godolphin Ara-
bian, one of three stallions from whom all Arabian thoroughbreds de-
scend (EB, "horse": "history"). If so, this figure of peace is another
species, dead yet still alive in its progeny, elite, and familiar chiefly to a
small circle.

"its cloth / Generations of the imagination," "stitchings," "thread," "weav-
ing": the garment for "peace after death" recalls older elegies, where
tropes of sewing and weaving also evoke the act of making a text, as of
mourning.

"doom": including its old sense of "destiny."

"A bee": we burrow like bees in the sewn flowers that embody a life now ended;
also punning on B ("an alphabet"), and cf. "bee . . . be" in NSF II.ii.

"in the summer of Cyclops / Underground": an unusual combining of a sense
of the cave of Cyclops, the one-eyed giant who imprisoned Ulysses, and
Pluto's underworld, where Persephone must live during the winter
months. In both legends, those imprisoned get out, at the least for a sea-
son. So combined, the legends catch effectively the ongoing life in mem-
ory of our cherished dead.

V

"exhalation": recalling "the syllable between life / And death" as in a last
breath; contrast "inhalations" ("Credences of Summer" 1) and "inhale a
health of air" (OE viii).

"fling without a sleeve": cf. "a body wholly body, fluttering / Its empty
sleeves" ("The Idea of Order at Key West," ll. 3–4).

VI

A canto that opens with a strange phrase in a lexis that calls attention to it-
self: "monsters of elegy." The phrase requires the reader to choose a defini-
tion of "monster" in accord with the poem. In a nonpejorative sense, a mon-
ster is a legendary creature combining attributes of different natural species,
like the sphinx or griffin (both ancient tomb-guardians). As the canto con-
tinues, Stevens expands on these "monsters of elegy" and, in the very moving
closure, they become one with the "people . . . by which it [the mind] lives
and dies."

Saint John and the Back-Ache

Modern American Poetry, ed. B. Rajan (London: Dennis Dobson, [May] 1950, with "Credences of Summer," "Imago," and "Celle Qui Fût Héaulmiette"; CP 436–37, LOA 375–76.

A remarkable debate-poem on the question of pain, still in need of good exegesis.

"Saint John": unspecified (the Baptist? the Evangelist? the Divine?); probably the putative author of John's Gospel. (In 1922, Stevens described the title, "Klenken's Presse Evangelium Sancti Johannis," as the "sweetest line of poetry," adding how much he would like to have the book [LFR 401].)

"The world is presence and not force": for any St. John, world as presence is associated with the presence of God, as through the biblical books or in the Eucharist.

"*Kinder-Scenen*": (Ger.) literally, "scenes from childhood"; the old spelling (not modern-*szenen*) indicates an allusion to Schumann's well-known piano sequence. If "Presence is *Kinder-Scenen*," literally, then the Back-Ache is scoffing at its significance as mere "scenes from childhood." But the allusion undercuts his assertion by implicitly conceding how far (and how) such presence might work, when confronted by the force of pain. How far (and how?) does music help with pain? How far (and how) does a music that might be called "scenes from childhood" help?

"I speak below / The tension of the lyre": St. John as poet, in a memorable sentence. As with all stringed instruments, the tension of the strings determines the pitch; a string with no tension makes no sound. Compare also St. Paul speaking on his own "and not of commandment" (I. Cor. 7:6).

"turtle": possibly the turtle on whose back the world rests, in Amerindian legend.

Celle Qui Fût Héaulmiette

Ibid.; CP 438, LOA 376.

Stevens wrote that the poem was suggested by Rodin's sculpture, *Celle qui fût la belle heaulmière* (*She Who Was the Helmet-Maker's Beautiful Wife*), a work that Rodin sometimes called "Winter" (Lensing [2001], 256; Baird,

The Dome and the Rock [1968], 87n.). Villon's *Testament* includes two series of poems called "Les regrets de la belle Hëaumière" ("The Regrets of the Helmet-Maker's Beautiful Wife") and "Ballade de la belle Hëaumière aux filles de joie" ("Ballad . . . to Women of Pleasure"); for the original Hëaumière, see François Villon, *Poésies*, ed. Dufournet (Paris: Gallimard, 1973). Stevens owned a copy of Villon's *Poésies* (sold at auction by Parke-Bernet in 1959).

TITLE: (Fr.) "She Who Was Héaulmiette"; a *héaume* is a helmet; the *l* indicates Old Fr., as in Rodin; Stevens's "-iette" and his text suggest a young girl, perhaps the daughter of *la belle héaulmière* or the woman herself when young.

"gilderlinged": with "entinselled," suggesting "gild" as "gold-washed," and a gilderling as one who does this (cf. "worldling"); evoking Old Eng. rather than Old Fr.; "-ling" is sometimes a pejorative suffix, so here leads into the defensive irony of "American vulgarity."

"native shield": cf. "nature," "natives" in "A Primitive Like an Orb" (VIII.5–6); "shield" adds to her helmet.

"a mother with vague severed arms": resembling Rodin's figure less than the Venus di Milo; Venus is sometimes a universal mother, source of all generation.

"a father bearded in his fire": cf. "The Auroras of Autumn" IV.

Imago

Ibid.; CP 439, LOA 377.

Linked with the preceding poem by stanzaic and rhythmic forms, as well as the interaction of early-spring landscape and the imagination.

"Who can pick up the weight of Britain," etc.: echoing the questions in Job, chap. 38, appropriately asked about countries still recovering from the ravages of World War II.

A Primitive Like an Orb

Printed for the Gotham Book Mart as a pamphlet (New York: Banyan, 1948); CP 440–43, LOA 377–80.

The poem considers and expands statements about "the essential poem" and "the central poem." Stanzas VII through IX consist of one 24-line sentence, ending with both a child's and a high sublime delight. The combination of "whirroos" and "the serious folds of majesty" is typical of Stevens's tone, and of his convictions. Familiar tropes from earlier poems help to focus the concerns of this one. The iambic pentameter is more regular than usual for Stevens.

"primitive": as a noun, usually an aborigine, an ancestor, or a pre-Renaissance (or else naïve) European painting; at the end, all three meanings converge in the giant.

"fiddlings": submerged pun on "fidgetings" (cf. OE xxxi), and a slight disjunction from "arias" (usually sung).

"gorged the cast-iron of our lives" etc.: literal cast-iron makes a good cooking pot, by which we may gorge our stomachs; if we are fortunate, our stomachs are like cast iron; Stevens is considering spiritual food.

"pale air": cf. the "pale head" of "To the One of Fictive Music."

"as it was / Oh as": cf. the play on "As it is" in OE xxviii.

"The lover, the believer and the poet": another allusion to "The lunatic, the lover, and the poet / Are of imagination all compact," etc. (*A Midsummer Night's Dream* V.i.7–8).

"a light apart, up-hill": as, e.g., in Matt. 5:14.

"virtue": echoing latinate "vis" (force, power) earlier and "virtuoso" later; linked thereby with "power" at the end of the same stanza.

"eccentricity": playing against the poem's concentration on "centre," "central," etc.

Metaphor as Degeneration

American Letters 1 (Apr. 1949); CP 444–45, LOA 381.

The poem questions its title, which thereby hangs as a reproach or challenge at the start. Stevens's main affirmation comes in the opening 9-line sentence, and culminates in lines 8–9. Most stanzas have two assonantal or other rhymes.

"brooding": as transitive verb, "to brood," as eggs in a nest.

"Swatara": see note on this name in "The Countryman," above.

"round the earth and through the skies": recalling Oceanus, for which see note on the last line of "The River of Rivers in Connecticut," below.

"flock-flecked river": cf. the "flecked river" of Heraclitus in "This Solitude of Cataracts." Stevens's compound invention gives him a spondee in the line, as do other compounds here.

The Woman in Sunshine

Written by August 1948 and submitted for publication, with the next four poems, under the title "The Bouquet" or else "Poems from Hartford"; apparently not published (L 609n., 615); CP 445, LOA 381–82.

"image": cf. "images" in the preceding poem.

Reply to Papini

Ibid.; CP 446–48, LOA 382–84.

A defense of poetry, paying the fictitious Pope Celestine VI the compliment of responding seriously to his supposed procurator's directive. This is a poem that should be better known, especially for its precision, directness, and intelligence. It includes some memorable formulations (see, e.g., lines 5–6 on "the way through the world" and "the way beyond it" and "a politics / Of property").

EPIGRAPH: "Papini": Italian essayist and philosopher (1881–1956); the epigraph translates excerpts from his 1946 *Lettere agli uomini del papa Celestino sesto*, chap. X, "To the Poets," which differs slightly from the 1948 translation (*Letters to Mankind from Pope Celestine VI*). Pope Celestine VI is invented, though the name is valid for a new pope.
"Celestin, the generous, the civilized": in accordance with Papini's description in his preface.
"angry day-son clanging at its make," etc.: the change in diction itself clangs and also echoes, as the poet, son of the day, sounds out like a clarion, carillon, tocsin, etc.; cf. "angering" in "Nomad Exquisite"; note the double sense of "clanging at" (at the time of, against); "make": (Middle Eng.) "mate."

The Bouquet

Ibid.; CP 448–53, LOA 384–87.

One of several poems where a bouquet is closely observed and sensuously apprehended, while also providing the focal point for a meditation and/or an inferred plot. The few stage properties are revealed gradually, as if being seen in a play or a painting. The diction includes a number of words unusual enough to sound like neologisms. In Stevens's early "Bowl, Cat and Broom-stick," a poem called "Le Bouquet" parodies extreme Imagist effects (OP 174, LOA 630–31, 1917).

"medium nature": not "major" but equally, not pejorative; cf. "medium man" in "Imago"; playing against "extreme."

"apparitions": cf. the behavior of the "apparition" in the final poem of *The Auroras of Autumn.*

"the other eye": gradually defined in what follows.

"meta-": (Gk.) "beyond," as in "metaphor" (ll. 4–5); "para-": (Gk.) "beside," as in "parallel," and note echo of "apparitions" (l. 6).

"prevents": also in the etymological sense of "anticipates," as in Eliot's theological use in *East Coker* IV.

"choses of Provence": (Fr.) "things," unspecified except by contrast; Eng. "of " rather than Fr. *de* breaks the phrase oddly.

"centi-," "mille-": literally, "hundred-" and "thousand-" in continuing play with the prefix or "the fore" (next line), so to speak.

"a sovereign of souvenirs": cf. work with these two words in "Lions in Sweden."

"real . . . seen in insight": cf. the philosopher, H. D. Lewis, "If I am right, the essence of art is insight of a special kind into reality" (quoted in NA 99, LOA 703, 1948).

"facture": note also the meaning, "the quality of the execution of a painting."

"farced, finikin . . . flatly": extending the pronounced effects of earlier *f* words; the adjacent adjectives have contrary associations; cf. "finikin" elsewhere in Stevens's poetry, especially in OE XXXI, and "finical" used of Marianne Moore's work (NA 97, LOA 702, 1948).

"splashings in a penumbra": as in seeing the aurora ("splashed," "The Auroras of Autumn" VI).

"A car drives up": the cryptic closing cinematic scene recalls this poem's post-war date.

World without Peculiarity

Ibid.; CP 453–54, LOA 388.

Stevens divides the tercets of this simple, forceful, memorable poem in the 4/3 proportions of an Italian sonnet, with the turn coming after stanza 4. He allows a rare glimpse into things close to his heart, albeit abstracted and disciplined by the demands of his art. One response (to "she that he loved") does an astonishing amount of work in eleven syllables, encompassing a subject for an entire short story or novel.

TITLE: cf. the possible title, "A Poet without Peculiarity" (Lensing, *Southern Review* [1979], 889, and 1986, 174).

Our Stars Come from Ireland

CP 454–55, LOA 389–90.

I.

EPIGRAPH: an oblique dedication; "*Tom McGreevy*" (1893–1967) was a correspondent and friend, a writer, and the director of the Irish National Gallery.

II. *The Westwardness of Everything*

TITLE: "*Westwardness*": McGreevy commented on his own westwardness because of living close to the Shannon Estuary. Stevens was interested because his boyhood house faced west, and he instinctively tried to pull any house he lived in later "round on an axis" to make it straight (L 618, 1948).
"Mal Bay": north of Tarbet (l. 8), mentioned in McGreevy's poem "Recessional" (1934).
"Over the top of the Bank of Ireland": see Stevens's comments on McGreevy's "High above the Bank of Ireland / Unearthly music sounded, / Passing westwards," from his "Homage to Hieronymus Bosch" (L 596, 1948).
"Tarbet": McGreevy's birthplace in Ireland.
"Swatara // And Schuylkill": rivers in Pennsylvania; see "The Countryman" and "A Completely New Set of Objects," etc.
"fitful-fangled": invented compound like "new-fangled" (see note on "fire-fangled," "Of Mere Being," below).

Puella Parvula

Voices 136 (winter 1949); CP 456, LOA 390.

Another poem that should be better known, of great force and directness. The opening stanza is a tour de force. The poem embodies the necessary and enabling struggle of a powerful sense of vocation. Stevens's imperative to the "wild bitch" introduces utterly unexpected diction, even though the term of abuse is not the primary meaning.

TITLE: (Lat.) a very small girl, either a child or a young woman (Catullus calls his lover *puella*).

"caterpillar . . . devoured": one of nine names in the English Bible translating grasshoppers of the family Acrididae, order Orthoptera, that can indeed "devour" parts of Africa and elsewhere; more familiar as "locust" (see OED or Webster, "locust," and Joel 1:4).

"elephant," "lion": cf. NSF I.v.

"Write *pax* across the window pane": (Lat.) "peace"; *pax* is on a window in Harvard's Memorial Chapel, and doubtless in other similar settings.

"*summarium in excelsis*": (Lat.) "abstract (or summary) in the highest," echoing familiar liturgical Latin like "hosanna in excelsis," but using a noun that is unfamiliar in this combination.

The Novel

Privately printed (L 617n., 1948); CP 457–59, LOA 391–92.

"*Mother was afraid . . . away*": the italicized words quote or closely paraphrase José Rodríguez Feo's letter to Stevens of 21 Sept. 1948 (L 617n.).

"*Olalla blanca en el blanco*": (Sp.) "Eulalia white in the white," from Garcia Lorca's "Martirio de Santa Olalla" ("Martydom of Saint Eulalia" III.22), a vivid evocation of the saint's grisly martyrdom; cf. Eulalia in "Certain Phenomena of Sound" III.

"the Arcadian imagination": the ideal imagination, Arcadia being the projected ideal place for classical writers of pastoral; "Who inhabited Arcady?" (L 120, 1900).

What We See Is What We Think

Botteghe Oscure 4 (autumn 1949), with the following five poems, all under the title "A Half Dozen Small Pieces" and accompanied by Italian translations; CP459–60, LOA 392–93.

Stevens's title for the grouping implies that the six poems are slighter than his most concentrated work. See L 642–43 (27 July 1949), which confirms this, while noting that the poems "came into my head" and pleased Stevens. The six poems are linked, chiefly by tropes of sun or sunny days and moon or moonlit nights. All six take the same form of six tercets with iambic pentameter lines, nearly all unrhymed.

"phantomerei": a coinage with the Ger. suffix "-erei" (cf. "Schwärmerei," NSF I.vii), based on "das Phantom" and meaning "things concerning or brought about by phantoms."

A Golden Woman in a Silver Mirror

Ibid.; CP 460–61, LOA 393–94.

"Au Château": the first of three stage directions for different golden women. At the Castle. A Salon. Gawks of hay.

"Augusta Moon": a personified August moon or a woman like that, with memories of "the old Lutheran bells / At home," like Stevens's own memories and his wife's.

"belle Belle": beautiful Belle or Beauty.

"Abba": transliteration of Aram. for "father," familiar from the New Testament (e.g., Mark 14:36), used in direct petition to God the Father.

"Ababba": playing on "abba"; "ab" is Heb. for "father"; see also OED, Webster, for similar words; setting up an echoing play on the first letters of the alphabet, and a mirroring relation (ab ba). On the desire for a queen to appear, cf. "Depression before Spring" and "Description without Place" 1.

The Old Lutheran Bells at Home

Ibid.; CP 461–62, LOA 394.

Title from previous poem, hence as if hummed by a character. In 1922, Stevens thanked a friend for his letter, which, he said, reminded him of attending the Evangelical Church in Reading, and hearing the pastor "preach in German on the text 'Ich bin der Weg, die Wahrheit, und das Leben'" (LFR 401; "I am the way, the truth, and the life"). A little later, he wrote that Martin Luther could not really be called a Pennsylvania Dutchman, but was nonetheless "a native element of the Pennsylvania Dutchman's [soul?]" (LFR 405, on receiving a copy of John's Gospel in German, clearly from the standard German Luther Bible; see also L 602, 1948, and NA 100, LOA 704, 1948).

"Paul" etc.: The references are to St. Paul the apostle, author of most epistles in the New Testament; probably St. John the Evangelist, author of the fourth Gospel (see title-note to "Saint John and the Back-Ache," above); St. Jerome, Church Father and translator of the Bible into the Latin Vulgate; St. Francis of Assisi; Martin Luther; the Spanish St. John of the Cross.

"scrupulous Francis": because of "those bells . . . around his ankles to warn crickets and other creatures" (to Sister B. Quinn, 2 Oct. 1950, courtesy of Dartmouth College Library), thus another bell-ringer.

"fortress": cf. Luther's well-known hymn, "Ein' feste Burg ist unser Gott," often translated as "A mighty fortress is our God," and quoted by Stevens in 1942: "one's own fortitude of spirit is the only 'fester [sic] Burg'" (L 403). His German was a little rusty, so that the shortened feminine article *ein'* is misread as masculine *ein* (followed by masculine *fester*); he was perhaps confusing *eine Burg* and *ein Berg* ("mountain, hill").

"pastors . . . shepherds . . . sheep": biblical pastoral language, also used elsewhere by Stevens.

Questions Are Remarks

Ibid.; CP 462–63, LOA 394–95.

"enfantillages": "childishnesses" in a more elegant Fr. form, leading into "infant" (l. 18).

"grandson": reference to Peter Reed Hanchak, Stevens's grandson, then aged two.

"voyant": a perceiver, someone who sees (not a voyeur); on 3 Dec. 1948, José Rodríguez Feo addressed Stevens as "My dear Voyant" (LWSJRF 145).

"aetat.": short for Lat. "aetatis," or "of the age . . ."

Study of Images I

Ibid.; CP 463–64, LOA 395–96.

First of a linked pair with painterly titles, the first on images of the sun, the second on images of the moon.

"bella": (It., fem.) "beautiful," and so a beautiful woman.

Study of Images II

CP 464–65, LOA 396.

"drop / From heaven": cf. "Le Monocle de Mon Oncle" VIII.

"mannequins": figures of the moon often include "pearly women" and "witches," but figures for a "brown" moon are less frequent (cf. "brown moon," in "God Is Good . . .").

"ice-month": the Dutch used to call January *Lauw-maand* ("frosty month") (Brewer).

"Rose—women as half-fishes of salt-shine": the Venus image modulates by the dash into mermaids, reflecting the moon in the sea.

"bearing birth of harmony": Harmonia or Concord is a daughter of Venus and Mars.

An Ordinary Evening in New Haven

Transactions of the Connecticut Academy of Arts and Sciences 38 (Dec. 1949), a shortened eleven-canto version, differently ordered (see LOA n. 397.1): I, VI, IX, XI, XII, XVI, XXII, XXVIII, XXX, XXXI, XXIX; CP 465–89, LOA 397–417.

A meditative poem that is set in New Haven, though this is not apparent for some time. An evening walking-poem, in which physical characteristics of New Haven may be ascertained (once-plentiful elm trees, the Long Island Sound, chapels and schools, statues) and one professor, Professor Eucalyptus. The sequence includes a walk with various sounds and sights (such as seeing the evening star and hearing the rain), time in a hotel room, memories of the day, retiring to bed, thoughts of other cities compared with New Haven as well as the earthly paradise, and a summing up in an autumnal vision (XXX), a vision that is like "an evening evoking the spectrum of violet" (XXXI).

These are all seen through a mind meditating on the reality that informs them, including the historical reality. What is the reality of New Haven now? Older New Haven built itself on a biblical perspective that culminated in the vision of the New Jerusalem in Revelation. That was their ultimate reality. Thus the "heaven" / "New Haven" pun in XV, Alpha and Omega in VI, the "Eucalyptus" / "apocalypse" pun in XIV and XXII. This poem, however, is anti-apocalyptic, though not by simply reversing direction and going down instead of going up. Stevens's "serious reflection" moves away from apocalyptic thinking and turns to the wisdom of the "ordinary" and "commonplace" (XVII). That too has biblical roots. Hence the appearance in canto XIX of the Ecclesiast or Preacher, author of Ecclesiastes and Proverbs, i.e., biblical wisdom literature. The last four cantos move toward a new, contemporary sense of reality for Stevens's "poetry of the earth."

Stevens stated that his desire in this poem was "to try to get as close to the ordinary, the commonplace and the ugly as it is possible for a poet to get." It was not a matter "of grim reality but of plain reality." Then, in an important use of the verb "purge," he added that the aim was "to purge oneself of anything false" (L 636, 1949). On the concept of purging as an artistic discipline, cf. remarks on how poets "purge themselves before reality, in . . . saintly exercises" (OP 227, LOA 790, 1936).

The poem must be read as slowly as "Notes toward a Supreme Fiction." While sometimes dense, it is also often rich, with some memorable lines and phrasing. It is also sometimes relaxed and funny. Readers are especially drawn to many of the earlier cantos (e.g., I, V, VI, VIII–XII) as well as the closing ones (XXVIII–XXXI).

TITLE: Ordinary: An "ordinary day" did more for Stevens than an "extraordinary day," just as "the bread of life is better than any souffle" (L 741, 1952).

I

Cantos I through V look at the "actual scene" with a "never-ending" question of what ultimate reality informs it. A biblical sense of reality provides one older point of reference (e.g., the biblical text, "I saw a new heaven and a new earth" [Rev. 21:1, etc.]). Canto VI works out from "I am Alpha and Omega, the beginning and the end" (Rev. 21:6). After this, the poem's persona begins to look more particularly at aspects of New Haven, and begins his walk.

"eye's plain version": a packed opening sentence, requiring thought, as do the various qualifications of "and yet, and yet, and yet—"; note the later poem, "The Plain Sense of Things."

"apart": apart from ultimate reality (which is unknowable); the Heb. word for holy, *godesh*, like Lat. *sacer*, means "set apart"; note both the likeness and difference here.

"vulgate": written in the common or vulgar tongue, hence accessible; recalling the Vulgate, Latin translation of the Christian Bible, especially Jerome's; so called because Latin was for centuries the common language for literate people in Western Europe and beyond. "The eye's plain version" is always some kind of translation, but what kind?

"house": in the widest sense, including the body as house, house as a structure of belief ("house built on sand," Matt. 7:26), etc., here with actual houses before the mind's eye; see also OP 258, LOA 840 (1951) on "dwelling-places" and "abodes of the imagination."

"composed . . . of the sun": with Stevens's long-standing sense of "compose" as "put together" in various contexts, and his longstanding use of the sun as origin and ultimate cause of life.

"Mythological form . . . beard," etc.: cf. the description of Jove, OP 259–60, LOA 841–42 (1951); on "giant," note the description of the old gods as "giants" and remarks on the end of the gods (ibid.), a useful gloss on I.

II

The sole one-sentence canto, examining the hypothesis that reality is defined by radical idealism of a Platonic or Christian kind, which Stevens treats as radical subjectivism. Shaped like a standard geometrical or Euclidean hypothesis

("Suppose that X . . ."), canto II repeats diction from I ("compose," "come together," "apart"), but changes the context. Here houses are composed, not of the sun, but of ourselves. Unlike I, this canto moves away from palpable time and place. Grammar, rhetoric, and logic flow easily, with no "and yet," unlike most of the other cantos.

"point / Of the enduring, visionary love, / Obscure": "point" as in Dante's *punto*, or "point," which is God, or Plato's vision of the Good. The word "obscure," emphasized by enjambment, darkens this vision, recalling Dante's *selva oscura* or "dark wood" (see note on "Esthétique du Mal" v, above).

III

Redefining the "point / Of the enduring, visionary love" (II) by including desire, rather than excluding it as Eliot does (see *Burnt Norton* v). The canto comes to focus on the word "desire" as a spiritual hunger, in language as passionate as its subject.

"hill of stones": cf. "dilapidate" (etymon "stone") in I.
"If it is misery . . .": cf. "So that he that suffers most desires / The red bird most," etc. ("On the Adequacy of Landscape").
"next to holiness . . . next to love": cf. NA 171, LOA 748 (1951) on the imagination as "the next greatest power to faith: the reigning prince."
"cannot / Possess . . . Always in emptiness": cf. "The Poems of Our Climate."
"A porcelain as yet in the bats": porcelain as a work of art, also figuratively as what human clay may become.

IV

Returning to the word "plain" in I, and positing an unexpected definition of it as "savagery." In turn, "savagery" is developed unexpectedly. See "savage" and "barbarian" as describing Stevens's own intense desire in 1948 (L 624). The canto focuses on the fight against illusion, as Stevens continues clearing the ground for his meditation to proceed.

"a savage assuagement": not an oxymoron in some contexts, e.g., sexual.
"children's tale of ice . . . a sheen of heat romanticized": if a specific tale, perhaps like Andersen's fairy tale, "Snow Queen."

V

Linked with IV by the word "romance," now "Inescapable romance," as Stevens's quest enlarges its sense of human reality. Here, it includes things of our common earth and also our search for some majesty for our lives. The long opening sentence accepts romance, dream, and illusion as part of our reality, at least for the nonquesting or "inexquisite eye" (played against "inquire"). Stevens works with the preposition "in" (plus the negative prefix "in-") and tropes of inside and outside.

"glassy ocean": Long Island Sound, and cf. the "sea of glass" in the Apocalypse (Rev. 4:6).

"hanging pendent": echoing Milton: "hanging in a golden chain / This pendant world" (*PL* II.1051–52, adapting Homer's trope of the earth on a golden chain, *Iliad* VII.19); modified in various ways by "in a shade"; free-floating grammatically, without a main verb.

"Who has divided the world": e.g., Satan? Descartes?

"entrepreneur": a divider of sorts, playing on the literal Fr. meaning, "one who takes [something] between"; properly "one who undertakes."

"No man": perhaps Stevens's favorite, Ulysses, in his punning answer to the Cyclops in *Odyssey* XIX, often rendered in English as "Noman" and "no man." If so, this should be read two ways, with Ulysses as one "chrysalis of all men" who "held fast . . . in common earth" (Ithaca and Penelope) and also "searched out . . . majesty." Ulysses is appropriate in this canto as hero of the archetypal romance of Western literature.

"chrysalis": usually the symbol of a temporary human state that will finally discard "common earth" (cf. Tennyson, *In Memoriam* LXXXII). Not for Stevens.

VI

In the shortened version, this was number II; it initiates a new movement, VI–IX. The canto rewrites Christ's saying, "I am Alpha and Omega, the beginning and the end" (Rev. 1:8, 21:6, 22:13). Alpha (A) and Omega (Ω) are the first and last letters of the Greek alphabet. Here Alpha represents beginnings, not the beginning, while Omega or English Z represents teleological ends, not the end. As against the Book of Revelation, this canto locates reality in the beginning, not the end; it favors Alpha and tests Omega, while acknowledging that both have due place.

"infant A": as in any new beginning (cf. depictions of the New Year as an infant in diapers); as in the letter A, which looks like a baby's legs when it is learning to walk. The letter Z resembles a "twisted, stooping" aged man.

"characters": both personified dramatic characters and characters meaning letters, hence encompassing the full alphabet and thereby all words.

VII

The architecture of New Haven revisited, both in its actual and symbolic form, and as a trope for mental structures. There is a play throughout of the miraculous embodied in the commonplace, as indicated by Yale's and New Haven's architecture.

"such chapels and such schools": in Yale University, as well as the New Haven
    Green, etc.
"antic symbols": perhaps architectural; possibly gargoyles, as on Yale's Law
    School.
"new mornings and new worlds": cf. "a new heaven and a new earth."
"The tips of cock-cry pinked out pastily": a crowded line, drawing together
    cock-cry as heralding "new mornings" and the cock as church-spire deco-
    ration ("pinked out"); "pastily" is not in OED or Webster: like a "pasty"
    or "pastil"?

VIII

One of the most accessible cantos. The real is personified as a beloved, with the lover of the real passionately desiring to speak to her. The 11-line sentence ending the canto is among Stevens's most moving on desire and true intimacy (artistic desire is troped as erotic). The canto works with tropes of breathing, for poetry is "not some breath from an altitude" (NA 45, LOA 670, 1943), but essential as actual breath.

"this form": presumably "credible day" (VII.18), hence "the real" (VIII.3).
"inhale a health of air": see L 423 (1942) on Stevens walking to the office in
    an October morning, when "it was easy to inhale health."
"our sepulchral hollows": our lungs, cave-like places where we would die
    without air; cf. "the marriage of / Flesh and air" ("Life Is Motion"); even-
    tually, the tomb of our dead spirit.

IX

Both cantos IX and X show how aware Stevens is of the pitfalls of his subject. Canto IX works against one hazard of antiapocalyptic writing, the shearing off of all ideas of heaven, saints, etc., if the human spirit needs them. These too may be part of our imagined reality, and they are troped expansively in the last sentence.

"pure reality, untouched / By trope or deviation": impossible, but an ideal
    by which to test tropes; "deviation": astronomically a swerving of the

eccentric, and so related to the eccentric/center/point troping of the poem.

"alchemicana": a neologism, including "alchemy-can," "all-chemi[stry]-can," and inviting more.

"The coming on of feasts": reality here includes the "festival" of cantos I and X; "movable . . . feasts" (16–17) are feasts whose calendar date changes (e.g., Passover, Easter).

"the habits of saints": both their practices and their garments.

X

Written against any idea of constant change, even if the "permanence" and "faithfulness" here are not those of the old faith. The moon is commonly a trope for changefulness and mutability. As in "The Man with the Blue Guitar" and elsewhere, Stevens also tropes it as unconnected to reality (the sun's world) and so possibly hazardous.

"fatal": cf. Crispin's journey from romance through disillusion through realism to fatalism (L 352, 1940), including his time with the "book of moonlight" ("The Comedian as the Letter C," III.1); on going to the moon, cf. "Extracts to the Academy of Fine Ideas" VII.

"allons": (Fr.) "come on," "nonsense."

"hallucinations in surfaces": here as elsewhere, Stevens works against the stereotyped metaphor of surfaces as shallow and depths as profound, hence of mere appearance with a hidden underlying reality; cf. Valéry, "le plus profond, c'est la peau" ("the deepest thing is the skin"), cited Deleuze in *Textual Strategies* (ed. Harari [1979]), 281.

XI

A vigorous and accessible walking canto in the "metaphysical streets" of New Haven. It grows out from the biblical phrase below, ending with the human need that this phrase once addressed.

"Lion of Juda": the Lion of Judah is a figure for Christ in Rev. 5:5 (cf. Gen. 49:9); Stevens took the phrase from an Easter card from Sister Bernetta Quinn (L 634–35, 1949); hence the unusual spelling, which follows the Vulgate's Latin. (Latin was still the language of worship in the Roman Catholic Church in 1949.) More generally, a powerful spiritual leader (cf. C. Bronte, on seeing Lawrence's portrait of Thackeray: "And there came up a Lion out of Judah!" [Gaitskell, *Life of Charlotte Bronte*, chap. 12]). The lion, kept strong by purging it "of anything false" (see head-note,

above), becomes a type of the great cat of poetry (cf. the endings of "Po-
etry Is a Destructive Force" and "Montrachet-le-Jardin").

"clou": central idea (OED), point of chief interest (Webster), literally "point"
or "nail" (Fr. *clou*).

"majesty": associated with the lion; cf. the last line of v and NSF III.viii; bib-
lical and Miltonic resonance, and cf. also Wordsworth on "aspirations of
the soul / To majesty" (*Prelude* VII.755).

"wafts of wakefulness": José Rodríguez Feo "creates by mere will a total
wakefulness," as against Eliot and Blackmur, who, said Stevens mischie-
vously, "step into their nightshirts and . . . say their prayers" (L 624,
1948).

XII

Among the most powerful cantos of the series, and deservedly well known; in
the shortened version, canto v. We so commonly say a poem is "about" some-
thing that our formulation goes unobserved. Stevens challenges it, then
moves on, expanding into a visionary moment, as if a new poem were being
born.

"cry": a key word in the sequence, as also in Stevens's poetry; already intro-
duced in IV and VIII; see also note on "leaves," below.

"res": (Lat.) "subject-matter," later "thing" or "object," now chiefly legal; for
its wide significance, see *Black's Law Dictionary*.

"about": the poem is not *about* its subject, but part of it, just as we do not say
a cry of pain is *about* pain, but part of it; similarly love, sex, or a jazz im-
provisation are not per se *about* something; they simply are.

"The mobile . . .": note the precise diction and grammar of this long sen-
tence, which ends with a clause governed by "as if "; see Vendler (1969)
275–78 on how the many appositions work.

"the area between is and was": on the fact that "we never see reality immedi-
ately but always the moment after," see L 722 (1951), where Stevens calls
it "a poetic idea."

"leaves": Stevens's favorite topos of the fallen leaves that moves from Homer
to Virgil to Milton to Shelley to Whitman and through many more; see
note on "Domination of Black," above. Shelley's apocalyptic leaves recall
and revise Isa. 40:6–8 and its "cry" ("All flesh is grass"), ending with a
prophecy of spring. Whitman's title *Leaves of Grass* (where we expect
"blades of grass") also recalls and revises Isa., evoking the meaning of
"leaves" as "pages" of a book, as well as human bodies or "lives." Stevens's
leaves remain autumnal. Compare also Eliot's use of leaves in *Little Gid-
ding* IIb (1942).

"a casual litter": "leaves" also as leavings or "litter" (cf. "littering leaves," "Sunday Morning" v), and see the note on "casual" (ibid., VIII), above.

XIII

A return to a more casual tone in this descriptive walking canto, after the climactic canto XII.

"ephebe": much strengthened since NSF I and now a "strong mind in a weak neighborhood."

"seeks out / The perquisites": more work with words from Lat. *quaerere*, "to seek" (cf. "inexquisite," "inquire," "searched out" in v).

"journalism": as the daily and passing record (Fr. *jour*, "day"), cf. "newspapers" in XII.

"neither priest nor proctor": i.e., not belonging to the "chapels" and "schools" of VII.

"under the birds, among the perilous owls": related to Yale's carved stone owls, symbols of wisdom, on various buildings?

"difficulty": cf. "these difficult objects" in I. On the importance of believing that "the visible is the equivalent of the invisible," see NA 61 LOA 681 (1943); by so doing, we destroy "the false imagination." The reality of Stevens's religious ancestors "consisted of both the visible and the invisible" (NA 100, LOA 703, 1948).

XIV

Continuing work with the word "cloud" and the apocalyptic, Stevens invents Professor Eucalyptus, whose way of thinking is the focus of XIV and XV; he reappears in XXII, but is not the poem's final focus.

"Eucalyptus": as against apo-calypse (Gk., a "sudden uncovering," especially the cataclysmic Christian Apocalypse), the eu-calyptus flower is well-covered and gradually unfolds, thereby offering a figure for natural progressive revelation. (This last was much favored in the eighteenth century; see the end of Newton's *Optics*.) Borges also uses the pun in "Death and the Compass." Compare Stevens's early implicit pun on "eucalyptus," "Primordia" VI, *"In the South"* (OP 26–27, LOA 535–36).

"not grim / Reality": see Stevens's remarks on "grim reality" in head-note to this sequence, above.

XV

"heaven . . . earth . . . New Haven": see head-note to this sequence, above.

"tournamonde": the world as a place where "things revolve" and so an apt word "in the collocation of is and as"; Stevens's invention, starting with "mappemonde," then Fr. *tournemonde*, then "tournamonde." He added that a number of words in his poems "come to me from French origins" (L 699n. and 699, 1950).

"heaviness": cf. the way that imagination can come " 'in a leaden time' " to a world that has been brought to a standstill by " 'the weight of its own heaviness' " (NA 63, LOA 682, 1943).

"hand": Stevens is sensitive to the language of hands, like Milton, whom he faintly echoes here in unusually personal language.

XVI

On paradoxes of youth and age in nature, e.g., ever-fresh, ever-youthful new days, which are nonetheless an ancient phenomenon.

"youthful sleep . . . eyes closed": with the trope of a daylight sky making love to the sea, cf. Shelley's earth-ocean embrace in "the Earth and Ocean seem / To sleep in one another's arms, and dream . . . all that we / Read in their smiles, and call reality" ("Epipsychidion" 509–12).

"Oklahoman . . . Italian": see note on "Oklahoma" in "Earthy Anecdote," above.

"bough in the electric light": recalling and revising Shakespeare's tropes of aging in sonnet 73, "That time of year thou mayst in me behold": first, leaves dropping until a bough is bare ("those boughs . . . Bare ruined choirs"); second, loss of light "after sunset fadeth."

"eaves": in 1930, Stevens remarked on how the wind in Florida "cries in the eaves in a most melancholy manner" (L 258); an echo of "leaves," given the cross-line assonantal rhyme with "leaflessness." This part of the sequence is the most "leafless" and ascetic part.

XVII

A canto that moves from an initial sense of failure toward the commonplace, rather than comedy or tragedy. This is the commonplace in the best sense, as, e.g., in wisdom literature. The last sentence locates the genre of the whole poem, and establishes its dominant tone.

XVIII

A somewhat pedestrian canto on trying to see and live in the present, which is defined as a thirty-year span of generation.

"this carpenter": unidentified, though an anonymous carpenter is likely to evoke Jesus; note the difference if "this" is stressed. The poet is troped as a carpenter in Dickinson (no. 488).

"depend / On a fuchsia in a can": the construction recalls Williams's "The Red Wheelbarrow"; Stevens noted "Carpenter and Fuchsia" as a possible title or subject (Lensing, *Southern Review* [1979], 878, also 1986, 166).

XIX

On the center or axis or radial aspect of a given time, see also "Description without Place" III. With the last two stanzas, and the figure of Ecclesiast, the poem moves toward the possibility of an answer to its quest, though in the future. Similarly with the youth in the essay, "The Figure of the Youth as Virile Poet."

"radial aspect": Stevens called Milan "a great radial focus," if not a great place (L 645, 1949).

"Ecclesiast": the Preacher or Solomon, author of Ecclesiastes. In NA 78, LOA 690 (1947), Stevens quotes Ecc. 12:6, commenting on how it provides "the pleasure of 'lentor and solemnity' in respect to the most commonplace objects." The reference helps to confirm that he is locating the genre of this poem within wisdom literature.

XX

In cantos XX–XXVII Stevens avoids the familiar shaping of comedy and tragedy, but this does not bring him to a standstill as it does at the end of "The Comedian as the Letter C." Instead he works with the commonplace. He experiments with different "models" (XVIII) in this occasionally ascetic portion of the series, looking for a "radial aspect of this place" (XIX).

Canto XX treats the will and the possibility of escaping from it, which canto XXI denies. On "the will, as a principle of the mind's being," see NA 10, LOA 648 (1942), referring to Richards on Coleridge; Stevens marked in his copy of I. A. Richards's *Coleridge on Imagination* the famous quotation on fancy and imagination, where the secondary imagination is "co-existing with the conscious will" (*Biographia Literaria*, chap. 13; copy at the Huntington Library).

"imaginative transcripts . . . / Today": as if the speaker kept a daily journal, noting events of the imagination.

"residuum": cf. Stevens's view that "a residuum will eventually emerge" from a number of scattered phenomena (L 508, 1945).

"when it was blue": as usual, blue is the color of the imagination, which includes the religious imagination.

XXI

As elsewhere, Stevens can be cryptic when eros is involved. For all its mysteriousness, a strong canto in its affirmations, as befits poetry on the subject of the will. The ending is a surprise, given the bleakness at the end of xx, yet also a typical move for Stevens. It speaks to the power of "another isle" and "the alternate romanza."

"will of wills— / Romanza": a pregnant dash, as Stevens moves to an example of will that cannot be evaded, the force of romanza (It. musical term, denoting a romance or song or ballad).

"black shepherd's isle . . . his black forms": see note on Cythère, below. Why "shepherd"? Probably as amorous lover, pastoral variety, given to singing.

"the will of necessity, the will of wills": as in Ananke, goddess of Necessity (see note on "Like Decorations in a Nigger Cemetery" xii, above).

Cythère: the Fr. form of Venus's isle, with "black," suggests Baudelaire's "Voyage à Cythère" with its "île triste et noire" ("dreary island, the black one there" [Richard Howard]), which makes everything "noir et sanglant" ("black and bloody"). For Stevens's early view of Cytherea, see "Carnet de Voyage" vi (OP 7, LOA 523, 1914); for Crispin's early view, see "From the Journal of Crispin" II (OP 50, LOA 988, 1921), cut in "The Comedian as the Letter C" along with all references to Crispin as lover and to the genre of romance.

"Out of the surfaces": cf. note on x, above echoing the well-known opening of Psalm 130:1, "Out of the depths have I cried unto thee" (Lat., "*De profundis, clamavi*," a Baudelaire title).

XXII

"a daily sense": hence the importance of diurnal observations and tropes throughout; cf. "oldest-newest" in xvi.

"lone wanderers": in context, not so much a solitaire or a Wordsworth ("I wandered lonely as a cloud," etc.) as an isolated wanderer, especially isolated from the actual world; the planets are also called the "wanderers," though none is a lone wanderer.

"the evening star": the planet Venus, linking this canto with the previous one (cf. the early poem, "O, Florida, Venereal Soil").

XXIII

An evening canto, whose long third sentence repeating "sound" suggests Long Island Sound, sometimes like charm verse. The canto provides a very effective mimesis of going to bed, musing on the day, dozing, and slowly approaching sleep.

XXIV

"The consolations of space": a revisionary echo of Boethius, "The Consolation of Philosophy."

"The statue of Jove": as elsewhere, a statue embodies something long gone that is now unreal (cf. NSF II.III).

"Incomincia": a latinate neologism, presumably "things that are incoming," etc.; cf. "a coming on and a coming forth" (xxx), "edgings and inchings" (xxxi), etc.

"the hand was raised": in context, suggesting the common gesture that signals a beginning, as before a speech, or a conductor's first movement, or a bell-ringer's for the "first bells."

XXV

A simple, beautiful, and memorable canto on Stevens's inner artistic conscience, personified.

"fixed": a strong word for Stevens; cf. his observation in 1948 about certain painters who appeared to be deviating from reality, but in fact "were trying to fix it" (L 601, 1948).

"C'est toujours . . .": (Fr.) "It is always life that is watching me."

"unfaithful": "to every faithful poet the faithful poem is an act of conscience" (OP 253, LOA 834, 1951).

"this hidalgo": less a muse figure than "a companion of the conscience" (ibid.), and cf. L 692 on how "the conscientious artist must please himself " (1950). See biography and also SPBS 93 (1948) on the characteristics of the "deep Spanishness" of Santayana and Picasso.

"The commonplace became a rumpling of blazons": offering many possibilities for word-play linking "commonplace" and "blazons."

"hatching that stared . . .": cf. "looks that caught him" in l. 4, and "The eye of a vagabond in metaphor / That catches our own" (NSF II.x), in a submerged "hatch" - "catch" rhyme; hatching is also a drawing technique.

XXVI

On "the earth / Seen as inamorata," both afar and nearby. The ending resembles the ending of xv, and similarly is unexpectedly moving.

"the afternoon Sound": punning on Long Island Sound, the location of New Haven, and the sounds here and elsewhere.

"transcendent": cf. the end of "Effects of Analogy" (NA 130, LOA 722–23, 1948).

"inamorata": a beloved (female), here the earth, both in its sublime aspect and its everyday impoverished aspect; cf. reality as the poet's "inescapable and ever-present difficulty and inamorata" (OP 256, LOA 838, 1951).

"naked or in rags": cf. the poor items at a farmers' market that nonetheless have extraordinary emotional power (OP 248, LOA 820, 1948); a resonance of language from the Gospels, used of the needy who require help for body and spirit.

"gritting the ear": see note on "grates" in "Autumn Refrain," above; a rehabilitation of the word and the effect.

XXVII

A canto close to a parody of the marriage of the Spirit and the Bride in the Book of Revelation, though the tone does not sound parodic. Perhaps it is deliberately dry after the emotion of xxvi.13–18 and before the accumulating force of the last four cantos.

" 'lies at his ease beside the sea' ": cf. major man in the form of the McCullough, who "lay lounging by the sea," where language may speak "with ease" (NSF I.viii).

XXVIII

The first of four powerful closing cantos. Note the careful construction of the remarkable closing sentence, a key sentence for Stevens's work.

"the tin plate," etc.: as in actuality, and also in paintings by Picasso, etc.

"Misericordia": (Lat.) "pity, compassion, mercy"; in capitalized form, the goddess of pity.

"Bergamo on a postcard, Rome . . . Salzburg . . . Paris": Stevens enjoyed postcards from abroad, which stimulated his sense of place. Paris and a few other sites became places he could visit imaginatively (L 605, 1948); when a friend was at Bergamo, he "looked up the place" (L 645, 1949); a "postcard from Rome set me up" (L 629, 1949); and cf. "a postcard from . . . Salzburg" (L 613, 1948); for Paris, see, e.g., index to L, "Paris," especially letters to Anatole and Paule Vidal, and to Barbara Church.

"longed-for lands": Stevens has already evoked Patmos (where the Apocalypse was written) and Cythère with the other isle, as well as Paris in the present and Long Island through a pun.

"intricate evasions of as": "evasions" is not necessarily a pejorative word for Stevens; "as": not only the preceding "as," but also the "as" of all similitude; note how the grammar ("of life, // As it is, in the intricate evasions . . .") complicates things.

"created from nothingness": as elsewhere, revising the sense of creation ex nihilo, the orthodox Christian doctrine of creation.

XXIX

A bewitching canto, capturing the sense of many of the contraries in this poem, which test an ideal world against this present one in its plainest aspects. In the end, the earthly paradise and this actual earth are one and the same, "except for the adjectives"—a large exception.

"land of the lemon trees": a compendium of earthly paradises, most immediately Goethe's, in Mignon's well-known song, "Kennst du das Land, wo die Zitronen blühn" ("Knowst thou the land where the lemon trees bloom"), from *Wilhelm Meisters Lehrjahre* (*The Apprenticeship of Wilhelm Meister*), associated with Italy.

"citron-sap": also recalling Milton's citron trees in Eden, which lie behind Goethe's.

"mic-mac of mocking birds": setting up multiple word-play; also reminding us that the North American mockingbird corresponds to the European bird associated with an earthly paradise, the nightingale (as in Milton, Keats, etc.). (It is sometimes called "the American nightingale," and see Whitman, "Out of the Cradle Endlessly Rocking," and others.) Note also the sound effects, as of bird song or cry.

"land of the elm trees": New Haven as Elm Tree City (as it was once known), i.e., this earth.

"Wreathed round . . . round wreath": autumn in New Haven through the eyes of an heir to a Spenser-Keats line of succession, in the conventional figure of an autumn wreath ("Mutability Cantos" 7.30.1–9, "To Autumn"); it is presented in a scheme of chiasmus, another example of going "round and round."

"They rolled their r's there": again, multiple word-play (a Mediterranean Romance language, an etymological pun on "voluble," an echo of "cigars" and so an idealized South, perhaps Milton's reported pronunciation, etc.).

"folded over, turned round": a play on "elm" / "lemon" and on "folded" (enigmatic) and "turned" (reversed and troped) language. The linguistic play offers a trope for the relation of this actual earth and an earthly paradise.

XXX

The bareness of late autumn provides a figure for the clearing or purging of sight that is given as Stevens's aim at the start.

"là-bas": (Fr.) "down there," often used of an ideal place (see note on NSF II.v).
"a coming on": cf. "Incomincia" (xxiv) and also "sweet the coming on / Of grateful evening mild" (*PL* IV.646–47).
"squirrels": cf. Dickinson, no. 131.
"hundreds of eyes, in one mind": not just one hundred eyes in one man, Argus.

XXXI

At the end of his long sequence, Stevens seems content to leave the building of a new common mythology to a future generation. Similarly in the essay, "The Figure of the Youth as Virile Poet," where the focus is on one imaginative leader, not a community as here. Most of the canto is a 15-line sentence whose subject is given in lines 10–12 ("the edgings . . . statements").

"legible," etc.: the opening examples both pun and cross sense-effects as in synaesthesia; e.g., "reds" with "legible" puns on "reads," "sheets of music / In the strokes of thunder" suggests sheet-lightning, etc.
"Constantine": the emperor Constantine (288?–337), instrumental in decreeing the acceptance of Christianity within the Roman Empire (313) and convening the first ecumenical council (Council of Nicaea, 325); suggesting a parallel of early Christianity and the mid-twentieth century; playing also on "constant" elsewhere.
"Mr. Blank": as with "blank" elsewhere, the reader is invited to fill in the blank, and perhaps to consider other memorable uses of "blank" (see note on "The Auroras of Autumn" II, above).
"a woman writing a note": on realizing "the poetic act" in ordinary things such as "writing a letter to a person at a distance," see OP 255, LOA 836–37 (1951).
"a solid": Stevens quotes Joad on the misperception of the world "as a collection of solid, static objects" (NA 25, LOA 658, 1942).
"dust": in biblical use including humankind (cf. "Ashes to ashes, dust to dust" in many Christian burial services). Compare also Stevens's troping on "dust" and "shade" throughout his writing.

"force": any force that "traverses a shade," e.g., a brain wave. Stevens's hypo-
thetical definition of reality is "a shade that traverses" or "a force that trav-
erses," a definition that also accords with modern physics. On a wave as a
force rather than solid water, see NA 35, LOA 665 (1942).

Things of August

Poetry 75 (Dec. 1949); CP 489–96, LOA 417–22.

Stevens moves from bare autumn back to late summer, in these sharply real-
ized August sounds, sights, weather, etc., with intimations and memories
therefrom. The tone is generally more relaxed than in "An Ordinary Evening
in New Haven," and sometimes exhilarated. There is much humor in the ten-
part series, though the end is touched with melancholy. While the series is
uneven, some parts deserve to be better known, particularly cantos I, II, V, and
X. Some portions read like commentaries on the long sequence just preced-
ing. Note the variation in person throughout.

I

"Locusts": cicadas (American usage); see note on "Certain Phenomena of
    Sound," above. Not biblical locusts (family Acrididae), who do not sing,
    and include destructive pests, as in the plague of locusts (Ex. 10:5–6,
    12–15, and see "Puella Parvula"); but they do give biblical resonance to
    "day" and "night" in line 1, echoing the pillar of cloud by day and of fire
    by night (Ex. 13:21–22); the echo is appropriate as these sounds also are
    guides to another place, perhaps a home.
"By a pure fountain, that was a ghost": playing against the well-known
    French-Canadian folksong, "A la claire fontaine" ("By a pure fountain"),
    with a refrain, "Il y a longtemps que je t'aime / Jamais je ne t'oublierai"
    ("Long ago I loved you / Never will I forget you").
"honky-tonk": ragtime or jazz, usually on the piano and of a kind played in a
    honky-tonk, i.e., cheap nightclub, etc.; the word in the sense of "music"
    was first recorded in 1933, according to the OED.

II

The world as an egg is a common trope. Stevens's troping also makes use of a
breakfast egg, cracked and then poached or fried ("spread white," etc.). The ex-
ultant ending celebrates this example of a "poetic act" in an ordinary occasion.

"myrrh and camphor": both intensely aromatic; linked in sound with the
    word "summer," hence a "variation"; "myrrh" breaks with the familiar

December myrrh of the Three Wise Men and moves toward the second syllable of "summer" (as well as Keats's "summer mirth" in "To Autumn").

"And Adirondack glittering": the Adirondacks become one in a collective metaphor, and a radical change of perspective, a mountain within an egg; note the scheme "And Adiron- ," which is another type of "variation" and initiates a series of sound-schemes here.

"cat hawks it . . . hawk cats it": as if the Adirondack brought its animal life with it; another variation, where words "spread sail" and play with grammar; as if the hawk is a flying cat, etc.; suggesting how hawks and cats resemble each other, notably in eyesight, claws, and pouncing on prey; similarly with the writer, and so recalling Stevens's use of both creatures as figures for the poet or poetry; through chiasmus, pulling the inner eye up and then down, and around in a circle, like the governing trope of egg as world. All this and more, in the sheer fun of nine words.

III

Compare the contrast (with a difference) in MBG XXIII.

"High . . . low": already exemplified in the poem's high and low diction.
"Mediterranean": as elsewhere, the etymological meaning is in play, (Lat.) "middle of the land."

IV

An intriguing canto, not yet well read. Stevens analyses a fragrance that brings back memories, like the odor of Proust's madeleines. As in Proust, the memories evolve into filial ones, but less happily. It is uncertain how far the parent-offspring relation is personal and/or generally individual and/or metaphoric, as, e.g., with God the Father. Stevens leaves open the question of how the desired lilacs at the end might help. (See also the father figure in VIII.) This is the only canto using "One" as person.

"The sad smell of the lilacs": a spring-time fragrance remembered in August. "Sad" recalls both Stevens's own associations with the fragrance (see note on "Last Look at the Lilacs," above) and Whitman's in his elegy for Lincoln, "When Lilacs Last in the Dooryard Bloom'd."

"Not as . . . Persephone . . . a widow Dooley": Persephone returns from the underground in the spring, thanks to "parental love." The reader must infer Mrs. Dooley's character; if she is the widow of the sardonic political commentator, Mr. Dooley, he may have influenced her. (See Finley Peter Dunne's once-popular series on Mr. Dooley.)

"rich earth . . . brown wheat": with these lines, cf. the passage on "autumn umber" (NSF I.1).

"the fatal . . . An arrogant dagger . . . In the parent's hand": cf. "Esthétique du Mal" XIII on father and son.

V

By contrast, Stevens's favorite wisdom figure and mentor, the rabbi, fills this canto with happy satisfaction. The tone gives Stevens's own flavor of wit and humor, easy intelligence, accommodation of high and conversational diction, and sense of pleasure. Compare with the tone of II.

"Weisheit": (Ger.) "wisdom," part of Stevens's exuberant *w* series; wisdom with German connotations, as with a learned rabbi.

"wears the words . . . to look upon / Within": an expansion of the word "insight," whose metaphoric base is now dead, and which ends the canto; see also next note, below.

"crown," "garment": for the metaphor of wearing wisdom as a garment and crown, see, e.g., the apocryphal book of Ecclesiasticus, 6:31.

VI

As if extending the word "fatal" in IV, and contemplating its influence in a life.

"frere": (Fr., *frère*) "brother," accent omitted; alliteratively linked to "fields" as "mechanic" is to "mountains."

VII

A rather flat canto. Nonetheless it catches the mixed response of returning to nearby familiar life after contemplating the world at large. Compare the tower in "Credences of Summer" III.

VIII

"We resembled one another," etc.: starting a new stanza, as in LOA.

IX

A single 20-line sentence, marked by a large proportion of monosyllabic words.

"A new text of the world": cf. "an Ordinary Evening in New Haven" I.

"hermitage": cf. "Hermitage at the Centre."

X

A canto moving back toward more realistic mimesis, as in canto I.

"The mornings grow silent": early-morning birdsong, so loud in spring, wanes during the nesting and fledgling season, until it falls virtually silent in August.

"the never-failing wonder": Stevens's syntax is built so as to offer two possible meanings of "wonder," birdsong or the cycle of song and silence.

"tricorn": a three-cornered hat, literally "three horns," playing on the epithet of the moon as "triform" because it is "either round, or waxing with horns towards the east, or waning with horns towards the west" (Brewer).

"Impolitor": an invented noun from Lat. adj. *impolitus, -a, -um*, "rough, plain, unadorned," perhaps by analogy with Imperator (Emperor). Instead of a "rex Imperator," a king Emperor, Stevens offers a king Rough; in context, rough plain king Winter or king Death.

"what she was": a contrast in dazzling brilliance, love, and generosity with the rex Impolitor who will follow. Perhaps August at month's end. Perhaps an August muse like the one of fictive music. Perhaps both.

"exhausted and a little old": as of August, as of any woman, in contrast to the "never-tiring wonder" in l. 1; the contrast resembles that in Keats's "To Autumn."

Angel Surrounded by Paysans

Poetry London 17 (Jan. 1950); CP 496–97, LOA 423.

A central and moving poem. Stevens chose a phrase from it, "the necessary angel," as title for his collection of essays in 1951, a phrase that needs to be read in its full context. (See the couplet where it appears, as in the epigraph to *The Necessary Angel*; see also note on "angel of reality," below). The poem grew from a still-life painting by Tal Coat, purchased by Stevens in September 1949. He titled it *Angel Surrounded by Peasants*, calling the "Venetian glass bowl on the left" an angel and "the terrine, bottles and the glasses that surround it" peasants. He added that the title tamed the painting (L 650, 1949). See also L 652–54, 655–56, 661.

"paysans": (Fr.) "peasants, countrymen"; cf. Dickinson; "How far the Village lies - / Whose peasants are the Angels" (no. 7).

"There is / A welcome at the door . . . ?": cf. Rev. 3:20, " 'Behold, I stand at the door, and knock,' " etc., and the once-famous Holman Hunt painting by that title. As is appropriate, it is impossible to tell who is inside the door and who is outside—or rather if there is an inside and outside at all in the allegorical sense of Hunt's painting.

"I am the angel of reality": note Stevens's important statement that the necessary angel "will appear to be the angel of the imagination" for nine readers out of ten and for nine days out of ten. But, he adds, "it is the tenth day that counts" (L 753, 1952).

"no wear of ore": that is, an earthly figure with no golden crown or similar adornment, not a heavenly creature (L 661, 1949).

"tepid": on Stevens's awareness of lexis here ("paysans" and "tepid"), see his amusing p.s. to Nicholas Moore, *Poetry London* (L 650, 1949).

"Rise liquidly . . . watery words": as in a new creation, echoing Milton's creation story (see note to "Looking across the Fields and Watching the Birds Fly," below).

"half of a figure of a sort": part of a cunningly shaped question; "figure" in multiple senses, including (1) a personified angel; (2) a ghost ("apparition"); (3) a figure of speech, alliteration (see next note, below); and more.

"apparition apparelled": cf. "glorious Apparition," used of the archangel Michael (*PL* XI.211), and cf. "Apparelled in celestial light" (Wordsworth, "Ode: Intimations of Immortality" I.4).

"lightest look": as in "sheerest, hardly perceptible," "ghost-like"; as in a look that is light; as in a look full of light like Wordsworth's celestial light.

"a turn / Of my shoulder": also a turn of enjambment over the line, and a turn of the page, the last page of *The Auroras of Autumn*. The figure, which has metamorphosed into something like a ray of light or a fugitive ghost-like glimpse of some thought, now reappears as a body, with shoulders. Like the body of the poem, it turns sideways when the page is turned, becoming wafer-thin and vanishing, except where it lives on in memory.

"The Rock"

Title for the final section of *The Collected Poems of Wallace Stevens* (New York: Alfred A. Knopf, 1954), consisting of twenty-five poems written after *The Auroras of Autumn* (1950). A three-part poem titled "The Rock" is one of them. The poems include some of Stevens's most vigorous and moving work.

An Old Man Asleep

Nation 175 (6 Dec. 1952), "Poems," consisting of the first seven poems of "The Rock"; CP 501, LOA 427.

Another poem that moves like river motion, with increasing repetition and undulating rhythm.

"the river R": the capital-R typic river, any R river (Rio Grande), "R" as the sound of a sleeper gently snoring, pun on second-person "you are." The poem closes with "the river R," so that all these meanings seem to continue on after the poem ends.

The Irish Cliffs of Moher

Ibid.; CP 501–2, LOA 427.

One of Stevens's parenting poems. Jack Sweeney sent him a postcard from County Clare in Ireland with "the worn cliffs towering up over the Atlantic." It felt to him "like a gust of freedom," in the sense of returning Stevens to memories of "the spacious, solitary world in which we used to exist" (L 760–61, 1952). The card was the starting-point for this poem (L 770, 1953). The Cliffs of Moher are listed as one of Ireland's "attractive . . . localities" in Joyce's *Ulysses* (p. 726). Note the use of the colon in effecting closure.

"somnambulations": cf. preceding poem, also "Somnambulisma."

The Plain Sense of Things

Ibid.; CP 502–3, LOA 428.

A striking poem on the end of the imagination. The poem turns direction with the astute argument that "the absence of the imagination had / Itself to be imagined." It is thereby both like and unlike many poems on the same subject, e.g., Coleridge's "Dejection Ode." The lexical precision and play are remarkable.

TITLE: "plain" in several connotations, as glossed by the rest of the poem; cf. "The eye's plain version" (OE I), also John Ashbery's "This poem is concerned with language on a very plain level" ("Paradoxes and Oxymorons," *Shadow Train* [1981]).
"Inanimate in an inert savoir": distinctly un-plain diction, rhyme, and sound effects; "savoir": (Fr.) "knowledge."
"blank": the chosen adjective (l. 5), yet suggesting something absent, a blank on the page; cf. "blank" elsewhere, and see note on "The Auroras of Autumn" II, above.
"great structure": cf. houses and dwelling-places elsewhere ("A Postcard from the Volcano," NSF I.vi, etc.).
"turban": synecdoche for an exotic or colorful figure, as in "The Load of Sugar-Cane."
"fantastic": as of a fantasy, not in the modern colloquial sense.
"repetition . . . repetitiousness": note difference in meaning between the two words.
"of men and flies": cf. "As flies to wanton boys are we to th' gods" (*King Lear* IV.i.36).
"great pond," etc.: inviting comparison with Eliot's pool in *Burnt Norton*, especially given the rat in l. 17 (Eliot's earlier rats are memorable).
"inevitable knowledge": moving on from the kind of knowledge in "Inanimate . . . savoir."

One of the Inhabitants of the West

Ibid.; CP 503–4, LOA 428–29.

Another angel poem, another reader poem, another poem meditating on day's end, here as if on the edge of Western Europe. If it is touched by any sense of "Westward the course of empire" (Berkeley, 1752, and see Bartlett), there is no sense of triumph. The poem breaks in form, import, and tone with the text of evening written or read by its archangel. Medusa is startling; the evening star even more so, as praise gives way to troping the star as a drop of blood, an apocalyptic image. The varying dimeter and trimeter lines use occasional tetrameters for emphasis.

"evening's one star": the evening star is Hesperus or Venus, familiar from Sappho through to Tennyson ("Crossing the Bar") to Eliot.

"its pastoral text": "Evening star that bringest [home] . . . the sheep . . . the goat" (Sappho 149, *Lyra Graeca*, Loeb Classical Library, quoted by Stevens, L 248, 1926; cf. Milton, *Comus* 93; Eliot, *The Waste Land* III.221); on "pastoral," see note to "The Old Lutheran Bells at Home," above.

"Horrid figures of Medusa": Lat. *horridus* means "causing fear," "shaggy," or (of hair) "standing on end," all appropriate for Medusa's snake-hair and its effect; "figures": also rhetorical figures, e.g., tropes of evening; "of": of Medusa herself or petrified by her.

"banlieus": (Fr.) "suburbs, outskirts"; Stevens noted that it has appeared as an English word and hence "the justification for the final s instead of x" (L 764, 1952); not in the OED, but in Webster, which cites Max Beerbohm's use.

"men of stone": including men who looked directly at Medusa.

"well-rosed two-light": a double light made rosy from sunset and/or rose-colored glasses; recalling "fall"; playing on "twilight" (etymologically "between-light," cf. "Delightful Evening").

"I am the archangel of evening": cf. the very different "I am" sentences of the angel in "Angel Surrounded by Paysans."

"a drop of blood": cf. Joel 2:31, where the moon is turned into blood. World War II ended in 1945; its devastations were still widespread in 1952.

Lebensweisheitspielerei

Ibid.; CP 504–5, LOA 429–30.

A poem of human life that is all the more cherished because of its diminishments. Sentence coincides with stanza, except for the first.

TITLE: (Ger.) "Practical Wisdom's Amusement," compound apparently invented by Stevens; *Lebensweisheit* is common, as is *Spielerei*, but not the combination; contrast "Weisheit" in "Things of August" v.

"poverty / Of autumnal space": autumn is also troped as diminishment in adjacent poems, as if in anticipation of old age.

"What he is and as he is": cf. Stevens's "I am" formulations in NSF, and their revision in "The Sail of Ulysses."

The Hermitage at the Center

Ibid.; CP 505–6, LOA 430.

An intertwined double poem in stanzas 1–4, with one poem consisting of line 1 of each stanza, the other of lines 2–3 as marked by dashes and indentation; lines 2–3 also gloss line 1. Stanza 5 locates the two fugal voices as an end and a beginning, and speaks with one voice in unison. As with many other poems of this period, this one is marked by memories from Stevens's early poems and days. It is also marked by the reappearance of birdsong.

TITLE: cf. "hermitage" elsewhere, especially "Things of August" IX.
"leaves on the macadam": cf. the wide troping of leaves throughout Stevens's work, also "Tea."
"attends": also in the Fr. sense of "wait for;" cf. the sense of waiting in "The Paltry Nude . . . ," "Peter Quince at the Clavier," and "Gray Room" (OP 28, LOA 537–38, 1917).
"tintinnabula": (Lat., plural), "bells, signal-bells."
"intelligible twittering," etc.: with "tintinnabula," "wit," etc., providing internal rhyme, much echoic sound, and a memory of Stevens's favorite Keats poem, "To Autumn."

The Green Plant

Ibid.; CP 506, LOA 430–31.

"Out-bre": see note on "Metamorphosis," above.
"lion-roses . . . paper": presumably red roses, late-blooming, now withered and paper-like (cf. "Extracts . . ." I).
"glares": as in the sun, as from an angry person, as if "angering for life" ("Nomad Exquisite").

Madame la Fleurie

Accent 11 (autumn 1951); CP 507, LOA 431–32.

A haunting terrible-mother poem, where the powerful mother-figure is identified as earth, though hardly a generative Mother Earth (cf. "In the Carolinas").

This Mother Earth is the one who awaits our end. She is seen here as a destructive force, like the wicked mother in some myth or fairy-tale. Stevens makes clear that she need not be seen in this light. The two quatrains and one quintain have exceptionally long lines, chiefly hexameter; Stevens's great skill in the use of repetition is evident.

TITLE: Fr. "Madame" changes the stress from Eng. "Madam," as in NSF III.x; "Fleurie": (Fr.) "flowery, florid," hence a late metamorphosis of Florida; cf. Flora Lowzen in "Oak Leaves Are Hands."

"Weight him down," etc.: note the force of an opening imperative, of repetition (three times, with a spondee in l. 5), of internal rhyme and near-rhyme ("weightings," "thought," "waiting"); "weight" as mental and spiritual burden, also evoking burial.

"O side-stars": as if in attendance on the great mother like "side-cars"; "side" echoing "sideral" (including malign influence) and "sidereal."

"His crisp knowledge is devoured by her": like some lettuce eaten by a caterpillar (cf. "devoured" in "Puella Parvula"; see note on "crisp" in "The Comedian as the Letter C" I, above).

"a glass": on the perils of living as in a glass or mirror, cf. NSF I.iv; for Stevens, both the reality of the earth and the imagination that interacts with it are needed for full human life.

"black fugatos": cf. the function of "black" in "The Countryman," "The River of Rivers in Connecticut," and "The Sick Man."

"lie there": contrast with how "he lies" in "The Sick Man."

"say the jay": as in MBG XXXIII or "The Sense of the Sleight-of-Hand Man"; double sense of "say" as example and as speaking.

"feed on him": including literally, in the dissolution of the body after death.

"dead light": as against opening "weight," and playing on "dead weight / dead wait"; ghost-rhyme of "weight-light-late."

To an Old Philosopher in Rome

Hudson Review 5 (autumn 1952), "Eight Poems," together with the following seven poems (order of the next two reversed); CP 508–11, LOA 432–34.

A moving poem addressed, though not by name, to George Santayana, American philosopher of Spanish origin (b. 1863) and Stevens's teacher at Harvard; he also wrote poetry. He returned to Europe in 1912 and lived secluded in a convent in Rome, where he died in 1952. Robert Lowell wrote in 1952 that Santayana "sternly remained an *ideal* but unbelieving Catholic" (*Letters*, ed. Hamilton [2005], 196). The poem is remarkable for its imaginative apprehension of a peaceful death-bed and a waning life on the threshold of death. Threshold imagery, where "two worlds" meet, runs through the poem, as does a contrast of what is small and shrinking with what is large and long-lasting. Two very long sentences contrast with short one-line sentences.

"Rome, and that more merciful Rome / Beyond": Rome and heaven or the New Jerusalem as a perfected Rome; thus Augustine, *De civitate dei* (*On the City of God*), Dante, *Purgatorio* 32.102, etc.

"The newsboys' muttering": as elsewhere, newspapers provide a figure for life's daily passing concerns ("The Emperor of Ice Cream," OE XII).

"fire . . . symbol": fire is traditionally the symbol of the "celestial" (Dante, Eliot, etc.); Stevens's "celestial possible" allows room for both the tradition and a more tentative imagined celestial.

"Be orator": the second imperative that is addressed to the dying man, and the start of a 20-line sentence that imagines, as if it is in the very room, what the dying man may be feeling, as it responds to his life, both past and present.

"with an accurate tongue / And without eloquence": how Stevens's ideal "orator" speaks; cf. "accurate" in NSF I.IX, and Stevens's suspicion of eloquence in, e.g., "Thirteen Ways of Looking at a Blackbird" X.

"the blood of an empire": the sense of a present Rome, where Rome's long history is also embodied, runs throughout; similarly, a person's own history is embodied in the present, here in a dying body.

"Of bird-nest arches and of rain-stained-vaults": accurate description, also recalling Shakespeare's famous sonnet 73.

Vacancy in the Park

Ibid.; CP 511, LOA 434–35.

Another fine March poem, eliciting a late-winter feeling of absence, chiefly from a set of footprints in the snow. Among the "Eight Poems," Stevens mentioned liking "Vacancy in the Park" (to Babette Deutsch, 31 Oct. 1952, New York Public Library, Berg Collection).

"four winds": from all four directions, as traditionally shown on old maps, in the turbulence of March.

"mattresses of vines": grape or other vines, dense and now leafless, provide a winter mattress for dead leaves or sheltering birds, awaiting spring and resuscitation.

The Poem that Took the Place of a Mountain

Ibid.; CP 512, LOA 435.

Stevens moves into the subject of mimesis suggested by his title, illustrating its immense force, first by statement, then by leaving it behind and entering the world it has made. The first two stanzas, each a sentence, are set in two worlds simultaneously; the last five stanzas, all one sentence, move fully on to the poem-mountain.

TITLE: a stimulating, even provocative, title, in itself slyly humorous, though its poem is not.

"his own direction": cf. the use of "direction" in "Credences of Summer" IV.

"right," "exact," "inexactnessess": Stevens's constant emphasis on accuracy becomes more pressing as he grows older, especially in writing where he seeks a sense of completion and of home, as here.

"pines," "rock": cf. earlier pines (e.g., end of MBG) and "rock" elsewhere (e.g. in "The Rock").

Two Illustrations That the World Is What You Make of It

Ibid.; CP 513–15, LOA 435–37.

A winter-summer pair, working from the contracted world of winter and the plenitude of summer. The pair offer two different readings of the common idiom in the title, including "make" as a form of sculpting. Part I ends with a 12-line sentence.

I *The Constant Disquisition of the Wind*

EPIGRAPH: "disquisition": another *quaero, quaesitum* word (Lat., "to seek") from the family Stevens liked (cf. "Nomad Exquisite," etc.); not his inquiring wind this time, but a pronouncing wind whose breath nonetheless is not human.

"animal": the wind may be *anima* (Lat.) but is not animal, not human; cf. MBG XVII.

"a Sunday's violent idleness": ending on a surprising oxymoron, with memorable internal rhyme.

II *The World Is Larger in Summer*

"half a shoulder and half a head": recalling Shelley's "Ozymandias."

"bellishings": Stevens's blue, color of the imagination, expands into exuberant *b* sounds, including this obsolete Eng. word without the usual *em-* prefix and so closer to Lat. *bellus* ("beautiful") and Eng. "bells."

"mastery": as elsewhere, the inheritance from real mastery is necessarily limited, once the master has died; cf. generally "A Postcard from the Volcano," and in particular, the loss of the "master and commiserable man," Santayana, in "To an Old Philosopher in Rome."

Prologues to What Is Possible

Ibid.; CP 515–17, LOA 437–39.

A powerful two-part poem. Note the force of the word "possible" in Stevens (NSF III.vii, "To an Old Philosopher in Rome," etc.). The possible here includes what is just beyond ourselves, yet perhaps attainable; also the possible that governs the world of imagination (not so much "This is," as "This is like" or "Let this be"). Part i evokes an immense range of the possible, while Part ii evokes Stevens's own possibilities as a writer. The lone figure in a boat bears comparison with Ulysses, who appears in several late poems. The magic boat suggests the genre of romance, a quest that will fulfill itself by shattering the boat on arrival. With the shattering attainment of the syllable that lures, cf. "The Motive for Metaphor." Both poems suggest the force and the price of making art; the second also extends this into the wider domain of human experience. In some of Stevens's best late poems, the force of life is troped as a journey on a powerful river or sea. (Compare earlier, less weighted, water journeys in his work.) Stevens's very long lines include many trisyllabic feet, and a strong rowing rhythm in part i.

I

"an ease of mind that was like . . .": the starting-point, governing the full 18-line sequence of part i.

"a boat carried forward by waves": suggesting briefly Rimbaud's "bâteau ivre," then quickly moving away with another simile that makes the waves into rowers. Stevens's enjambment changes the context with each line, moving the poem further into the world of "an ease of mind."

"destination": governed by a third trope ("as if "), then developing so that we forget the waves (and Rimbaud) and see the strong rowers.

"The boat was built of stones": not an old stone-boat, but a magic one. On an early conjunction of sea, stone and syllable, cf. "Le Monocle de Mon Oncle," stanza I.

"He belonged . . . and was part": governing the final 9-line sentence, with its series of dependent phrases and clauses. The man is gradually perceiving as one with his vessel, as he travels on the sea of a mind at ease, intense, focused, and searching. Compare Stevens's uses of "part of " in *Parts of a World* and elsewhere.

"speculum of fire": a brilliant trope, with all three meanings of "speculum" in play (a mirror, part of a bird's wing, the medical instrument whereby internal parts of the body may be seen); the trope suggests ways of voyaging to unknown places in order to attain new insight.

"glass-like sides": with "brilliance" and "speculum of fire," gradually suggesting an approach to some otherworldly state, as in the similar imagery of Yeats's "Byzantium."

"like a man lured on by a syllable without any meaning": the fourth simile, once again shifting the focus, here to the lure and the arrival; the grammar also acts as a trope that embodies the action, as the man enters into the simile-world; "lured" makes the syllable sound like a Siren; later poems develop the similes here in different directions, e.g., the Sibyl (cf. a "syllable"/ "Sibyl" scheme in "The Voyage of Ulysses") and "without any meaning" (cf. "without human meaning" in "Of Mere Being").

"shatter," etc.: cf. the end of "The Motive for Metaphor"; entering another state means shattering normal existence. Compare the trope of "splitting" the atom. To enter into the atom or inner meaning of a syllable would be like splitting it.

"central," "moment": weighted words for Stevens, especially in contexts of finality; cf. "Final Soliloquy of the Interior Paramour."

II

"The metaphor stirred his fear": which of the metaphors? All as part of one, surely. A startling reaction to metaphor; cf. the unexpected fear at the end of "Domination of Black," which is however more explicable. The powerful near-visionary experience here is too strange, shattering the sense of limitless metaphoric possibilities; the boundaries of the man's imagination have been made apparent, though not closed entirely.

"speculated": contrast with "the speculum of fire" in I.

"What self ": the self, in defense, works within "the enclosures of hypotheses" in a new quest.

"that had not yet been loosed, / Snarling in him for discovery": among Stevens's selves is a fierce animal, the dog or lion of poetry that has now become internal ("Poetry Is a Destructive Force," the end of "Montrachet-le-Jardin"); cf. "Be quiet in the heart, O wild bitch" ("Puella Parvula"), as well as the early firecat in "Earthy Anecdote."

"as if ": another simile governing the final 10 lines, where the smallest change can be momentous, as in metaphor, now no longer fearful.

"dithering . . . smallest . . . puissant flick": cf. the ending of OE, with the little more that matters greatly; re "ordinary," "commonplace," see also OE.

"earliest single light in the evening sky, in spring": the planet Venus, also known as the evening star; cf. "Final Soliloquy of the Interior Paramour."

"Creates . . . out of nothingness": as elsewhere, revising the Christian doctrine of creation ex nihilo.

"a look or touch": contrast with the end of part I, "Removed . . . from any man or woman."

"magnitudes": also used of stars.

Looking across the Fields and Watching the Birds Fly

Ibid.; CP 517–19, LOA 439–40.

On the relation of humans to the natural world around them and the universe beyond them. Despite Stevens's engaging invention of Mr. Homburg of Concord, the poem remains opaque and not very satisfying. Stevens fails to make sufficiently clear his disagreement with Mr. Homburg. His much-favored grammatical construction, apposition, here tangles the line of thought rather than spinning it out suggestively. Stevens disliked the sense of the transcendental in traditional Christian doctrine, but the radically revised Transcendentalist viewpoint does not fare much better here, at least in Mr. Homburg's thought.

"Mr. Homburg," from Concord, is presumably one of the Transcendentalists of Concord, though he has left home. He may be a post-1894 variety, as the Homburg hat appeared only then, to follow the OED. Perhaps a suitably Germanic heir to Emerson and like-minded thinkers. The hat suggests the character.

"Or we put mantles on our words because / The same wind, rising and rising": echoing Milton's creation story, ". . . at the voice of God, as with a mantle, didst invest / The rising world of water dark and deep" (*PL* III.9–11).

Song of Fixed Accord

Ibid.; CP 519–20, LOA 441.

A charming evocation of the sight and sound of mourning doves, enfolding touches of the old iconographies of the dove into Stevens's rich "ordinariness."

Appropriately, Stevens uses imitative sound, and much internal, assonantal, and near-rhyme. The dimeter stress in the first stanza is altered for the female dove's stanzas, and also later.

TITLE: "accord" as both "being in tune" and "tuning"; "of ": a song about fixed accord, a song with no variations in the tuning.

"Rou-cou": "coo," adapted from the similar Fr. echoic verb, *roucouler* ("to coo").

"sooth lord of sorrow": the mourning dove, in archaic guise, expanding through "sooth love" to the dove as bird of love (e.g., Venus's birds).

"hail-bow, hail-bow": the repeated bobbing motion of this bird, adapted to its personified self.

"fixed heaven": fixed in a general sense, and as in the old Ptolemaic cosmology with fixed stars.

"Day's invisible beginner": a fruitfully ambiguous phrase: invisible to those lying in bed and hearing dawn birdsong, in which case this is the male bird; invisible like the sun's warmth (cf. the sun as Ulysses in the following poem); whether the Holy Spirit as impregnating dove was visible or not is a moot point; the visible beginner of day is the sun.

The World as Meditation

Ibid.; CP 520–21, LOA 441–42.

An exquisite poem of hope and patient waiting for something greatly desired. The faithful Penelope here personifies any such faithfulness, and a Ulysses-sun figure personifies what is so desired. (Compare the use of the word "faithful" for the calling of an artist.) Stevens draws on the intensely moving reunion of Penelope and Ulysses in Homer's *Odyssey*. A favorite stanza, the unrhymed tercet, here has very long lines with varying stress. The syntax shows a high proportion of short sentences for Stevens, twenty in a 24-line poem.

TITLE: the unobtrusive title raises questions: what world? (More than one would qualify here.) In what ways can any world be "as meditation"?

EPIGRAPH: "J'ai passé . . . ENESCO": (Fr.) "I have spent too much time working with my violin, traveling. But the essential exercise of the composer— meditation—nothing has ever suspended that in me. . . . I live a permanent dream, which stops neither by night nor by day." Georges Enesco (or Enescu: 1881–1955) was a Romanian violin virtuoso and composer.

"interminable adventurer": the phrase works for both Ulysses and the sun.

"trees are mended": in a seafaring context, we expect to hear that the nets are mended, as in "Continual Conversation with a Silent Man."

"savage": see note on "savage" in OE IV.

"Companion," "friend and dear friend": cf. NSF II.IV, "companion," etc. Compare also the opening terms, which work for the "opposite natures" here, though the emphasis and tone differ.

"inhuman meditation": the world, like Penelope, meditates, awaiting the sun and the change of seasons; "inhuman": cf. "Of Mere Being."

"fetchings": fine ambiguous play on "far-fetched," on "fetching" as "charming," and on a "fetch" as someone's ghost or double.

"His arms would be her necklace": the implicit trope of "Auroras of Autumn" III.12 is here explicit.

"belt": cf. the garments of Nanzia Nunzio (NSF II.VIII); generally, evoking the magic belt or girdle of Venus.

"barbarous": corresponding, and responding, to the "savage presence" of the Ulysses-sun.

"as she combed her hair": in Stevens, sometimes a memorable act, e.g., "a woman / Combing. The poem of the act of the mind" ("Of Modern Poetry").

"with its patient syllables": patience is a predominant virtue of Penelope's. She and the Ulysses-sun figure appear to come together, yet remain distinct, rather as Stevens's late landscapes hold reality and imagination in one.

Long and Sluggish Lines

Origin 2 (spring 1952); CP 522, LOA 442–43.

Another February poem, with a strong second half, at first masquerading as simply an older man's sense of déja-vu. The first stanza is especially fine. A sense of coming rejuvenation begins with the challenge in stanza 5. Compare "A Discovery of Thought."

TITLE: The lines are shorter on average than those in "The World as Meditation," in case we suppose long lines must be sluggish. Compare also the lines of smoke, etc., as if in "earth-lines, long and lax, lethargic" ("Stars at Tallapoosa").

"Wood-smoke": cf. Stevens's favorite du Bellay sonnet, "Ulysse . . ." (see note on "A Dish of Peaches in Russia," above), also "Death of a Soldier."

"—essent—issant pre-personae": "-essent" is a common suffix, to which we can add any appropriate prespring start; "issant" is Stevens's own coinage, as is "spissantly" in "Snow and Stars," unless of course it is Fr. as in *florissant*.

"infanta": (Sp.) "infant, princess," playing on "infant," "infantine," as elsewhere in Stevens (see Concordance, also note on "Infanta Marina," above); on "infantine" as looking to the future, see L 367 (1940).

"Babyishness of forsythia": one of the first shrubs to bloom in spring, with
    swollen flower-buds in February; commonly forced for indoor late-
    winter bloom; yellow, like the "yellow patch."
"spook . . . of the nude magnolia": like forsythia, magnolia blooms very early
    in the spring; in February, its candle-like buds may look like ghosts of its
    forthcoming flowers.
"pre-history," "not yet born": life in February as, first, the time before recorded
    history, then as life still in the womb or "this wakefulness inside a sleep."

A Quiet Normal Life

Voices 147 (Jan.–Apr. 1952); CP 523, LOA 443–44.

Another poem of place and one of Stevens's quiet-evening-at-home poems,
with unexpected reverberations. The title suggests an exercise: write down ex-
amples of a quiet normal life, then read this poem. Do the examples need re-
vising or enlarging? Until the end, the poem does not disclose whether the
quiet normal life is tedious and deprived or not. The end raises the question of
how many such lives include a similar flame of life. The poem is another ex-
ample of Stevens's work with the words "normal," "ordinary," and "common."

"not," "naught": homophonic rhyme, unusual in Stevens, emphasized by in-
    ternal rhyme with "thought."
"peaked," "cut": the two end-words may each be read in a destructive or a
    constructive sense, e.g., "cut" as in wound or as in diamond-cutting.
"gallant notions": "gallant" takes a full range of meaning, in a contrast of nat-
    ural phenomena and a domestic setting. The contrast is heightened by
    the near-repetition of l. 6 in l. 11. Compare the very different ending of
    "Domination of Black," another poem where natural outside phenom-
    ena surround a room containing a fire.
"candle . . . artifice": see also the following poem for a candle of great force, a
    trope for the strength of the imagination. Compare the earlier and
    weaker "Valley Candle."

Final Soliloquy of the Interior Paramour

Hudson Review 4 (spring 1951), "Two Poems," with "The Course of a Particular"; CP
524, LOA 444; final poem in Stevens's selection of "representative" work for the 1953
Faber and Faber *Selected Poems* (L 732n.).

One of Stevens's beautifully realized and affecting late poems, something of a
Credo for him. (James Merrill said that "Sometimes I feel about this poem

the way others feel about the Twenty-Third Psalm" [see Katha Pollitt, "Poetry on Location," *Nation* 246 (16 Apr. 1988)].) Its strength lies partly in its sure measured judgment about how much, and how, to claim for the imagination. Compare the dedicatory poem to NSF.

TITLE: a soliloquy, in dramatic terms, is spoken to oneself alone (unlike a dramatic monologue, which implies an auditor). Why then does the speaker use the first person plural and open with an imperative, as if to another person? Because the paramour is interior, a muse figure, a crucially enabling part of one's own self. Stevens defined earlier "paramours" as "all the things in our nature that are celestial" (L 367, 1940). Given her importance, a "final" word requires close attention. Does Stevens anticipate that she will vanish? Not necessarily.

"Light the first light": a simple domestic act that faintly echoes God's primal act of creation, "Fiat lux," "Let there be light" (Gen. 1:3).

"ultimate good": as in *summum bonum*.

"in that thought," etc.: the prepositions are important throughout, for a sense of the right placing of this poem's affirmations.

"since we are poor": on poetry as "a purging of the world's poverty" and something that helps "the irremediable poverty of life," see "Adagia" (OP 193, LOA 906).

"God and the imagination are one": the noun clause is one of two "Propositia" in "Adagia" (OP 202, LOA 914) where it stands as an independent sentence; note the effect of adding "we say."

"How high that highest candle lights the dark": echoing Portia's "How far that little candle throws its beams!" (*Merchant of Venice* V.i.90).

The Rock

Trinity Review 8 (May 1954), with "Not Ideas about the Thing . . ."; CP 525–28, LOA 445–47.

A three-part poem, explicitly from someone in his seventies. The rock as the ground of being is here "the gray particular of man's life," "the stern particular," but then "the habitation of the whole" (III). Contrast the frequent symbolism of a rock as comforting stability or the biblical tradition of God as a rock (cf. Eliot's 1934 *Choruses from "The Rock"*). The central metaphor of leaves covering, then curing the rock, is developed in a way that is a shade doctrinal. The poem intimates that the desire to cover the rock is not only human, but also a wider desire within nature (cf. Frost, "West-Running Brook"). Compare also the introduction to *The Necessary Angel* on poetry as illuminating "a surface, the movement of a self in the rock" (NA viii, LOA 639, 1951).

I *Seventy Years Later*

On the sometimes unreal effect of old memories, when examined by some-body over seventy.

"rigid . . . no longer remain": on how memories change over time, cf. "A Postcard from the Volcano" with "The Auroras of Autumn" III.

"absurd": Stevens, on his birthday in 1939, wrote that a poet should be thirty rather than sixty. It seemed "incredible" to him that he was sixty (L 343).

"an illusion so desired": note the move from an unmodified "illusion" in l. 1. For Stevens, illusion is not necessarily negative; he offered "the idea of God" as an example of "benign illusion" (L 402, 1942).

II *The Poem as Icon*

"cured . . . by a cure": cf. "Adagia" on poetry as "a cure of the mind" (OP 201, LOA 913).

"a cure of the ground": ground in multiple senses, chiefly the ground of be-ing, philosophical ground, agricultural ground, etc.

"the pearled chaplet of spring, / The magnum wreath of summer, time's au-tumn snood": as if in a painting of the iconography of the seasons, shown in head-dresses; note also the likeness to flower buds or dew. A snood gathers in the hair as if gathering in harvest (see also note on "snood" "Late Hymn from the Myrrh-Mountain," above).

III *Forms of the Rock in a Night-Hymn*

"the gate / To the enclosure, day, the things illumined by day . . .": another ex-ample of Stevens's liminal imagery for intensely apprehended, significant moments of existence ("the fragrant portals" at the end of "The Idea of Order at Key West," "in-bar" and "ex-bar" in "Esthétique du Mal" v, etc.).

"midnight-minting fragrances": playing on "newly minted" at the portentous midnight hour, when a new day begins, and on the aromatic family of herbs.

St. Armorer's Church from the Outside

Poetry 81 (Oct. 1952); CP 529–30, LOA 448–49.

Within the topos of a ruined building, a church, Stevens devises new life, a chapel "of breath." (On responses to a ruined ecclesiastical structure, cf.

especially Wordsworth's "Lines . . . [on] Tintern Abbey.") The Episcopalian Church of the Good Shepherd in Hartford was built in memory of Col. Samuel Colt and three children who died in infancy. Much of the architecture, carving, and stained glass represents peace (the church was consecrated in 1869) and also Christian pastoral care, including the text, "Feed my lambs" (quoted by Stevens in his "Adagia"). The architect liked to include details relating to his patron's life, so that one entrance, "the armorer's porch," includes stone carvings of gun barrels, pistol handles, and so on, together with crosses and other religious symbols (see goodshepherdhartford.org). After floods in the 1930s, the church's foundation began to rot and the 150-foot steeple began to lean noticeably. The building presented a standing allegory for Hartford inhabitants. The multiple ironies need no further comment.

"an immense success": a tell-tale phrase, like the adverbs in the next line; this church once liked such trite and inappropriate self-congratulation.

"fixed one for good": punning on the usual idiom, applying it to the graveyard and heavenly destiny.

"geranium-colored": the geranium is also associated with "our more vestigial states of mind" in NSF II.III.19.

"Terre Ensevelie": (Fr.) "Earth Entombed."

"Matisse at Vence": the chapel of the Dominicaines at Vence, where the wall paintings, stained glass, and more were designed by Matisse; it is full of light. Matisse (1869–1954) completed it in 1950.

"The *vif*": (Fr.) "the quick" (as in flesh), a living person.

"sacred syllable rising from sacked speech": the alliteration slows the pace, and focuses attention on the unusual trope of sacking speech; sacking a city like Troy or Rome meant a radical change of civilization (cf. the preceding line).

"The first car out of a tunnel": a fine shift to a modern trope of emergence from the dark.

"achieved, / Not merely desired, for sale": playing against biblical "first fruits" and fruits of the spirit, i.e., St. Armorer's fruits.

"market things / That press": see "John Crowe Ransom, Tennessean," OP 248, LOA 820 (1948) for Stevens's intensely emotional response to a farmers' market with poor produce.

Note on Moonlight

Shenandoah 3 (autumn 1952); CP 531–32, LOA 449–50.

"It is as if being was to be observed": recalling Bishop Berkeley's philosophical dictum, "*Esse est percipi*" ("To be is to be observed").

"the arbors that are as if of Saturn-star": i.e., of the planet Saturn, the farthest of the seven known planets in ancient cosmology; Saturn is also an old Roman god, sometimes of seed-time, and so appropriate for arbors (see OCD). Compare also the play on Saturn in NSF II.1. There is pronounced near and partial rhyme throughout ll. 16–18.

"in a corner of the looking-glass": on light effects caught this way, cf. "Esthétique du Mal" 1.5–6.

The Planet on the Table

Accent 13 (summer 1953); CP 532–33, LOA 450.

If the work of a good poet embodies a world, then it can be a planet, like a globe that sits on the table. Adopting a persona of the young Stevens, this poem on his body of work is at once valedictory and celebratory. Its judgments, like those in "Final Soliloquy of the Interior Paramour," are measured, sure, and memorable.

"Ariel": Shakespeare's engaging spirit of air in *The Tempest*, and Stevens's early name for one of his writing selves (L 123, 1909, also L 124).

"ripe shrub writhed": unusually emphatic, with three adjacent strong stresses in a short line (cf. Keats's "And no birds sing," the last line of "La Belle Dame Sans Merci"). With the trope and assonance, cf. Browning's "How the vines writhe," where nature similarly mirrors a state of mind ("James Lee" III); see also l. 1 of "The Ultimate Poem Is Abstract."

"His self and the sun were one": a constant perspective in Stevens, from "Sunday Morning" in 1915 onward.

"if only half-perceived": echoing and revising "all the mighty world of eye, and ear—both what they half create, / And what perceive" (Wordsworth, "Lines . . . [on] Tintern Abbey," 105–7); the internal rhyme with "affluence" mitigates the fractional sense of "half."

The River of Rivers in Connecticut

Inventario 5 (summer 1953); CP 533, LOA 451.

One of Stevens's last and greatest river poems. A powerful assertion of the astonishing force of life, all the more evident and necessary as death approaches. The awareness of death is constant for the first four tercets, but rebuffed by the movement of this "great river." The Connecticut River, which flows through Hartford, is realized as both actual and metaphoric at once, taking on the mythic force of the "fateful" Stygia and conquering it. The iambic pentameter line includes a number of spondees (striking in l. 7) and opening stressed syllables for emphasis. Four negatives define this river and defy death in ll. 7–10. Note also the grammatical moods, and the use of repetition, culminating in the explicit "once more" and "again and again."

"Stygia": the area of the Styx, the river that circles Hades nine times, black and
    gloomy. The great oath of the gods was taken in the name of the Styx, "eld-
    est daughter of Oceanus" (Hesiod, *Theogony* 776; Homer, *Iliad* XIV.271).
"mere": see note on "Of Mere Being," below.
"No shadow walks": as at noon, and much more "no shadow" as a shade or
    ghost of the dead.
"fateful, / Like the last one": the force of life is just as "fateful" as the force of
    death.
"no ferryman": no Charon, who ferries the dead across the last river, for a fee.
"bend against": as a rower, and also as a mythical figure who reflects the force
    of the last river, death; etymologically, "reflect" is "bend back or aside"
    (cf. "reflecting," l. 16).
"Farmington": on the Farmington River, a tributary of the Connecticut River,
    upstream from Hartford; "Haddam": on the Connecticut River, down-
    stream from Hartford; the place-names stress that this is not an other-
    worldly river, but the actual one, seen by an imaginative man.
"third commonness, with light and air": cf. the epigraph to "Evening without
    Angels."
"curriculum": a running (Lat. *cursus*), like a river.
"The river that flows nowhere, like the sea": and like the bloodstream; recall-
    ing the Styx; recalling also Oceanus, the circumambient ocean-river that
    encircles the earth and is a source of life in Homer, Hesiod, etc. (OCD,
    "Oceanus," both entries). (See also "flows round the earth" in "Metaphor
    as Degeneration.") Stevens drew a diagram of Achilles' shield in the back
    of his college copy of *The Laocoon, and other Prose Writings of Lessing*,
    trans. and ed. W. B. Rönnfeldt (London: Walter Scott, n.d.); he penciled
    in the name "Oceanus," which surrounds the interior scenes of the shield
    (copy at the Huntington Library).

Not Ideas about the Thing but the Thing Itself

Trinity Review 8 (May 1954), with "The Rock"; CP 534, LOA 451–52.

On a common, happy, late-winter dawn experience: the first cry of a newly arrived bird, which heralds the start of the eventual loud chorus of spring birdsong at daybreak. The six mostly unrhymed tercets have unusually short lines; "outside" appears as an end-word three times, an emphatic positioning; note also the use of sibilants and hard *c* sounds. The technique works to provide a strongly affirmative, clear poem.

TITLE: cf. "Part of the res itself and not about it" (OE XII); prepositions are important throughout the poem.

"seemed like a sound in his mind": a common phenomenon when waking from sleep.

"panache": see OED or Webster on the two meanings; note etymology (Lat. *penna*, "feather"), and also the connection with knightly splendor, as in Stevens's various Dons, who are often associated with the sun.

"papier-mâché": in a recording, Stevens uses Fr. pronunciation, as the accents suggest.

"A chorister whose c preceded the choir": recalling and surpassing the sound effects of "The Comedian as the Letter C"; pun on "pre-c-eded," as if the act of preceding included the letter c, to which the choir of birds will be tuning, as a modern orchestra tunes to A above middle C.

"part of the colossal sun": in nature, dependent like all life on earth upon the sun; as if singing a hymn of and with the earlier-rising sun; as if rewriting Milton's morning hymn (*PL* V.153–208).

"like / A new knowledge of reality": a simple simile that captures this common, joyful experience, and a powerful closing sentence to Stevens's *Collected Poems*.

Late Poems
from "Three Academic Pieces"
(1947) and from 1950–55

With the exception of the poems from "Three Academic Pieces," (see the first entry, below) these poems follow the selection and order in the LOA edition, "Late Poems," 453–77. A number of them were written after Stevens's 1954 *Collected Poems* went to press; at least one, "The Course of a Particular," was omitted inadvertently (L 881, 1955).

Someone Puts a Pineapple Together

Part 2 of "Three Academic Pieces," NA 83–87, LOA 693–97.

This poem and the following one constitute Parts 2 and 3 of "Three Academic Pieces," extending and exemplifying the essay of Part 1, which in turn provides a vital gloss on the poems. The opening argument of Part 1 governs the whole: "The accuracy of accurate letters is an accuracy with respect to the structure of reality," etc. Part III of this poem includes the tour de force of 12 one-line metaphors for a pineapple (an exercise worth trying for any apprentice poet using any suitable object).

TITLE: cf. "Piece the world together, boys," etc. ("Parochial Theme") and other synonyms of the latinate word "compose" in *Parts of a World*; the word "pineapple" is itself put together out of "pine" and "apple."

I

"O juventes, O filii": (Lat.) "O youths, O sons"; cf. the opening tutelary address in NSF I.i.1, "Begin, ephebe."
"a wholly artificial nature": wherein a natural object may appear as if it were man-made, perhaps by isolating it "on a table"; wherein a natural object inspires the mind with resemblances or metaphors (cf. "the mind begets in resemblance," NA 76, LOA 689, 1947) in such a way that nature and

artifice appear as one whole when contemplated; an apparent oxymoron catches the condition.

"The profusion of metaphor has been increased": on how "the proliferation of resemblances extends an object" and gives pleasure, see NA 78, LOA 691 (1947).

"the angel at the center of this rind": as, e.g., the angel of reality in "Angel Surrounded by Paysans"; grown perhaps from the X shape in pineapple rind that resembles a simplified angel form with outspread wings and garment, as in Christmas-tree decorations.

"Himself, may be . . .": the tuft transmuted into a tuft of hair on a pineapple-head; the self as origin of the preceding "profusion of metaphor."

"a jar of the shoots of an infant country": with the contrast of "jar" and "urn," "infant" and "venerable," cf. OE vi; as often in Stevens, "infant" puns on Lat. *infans*, or "not speaking," here shoots (or metaphors) being propagated and not yet rooted or developed into their full potential.

"from the ash within it, fortifies": on phoenix-like renewal from ashes, cf. "Of Mere Being"; wood ashes do actually fortify plant growth, being rich in phosphate.

"the chance / Concourse of planetary originals": cf. Stevens on Bishop Berkeley and what he might have dubbed "a fortuitous concourse of personal orders" (L 293, 1935).

"of human residence": part of Stevens's lifelong work on what makes a true human dwelling-place; numerous types of residence abound in his poems.

II

"true": in a capacious sense that includes true metaphor, not simply "true" as fact or information.

"defy / The metaphor that murders metaphor": a challenge to the reader, especially if tempted to think of all metaphors as alike. If weak or hackneyed metaphors may eventually murder metaphor, do they need defying rather than simply avoiding? Compare also "metamophorid" and "Mac Mort she had been" ("Oak Leaves Are Hands").

"truth's most jealous subtlety": "jealous" as "zealous, vigilant on behalf of."

"erudite . . . scholia . . . scholar": "Poetry is the scholar's art" ("Adagia," OP 193, LOA 906).

"capital": as a city, with arrondissements like Paris; also etymologically, as the head (Lat. *caput*).

III

Lines 1–12 provide an extraordinary series of one-line, mostly one-sentence, tropes for a pineapple, numbered as if an exercise in poetry-writing.

"island Palahude": not traced in this spelling; "Pulau" is the word for "island" in the Pacific around Malaysia and the Philippines; there is a Pulau Ubin in Singapore and a Palau is part of Micronesia; the area was part of the Pacific war zone in World War II, and much in the news; pineapples grow in the region.

"tropic of resemblance . . . Capricorn": playing on "trope," as elsewhere, and on the tropic immediately south of the equator, a pineapple-growing area, where Palahude is likely to be located; playing also on meanings and cognates of "Capricorn."

"In the planes that tilt hard revelations on / The eye": cf. the painter's discipline of looking intently at plane surfaces; cf. also Cézanne as quoted by Stevens in 1951: ' "I see planes bestriding each other' " and ' "The colored areas where shimmer the souls of the planes' " (NA 174, LOA 750).

"ellipsis . . . planes . . . geometric . . . cones": in his copy of Adams's *Vico*, Stevens marked the sentence, "to exercise, and at the same time restrain and curtail the imagination, an adolescent should study geometry" (H. P. Adams, *The Life and Writings of Giambattista Vico* [1935], 87; copy at the University of Massachusetts, Amherst, Library).

Of Ideal Time and Choice

Part 3 of "Three Academic Pieces," NA 88–89, LOA 697–98.

A gloss or scholium on "Someone Puts a Pineapple Together," as well as a poem on its own. Like the preceding poem, this one is written in unrhymed tercets with an iambic pentameter base. Ten stanzas out of eleven comprise one 30-line sentence that ends with interrogation. The poem covers familiar Stevens territory, freshly reimagined.

"Since thirty mornings are required . . . thirty summers . . . thirty years": cf. Housman's tabulation of time in "Loveliest of trees."

"lapised and lacqued": cf. the blue woman of NSF III.ii, "linked and lacquered."

"clear revolving crystalline": see note on "crystal" in NSF III.x, above, and cf. "an inchoate crystal tableau" in "Someone Puts a Pineapple Together" III.

"inhuman making choice of a human self ": on an inhuman (but not inimical) force in the universe, especially in Stevens's late poetry, cf. "The World as Meditation" and "The Sail of Ulysses"; the meaning of "inhuman" develops through his work.

The Sick Man

Accent 10 (1950); OP 118, LOA 455.

A poem whose development is embodied in its sentence structure: (1) two sentences of music heard or recalled that coincide with stanzas 1 and 2; (2) one 9-line sentence, no longer passive but gathering strength as unison is anticipated, and, much more, anticipated words for a distant or even a final bed.

"the dissolving chorals": this variant spelling of "chorale" is often associated with German *Choral-gesang*, or "plainsong," such as Luther's "Ein' Feste Burg"; thus in Longfellow, trans., "The Children of the Lord's Supper" (Tegner), "Tuned to the choral of Luther." The association is especially pertinent for a speaker in a Stevens poem; see references to Luther and to this well-known hymn in "The Old Lutheran Bells at Home."

"the listener, listening to the shadows, seeing them": cf. "The Snow Man," also "shadows" as shades or ghosts of the dead.

"Choosing out of himself": both the participle (not passively accepting others' speech) and the pronoun (not out of an outside source) indicate inner strength in facing illness.

"good hail": "hail" is both "health" (obs.) and a salutation (cf. Lat. *salve* or *salute*, also "hail" in "Hymn from a Watermelon Pavilion"); the grammar works whether the sick man will recover or will die, and indicates he is preparing for both.

As at a Theatre

Wake 9 (1950), with the following five poems, all under "Six Poems"; OP 118–19, LOA 455–56.

"outre-terre": outside the earth, Stevens's coinage, modeled on Fr. "outre-mer," "overseas"; he knew the term and used it in a letter to Barbara Church, "Your first letter *d'outre mer* . . ." (L 787, 1953).

The Desire To Make Love in a Pagoda

Ibid.; OP 119, LOA 456.

Stevens plays with a possible ambiguity in "in": a human desire to make love in a pagoda or a pagoda's own desire to make love. Make love to what? Surely the sky, as in the long-standing trope of hills, trees, buildings, etc., meeting the sky (e.g., "heaven-kissing hills," *Hamlet* III.iv.60). Stevens, like Shakespeare, personifies the earthly object. Generically, close to a riddle poem. A Chinese pagoda was constructed on Mount Penn near Reading in 1906–8, and Stevens records walking with Elsie up to "the dark Pagoda, black in a night full of mysterious calm and heavenly beauty" (SP 226, 1909). A witty, erotic, layered poem on desires of the body and of feelings; on a primal desire for morning, which a temple might desire, as in love.

"rioter": also a near-anagram for "erotic," "when things are changed."
"alien freedom": a pagoda is a foreign or "alien" temple; here, the body is not "the temple of the Lord" as in biblical usage, but behaving more like a pagoda.
"peak": in the different senses of making love and of the top of a pagoda.

Nuns Painting Water-Lilies

Ibid.; OP 120, LOA 456–57.

Based on actual observation of a group of nuns who came to Elizabeth Park several mornings "to paint water colors especially of the water lilies." The sight always gave Stevens a sense of chasteness, which, he added, reminded him of "the chasteness of the girl in Oscar Wilde who spent her time looking at photographs of the Alps." Then, one morning, "even these exquisite creatures" had vanished (L 610, 1948).

"pods": literally, the prominent seed-pods of water-lilies; figuratively, new life, as of water-lilies in paintings, a subject dominated by Claude Monet.
"queer chapeaux": the head-dresses of nuns vary according to their order; "chapeaux": (Fr.), "hats."

The Role of the Idea in Poetry

Ibid.; OP 120–21, LOA 457.

Reversing "the role of poetry in philosophy" or in whatever (cf. A. R. Ammons, "The Role of Society in the Artist"). The poem assigns a dramatic rather than an abstract role to "Idea," as "poetry" becomes a drama or a stage or a world.

Americana

Ibid.; OP 121, LOA 457–58.

"Flaunts": the subject is "hoop-la" in a somewhat confusing syntax, as Stevens plays on various ambiguities.

The Souls of Women at Night

Ibid.; OP 122, LOA 458.

Spoken by an "I" of Spanish origin, one of Stevens's women with mysterious night-lives, who go back to "The Ordinary Women." On owls and women, cf. "Hoot, little owl, within her" ("Woman Looking at a Vase of Flowers"). This female may be a prototype or the cata-sisters may explain the plural in the title.

"much-horned night": as of the "tuft-eared" or horned owl (l. 3), as of the horned moon, as of cuckolds.
"cata-sisters": "cata-" (Gk.), prep., "down" in various senses, "reflecting on," etc.; echo of "cat" (perhaps because they are also night-time prowlers who can see in the dark like owls).
"amigas": (Sp.) "female friends."

A Discovery of Thought

Imagi 5 (1950); OP 122–23, LOA 459.

A simple but passionate anticipation of new birth: of spring while icebound in winter, as well as of the true best word for a writer. (Stevens himself became a grandfather in 1947.) As with "Notes toward a Supreme Fiction," every word of the title matters. Contrast with the following poem, and cf. both with "The Snow Man." As anticipation grows, the sentence-rhythms lengthen; the last two-thirds of the poem contain a 9-line and a 7-line sentence.

TITLE: "A," not "The"; "Discovery" is a strong word in Stevens: cf. "discover" as against "impose" in NSF III. vii, and "surrealism . . . invents without discovering" ("Materia Poetica," OP 203, LOA 919). "Of " is used in both senses, so that we discover something in or about thought, while thought itself also makes a discovery; the double meaning catches mental experience.
"At the antipodes of poetry, dark winter": the word "antipodes" echoes regularly, inviting us to test later uses against our expectations in l. 1.
"the trees glitter with that which despoils them": the aftermath of an ice-storm, as also in the following lines.
"Daylight evaporates": a fine trope for shortened daylight hours in winter, and for frequent waning light during the day; the trope also briefly anticipates the different evaporations of early spring, only to be cut off by another trope on the very different evaporations one experiences in sickness.

"One is a child again": icebound winter readily evokes childhood responses to a seemingly magic landscape. Note grammatical person throughout: "One is," "One thinks," "One thinks" (all at the start of the line), then the quiet shift to first person with "ours" in l. 19.

"infancy": as elsewhere, with a sense of "unable to speak" (see note on "Infanta Marina," above), though only in retrospect.

"One thinks": note the change from "thought" in the title to the verb "think"; each of the following appositions tropes on and also delays the coming of the "first word"; the core sentence moves from l. 12 to l. 14–15.

The Course of a Particular

Hudson Review 4 (1951), with "Final Soliloquy of the Interior Paramour," both under "Two Poems"; OP 123–24, LOA 460.

Stevens returns to the topos of the leaves in this compact, slowly paced, memorable poem. He starts with a memory of "The Snow Man" (l. 2), where the sound of winter leaves also provides a starting-point. No attribution like misery is heard in the sound here, though the trope invites it: "The leaves cry." The sentence "The leaves cry" and the word "cry" echo throughout. The stress in the 12–14-syllable lines varies greatly.

TITLE: playing against expectations, as so often; not "The Course of a Particular X," but "particular" as noun; in logic, the particular is contrasted to the universal, a meaning that is in play here, as Stevens repeatedly declines to attach any universal significance to the cry.

"the nothingness of winter": recalling, but altering "The Snow Man" ("nothingness" this time).

"shapen": usually in combination (e.g., "ill-shapen"); here the reader may provide kinds of shaping.

"declines": in the two related senses of "lessens" and "says no."

"the smoke-drift of puffed-out heroes": smoke as from a chimney or a smoker, playing on various meanings of "puffed-out."

"in the final finding of the ear . . . at last," a moment that Stevens leaves to the reader to decide.

"in the thing / Itself ": note the different relation of the thing itself to a cry in "Not Ideas about the Thing But the Thing Itself."

How Now, O, Brightener . . .

Shenandoah 3 (1952); OP 124, LOA 460–61.

"Brightener" is another epithet for the sun in another sun-and-spring poem. Here the mind does not "lay by its troubles" as in "Credences of Summer" I. Instead it offers "a residue, a land," and much more, for the "spectra," even in the life of springtime. The remarkable series of tropes explores the kind and degree of the mind's trouble. The poem consists of one 12-line sentence that develops its logic in unexpected ways, including a surprise ending.

"the green-edged yellow," etc.: such simple naming of color, as if in a painting or photo, is a favorite technique (cf. "Nomad Exquisite" or OE XXVIII).

"apparition": linked with "nourishing element / And simple love," and so comparable to the apparition in "Angel Surrounded by Paysans" or the benign ghosts in "Credences of Summer" I.

"spectra": a fine play on the plural of "spectrum" and "specter," in a link with "apparition."

"take from . . . stunted looks": "take from" at first sounds like "detract from," until the last line shifts the meaning and diminishes the force of any inimical ghosts among the spectra.

The Dove in Spring

7 Arts, ed. Ferando Puma (Garden City, N.Y.: Perma Books, 1954); OP 124–25, LOA 461.

Another poem of birdsong in spring, another dove poem, another poem of predawn consciousness, well caught in the closing two lines. The poem reflects on how dove-sounds might resemble some human thought processes.

"Brooder, brooder": playing on the double sense of meditating in a moody or morbid way and brooding on eggs in a nest (cf. Milton's Holy Spirit, who "Dove-like satst brooding on the vast Abyss," *PL* I.21); the emphatic opening trochees also echo dove-song, as conventionally rendered in English, "coo, coo."

"small howling": a fine trope for the maddeningly insistent song of the mourning dove, also treated in the more powerful poem, "Song of Fixed Accord"; this is howling as of a ghost, not a child or a hyena.

"outer bush": the dove, like a human, thinks of a vast outer world, perhaps transcendent, say, of Milton's Dove, the incarnate form of the Holy Spirit.

"a place / And state of being large and light": as in the invocations to *PL* I
   and III.

Farewell without a Guitar

New World Writing (n.p.: New American Library, 1954); OP 125, LOA 461–62.

A spring poem that is also a moving valedictory poem for Stevens's Spanish
self, seen earlier in several Dons, the hidalgo, etc. The riderless horse marks a
death; the absence of a guitar, so often the instrument of earlier poetic voice,
marks the death even more sharply. The five tercets retain a strong pulse in
lines varied from four to eleven syllables.

"the thousand-leaved green . . . red": more familiar as the botanical name for
   common yarrow (millefolium), here finely adapted to the leaves of spring
   and fall.

The Sail of Ulysses

OP 126, LOA 462–67 (a version was read in 1954, L 834–35).

The culmination of Stevens's quest poems, starting with the early "Nomad
Exquisite," and of his Ulysses figure. Ulysses as "symbol of the seeker" is the
Ulysses familiar from Tennyson's dramatic monologue by that name, not
Dante's Ulysses, who is possessed with overweening pride. It is written by a
man in the later years of his life, not by a man of twenty-four, as Tennyson
was. Stevens takes for granted the governing trope of the wind as breath, in-
spiration, and/or spirit that moves the sail, as in, e.g., "Sailing after Lunch."
The sail in turn moves the craft as ship, as the human body, and as the artistic
craft of the poet. The poem is a soliloquy in the form of an eight-part medita-
tion on Ulysses' statement, " '*As I know, I am and have / The right to be,*' " and
framed by two six-line, third-person stanzas. From "Notes toward a Supreme
Fiction" onward, Stevens had been thinking about his own version of God's
"I am that I am" (Ex. 3:14, and see NSF II.viii, III.viii, III.x). Here, two
terms enter the affirmation: knowledge and "the right to be." Stevens's head-
ings to each section on his typescript (OP 324, LOA 462–67) are listed with
the stanza numbers, below.

"*Under the shape of his sail* . . . he said": "The place of the poem. Its theme."
"*shape of his sail*": on the poet as shaper or maker, see note on "The Idea of
   Order at Key West," above.
"*The giant sea*": for Ulysses in legend, the Atlantic, beyond the Mediter-
   ranean, through the Pillars of Hercules at Gibraltar.

"*the middle stars*": not the most distant, which elicit thoughts of infinity and
eternity.

I "To know is to be."

Knowledge as "the only life" appears to be full knowledge of people and
places; not only detached empirical and theoretical knowledge, but also
knowledge through imaginative identifying, etc., in a wide sense of the word.
The section consists of one 11-line sentence, with three parallel conditional
clauses, in an "if—then" logical construction.

II "To know is the force to be."

Also a single sentence, here 13 lines long.

"the inner direction on which we depend": see Stevens's moving letter to his
daughter, trying to persuade her to stay at university (L 425–26, 1942);
"inner direction" also as in sailing.

III "The true creator."

Two sentences, the first followed by an ellipsis without a stop; Stevens's el-
lipses usually call for a noticeable pause.

"created from nothingness": as elsewhere, an allusion to the Christian doc-
trine of creation from nothingness, or ex nihilo.

IV "The center of the self."

Again, a 13-line sentence, as with II, this time without a main verb. Eden is
conceived as "Morningside" and thereby plays between an imagined earthly
paradise (where the earth is fresh and new, as if in the morning of its exis-
tence) and an actual place. Stevens first read the poem at Columbia Univer-
sity, which is located in Morningside Heights, New York City.

"the order of man's right to be / As he is": extending Ulysses' opening state-
ment, in a familiar line of thought for Stevens.

V "Except for illogical receptions."

Another kind of life, also known, but not by will. Yet the description of the
ideal life (to call it that) seems more willed than realized, and the poem be-
comes slightly prosy in this section. The syntax changes sharply, with a num-
ber of short sentences and nine sentences in all in 31 lines. From here on, the
syntax remains similarly varied, including, e.g., several one-line sentences.

VI "Presence of an external master of knowledge."

"crystal": see note on "crystal" NSF III.x, above.

"the John-begat-Jacob of what we know": echoing once-familiar biblical language that lists the generations of men; a figure for accumulated familiar knowledge and tradition.

VII "Truth as fate."

"Plantagenet abstractions": still unread; a type of older reigning abstraction like the House of Plantagenet?

"the difficult inch": cf. the last canto of OE.

"a giant's back": cf. OE I.

VIII "Shape of the sibyl of truth."

A section that reads freshly, especially at the start.

"Not, / For a change, the englistered woman," etc.: not the traditional Sibyl, priestess of Apollo, uttering prophecies in mysterious language, and adapted to Christian use (as in Dante at the end of the *Paradiso*).

"a blind thing fumbling for its form," etc.: neither is this sibyl of the self similar to the desiccated sibyl of Petronius, which Eliot used in the epigraph to *The Waste Land*.

"*with an enigma's flittering . . .* ": again, the ellipsis requires a conscious pause; with this use of "enigma," cf. the three other late uses in the poetry ("Credences of Summer" IV, OE x, and "The Auroras of Autumn" IX), and also in NA 67, LOA 685, 1943); each use is distinct, on which see Cook, *Enigmas and Riddles in Literature* (2006), 210–25.

"*As if*": the ending itself affirms an imaginative way of thinking and knowing through "as."

"*and clumped stars dangled,*" etc.: cf. the final line of "Of Mere Being."

Presence of an External Master of Knowledge

Times Literary Supplement (17 Sept. 1954); OP 131–32, LOA 467–68.

Framed by two stanzas very close to the framing stanzas of "The Sail of Ulysses," and so inviting comparison. The two inner stanzas also form a short soliloquy, in a very condensed form of the longer poem.

TITLE: heading to section VI of "The Sail of Ulysses," and cf. "Final Soliloquy of the Interior Paramour."

A Child Asleep in Its Own Life

Ibid.; OP 132, LOA 468.

The title repeats a line from "The Sail of Ulysses" VIII, repositioning it in a new context, at first puzzling. What is the relation of the title to the "old men" that are the poem's subject? It helps to recall Wordsworth's "The child is father of the man," and to remember that all human beings contain different, though inter-twining, selves. An older man, as Stevens was when he wrote the poem, consists of several older men. So read, the poem is also about a child who will become an old man some day, like "the old men that you know." All the more so, if he knows a grandfather like Stevens, who is by definition part of himself. (Note the effect when the title is inverted, as in Mark Strand's "An Old Man Awake in His Own Death.") The "unnamed . . . single mind" is sometimes read mythically.

"a single mind": cf. elsewhere the working of one powerful single mind, sometimes human, sometimes more than human (e.g., "Metaphor as De-generation").

Two Letters

I *A Letter From* and II *A Letter To*

Vogue 1 (Oct. 1954); OP 132–33, LOA 468–69.

A study in contrast, on the subject of desire for an ideal place. "A Letter From" goes over familiar terrain in a slightly stale way, alluding to "The Po-ems of Our Climate" and echoing, e.g., "Final Soliloquy of the Interior Para-mour." "A Letter To" is centered on a female rather than "one," and invites comparison of its different and quite compelling ideal place. Despite the title, not in epistolary form, unless modulated (see Fowler, 108).

"dulcied": reinvented from the common Lat. root, rather than the unsweet-sounding "dulcified."

Conversation with Three Women of New England

Accent 14 (1954); OP 134–35, LOA 470–71.

TITLE: again a title indicating genre, this time the conversation poem (see NPEPP), whose modern form originated with Coleridge. Compare "Continual Conversation with a Silent Man."

Dinner Bell in the Woods

Perspective 7 (1954), with the following poem, both under "Two Poems"; OP 135, LOA 471.

Compare other scenes of meals in the woods, notably in NSF III.ix. The point of "the way he heard it" is left to the reader to imagine.

"belled the glass": made the glass into a bell by tapping on it; also playing on "belle," "belly," as well as on "Came tinkling on the grass," itself playing on the movement of small children.

Reality Is an Activity of the Most August Imagination

Ibid.; OP 135–36, LOA 471–72.

On the effects of driving in a car through the countryside late at night. This is a poem full of rushing movement, both of the car and of the night sky. The "big light" (l. 1) remains unspecified, so that the reader is invited to recall clear nights with glittering stars, and the effects of either the northern lights or a full moon, with clouds scudding across it. The language suggests the auroras. Stevens anchors the poem in a specific time and place and experience, where the "big light" is not fearsome, as in "The Auroras of Autumn," but exhilarating. The first stanza is striking, both for its casual tone and for its skilful execution. The words "night" and "light" echo through the opening and the closing lines.

TITLE: a sentence-title that is also a proposition; a pun on the month of August may be in play, as the season for the auroras at the Cornwall-Hartford latitude starts in late summer.

"Cornwall to Hartford": Cornwall, Conn., is "about an hour's drive from Hartford" (L 827, 1954), due east. Stevens spoke of spending "several week-ends, at Cornwall" with his friends, James A. and Margaret Powers, who owned a farm there "at which to loaf." Stevens especially enjoyed the sight of the power mower; it stood out on the lawn and Powers referred to it as "the statue." "Nothing," said Stevens, "could be more comatose" (L 795, 7 Aug. 1953; see also L 827, 1954; L 853–54, 1954). For Margaret Powers's reminiscences of Stevens's visits, see Brazeau 92.

"a glassworks in Vienna / Or Venice": both cities are renowned for glass design.

"a crush of strength in a grinding going round": as in a glassworks during production, as in a car driving quickly, as in the revolution of the stars and planets.

"argentine abstraction": displays of the auroras are commonly white, except in the far north.

On the Way to the Bus

OP 136, LOA 472.

The opening one-line sentence establishes the scene and conditions ("light snow"). The remaining 13-line sentence of this 7-couplet poem develops a response, notable chiefly for the penultimate line.

"journalist": as elsewhere, the part of Stevens's persona that notes events of the current day (Fr. "jour," day); cf. OE XIII.

The Region November

Zero 2 (1956), sent by Nov. 1954, see OP 324; OP 140, LOA 472–73.

Compare Stevens's other November effects, e.g., "Metamorphosis"; cf. also the more powerful poem "The Course of a Particular." Stevens deploys charm effects, echoing "sway" and "say," as well as the adverbs "deeply" and "loudly," which he converts into one-word comparative forms. The strong couplets follow the November rhythm of the poem.

Solitaire under the Oaks

Sewanee Review 63 (1955), with the following three poems, all under "Four Poems"; OP 137, LOA 473.

On solitaire as both a card game and a solitary (cf. "The Place of the Solitaires"). The word "cards" plays on *des cartes* (Fr. "playing-cards") and René Descartes; "principles" and "to principium, to meditations" refer to Descartes' *Principia philosophiae* and *Les Méditations*. Stevens owned and annotated Leon Roth's 1937 *Descartes' Discourse on Method* (copy at University of Massachusetts, Amherst, Library), and quoted it in 1943 (NA 55–56, LOA 677, 1943). He also owned a copy of Descartes' *Traité des passions* (sold at auction by Parke-Bernet in 1959). See also notes on Descartes in "Winter Bells" and NSF I.IV.

What card-game would M. Descartes play? Solitaire, surely (I think, therefore I am). The poem observes what this game omits and what it offers. The poem is itself a game, generically a riddle-poem, but in a simple and accessible guise even without its punning brilliancies.

Local Objects

Ibid.; OP 137–38, LOA 473–74.

The word "foyer" opens the poem, widens its context, then closes the poem. Compare the foyer of the spirit "at the end of thought" in "Crude Foyer." Note also the etymon, Latin *focus*, "hearth," and by extension, "home." The phrase "local objects" suggests objects that are largely unimportant except for their sentimental value, as against universal or classic objects. Stevens reverses such an assumption in a move typical of his late writing.

"that serene": for Stevens's varied uses of the word "serene," see the Concordance.

Artificial Populations

Ibid.; OP 138, LOA 474.

A poem that reads as if it followed on from the preceding poem. That poem's middle style continues here, adding a conversational second thought, as if the poem is thinking out loud: "Well, more than that," etc. Incorporating second thoughts into a poem is a movement that Elizabeth Bishop also liked.

A Clear Day and No Memories

Ibid.; OP 138–39, LOA 475.

The third interconnected poem, this time through "weather after it has cleared" and "air [that] is clear of everything." Stevens's wide use of the word "weather" is apparent, and in turn suggests a wider reading for "Artificial Populations." Note the work with negatives. Stevens catches a feeling of older people that is not often mentioned: that it may be a relief, at least briefly, to be rid of the memories of the long-known dead.

"Here before / And are not now": a surprising turn of thought, quietly introduced over the turn of the line.

Banjo Boomer

Atlantic Monthly 195 (Mar. 1955); OP 139, LOA 475.

Another poem with charm effects, this time a song with a strong beat and an appealing refrain. Repetitions propel the poem, which gradually becomes shadowed, though only a little, by the metaphors of stanzas 3 and 4. Stanza 4 touches lightly on the theme of how nature speaks and does not speak (cf. "The Course of a Particular," "The Region November," etc.). The near-rhyme of "shape" and "shade" links this theme to the refrain.

TITLE: Stevens told a 1954 interviewer that he had never played a banjo, though he used to play a guitar (Lewis Nichols, *New York Times*, 3 Oct. 1954).

"double tree": the mulberry as a double tree is not the legendary tree whose white flowers turned red with the blood of Pyramus and Thisbe (see Brewer); the sense of doubleness here is indicated in ll. 9–10.

July Mountain

Ibid. (Apr. 1955); OP 140, LOA 476.

A one-sentence, 10-line poem on the full mental world in which we live, and how we continually put it together. The stress is greatly varied.

"patches and pitches": see note on "patches . . . together," NSF epilogue; "pitches" adds the motion of "throws" (cf. l. 10) and also musical pitch (cf. l. 4).

"Vermont throws itself together": Vermont as reality composes itself ("patches"), and, as a word, "throws itself together" with two Fr. words, *vert* (green) and *mont* (mountain).

[A mythology reflects its region.]

OP 141, LOA 476.

The thesis of this untitled poem is familiar throughout Stevens's work. The poem leaves open the question of whether Connecticut might achieve a modern mythology.

"we": the pronoun unobtrusively raises questions of time and place; are these European settlers and their descendants and/or aboriginal inhabitants (who did have a mythology) and their descendants?

Of Mere Being

OP 141, LOA 476–77.

One of Stevens's most memorable poems and one of his last, written before entering hospital for surgery in April 1955. The mysterious bird sings in an otherworldly setting like that of Yeats's bird in "Sailing to Byzantium." The poem's metrical variation in a mere twelve lines is notable: regular, irregular, even strong-stress meter.

TITLE: "mere" takes its double meaning of "only, just" (often pejorative) and "essential, very."

"the end of the mind": "end" as the limit of reason and "end" as near death; similarly "last" (l. 2).

"fire-fangled": a neologism, combining "fire-fang" (obsolete, "caught by fire, singed, scorched") and "new-fangled" (derisory, from Old Eng. *fangol*, "inclined to take") to create the double meaning of "burned" and "inclined to take fire." Such language works for a mythological bird like the phoenix, while the new word itself rises fresh from the ashes of obsolete and derisory language.

"dangle down": emphatic internal rhyme, suggesting further rhymes like "dangling and spangling" (OE XXIX), in a strongly stressed line.

How To Read Poetry, Including Stevens

1. Preliminary

As it happened, I came to poetry late. Of course I heard some, starting with nursery rhymes, and I read some and even wrote some, aged eight. But I didn't read it in any full sense of the verb "to read." Most of it did not speak to me (as we say), though some of Shakespeare did and some Romantic poetry too. (These were the staple diet in the Ontario school curriculum in my generation.) And some minor verse stuck in my head because the rhymes were funny, sometimes unintentionally funny. I can still recite reams of Pauline Johnson's "The Song My Paddle Sings."

But poetry was mostly taught as High-Sounding Ceremony then. Stories and novels were different. They were gripping. They were irresistible. For them, we stayed up late reading under the covers. Poetry was something to quote on solemn occasions or in a political speech. It gave tone. Privately I thought a certain amount of it was self-indulgent nonsense—always excepting Shakespeare. This says a lot for the staying power of Shakespeare and for good teaching, since the Shakespeare I saw on the stage was declaimed as high-sounding ceremony by humans acting like wooden mannequins. Somehow the revered Shakespeare called for reverential treatment. So did the great Romantics, whose genius we all accepted as a matter of course, and whose work we duly memorized as required. (And for this requirement, I've always been grateful. So were my students, to my surprise, when I tentatively required a little memory-work in a first-year course. It gives us something to remember, they said.) But we didn't go to the library and hunt down books of poems. And we didn't stay up late reading poetry under the covers.

For me, all this changed when I was about twenty. There were a couple of reasons and I remember their occasions very well. I remember pacing up and down by a bus-stop in north Toronto, running a few lines by Browning through my head. I was trying to get a handle on an essay assignment. I began to think about exactly what those lines were saying, because the argument was not obvious. It didn't ooh or aah over trees, or beat the breast over unrequited love. It seemed fairly tough-minded, and it sounded as if it meant what it said. I thought to myself: why, one should take this stuff as seriously as prose. And I found myself fascinated.

The second occasion came about a year later. I was in Europe for the first time, and I went to see Shakespeare's *Much Ado about Nothing* because the two lead roles were being played by Peggy Ashcroft and John Gielgud. Do I need to say that they didn't declaim, that they weren't wooden mannequins? The audience fell in love with them, with the play, with Shakespeare. I thought, like many another: this is how we would all speak, if only we could. The curious thing is that there *was* ceremony, certainly. But this ceremony was different. It was not high-sounding. It seemed like true human ceremony, as required, intelligently sustained, tested as necessary. And with the understood liberty to be unceremonious, as required. This sense of poetry speaking as we would if only we could: this has stayed with me from that time on. Every time that I read or hear a new poem that works wonderfully well, I think something of the sort.

Most of my students are somewhat like my younger self in their attitude to poetry. The Ontario school system, though admirable in many ways, currently deprives its students of basic knowledge in grammar and poetics. Other jurisdictions apparently do so too. Students come like starved creatures to the pleasure and challenge of precise knowledge, for good poetry is very precise and the most highly organized of all verbal forms. Once I was yawning and squirming my way through a graduation ceremony, where Mavis Gallant was to be the speaker. She rose and spoke a living English, whereupon boredom and fatigue vanished instantly. The audience was energized, their brains released from the forced labor of cliché and allowed the pleasure of true work and play. So too with my students who begin to be able to read good poetry.

2. On Approaching Stevens's Poems for the First Time

How to approach this body of poetry, which does not reach out its hands in familiar poetic gestures? Perhaps something has attracted us, say, the slightest glance of a joke or a thought—something that catches our eye, like "The eye of a vagabond in metaphor / That catches our own" (NSF II.x). Once caught, we want to know more.

We may be attracted to one of Stevens's brief memorable phrases:

> the malady of the quotidian
> a mind of winter
> complacencies of the peignoir
> one's tootings at the weddings of the soul
> a supreme fiction

Or by some of his surprising titles:

> No Possum, No Sop, No Taters
> Thirteen Ways of Looking at a Blackbird
> Extracts from Addresses to the Academy of Fine Ideas
> Man Carrying Thing
> The River of Rivers in Connecticut

Or it may be a rhythm that catches our ear, in the way that Langston Hughes can start a blues rhythm in our heads with "The Weary Blues."

There are seasonal poems. There is pure fun. There are figures: angels, rabbis, giants, jack-rabbits, Lenin, Luther. There are irresistible names: Nanzia Nunzio, Mr. Homburg, Alpha and Omega. There is the prolonged reflection on "a supreme fiction." There are questions and there are hypotheses.

Or perhaps we are simply curious.

Sampling Stevens for the first time can be a somewhat odd experience. He does not sound like anyone else. It is not that his words are strange, though a few are decidedly so. It is that they are often in a strange relation to each other. Suppose we start with "imagination" and "reality" and the "interaction" between them. The interaction of imagination and reality can produce something new, say, a poem.

Some kinds of interaction are so familiar that we stop thinking of them as interaction at all. We simply think of them as the way things are, or reality that may be "expressed" in poetry. This is the way that a good deal of Wordsworth or of Frost strikes us. Or a good deal of TV or the Internet. ("Some students even SEE flowers still," Elizabeth Bishop wrote in 1979, "although I know only too well that TV has weakened the sense of reality so that very few students see anything the way it is in real life" [*One Art: Letters*, ed. Giroux (1994), 638].) Or we may think of a physicist's or a biologist's construction of nature as the way things really are, in spite of all that physicists and biologists tell us. "Physical concepts are free creations of the human mind, and are not, however it may seem, uniquely determined by the external world" (Einstein and Infeld, *The Evolution of Physics from Early Concepts to Relativity and Quanta* [1938], 31). Or consider Sue Hubbell:

> These names that we use for orders—Lepidoptera, Coleoptera,
> Diptera, and all the others . . . are sorting words, or taxa, that we
> humans use to group a dizzying array of individual bugs. . . . We have
> sorting kinds of brains and feel more comfortable if we put what we
> see in the world into various piles and categories. . . . But this says
> more about us and our brains than it does about the world outside our
> heads. And we shouldn't mix up these categories—the taxa—with
> reality. (*Broadsides from the Other Orders: A Book of Bugs* [1993], 22)

Stevens's poetry makes us aware of the process by which the imagination translates reality into a poem. One of my students once said: Stevens doesn't just care about what words *mean*; he cares about what words *are*. She was quite right, though a more advanced student would say: yes, and what they are is part of what they mean. Stevens so highlights the often-hidden process of translating into words that we become conscious of what and how words are.

In *Harmonium*, the interactions between imagination and reality range from familiar to striking to strange. Here are some examples, beginning with the more familiar, and arranged in order of writing: "Deer walk upon our mountains," and quail utter "spontaneous cries." These lines are from the last stanza of "Sunday Morning," and the full seven-line sentence translates readily from out there to in here. A few words give pause (e.g., "spontaneous"), but nothing stops us short. The rhythm, undulating like the flocks of birds at the very end, is satisfying. This is an early poem, from 1915.

The 1919 poem, "Nomad Exquisite," is built on a simile, "As," "As," "So." It opens: "As the immense dew of Florida . . ." Again the line of thought is straightforward, the words easily comprehensible. But here, the combination of words is marked more loudly—"immense dew," for example. Or in the startling participle in the "green vine angering for life." For one thing, its grammatical function has shifted, for the verb "to anger" normally takes a direct object. And the meaning? We are accustomed to "hungering for life," "yearning for life," and so on. But this?

Stevens can also start a poem with familiar descriptive language, then move in a figurative direction, as in another 1919 poem, "Ploughing on Sunday": "The white cock's tail / Tosses in the wind." At the end, the same tail "streams" all the way to the moon, while wind "pours down" rather than the expected rain. The stanzas between are exuberant and hyperbolic, including the lines addressed to Remus telling him to blow his horn. Some of Stevens's poems are like this. They sound like folk songs, a kind of interaction that is familiar to us. Stevens enjoyed animal figures out of tall tales, American style—the animal figures that children know from cartoons nowadays: rabbit, bucks, cocks, bantams. Or the jack-rabbit that sings to the Arkansaw in a flourish of puns in 1918, warning him about buzzards ("The Jack-Rabbit").

But if these activities sound a bit strange, try this tour de force, the opening lines of "Bantams in Pine-Woods" (1922):

> Chieftain Iffucan of Azcan in caftan
> Of tan with henna hackles, halt!

This offers one of Stevens's own flavors: an unusual mix of something colorful, often witty, unexpected to the edge of being bizarre, yet with a curious staying power. For such strange kinds of translation, the best rule of thumb for me is to ask exactly what we expected to find. Sometimes we then discover that Stevens is exploring some emotion or thought or sense effect that we've taken for granted. He can explore it obliquely, by stopping our usual translations short and enticing us into new ones.

Take "Nomad Exquisite" again. As Stevens develops his similes about Florida, with its "immense dew" and so on, nothing really startles us until lines 10–11. In line 10 we are told of "blessed mornings," the world all alive and new and full of energy. These mornings, the next line continues, are "Meet for the eye of the young . . ." The eye of the young whom or what? Let's see. Of the young lover, the young poet. Of the young girl singing to herself. Of the young egret or ibis. No, none of these. "Meet for the eye of the young alligator." See what that touch of reality does to the tone. It reminds us of nature red in tooth and claw. Not too somberly, however, given the submerged pun on "meet" and "meat." The short poem ends with a writer's creative energy to match Florida's own. A poet's creative work also has its alligator eye—providing for "a gobbet in my mincing world" ("Le Monocle de Mon Oncle" XII).

What else seems strange about Stevens's work on first encounter? The personal pronoun, for one thing. Who is this "he," that "I"? They arrive without introduction, but then so do many a "he" or "I" of the modern short story, as it places us in the middle of things. We are familiar with the technique, and we set about ascertaining from the plot what kind of person the "I" or "he" is, what point of view is prevailing. So with each of Stevens's poems where an unidentified person acts or thinks or feels. It is, so to speak, a short story in little, perhaps a crucial episode. Stevens sometimes likes to make his "he" or "I" or "we" the subject of some form of the verb "to say": "he said," "we say," etc. It is a familiar distancing device in his work. The reader is implicitly invited to consider a given statement as perhaps hypothetical or conditional, and to consider how and why.

Stevens's "speaking names" are something other, suggesting through their names what role they may be playing among the dramatis personae of his work. Sometimes they are parts of Stevens's own self, for he talked about how we all carry within us a trunkful of characters (L 91, 1906). A great many have humorous names.

Another characteristic is the way that Stevens exploits the unobtrusive work of prepositions. Sometimes this work is highlighted, as when normal usage is slightly skewed. Sometimes it is not apparent at first, as in Stevens's use of the double sense of the preposition "of," subjective and objective. ("The love of X" may mean X's love for Y or equally Y's love of X.) This last is one of Stevens's favorite devices. "Credences of Summer," for example, reads as both summer's own possible credences and some person's credences in summertime (or some person's credences about summer). Such hovering imitates the mutual give-and-take of an outside world and our own responses to it. So compact is this effect that it passes almost before we realize it. So also our senses and imagination respond to summer without pausing to reflect on the relation of inside and outside worlds. Similarly in the title, "The Pure Good of Theory." Is theory in and of itself a pure good, as in some Platonic realm of Ideas? Or is this some person's sense that theory can be a pure good? (The adjective complicates things, by raising the question of whether some theory is relatively good, while Theory is purely good.) Again, the quiet work of a preposition catches the interaction of outside and inside.

Stevens once used the phrase, " 'in, on or about the words' "—"to say it as a lawyer might say it" (L 351, 1940), reminding us that a lawyer is aware of prepositions. But then a lawyer, to say nothing of the best surety claims man in the country, is aware of language at large. Some of Stevens's hypothetical cases, possible theories, and so on, in his poetry are laid out like legal propositions or case law.

But it is time to look more systematically at ways to approach a poem.

3. First Glances

What does the poem on the page look like? A box, a birthday present, an invention. May Swenson offers these similes when she reads the clues about what is inside the box (*The Contemporary Poet as Artist and Critic*, ed. Ostoff [1964], 12). Poems can look wide or narrow, in regular shapes or not, ponderous or flitting. Richard Wilbur also thinks of a poem as "a created object," say, "an altar-cloth, Japanese garden or ship of death. Not a message or confession" (ibid., 19).

Or what does a poem on the page sound like, if we read it as a musical score? This is Jon Stallworthy's suggestion—hearing the words aloud or in the mind's ear ("Versification," *Norton Anthology of Poetry*, 3d ed. [1970], 1403). How are the lines and sounds grouped, even on first glance?

4. Words: "The Enchantment of Accuracy"

In 1953, Stevens was reading Beucler and he kept wanting to run to the dictionary. Why? Well, for instance, to find out exactly what a "tailleur à façon" is. When he did run to the dictionary, he found a quarter of a page on different uses of *façon* and he studied them—"a word about which one had no feeling whatever previously" (L 769). Stevens was writing to his good friend, Barbara Church, who replied that a *tailleur* makes suits and coats, and also furnishes the cloth, whereas a *tailleur à façon* takes the customer's material and charges for the work only (WAS 3617, 11 Feb. 1953). She expressed no feelings about the word *façon*. She was not a poet.

Feelings about words. Most of us have feelings about people, and that is a good place to start. For, as the poet John Hollander puts it, poets know words as they know people (*Melodious Guile* [1988], 228). T. S. Eliot also thought of words as people. They are people who are at their best when they feel at home. Whatever their job or status, whatever their temperament or age or class or style, they live in harmony when they feel at home, supporting others in their community. And they enjoy dancing. This is when things are going well in their lives, "where every word is at home . . . dancing together" (see the whole passage in *Little Gidding* V). Of course, Eliot knew that things are not always like this. Sometimes words have to take on back-breaking labor, in hostile surroundings: "Words strain, / Crack. . . . Shrieking voices . . . assail them" (*Burnt Norton* V).

How do we develop a feeling for words? In much the same way as for people. By paying attention, by spending time with them. By following their stories, which are to be found in good dictionaries, especially in the best storyteller of all, the generous multivolume *Oxford English Dictionary*, now also on-line. The OED classifies meanings, or word-stories, as follows: (1) Identification, (2) Etymology, (3) Signification, and (4) Illustrative Quotations. Similar principles inform the large Webster's *Dictionary*. These word-stories include jobs (grammatical part of speech), status (an old family or nouveau), family roots (etymology), relatives in other countries (cognates), examples of behavior (illustrative quotations), as well as signification. This last is what we ordinarily call "meaning." But a full dictionary meaning takes in all the above, and a full poetic meaning takes in much more. Poets delight in all these word-stories. And they don't just follow dictionaries. They also help to make dictionaries.

Eliot once said that all "vital" developments in language were developments "of feeling as well" (*Selected Essays* [1951], 210). But he didn't think any old term was a vital development in language and feeling. He also wrote about "the vague jargon of our time, when we have a vocabulary for everything, and exact ideas about nothing" (ibid., 347). We sometimes attach labels to people or to poems, especially popular psychological or sociological labels. Have we then understood a person or a piece of writing? Maybe. But too often, the label substitutes for trying to understand.

Stevens's vocabulary is one reason for reading him. It delights, energizes, amuses, occasionally irritates. Sometimes it's the unusual word that draws us, the older or specialized or even new word. Stevens, like Shakespeare, invented language. In 1931, Richard Blackmur made a list of unusual words in Stevens's poetry: "fubbed," "catarrhs," et cetera. He realized that not one was used in a precious way or as some "elegant substitute for a plain term"; all the examples were dictionary words "definitely meant" in context (183). Stevens liked to work with a full range of unusual words, words that are "rare, obsolete, archaic, colloquial, dialectal," to quote the OED's kinds of status for words (in class 1 above). He started early. He was probably reading Walter Scott's *Antiquary* at sixteen when he began a description of his paternal grandmother this way: "A dame upon a bed of auld-ferrant marigolds" (L 9, 1896). Or did this Scottish grandmother use the expression herself? "Auld-ferrant" means "old-favoring" or "having the manners or sagacity of age" (OED). Did he see her beside a bed of marigolds and translate the picture into heraldic terms, with a suitably specialized adjective? Very possibly. He doesn't classify her in the heraldic terms "rampant" or "couchant"—a bit hard to classify your grandmother that way.

At the other end of the OED's scale, colloquial expressions also turn up in Stevens: "Shucks," "Pftt" ("Add This to Rhetoric"), and so on. These have the flavor of their time, the 1920s, and 1930s. A lot of our colloquial terms come and go, and are pretty inert anyway. But the example of Shakespeare reminds us not to reject colloquialisms out of hand, or to be astonished if the most accomplished poets use them. Which ones do contemporary poets use well? Try "slush funds," as in James Merrill's refrain, "Where is the slush of yesteryear?" ("Snow Jobs," *A Scattering of Salt* [1995]).

Then there is family history (class 2, OED, etymology). Stevens described his vocabulary as "more Latin than Teutonic," though he was not prepared to say why (L 302, 1935). He was referring to the two main word-families of the English language, the ancient families of Germanic or Teutonic languages and Latinate or Romance languages. The Anglo-Saxon and French branches of these two families joined to produce the wonderfully rich and flexible English language. (They did not marry because of a love match or a tranquil arranged match. They married because of William the Conqueror. Dictionaries are histories of warfare, among other things.)

Possibly, Stevens continued, "the language of poetry is never Teutonic." Then, in case his correspondent mistook his point, or had forgotten about people like Goethe, Stevens added that perhaps even "the sound of German poetry is not Teutonic." He added that these were offhand remarks, and that he simply liked "the sound of Latin" (L 302). This was in 1935. In 1951, he objected to the view that Anglo-Saxon words had "the right to higgle and haggle all over the page" Some poems need a "hierophantic phrase" (OP 259, LOA 841). Consistency in word-choice is needed for a well-made poem. It's not that easy to achieve.

What about "higgle and haggle"? "Haggle" is fine: of Germanic origin (Old Norse to be precise), it means "to dispute, especially over the price of something." Anglo-Saxon poetry works with repeated alliteration, so that "higgle" calls for a word like "haggle." But what's this "higgle"? It doesn't exist except as Stevens's invention, so that we hear "wiggle and waggle" or "giggle and gaggle," all four of which do exist. But they aren't nearly as good in the argument because Anglo-Saxon runs to H's, as in the characters in *Beowulf,* and as Lewis Carroll knew when he inserted relatives of Hengist and Horsa in *Through the Looking-Glass.* (The Anglo-Saxon messengers in chapter 7 are called Haigha and Hatta.) In fact Stevens was being a bit mischievous. He'd just ended a poem with "haggling," including exuberant haggling between Anglo-Saxon and Latinate words (see "Auroras of Autumn" X).

As for class 4, the OED's invaluable quotations, these give not only the first known printed use of a word (or last, for an obsolete word). More important, they help give the connotation or association of a word. A word's field of association is essential and cannot be learned quickly. It is slowly absorbed through reading and listening and conversing. Without this knowledge, nobody can translate well from one language to another.

It is not just Stevens's use of single words that is so striking. Even more, it is his way of combining words. Blackmur notes this, and it is one thing that James Merrill remembers learning from Stevens:

> his great ease in combining abstract words with gaudy visual or sound
> effects. "That alien, point-blank, green and actual Guatemala," or those
> "angular anonymids" in their blue and yellow stream. You didn't have to
> be exclusively decorative *or* in deadly earnest. You could be grand *and*
> playful. The astringent abstract word was always there to bring your
> little impressionist picture to its senses. (*Recitative* [1986], 75)

(The Guatemala line is from "Arrival at the Waldorf," while "angular anonymids" may be found in "A Lot of People Bathing in a Stream.")

As we become more familiar with this body of work, we start to notice repeated words, some of which sound like key words. We notice Stevens's pleasure in punning. We may notice some echoes from earlier writers, faintly sounding like ghosts through Stevens's lines. But this kind of familiarity comes a little later.

Marianne Moore once wrote to Stevens: "I ponder what you have from time to time said about life, its largesse and its deprivations. There is the enchantment of accuracy, which seems more imperative than the personal . . ." (WAS 53, 18 Sept. 1948). Nowadays we are deluged with the personal. What if Moore is right, and the "enchantment of accuracy" is more imperative. "The enchantment of accuracy": does that sound contradictory for poetry? Or does Stevens himself sound contradictory when he says: "My dame, sing for this person accurate songs" (NSF I.IX). Yet listen to Proust: "The only fault . . . is that he sometimes employs imagery which is not inevitable. For in literature 'almost-parallel' lines are not worth drawing. Water (given certain conditions) boils at 100 degrees. At 98, at 99 the phenomenon does not occur. It is better therefore, to abstain from imagery" (preface to Paul Morand, *Green Shoots* [1923], 44). Better, that is, if you can't get it exactly right. You have to know words well to do that.

Like any poet, Stevens works to prevent stock responses. Sometimes he stops us short, maybe because his diction or grammar or logic is so unexpected. ("Personally, I like words to sound wrong," he once wrote [L 340, 1939].) In *The Government of the Tongue* (1988), Seamus Heaney considers two types of poetry. One talks in the way we have heard poems talk before, "massages rather than ruffles our sense of what it is to be alive in experience." Stevens can write this kind of poetry, but more often he writes another kind, a kind that Heaney says may be even more necessary for poetry. This kind can be "antic, mettlesome, contrary . . . retain the right to impudence . . . raise hackles . . . harry the audience into wakefulness" (122–23). Either way, it's very hard to predict a good poet's choices.

One way of testing this is to follow W. H. Auden. He is said to have given his students an exercise in which certain words were omitted from poems, and they were asked to fill in the blanks. It's fun to try with Stevens.

5. Walking: Lines of Poetry

Thinking about single words has one hazard. Words in a poem exist in relation, never in isolation. "There are no good or bad words; there are only words in bad or good places," as Winifred Nowottny says (*The Language Poets Use* [1962], 32). We need to move beyond single words to larger units: to the poetic line, to the rhythmic beat, to sentences, to logic. These moves are something like computer choices between one unit and another. Choose the poetic line, and we are in the world of poetic forms and of rhythm. Choose rhythm and we are in the world of sound and of the body's own rhythms. Choose sentences and we are in the world of grammar. Choose logic and we are in the world of thought-as-argument. These units all interact. None exists alone.

In a computer program, we might use one basic division for all these units: sound and sense. This is a very old way to describe the twofold nature of poetry. In another division, threefold this time and also centuries old, words may be studied according to the following curriculum: grammar, rhetoric, logic. Grammar then included a lot more than it does now; rhetoric was not meant in a derogatory way; and logic included reasoning and debate. Both the twofold division and the threefold one consist of units that interact, that do not exist alone. So the next four sections may be read in any order. Poems can start out from any one of these units. Poets work with them all.

The poetic line is a verse unit, whether the lines are arranged in stanzas or in long verse paragraphs or in one of the patterns of free verse. The lines of poetry that we remember tend to be just that: lines. "Not with a bang but a whimper." "Things fall apart; the center cannot hold." "And fools rush in where angels fear to tread." Handling the single line is one of the challenges of writing poetry: trying to make each line rock or jump or glide or dance just as it should. Merrill said that he was "always open to what another poet might do with *the line*," adding that it is "always very important, the phrasing of the lines." Flat-footed poets seem unable to hear the line as such. By contrast, Bishop's "North Haven" seemed to Merrill a masterpiece: "Every line fell in the most wonderful way, which is perhaps something she learned from Herbert" (*Recitative* [1986], 79). It's the line that announces immediately, the first time we see it: I am verse and not prose. (This is true of verse that's heard too, though it may take a little longer to pick up the line rhythms.) In prose, as Christopher Ricks reminds us, "line-endings are ordinarily the work of the compositor and not of the artist" (*The Force of Poetry* [1984], 89, and see the entire essay on Wordsworth's lines).

When young, Stevens was a prodigious walker, and he walked all his life, apparently composing to the rhythm of his steps as he walked to work at the Hartford Accident and Indemnity Company. He never owned a car. Neighbors remembered his figure and his pacing.

> It was odd seeing a man walking to work; it just wasn't done in that neighborhood. My father explained that it was his time to think and write poems. . . . Every morning, like clockwork, he used to walk down Terry Road . . . about nine o'clock, just about the time I was standing by my kitchen sink. I'd always get a thrill. In the afternoon he'd walk back, this very slow stride of his . . . slow and rather symmetrical. He almost walked in cadences. . . . He was such a great big fellow, six foot three or four, and weighed two hundred and fifty. But he didn't look fat, just a big man, tightly bound and fully packed. I could never imagine Stevens running. It was this stately measured walk. (Brazeau 238, 239, 119)

Reading poetry is itself a kind of walking: we go along the line, take a long stride back to the left margin, and continue the walk. (At least, this is true in most European languages.) Some lines end with a grammatical pause or stop: a comma or phrase-ending or period. Other lines break into the grammatical unit. We pause, if only slightly, but do not stop. "Enjambment" or "striding-over," from French *jambe*, or "leg," is the term for walking over the end of one line to the beginning of the next without a stop. Walking our own eyes along a line of verse, then turning (and the word "verse" has the root meaning of "turn"), we can map the rate of our movement, the kind of movement, and the kind of turn too. If cars had been with us as long as poetry, we might talk about "hairpin turns" instead of "enjambment."

See, for example, Anthony Hecht's opening line in "The Cost," the first poem of his collection, *Millions of Strange Shadows*: "Think how some excellent, lean torso hugs. . . ." Hugs? Hugs a friend or child or lover? But usually arms do this. A torso hugging? What then? "Think how some excellent, lean torso hugs / The brink . . . ," as Hecht gives us a young Italian riding his

Vespa, plus an image of what his line is doing, as it circles back for another ride on the iambic, hugging the center of gravity in this poem.

With a good poet, it's always possible to savor that split second at the end of the line when we don't know what's coming next. Try guessing what follows these lines: "The moon follows the sun like a French" (see "Variations on a Summer Day" XI); "The whole race is a poet that writes down" (see "Men Made out of Words"); "The poem must resist the intelligence" (see "Man Carrying Thing"); "After the leaves have fallen, we return" (see "The Plain Sense of Things").

The iambic pentameter line is the traditional workhorse of English poetry. (Its basic pattern is da-DA—or one unstressed and one stressed syllable—five times.) It is Shakespeare's line, Milton's line, Wordsworth's line. You can hear their different pulses in their use of the line. Who would dare to work with it in the twentieth century? Stevens, for one, especially in his later work, notably in the long sequences of the forties. "My line is a pentameter line," he wrote in 1942, "but it runs over and under now and then" (L 407). That "over and under now and then" (beyond the usual "over and under") is one mark of Stevens's iambic pentameter line. When his line does settle into a regular five-beat iambic, it sounds all the more settled because of the unobtrusive variations elsewhere. "The holy hush of ancient sacrifice" is the first fully regular line of "Sunday Morning" and it is line 5. The preceding lines "mingle to dissipate" the settled effect of very regular iambic pentameter lines, just as coffee and oranges on a Sunday morning "mingle to dissipate" a memory of Sunday church observance. (For the settled effect of very regular iambic pentameter, see the opening stanza of Thomas Gray's "Elegy Written in a Country Churchyard.")

In another rare comment on his technique, Stevens explained some of his "metric solutions" for free verse to his Italian translator. "In all free verse poems, I have adopted a sort of loose line which, in conjunction with shorter fragments, evokes what Mallarmé used to call 'la reminiscence du vers strict'." "Vers strict," as Stevens explained, "is in Italian an equivalent of the English iambic pentameter" (Poggioli, 169).

Of course we want to remember line-beginnings as well as line-endings, for the very beginning claims our attention first. Words at the start and finish of a line need special watching. One forceful way to begin a poem is with an imperative: "Think how some excellent, lean torso hugs. . . ." "Do not go gentle into that good night." Stevens even begins one of his best poems with the injunction "Begin," as if he were conducting an orchestra ("Notes toward a Supreme Fiction").

The art of writing one line so happily that it falls into place and stays in our heads is a great and arduous art. How many words will each of us utter by the end of our lives? For all the words we spout, most of us will never achieve one such a line in a lifetime.

6. Listening: Sounds of Rhythm

Depicting something with great accuracy can be enchanting. But there is another way of representing something, and that is by miming it, acting it out, sounding it out. Poetry does both. Its rhythm calls to us: its sway or bounce or march or stately progress. See Heaney on Auden's sense of the double nature of poetry (*The Government of the Tongue* [1988]), 109). Or see Auden himself on wanting "every poem I write to be a hymn in praise of the English language" and hence his "fascination with certain speech-rhythms" (*The Contemporary Poet as Artist and Critic*, ed. Ostoff [1964], 207). (He also said that he found far too much self-dramatizing in serious contemporary poetry, and that he wanted his reader to react first and foremost by saying "That's true" or, even better, "That's true: now, why didn't I think of it for myself?" [ibid.].)

Something in a poem will "catch the eye," as we say. Or catch the ear, as Auden's new rhythm caught the ear of the young Heaney, with its sense of Anglo-Saxon meter and the "gnomic clunk of Anglo-Saxon phrasing" that pulled against ordinary speech, and against the iambic too (*Government of the Tongue*, 124). New rhythms give new life. We can hear kinds of rhythm, Eliot's ragtime rhythm, for example, in his well-known lines from *The Waste Land* I about "that Shakespeherian Rag."

Teachers who run spotting tests can be flabbergasted by their students' apparently deaf ears. Yet the same students may be trained musically, and could teach their teachers a thing or two about jazz or blues or baroque music. It's just a matter of training the eye to read poetry for the ear, that is, partly as a musical score, feeling for the rhythm. This is Stallworthy's suggestion, mentioned at the start.

Some poems announce themselves as much by their rhythm as their subject. Tum-ti-tum ones are obvious, and so are pom-pom-pom (drum-beat) poems. Stevens called these latter "decorous." He thought many people expected poems to be decorous, whereas by contrast "many lines exist because I enjoy their clickety-clack" (L 485, 1945). Eliot thought the invention of the internal combustion engine affected our sense of rhythm. Other rhythms are as old as words or older: water rhythms, body rhythms.

"Meter" (from Greek *metron*, "measure") is simply a way of measuring rhythms. Try the pleasures of Hollander's *Rhyme's Reason,* where patterns of metrical and unmetrical (or free) verse describe themselves, For example:

> The *ballad stanza*'s four short lines
>   Are very often heard;
> The second and the fourth lines rhyme,
>   But not the first or third.

Readers baffled by the term and idea of "free verse" will find eight different types of patterning here. It's worth saying nowadays that there is good metrical verse and bad metrical verse, just as there is good unmetrical (free) verse and bad unmetrical verse. There's no automatic virtue in either form, and many modern poets write in both. Stevens did. The poems in *Harmonium* show a mix of forms, much varied, in their formidable technique.

Every reader has favorites. My own rhyming and rhythmic favorites in Stevens include the opening lines of "The Pure Good of Theory" (Part I), the opening stanza of "Pieces," and "The River of Rivers in Connecticut."

7. Sentences: Lines of Grammar

Sentences are grammatical units, governed perforce by the grammar of a given language. And grammar is not, not, not a set of strictly prescribed rules. It's an attempt to describe, sometimes to program, one of the structures of words in a language. We can't get outside grammar, so we might as well have some idea of how it works. (Any student who can learn basic computer terms and functions can learn basic grammatical terms and functions. Schools have no right to deprive students of this knowledge, which is routinely taught in other parts of the world.) Better still, we might also learn how grammar works in other languages, for example, in Japanese. (See Geoffrey Bownas's fascinating introduction to the *Penguin Book of Japanese Verse*.) The Japanese adjective, to take one instance, acts much more like an English verb. It conjugates, not in order to indicate the time of an action (past, present, future, etc.), but to indicate many shades of volition. Expressions such as "probably will not" are plentiful. This means that "conjecture and imagination appear as second nature in poetry" (xliii–xlv). It also means that those interested in doing business with the Japanese might pay a little attention to this linguistic experience.

How might the grammar of the English language affect poetry? Here is one way. Merrill once visited a poetry workshop, where only one writer out of fifteen had not used the first-person present active indicative:

> Poem after poem began: "I empty my glass . . . I go out . . . I stop by woods. . . ." For me a "hot" tense like that can't be handled for very long without cool pasts and futures to temper it. Or some complexity of syntax, or a modulation into the conditional—*something*. An imperative, even an auxiliary verb, can do wonders. Otherwise, you get this addictive, self-centered immediacy, harder to break oneself of than cigarettes. . . . [Such a writer will] never notice "Whose woods these are I think I know" gliding backwards through the room (*Recitative* [1986], 21).

Try this out with Stevens:

1. person (singular: I, you, he or she or it; plural: we, you, they)
2. tense (past, present, future, for a start)
3. voice (active or passive)
4. mood (indicative, interrogative, imperative, exclamatory, for a start)

First-person singular present active indicative: "I measure myself / Against a tall tree," and so on, all in Merrill's "hot" tense. An early poem, but an apparent exception to Merrill's argument. Yet see the way the poem ends, as the "I" experiences an unexpected moment of unease ("Six Significant Landscapes" III). For a recommended "cooler" construction, a negative plus an infinitive, see "Thirteen Ways of Looking at a Blackbird" V on inflections as against innuendoes. In fact, first-person singular present active indicative is hard to find in Stevens. Even to search for the first-person singular present tense in other grammatical moods or more complicated grammatical structures is to see Merrill's point:

> . . . what I feel,
> Here in this room, desiring you . . .
> ("Peter Quince at the Clavier" I)

> What am I to believe? If the angel in his cloud
> Serenely gazing . . .
> ("Notes toward a Supreme Fiction" III.VIII)

As for the interrogative mood: we don't ordinarily think much about kinds of questions, except when listening to politicians ("just a rhetorical question") or making jokes (the old "Knock, knock, who's there?"). But there are whole families of questions, and ways of asking questions matter. Most of us know the trick question: "Answer yes or no. Have you stopped beating your wife?" Fewer of us think about nouns and how they affect questions. But Wittgenstein did. Nouns can even mislead us:

> The Blue Book . . . begins with "one of the great sources of philosophical bewilderment"—i.e. the tendency to be misled by substantives to look for something that corresponds to them. Thus, we ask: "What is time?", "What is meaning?", "What is knowledge?", "What is a thought?", "What are numbers?" etc., and expect to be able to answer these questions by naming some*thing*. The technique of language-games was designed to break the hold of this tendency.
> (Monk, *Ludwig Wittgenstein* [1991], 337)

Poets know all about this, and they too like language-games, for this reason among others. Moore offers an entire lesson in how to answer the question "What is mind?" and all in thirty-six lines in her "The Mind Is an Enchanting Thing."

But then, we've known for centuries about answers to questions like "What is X?" or "Who is X?"

> And, behold, a certain lawyer stood up, and tempted him, saying, Master, what shall I do to inherit eternal life? He said unto him, What is written in the law? How readest thou? And he answering said, Thou shalt love the Lord thy God with all thy heart, and with all thy soul, and with all thy strength, and with all thy mind; and thy neighbor as thyself. And he said unto him, Thou hast answered right: this do, and thou shalt live. But he, willing to justify himself, said unto Jesus, And who is my neighbor?
>
> And Jesus answering said, A certain man went down from Jerusalem to Jericho, and fell among thieves, who stripped him of his raiment, and wounded him, and departed, leaving him half dead. . . . (Luke 10: 25–30)

There are different ways of building sentences in poetry as in prose. There are short sentences and there are long, long sentences. Word order may be reversed, so quietly that we hardly notice when a sentence is entering the stanza backwards ("Whose woods these are I think I know"). One syllable may alter the inflection and thereby a whole train of thought and feeling. ("The Mind Is an Enchanting Thing / is an enchanted thing. . . .") Coordinate clauses joined by "and," "but," etc., give a different effect from one main clause modified by subordinate clauses beginning with "which," "when," etc. Parallel clauses and phrases build their own logic, as in the Hebrew Scriptures (on which see James Kugel's learned and fascinating *The Idea of Biblical Poetry* [1981]). It's worth noting where the full stops come in a poem, and what the core sentence is (subject, verb, object if any). The results may be surprising. One-line sentences can possess special force: see Frost, for example. For some of the most challenging sentence structures in all English poetry, try Dickinson's apparently simple sentence designs, especially in her later work.

Stevens's sentence structure is wonderfully varied, as we would expect, since a command of syntactical variety is one mark of a good writer. Just try imitating one. "Try to put into a sequence of simple quatrains the continuous syntactical variety of Gautier or Blake," Eliot once wrote (*The Egoist*, Apr. 1918).

Yeats said that he only began to make "a language to my liking . . . when I discovered some twenty years ago that I must seek, not as Wordsworth thought, words in common use, but a powerful and passionate syntax." (*Essays and Introductions*, 1937 [1961], 521–22). A powerful and passionate *syntax*! There's a thought to confound the antigrammar sentimentalists.

8. Logic: Lines of Thought

The evil of thinking as poetry is not the same thing as the good of
thinking in poetry. (NA 165, LOA 744, 1951)

Here is a sentence from Wordsworth that will surprise many readers: "The log-
ical faculty has infinitely more to do with Poetry than the Young and the inex-
perienced, whether writer or critic, ever dreams of " (*Letters* IV.546, 1827). Yet
Wordsworth was hardly the only one to say such things. More broadly and
more recently, here is James Wright: "What makes the new poetry so bad is its
failure to realize that there is no sound poetry without intelligence" (Mc-
Clatchy, *White Paper* [1989], 16). Stevens, offering advice to a young writer
and friend, José Rodríguez-Feo, confirmed a writer's insatiable desire to read.
But, he warned, you must also think. He then went on to speak of "the passion
of thinking" and recommended an hour or two a day, even if one is at first
"staggered by the confusion and aimlessness" of one's thoughts (L 513, 1945).
We need to remember this when we hear Stevens saying, "The poem must re-
sist the intelligence / Almost successfully" ("Man Carrying Thing"). *Resist*, not
ignore or flee. *Almost* successfully, but not altogether successfully. How long
was Stephen Hawking's book, *A Brief History of Time*, on the bestseller list?
And why was this, if not that people were hungry to know and to think about
what physicists make of our universe? Aged twenty-six, Stevens noted poetic
language that was "capable" and "marvellous," but also noted the lack of poetic
thought. Moods were fine in poetry, he wrote. "But it's the mind we want to
fill" (L 92, 1906). Aged sixty-five, he was convinced that "supreme poetry" re-
quires "the highest possible level of the cognitive" (L 500, 1945).

All good poetry requires thinking. Does this sound strange? We may have
to do battle with several stereotypes, as follows:

1. The stereotype where thinking is what you do in the physical and
   biological sciences or in mathematics or in philosophy or in
   psychology.
2. The stereotype where poetry is divided between "content"
   (associated with thought, themes, arguments *that are already in
   words*) and "form" (associated with ornament, purple passages,
   hyperbole, etc., that "express" what is already in words).
3. The stereotype of an easy division between thinking and emotion,
   where poetry is assigned to emotion, and judgments about
   emotions go unexamined.

To expand a little:

1. I used to say: Words are not as accurate as numbers. It took me quite
a while to see that this is a meaningless statement. For what did I mean by

"accurate"? I meant "accurate" in the sense that "$2 + 2 = 4$" is accurate. I meant "accurate" in the sense that numbers are accurate. But all I was actually saying was that words are not accurate in the same way that numbers are accurate—not exactly news. Of course, words and numbers work differently. But both poet and scientist are accurate, and the greater the talent, the greater the accuracy. Kepler said that numbers are the words of geometricians (*Weltharmonik*, trans. Casper [1939], 26).

Stevens worked with numbers, and worked well, or he could not have earned the reputation of being the best surety bond man in the country in his day. He knew of our lackadaisical habit of associating accuracy with numbers. Or else, if we do associate it with words, of reserving it for concepts, dictionary definitions, and the like, and keeping it away from emotion or song or imagery.

Baseball may help. Logically considered, it makes less sense than poetry. Grown men taking a stick of wood to a small object, and racing against a set of arbitrary rules? But it's intensely human, this exercise of physical and mental skill, and beautiful to watch when seemingly preternatural ability looks effortless. We know from our own softball games how gifted those Major League players are, and good commentators help us to realize this. So also with poetry. We all use words. Still, there's not much to encourage us to use them really well, let alone play games with them or write occasional poems. If we played softball games with words, and also regularly heard the Major League word-players, with good commentators. . . . It's a nice thought. Nobody supposes for a moment that baseball players don't think, even if they don't think in philosophical concepts or chemical numbers. They think in baseball: thinking-in-baseball, we might call it. Thinking-in-poetry is what poets do. Not "thinking *as* poetry," which Stevens rightly detested, but "thinking in poetry."

Movies might help too, except that there are so many third-rate ones around. But movies have the advantage of being one art form that people are relaxed about and will reflect on. That includes questions of technique. Why this shot and not that one? What precisely makes Griffith or Chaplin or Renoir or Hitchcock or Kurosawa or X, Y, Z so good? I've watched a number of student films from a very good film school. You can trace the progress in learning the mechanics of film-making. But the real challenge is different. It's *thinking*, imaginative thinking. It has to do with a sense of proportion, a sense of shaping. (Coleridge spoke of "My shaping spirit of imagination" in his "Dejection Ode," and Stevens of "a constructive faculty" [NA 164, LOA 743, 1951].) It has to do with attention, passionate attention, to details. It has to do with an active, examining, alive self, a thinking self, as against a passive self, which just accepts without thinking whatever the TV or movie or computer screen feeds it.

2. The useful distinction between content and form sometimes stops being a distinction and gets solidified as the way-things-are. Actually it's most often a buried metaphor, and the metaphor is nearly always based on a container-and-contained model. "Content" is the milk or beer or important substance, what sometimes gets wrongly called the "philosophy" of A or B. "Content" can be poured into all sorts of containers. The container or form is just what's convenient or pretty or even beautiful, but distinct from what is inside. Yet if we recall an Aristotelian idea of form, all this changes. The form of the oak tree is contained in an acorn. The form of an adult is contained in an infant. Form suddenly becomes something vital in these examples. Similarly with poems.

3. All too often, we separate the processes of thinking and feeling, but there is one great hazard in doing so. We are accustomed to rigor and discipline in thinking. We prize it, we strive for it. How often do we associate rigor and discipline with feeling? Our terms for the way that emotions work can be reduced to such notions as expression and suppression, as if these were the only alternatives or indeed were simple matters. Worse, "expression," any expression, becomes a good in itself in the ignorant anti-Puritanism of pop psychology. What happens, Eliot asked, when our feelings become separated from our thinking, and both from our senses, so that they function in different compartments? What happens to our capacity to feel? To use our senses? To think? Eliot distinguished between "thinking with our feelings" and corrupting feelings with static ideas. "Mr. Chesterton's brain swarms with ideas; I see no evidence that it thinks" (*Little Review*, Aug. 1918).

Poetry can help us to reflect more accurately on our feelings. This in turn affects feelings. How many of us can distinguish 824 different kinds and degrees of feeling? Here is the pianist, Karl Ulrich Schnabel, on teaching young musicians:

> I ask my students to get beyond generalized expression. I encourage
> them to write down as many different shades of feeling as they can.
> The first 20 are easy; after 50 it gets hard, but fascinating. One of my
> pupils is up to 824. I collect a whole range of emotions from life's
> experiences—sometimes they are rather elusive states of being—and
> store each one in a special niche of its own. I then select the one that
> fits the music best and relive it with all the intensity of the original
> experience. Some may find such a system ridiculous, but it seems to
> help my students. (*New York Times*, 16 Jan. 1994)

Browning would have known what he meant. "I know and use to analyse my own feelings," he once wrote to Elizabeth Barrett, adding with a smile, "and be sober in giving distinctive names to their varieties." Then, without a smile, or rather with a different kind of smile: "This is *deep* joy" (*Letters of Robert*

Browning and Elizabeth Barrett Browning, I.279, 17 Nov. 1845). My students are always fascinated by the fact that there are three different Greek terms for our one word "love": *eros, agape*, and *philia*. (Loosely, these signify erotic love, sometimes in a wide sense including matters of generation; heavenly or divine or radically selfless love; and love as in friendship or as in the love of wisdom ["philosophy"] or of words ["philology"].)

What happens when feeling seems to collide with thought or ideas? "Domination of Black," an extraordinary early poem by Stevens, is a useful case in point. Stevens himself directed readers away from "ideas," regretting that this type of poem had to "contain any ideas at all." He added that the poem was meant to fill the reader with its sounds and images, and *"you are supposed to feel as you would if you actually got all this"* (L 151, 1928, my italics). Try blanking out the word "afraid" at the end of the poem, and then surmising what feeling we are "supposed to feel." Just how do we know that such a feeling has developed rather than, say, a "delightful-evening" feeling? It's also worth thinking about different kinds of fear. See especially the six different sentences offered by Wittgenstein, all using the clause "I am afraid," together with his comment: "To each of these sentences a special tone of voice is appropriate, and a different context" (Monk, *Ludwig Wittgenstein* [1991], 547).

Tracing the line of thought in a poem is always necessary. See, for example, the implicit argument in "Tea at the Palaz of Hoon": "Not less because in purple I descended . . . not less was I myself." Why say this? What's the logic? The day and the place ("the western day," "there") will turn out to be extraordinary, but why this opening response? Has someone said, "You were less yourself that day"? Do we ourselves say, "I was less myself that day"? No, the usual expression is simply, "I wasn't myself that day," period. That's how we often take care of extraordinary days and experiences, ones that don't fit into our regular routine, ones that are better (or worse) than usual. And so we guard ourselves against our other selves, the other better (or worse) selves. Not Stevens. This means that his speaker can go on to talk about finding himself "more truly and more strange." And so we learn to think a bit before we say, "I wasn't myself that day." Weren't we, now?

For an experienced reader, tracing the line of thought in a poem becomes a matter of course, just as tracing the rhythm, the sentence structure, the exact form of verb and pronoun, the range of diction, and so on, become matters of course. Even if a poem has a minimal line of thought, we should register this. (X is a minimal-thought poem working with A or B or C.) Formal logic may help, though we need to know its limits in dealing with the alogical. Aristotle's categories of kind and degree are indispensable. It may be helpful to distinguish opposites and contraries. (See Fowler's *Modern English Usage* [1926] or Richard Wilbur's enchanting book for children, *More Opposites*.) Eventually we come to see how and where logic interacts with rhetoric, for neither can exist alone. Stevens spoke of "the good of thinking in poetry" (see epigraph, above) and he did not use the word "good" lightly.

9."Who Speaks?": Address, Voice, Manners

Who speaks? But it must be that I,
That animal, That Russian, that exile. . . .
("A Dish of Peaches in Russia")

Some poems sound as if they are addressed directly to the reader. Older ones may even say "Gentle Reader" or "My very gentle reader, yet unborn" (Cowper, *The Task*). Some poems sound as if they are addressed to thin air and we are overhearing them. Some poems are addressed to God or a public figure or a lover or a friend.

Shut, shut the door, good John! fatigu'd I said,
Tie up the knocker, say I'm sick, I'm dead.
(Pope, "Epistle to Dr. Arbuthnot")

In a dramatic monologue, there is by definition an addressee within the poem who conditions what is said. Fra Lippo Lippi speaks to a patrol that has caught him out on the streets in Browning's well-known dramatic monologue of that name. J. Alfred Prufrock speaks to himself, as we slowly realize in Eliot's "The Love Song of J. Alfred Prufrock"; this fact in itself tells us that Eliot is altering the usual dramatic monologue. See also the various addressees in Richard Howard's dramatic monologues, for example, in *Untitled Subjects* or *Like Most Revelations*.

Stevens's addressees are often unusual. "Begin, ephebe." Who is this ephebe? "O juventes, O filii." Who are these young people, these sons? "Wanderer, this is the pre-history of February." Who is this wanderer: the reader or somebody else? Sometimes Stevens is certainly not addressing the reader, or most readers: Timeless mother, Vincentine, Remus, Chieftain Iffucan of Azcan, nuncle, sister and mother and diviner love, Swenson, Master Soleil, Redwood Roamer, Mrs. Papadopoulos, Sordid (sordid!) Melpomene. An entire telephone directory is needed. Some of his addressees are even more unexpected. "Be quiet in the heart, O wild bitch" ("Puella Parvula"). Some are outsize and inimical. There are degrees of abstraction. There are degrees of humor. There are animals and landscape. A mountain is given a voice in "Chocurua to Its Neighbor," and it speaks of—what else?—lofty things. (See, for contrast, A. R. Ammons's comically disputatious mountain and speaker in his "Apologetics.")

What about the speaker who does the addressing? How far is that person dramatized? What about grammatical person such as an unidentified "he" or "she"? Is this some dramatized part of the writer's own psyche? Perhaps, perhaps not. Context should eventually indicate sufficiently.

Who speaks in a poem? A voice. A voice that we hear and deduce from signs on a page. Each poem has its own voice, and we hear it as we hear the voice of a friend or acquaintance or stranger. If a friend, we are familiar with the voice, recognizing affectionately its cadences and range of pitch, its ways of expression, how it sounds in amusement or elation or anger or grief or casual chat. So with poems. Eventually we come to recognize the distinctive voice of a poet in the work, if he or she is good enough.

Finding a voice of one's own is the hardest challenge for a writer. The voice that will cause a reader to say, ah yes, Frost or Tennyson or Moore, just as a listener to music will say, ah yes, Mozart or Miles Davis. Not because something is specifically identified, but because the style is identified. This will be partly an individual idiom and partly the idiom of the time, highly selected, heightened or condensed. It's the individual idiom because people naturally write and speak in idioms peculiar to themselves, as they develop (assuming they do develop). Nobody expects all their friends to talk in just the same way. And different occasions call for different kinds of talk: colloquial or business-like or ceremonious, as required.

Stevens, for example, disliked euphony. He coined the harsh phrase "the bawds of euphony" ("Thirteen Ways of Looking at a Blackbird" X), and commented later that in his poem these bawds might express themselves differently, "naturally, with pleasure, etc." (L 340, 1939). The euphony of 1917 would very likely sound phony to us. So does a lot of current euphony, though it may be sincerely meant. "Euphony" means "a pleasing sound," though not to Stevens in 1917. Nor always to the OED in 1893: "euphonious" is "often used ironically." Bawds are female pimps, go-betweens that sell sex. As with sex, so with poetry: it is not to be sold, used, pandered for. "Naturally, with pleasure" applies to both.

And the idiom of the time, the idiom natural to the time that will shift with the passing of generations? "Beyond all whooping," Stevens once wrote in a letter, meaning "joyous beyond all whooping or shouting." The only other person I have heard use this expression is my mother, a generation younger than Stevens, so that it did belong to the living vocabulary of older generations. And nowadays? Here are some different voices:

> The wind whines in the elevator shaft. The homeless
> squinny at us, mumbling.
>
> (Amy Clampitt, "The Prairie")

> Man is not a god, that's what you said
> After your heart gave out, to comfort me. . . .
> (Gjertrud Schnackenberg, "Laughing with One Eye," 3)

4 words only of *mi 'art aches* and . . . "Mine's broken,
you barbarian T. W.!"

(Tony Harrison, "Them and [uz]")

The old, the mad, the blind have fairest daughters.
Take Job.

(Jay Macpherson, "The Beauty of Job's Daughters")

Merrill wrote that "voice" is simply the democratic word for "tone."
" 'Tone' always sounds snobbish, but without a sense of it how one floun-
ders!" (*Recitative* [1986], 26). For Eliot, tone is the hardest challenge of all.
The words of a poem "come easily enough, in comparison with the core of
it—the *tone*." Nobody, he added, could help with that (*Letters*, ed. Valerie
Eliot [1988], 1 June 1919).

In the end, speaking "naturally, with pleasure," shows one's attitude to the
reader, one's manners in the true sense:

> Manners are for me the touch of nature, an artifice in the very
> bloodstream. Someone who does not take them seriously is making a
> serious mistake. . . . And manners—whether good or bad—are entirely
> allied with tone or voice in poetry. If the manners are inferior the
> poem will seem unreal. . . . Manners aren't merely descriptions of
> social behavior. The real triumph of manners in Proust is the extreme
> courtesy toward the reader, the voice explaining at once formally and
> intimately. . . . Proust says to us in effect, "I will not patronize you by
> treating these delicate matters with less than total, patient, sparkling
> seriousness" (Merrill, *Recitative* 33).

10. Who Speaks to Whom?: Genre

The most gifted adult beginner must assimilate quite a few forms
before he can hope to get far with the poetry of Wallace Stevens.

—Alastair Fowler

Fortunately for us, Fowler adds that "sometimes readers can grasp a genre
with mysterious celerity, on the basis of seemingly inadequate samples, almost
as if they were forming a hologram from scattered traces. . . . The explanation
may possibly be that literary types are in part learned indirectly: for example,
through conversation, subliterature, advertising, films, and other indepen-
dent forms" (45). We begin learning genres willy-nilly as children, listening to
fairy-tales or playing verbal games. We can't understand words without gen-
res. (Anyone who takes Alice's adventures in wonderland literally is in trou-
ble.) We hear parody because we recognize the genre. We recognize dominant

story-patterns on TV or in the newspapers. Some people know only a few simple stories, and if you wander into their territory, you'll become part of such a story and its genre, like it or not.

If genres are so many pigeon-holes, what is more boring? But if we can't even read or watch TV or the Internet without using them, if we're trained in them from our first fairy-tales on our parents' knees, then they're a different matter. Fussing over classification is not the point, as Fowler like others observes: "Genres have to do with identifying and communicating rather than with defining and classifying. We identify the genre in order to read the exemplar" (38).

There are ways of signaling genres. For example, how to signal in the movies that a dream or dream-vision is starting? The standard genre-signal is a dissolve, often preceded by a shot of someone falling asleep (see *The Wizard of Oz*). If you use harp music and/or a fogged image, you are risking cliché. In poems, genres may be named specifically, or they may be signaled through names of characters, standard formulae, and so on. "Once upon a time . . ." is a fairy-tale formula. Sometimes poems announce their genre in their title: "A Pastoral Monody," "A Monodrama": these are the subtitles for Milton's *Lycidas* and Tennyson's *Maud*. Twentieth-century poetry does not go in for such subtitles. Perhaps Lewis Carroll gave us pause in 1876 with *The Hunting of the Snark: An Agony in Eight Fits*. ("Fits"? First and foremost, just what we think. Second, a section of an old poem or song, as in "Dr. Percy has written a long ballad in many fits" [OED]. Third, a specialized mathematical use that actually fits—naturally, Carroll being a mathematician.)

What twentieth-century titles do name genres? How about invective, fabliau, colloquy, hymn, epigram, and soliloquy? Try them in the following combinations, all by Stevens:

> Invective against Swans
> Fabliau of Florida
> Colloquy with a Polish Aunt
> Late Hymn from the Myrrh Mountain
> Adult Epigram
> Final Soliloquy of the Interior Paramour

Pastoral terms run all through Stevens's work: "A Pastoral Nun," "The Pastor Caballero," and so on. In "The Old Lutheran Bells at Home," Stevens plays over the key words and conventions of Christian pastoral, in a memory of his childhood. He knew the tradition well. If its doctrine did not draw him, its faithfulness and work and visionary force did. He adapted them to his own vocation, in an echo from the Gospels: "(Poet,) feed my lambs. Feed my lambs (on the bread of living)" (John 21:15, "Adagia," OP 187, 202; LOA 914, first example omitted).

Pastoral, by the way, does not act like a genre, but instead like a "mode" in

Fowler's definition. Modes run through various genres, and are usually called by adjectives instead of nouns. The distinction is useful (56, 106–7).

Stevens also knew the tradition of classical pastoral, the tradition whose key names are Theocritus in Greek poetry and Virgil in Latin. Classical pastoral has been wittily and succinctly described as "a literary mode in which the lives of simple country people are celebrated, described, and used allegorically by sophisticated urban poets and writers" (*Victorian Prose and Poetry*, ed. Bloom and Trilling [1973], 731). In English, Spenser and Milton combined Christian and classical strains of pastoral. The Romantics, notably Wordsworth, changed pastoral once and for all. It remains a perpetually appealing mode, even if sheep-tending is no longer the usual fictional setting. (Cowboys rather than shepherds sometimes continue the pastoral mode in a modern vein.)

Sometimes generic or modal signals are not so direct in Stevens, for example, in "An Ordinary Evening in New Haven." Only when we hear the pun, "New Haven / new heaven," together with the echo of "a new heaven and a new earth," and only after we have met Professor Eucalyptus, do we recognize that Stevens is reflecting on apocalyptic matters. He had mixed views of our attraction to the apocalyptic. He did not even agree with Professor Eucalyptus, though he found him more congenial than some Professor Apocalyptus (see "The Doctor of Geneva"). In the end, Stevens valued wisdom literature and a true "commonplace" more than apocalyptic literature, more even than comedy and tragedy ("An Ordinary Evening in New Haven" XVII).

Knowing something about genre helps us read individual poems better, and helps us develop our generic repertoire. We read better because we start thinking of groups of poems and comparing them in kind. Elegy, for example, is a large generic class.

For one example that illustrates Fowler's remark about Stevens, see the gloss on "anecdote" in the first poem of *Harmonium*, "Earthy Anecdote." Stevens was clearly interested in the genre of anecdote about 1918 to 1920. (Or is it a subgenre, and of what?) It is certainly popular now. "The Secret History of X" is a formula for a bestseller. Stevens's secret histories are a little different.

11. Figures of Speech

"Fig.," says the dictionary, which we duly expand into "figurative," then go on to distinguish figurative from literal meaning. "Fig.," however, is only a first introduction to a large, vital class of meaning. So vital is this class that it can condition or prevent our thinking and feeling. Sometimes we do not recognize how far this happens or even that it is happening at all.

Take our casual view of the brain as a kind of machine. That is a metaphor, and all very well to a degree. But it can affect our view of brain-damaged people. When something goes wrong with machines, they have no way of adjusting themselves to compensate for loss. Brain-damaged people do. Oliver Sacks wrote a book about such people, and one of his aims was to undo the force of our unexamined metaphor, "The brain is a machine." " 'Deficit,' we have said, is neurology's favorite word—its only word, indeed, for any disturbance of function. Either the function (like a capacitor or fuse) is normal—or it is defective or faulty: what other possibility is there for a mechanistic neurology, which is essentially a system of capacities and connections? What then of the opposite—an excess or superabundance of function? Neurology has no word for this" (*The Man Who Mistook His Wife for a Hat, and Other Clinical Tales* [1987], 87). There are two possible responses to the brain-machine metaphor. One says: let's get rid of metaphors. The other, more experienced response says: let's look for a better metaphor, or use more than one metaphor. We can't get rid of figures of speech, even if we wanted to. Dead or alive, they're part of the language. Poetry works with them, and so alerts us to their power and their pleasure too.

Here is the biologist, Stephen Jay Gould:

> We often think, naively, that missing data are the primary
> impediments to intellectual progress—just find the right facts and all
> the problems will dissipate. But barriers are often deeper and more
> abstract in thought. We must have access to the right metaphor, not
> only to the requisite information. Revolutionary thinkers are not,
> primarily, gatherers of fact, but weavers of new intellectual structures.
> ("For Want of a Metaphor," *The Flamingo's Smile* [1985], 151)

Poets like to play with the word "trope" (see following section), and so they should: it's their chief business. Sometimes the word appears openly, as when Stevens was visiting his favorite Elizabeth Park, Hartford, and constructed a Theatre of Trope for himself, presumably with figures like metaphor acting on the stage (NSF II.x). Sometimes, almost as if speaking in code to other wordsmiths, poets will play with the word "trope." Thus Stevens writes two couplets, "Artist in Tropic" and "Artist in Arctic."

12. Scheming and Troping

The word "trope" has returned to our vocabulary, as we've slowly recovered some of the rhetorical knowledge that the nineteenth century threw away. In one older division of figures of speech, tropes made up one large class and schemes made up the other. *De tropis et schematibus* is the title of a short treatise on rhetorical figures by the Venerable Bede (673?–735). The handy division held for centuries, and it is a useful place to start when thinking about figures of speech.

In this division, a trope is a figure of speech in which meaning is turned or changed. (The word "trope" etymologically means "turn," from Greek *tropos* [τρόπος].) Metaphor is a trope ("Achilles is a lion"), synecdoche is a trope ("All hands on deck"). The word "scheme" survives in our phrase "rhyme scheme," but the oldest meaning of "scheme" denotes an entire class, of which a rhyme scheme is just one part. We can start reading figures of speech by distinguishing tropes and schemes. It's like distinguishing birdsongs and birdcalls. Schemes are all those figures of speech where meaning is not overtly changed or turned. Schemes play with the surface arrangement of words: their sounds or their looks. Rhyme is a scheme, alliteration is a scheme. "Moon" may rhyme with "June," but rhyming them does not change the ordinary meaning of the words. Still, arbitrary as they may be in some ways, schemes do speak to us. Rhyming "moon" with "June" says "See this tedious rhymester" or "See this ironic poet" or just possibly "See this brave poet." Tropes are essential for poetry. Schemes are needed but they are not enough in themselves. Anyone can make up a jingle using schemes, and writing a clever or funny one is a challenge. But tropes are the real challenge.

Schemes are handy to start with because they often stand out more than tropes. Tropes can hide themselves. Schemes like to show off a bit more. We tend to notice something like chiasmus, the scheme where words are arranged in an xy-yx pattern. Moore uses it in her poem "The Fish": "The water drives a wedge / of iron through the iron edge / of the cliff." (The second x term has lost its first letter, as if the eroding water had already removed the *w* from "wedge" and changed it to "edge.") Stevens imagined a chiasmus-shaped enigma: "The enigmatical / Beauty of each beautiful enigma." The scheme outlines the type of enigma here: a self-enclosed, self-mirroring enigma.

We all know something about rhyme schemes and can plot them: abab, abba, aabb, etc. Or the linked rhyming of terza rima, Dante's rhyme scheme: aba bcb, cdc, etc. Can we write nineteen lines using only two rhymes, and repeating two of the lines three times over? See Dylan Thomas, "Do not go gentle into that good night" or Elizabeth Bishop, "One Art." (The form is a villanelle.) Or try Merrill, "Snow Jobs," then Dante Gabriel Rossetti's "The Ballad of Dead Ladies" and possibly Villon's "Ballade des dames du temps jadis." (The form is a ballade.)

What's worth looking for in rhymes? Magic, wit, puns, reproach, paradox. In short, rhymes, like other schemes, are attractive in themselves. We laugh at unlikely rhymes, and for some reason we tend to find triple rhymes in English inherently funny. (Try some stanzas of Byron's *Don Juan* or W. S. Gilbert's patter songs in *The Pirates of Penzance* and elsewhere.) Rhymes are said to be more powerful when they use two different parts of speech (see W. K. Wimsatt's essay, "One Relation of Rhyme to Reason"). Or a poet may prefer quiet rhymes sometimes. Richard Wilbur offers a rare glimpse into a poet's workshop:

It is precisely in its power to suggest comparisons and connections—
unusual ones—to the poet, that one of the incidental merits of rhyme
may be said to lie. Say to yourself *lake, rake,* and then write down all
the metaphors and other reconciliations of these terms which occur to
you within two minutes. It is likely to be a long list, extending from
visual images of wind furrowing water, to punning reminiscences of
Lancelot and Guinevere. . . . When a poet is fishing among rhymes,
he . . . must reject most of the spontaneous reconciliations (and all of
the hackneyed ones) . . . and keep in mind the preconceived direction
and object of his poem. (*Responses: Prose Pieces* [1976], 191)

Schemes are especially interesting when they start turning into tropes or
telling fables; we can see the process starting in Wilbur's workshop. That is
why the definition of "scheme" has to include the word "overtly." Sometimes,
covertly, schemes are doing more than surface patterning.

Tropes "turn" ordinary meaning. Not that ordinary meaning is fixed and
immutable. On the contrary, it is really quite extraordinary. But for everyday
purposes we can distinguish between ordinary uses and figurative uses, even if
we nearly always underestimate the power of figuration. Of course, ordinary
use varies from culture to culture, and one culture's "ordinary" will be an-
other's "figurative." We classify mosquitoes and black flies and biting midges
in certain ways biologically. "The Algonquin Indians classed some insects by
their desire to bite us, lumping together the bugs we would separate and
name mosquito, black fly, biting midge. They called them *sawgimay,* which
means, roughly, small-person-who-flies-and-bites-so-fiercely" (Hubbell,
Broadsides from the Other Orders: A Book of Bugs [1993], 28). We might think
of this as metaphoric, a figurative description, but it is just as valid and useful
as our ordinary ones. Useful for what? If you want to avoid being bitten, the
answer is clear.

Poetic tropes are remarkable in that they go on generating thought and
feeling. Attending *Hamlet* or *Twelfth Night* for the umpteenth time, we still
delight in the troping. Dying metaphors are different. They turn into clichés
and provide targets for satire. (See George Orwell's famous essay, "Politics and
the English Language.") Dead metaphors are those buried in the language, es-
pecially in word-roots. Or buried in unobtrusive parts of speech like preposi-
tions. Why is "up" where heaven is and where we want to climb and where
things are better ("looking up")? Why is "down" discouraging? Prepositions
need watching.

Metaphor, easily the most prominent of the tropes (and historically some-
times the name for the whole class), is a complex process of identification. It
means "transport" etymologically—and literally in modern Greece, where
you may actually ride on a bus called *metaphora.* The classic formula is
$A = B$, which makes no sense logically but does metaphorically. The standard

school-book example is "Achilles is a lion," which is easy to explain. Not all metaphors are.

We should watch exactly how the A and B of metaphor are joined on the page. They are not always joined by "is" or "are," and the equation sign (=) hardly does justice to the different kinds of comparison and identification that we perform. Sometimes metaphor's two terms are simply juxtaposed, without any verb, as in A, B. One example is Stevens's title, "The Bagatelles, the Madrigals." We ourselves infer the likeness and difference. Sometimes the word "like" or "as" is inserted, as if we wish to describe the relation logically: A is like B. (This is simile, which for some is a subcategory of metaphor.) Sometimes there is a radical alogical kind of joining in "A is B." Watching just how A and B are joined is a good first step toward reading them more fully. Exercise: set a pineapple on the table. Write twelve one-line metaphors for the pineapple. Do they sound anything like Stevens's twelve lines in "Someone Puts a Pineapple Together"? ("1. The hut stands by itself beneath the palms. / 2. Out of their bottle the green genii come. . . .")

Metaphor appears in Stevens's poetry as its own named self, and Stevens talks about it, sometimes in very different ways. I have never figured out completely what is involved in the following examples, among others, and I expect I never shall. They continue to give pleasure and engender profit. Here are some of metaphor's appearances in Stevens's work:

> The twilight overfull
> Of wormy metaphors.
> > ("Delightful Evening")

> . . . The senses paint
> By metaphor.
> > ("Poem Written at Morning")

> The motive for metaphor, shrinking from . . .
> > ("The Motive for Metaphor")

> The eye of a vagabond in metaphor
> That catches our own.
> > ("Notes toward a Supreme Fiction" II.x)

> He must defy
> The metaphor that murders metaphor.
> > ("Someone Puts a Pineapple Together")

> The metaphor stirred his fear.
> > ("Prologues to What Is Possible")

In one sense, reading the fictive patterns of a poem—its figures and stories—is the real beginning of reading it. Yet we can't read figures and stories without seeing and hearing the words and sentences and rhythms and so on. After all this, we are ready to check biography and history and perhaps different critical viewpoints, then to think about their interaction with the words on the page. When we have lived with all this for a while, we may find ourselves coming back to the words on the page, starting to talk to them now, sometimes talking back to them. In turn, the words may reply. At this point, we realize that we are hooked, and settle in happily for the long run.

SHORT GLOSSARY

(See also appendix. For other literary terms or fuller discussion, see, e.g., Abrams. For more advanced discussion, see NPEPP.)

allusion: what a likely reader would likely hear at a given time and place, e.g., Faulkner's *The Sound and the Fury* as an allusion to Shakespeare's *Macbeth*. (See also "echo," below.) "Reference" in this context applies to examples where exact words are not repeated.

anaphora (anaphoric): repeating a word or phrase at the start of the line.

assonance (assonantal): rhyming of vowel sounds in adjacent words.

blank verse: unrhymed iambic pentameter.

echo: distinguished from quotation (indicated by italics, etc.) and allusion (see above), as quieter. Echo ranges on a scale from clear to faint. The word "allusion" is sometimes applied to the whole process of quoting, alluding, and echoing.

ellipsis: a break, marked by three or four dots or a line of dots.

enjambment: see appendix, "Walking: Lines of Poetry."

figures of speech: tropes and schemes. Rhetoric from the Renaissance and earlier sometimes offers a wider definition.

genre: kind of writing, e.g., elegy, epic, romance (see further in appendix).

lexis: diction; see "Lexis," NPEPP.

mood (grammatical): the four chief moods are the indicative, interrogative, imperative, and exclamatory verb forms; others are, e.g., the subjunctive.

pastoral: see appendix, "Genre."

persona (Lat. "mask," familiar from the *dramatis personae* or actors in a play): the implied speaker of a poem.

portmanteau word: term coined by Lewis Carroll for melding two words into one new word, e.g., "slithy" from "lithe" and "slimy."

scheme: see appendix, "Scheming and Troping."

topos, topoi: topic, literally a "place" (from Gk. *topos*), at first the "common places" (*topoi koinoi*) of argument (e.g., kind and degree); later in Lat. also a specific argument and a memory-place; in postclassical use, applied to themes and formulas in literature, not just in oratory. (See further in Cook [1988], 44n.)

trope: see appendix, "Scheming and Troping."

SELECT BIBLIOGRAPHY

(For primary sources, see abbreviations I.)

Reference

(See also works cited under abbreviations II. There are reliable encyclopedias of philosophy, of religion and ethics, of Judaism, etc., for checking general or specific knowledge.)

Abrams, M. H., *A Glossary of Literary Terms*, 8th ed. Boston: Thomson, Wadsworth, 2005.

Bible (AV): the Authorized (King James) Version (1611). All quotations from the English Bible are from this translation, which was part of the common tongue for some 350 years. (The original Scriptures are the Hebrew Bible, which in Christendom becomes the Old Testament, and the Greek New Testament. For Roman Catholic Christendom, the Bible was known for centuries in its Latin [Vulgate] version.)

Edelstein, J. M., *Wallace Stevens: A Descriptive Bibliography*. Pittsburgh: University of Pittsburgh Press, 1973.

Fowler, Alastair, *Kinds of Literature: An Introduction to the Theory of Genres and Modes*. Cambridge: Harvard University Press, 1982.

Hollander, John, *Rhyme's Reason: A Guide to English Verse*. New Haven: Yale University Press, 3rd ed. 2001.

Morse, Samuel, Jackson R. Bryer, Joseph N. Riddel, *Wallace Stevens Checklist and Bibliography of Stevens Criticism*. Denver: Alan Swallow, 1963.

New Princeton Handbook of Poetic Terms, ed. T.V.F. Brogan, Princeton: Princeton University Press 1994: essential excerpts from the *NPEPP*.

Serio, John N., *Wallace Stevens: An Annotated Secondary Bibliography*. Pittsburgh: University of Pittsburgh Press, 1994.

Walsh, Thomas F., comp., *Concordance to the Poetry of Wallace Stevens*. University Park, Pa.: Penn State University Press, 1963. (Entries for *Opus Posthumous* are keyed to the first edition, ed. Morse, 1957.)

Biography

See also below in Bates, Ellmann (in Doggett and Buttel), and Lensing.

Brazeau, Peter, *Parts of a World: Wallace Stevens Remembered*. San Francisco: North Point Press, 1985: an oral "biography" from interviews with contemporaries, whose evidence requires the usual scrutiny.

Poggioli, Renato, trans., *Mattino domenicale ed altre poesie*. Torino: Giulo Einaudi Editore, 1954, pp. 168–85, letters by Stevens to the translator.

Richardson, Joan, *Wallace Stevens: I: The Early Years, 1879–1923* and *Wallace Stevens: II: The Later Years, 1923–1955*. New York: Beech Tree Books, 1986 and 1988: beyond detailed biographical facts, especially valuable on Stevens's reading.

Sharpe, Tony, *Wallace Stevens: A Literary Life*. New York: St. Martin's Press, 2000.

Stevens, Holly, "Bits of Remembered Time," *Southern Review* 7 (1971): 651–57; "Holidays in Reality," in Doggett and Buttel, below, 105–13; for *Souvenirs and Prophecies*, see abbreviations I.

Brief List of Criticism

A few critical and scholarly works, some older and well-established, some more recent. There is a large amount of commentary on Stevens, of varying quality. Studies that are elementary or specialized are omitted here, as are most articles (see John Serio, above). Some of the best writing on poetry is to be found in the works cited in the appendix.

Bates, Milton, *Wallace Stevens: A Mythology of Self*. Berkeley: University of California Press, 1985.

Blackmur, R.P., "Examples of Wallace Stevens" and "Wallace Stevens: An Abstraction Blooded," in his *Form and Value in Modern Poetry*. New York: Doubleday, Anchor, 1957, pp. 183–212, 213–18.

Bloom, Harold, *Wallace Stevens: Poems of Our Climate*. Ithaca: Cornell University Press, 1976.

Brogan, Jacqueline Vaught, *Stevens and Simile: A Theory of Language*. Princeton: Princeton University Press, 1986.

Cook, Eleanor, *Poetry, Word-Play, and Word-War in Wallace Stevens*. Princeton: Princeton University Press, 1988; in *Against Coercion: Games Poets Play* (Stanford: Stanford University Press, 1998, chaps. 9, 12, 13 and passim.

Doggett, Frank, and Robert Buttel, eds., *Wallace Stevens: A Celebration*. Princeton: Princeton University Press, 1980. (See Ellmann's biographical essay, Hollander on Stevens and music, MacCaffrey on "Le Monocle de Mon Oncle," and Vendler on how Keats's "To Autumn" echoes through Stevens's work.)

Filreis, Alan, *Wallace Stevens and the Actual World*. Princeton: Princeton University Press, 1991; *Modernism from Left to Right: Wallace Stevens, the Thirties, and Literary Radicalism*. Cambridge: Cambridge University Press, 1994.

Frye, Northrop, "Wallace Stevens and the Variation Form" in his *Spiritus Mundi: Essays on Literature, Myth, and Society*. Bloomington: Indiana University Press, 1976.

Jarrell, Randall, "Reflections on Wallace Stevens" in his *Poetry and the Age*. New York: Noonday, 1953, pp. 133–48.

Kermode, Frank, *Wallace Stevens*. Edinburgh: Oliver and Boyd, 1960.

Lensing, George, *Wallace Stevens: A Poet's Growth*. Baton Rouge: Louisiana State University Press, 1986; *Wallace Stevens and the Seasons*. Baton Rouge: Louisiana State University Press, 2001.

Litz, A. Walton, *Introspective Voyager: The Poetic Development of Wallace Stevens*. New York: Oxford University Press, 1972.

Longenbach, James, *Wallace Stevens: The Plain Sense of Things*. New York: Oxford University Press, 1991.

MacLeod, Glen, *Wallace Stevens and Modern Art: from the Armory Show to Abstract Expressionism*. New Haven: Yale University Press, 1993.

Maeder, Beverley, *Wallace Stevens' Experimental Language: The Lion in the Lute*. New York: St. Martin's Press, 1999.

Vendler, Helen Hennessy, *On Extended Wings: Wallace Stevens' Longer Poems*. Cambridge, Mass.: Harvard University Press, 1969; *Wallace Stevens: Words Chosen Out of Desire*. Knoxville: University of Tennessee Press, 1984.

INDEX OF TITLES

(main entries)